EXTRAORDINARY GROUPS

An Examination of Unconventional Life-Styles

FOURTH EDITION

FOURTH EDITION

EXTRAORDINARY GROUPS

An Examination of
Unconventional Life-Styles

WILLIAM M. KEPHART
Professor Emeritus, University of Pennsylvania

WILLIAM W. ZELLNER
East Central University

ST. MARTIN'S PRESS
New York

Editor: Cathy Pusateri
Project editor: Erica Townsend
Production supervisor: Alan Fischer
Cover design: Darby Downey
Cover photo: © 1982 by Ira Berger, Woodfin Camp & Associates, Inc.

For information, write:
St. Martin's Press, Inc.
175 Fifth Avenue
New York, NY 10010

ISBN: 0-312-03169-6

Acknowledgments

Excerpts reprinted from *Shaker Communities, Shaker Lives* by Priscilla J. Brewer, by permission of University Press of New England. © 1986 University Press of New England.

Excerpts reprinted with permission of The Free Press, a Division of Macmillan, Inc., from *Gypsies: The Hidden Americans* by Anne Sutherland. Copyright © 1975 by Anne Sutherland.

CONTENTS

PREFACE

As the record indicates, *Extraordinary Groups* has had an extraordinary history. Although it was written by sociologists, the book has also been used in a variety of nonsociological courses, including anthropology, religion, history, and psychology. Due in part to this interdisciplinary appeal, *Extraordinary Groups* has now been adopted in more than five hundred colleges and universities—and the number continues to grow.

Another reason for the book's appeal is the fact that it is descriptive and explanatory rather than analytical. True, the description is interwoven with basic sociological concepts, but systematic analysis and inductive reasoning have been left to the discretion and orientation of the instructor.

The fourth edition of *Extraordinary Groups* contains a number of important changes. Because the modern communal movement is dead, or at least dormant, the chapter on modern communes has been eliminated. In its place, we have added two new chapters: The Jehovah's Witnesses, and The Hasidim.

Both of these groups are extremely interesting, as the reader will discover. Although they are in some ways outside the mainstream of American culture, both the Witnesses and the Hasidim are "newsworthy." It was recently reported, for example, that pop singer Michael Jackson and mystery writer Mickey Spillane had joined the Jehovah's Witnesses.

The fourth edition of *Extraordinary Groups* contains other changes and addenda; indeed, every chapter has been revised and updated. The Old Order Amish, to take another example, seem always to be in the news. In the latest turn of events, the Amish—probably the most conservative group in North America—are said to be relinquishing many of their olden customs.

Amish-watchers report that more and more of the Amish are using such things as power tools, modern medicine, and professional services. Newer Amish homes include up-to-date kitchens, modern plumbing and bathroom facilities, and attractive exteriors. Where the modernization trend will end—and what the effect will be on the Amish life-style— can only be conjectured. But one thing seems certain: there are seldom any uneventful years in Amishland.

The Mormons, also, are ever in the news. In addition to the never-ending controversy over the remnants of polygamy, Mormon problems have centered on the intellectuals and the ecclesiastical role of women. And in the late 1980s a major scandal erupted, involving forgery, church documents, charges, and countercharges—and murder. Known as the "Salamander Incident," the story created headlines for weeks on end. Nevertheless, in spite of their problems—old and new—the Mormon church has continued to grow at a prodigious rate: from 1 million at the outbreak of World War II to well over 6 million today.

Unlike the abovementioned groups, Gypsies, perhaps the most "extra-ordinary" of all, are seldom in the news—which is hardly surprising, given their rather elusive way of life. Even in the sociological journals, articles on Gypsies are few and far between. Fortunately, monographic material—together with information published in the *Gypsy Lore Society Newsletter*—contains some valuable information regarding boundary maintenance, fortune-telling, and other facets of Gypsy life.

One of the problems in any textbook revision is how to incorporate the various changes without altering the style and character of the basic book. Readability, conceptual clarity, and the liberal use of meaningful examples have always been the hallmarks of *Extraordinary Groups*, and we can promise that they remain so in this new edition.

Finally, the fourth edition of *Extraordinary Groups* has been strengthened by the perceptive comments and suggestions of a number of interested persons. Special thanks, in this respect, are owed to the following: Paul Brasky, Ulster County Community College; Ron Broce, Central Wyoming College; Tom Fitzgerald, University of North Carolina at Greensboro; Kathryn Johnson, Indiana University Northwest; Marvin Kroeker, East Central University; Rodney Metzger, Lane Community College; Timothy Miller, University of Kansas at Lawrence; Donald Mossman, Concordia College; Natalie Rosel, New College of the University of South Florida; and Marcia Segal, Indiana University Southeast.

William M. Kephart
Moylan, Pennsylvania

William W. Zellner
Ada, Oklahoma

EXTRAORDINARY GROUPS

An Examination of
Unconventional Life-Styles

FOURTH EDITION

INTRODUCTION

America is a land of fascinating cultural diversity. Scores of various ethnic groups, hundreds of different religious sects and denominations—the total seems almost inexhaustible. Indeed, it is this *tremendous range of associational groups* that sets America apart from most other societies.

Out of the multitude of different culture-groups that have appeared on the American scene, we have chosen eight for inclusion in the present volume:

The Old Order Amish
The Oneida Community
The Gypsies
The Shakers
The Hasidim
The Father Divine Movement
The Mormons
The Jehovah's Witnesses

All of these groups are important in their own right. Just as liberally educated persons should have some knowledge of other times and other places, they should also have an awareness of the subcultural diversity within their own society. The only question to be asked is this: Why were these particular groups chosen, rather than others? The answer is threefold.

Sociological Illustration

The first—and most important—reason pertains to sociological illustration. The groups were selected because *they illustrate major sociological principles in concrete form.* Let us look at some examples.

As used by sociologists, the term *primary group* refers to a small, face-to-face group whose members share experiences, confide in one another, lend mutual support and understanding, and so on. These primary-group needs, as they are called, are deep-seated. They are

1

characteristic of human beings everywhere. In most societies, the basic primary group is the family, and insofar as the personality structure of children is concerned, sociologists feel that the family has a lasting influence.

It stands to reason, therefore, that any culture or subculture attempting to eliminate the family must provide an alternative social mechanism for the satisfaction of primary-group needs. The Oneida Community is a good case in point.

In their attempt to create a utopian society, the Oneidans dispensed entirely with marriage, family, and parental child rearing. All males were permitted to have sexual relations with all females, and all children were raised communally. Undue affection between parents and children—or between a particular man and a particular woman—was severely censured. And since the Oneida Community lasted for some fifty years, with a total membership running well into the hundreds, the methods used to promote group solidarity were obviously effective.

Oneidans were all housed under one roof—the Mansion House—a building designed specifically to promote feelings of togetherness. Members ate in a common dining hall and held meetings in a community meeting hall. Activities such as smoking, drinking, and card playing were prohibited, since they were considered to be individualistic or antigroup. Conversely, musical presentations, theatricals, and other group activities were strongly encouraged.

In their day-to-day living, Oneidans totally rejected the concept of private property. They shared their material possessions, their wealth, their mates, and their children. Members held both a common economic philosophy and a common theology. So strong was their we-feeling that they were able to satisfy primary-group needs despite the large size of their community.

Let us look at one more example: *definition of the situation.* As W. I. Thomas, who coined the term, put it, "What men define as real is real in its consequences." And the Old Order Amish provide an excellent illustration, for they have defined the automobile as a threat to their social equilibrium—and they are acting accordingly.

Many permissive changes have taken place among the Amish, but one "contraption" remains taboo: the automobile. Members are not permitted to own them. And despite a variety of pressures, the Amish church has not yielded on this point—and probably never will.

The Old Order Amish have a close-knit family life. They are wedded to the soil, to the church community, and to the horse and buggy. And they feel that the auto would tend to disrupt their methodical and slow-paced way of life.

True, the Amish may be wrong in their judgment. The automobile might not bring with it the feared aftereffects. But that is irrelevant. They have already defined the situation, and they can hardly change the definition without also changing their entire social perspective.

Other sociological illustrations would include *culture conflict* among the Mormon polygamists; *reference group behavior* on the part of the Shakers; *social control* in the Gypsy community; *cultural theme*, as exemplified by the Father Divine Movement; *alienation; assimilation; conspicuous consumption; sanctions; folkways and mores; charisma; ethnocentrism; level of aspiration; values;* and *manifest and latent function.*

Various chapters in *Extraordinary Groups* contain a number of these sociological concepts around which are woven the threads and cultural fabric of the group in question. By associating the concept with the group or groups involved, the student is thus aided in the learning process.

Diversity

Although it would have been possible to select groups that were fairly similar to one another, such as many of the counterculture communes that materialized during the period from 1965 to 1975, we felt that—in terms of liberal arts values—diversity was much more rewarding. Accordingly, we chose groups that were markedly different from each other.

The Shakers were strictly a stay-at-home group, for whom travel was largely prohibited. Gypsies, on the other hand, may well be the world-champion travelers. The Oneidans adhered to a system of strict economic communism, while the Mormons believe just as strongly in free enterprise. The Amish are a rural group; the Father Divine Movement is urban; and the Hasidim might best be described as urban villagers. The Oneida Community practiced "free love"; the Shakers were celibate. Jehovah's Witnesses and the Mormons gain members through proselytizing, while the Amish and most Hasidic groups are content to let God increase their numbers.

Interest

The third and final reason for choosing these particular groups was simply that *they are interesting.* This we know, since many of the accounts in *Extraordinary Groups* were based on personal experience. For example, we were born and raised in Pennsylvania, and our fascination and conversations with the Old Order Amish have spanned many decades. It was also possible on a number of occasions to talk with Father Divine and his followers. The association with Mother Divine continues.

Our interest in the Oneida Community also goes back many years; in fact, a number of the surviving members were actually interviewed, as well as their descendants. Talks with the Shakers—there are only a handful left—were most rewarding. Interviews and association with Jehovah's Witnesses were also quite revealing; indeed, with the exception of the Amish, more time was spent with the Witnesses than with any of the other groups.

We wish we could say that our relationship with the Gypsies was similarly rewarding, but—no pun intended—it was not in the cards. Both physically and conversationally, Gypsies are elusive. A good many of the interviews were out-and-out failures. Fortunately, a few of the interviewees were cooperative. Also, some invaluable fieldwork on the part of other investigators was available.

Sociological principles are not difficult to learn. The trick is to make them meaningful in keeping with the best traditions of a liberal education. And we do hope that a study of the following "extraordinary groups" will result in a meaningful grasp of the subject. Also, in terms of the cultural diversity mentioned earlier, a consideration of these groups may permit us to feel a little less smug about our own way of life.

CHAPTER ONE

THE OLD ORDER AMISH

The Amish are descendants of the sixteenth-century Swiss Anabaptists. Many of the latter came to be known as Mennonites because of the strong leadership of Menno Simons. In this sense, the Amish are a branch of the Mennonites, and the two groups have much in common, especially in a historical sense.[1]

Menno Simons was born in 1492 in the Netherlands. He was ordained a Roman Catholic priest, but broke with the church and eventually formed his own movement. His teachings included separation of church and state, adult baptism, and refusal to bear arms or take oaths. He died in 1561.

Although space does not permit an analysis of Menno Simons's theological and secular beliefs, one point should be mentioned. He was a firm believer in the *Meidung*—the shunning or avoidance of excommunicated members. It was the *Meidung* controversy that eventually led to the formation of the Amish.

Early History

Jacob Amman was a Mennonite preacher. Little is known of his early life, although he seems to have been born in Switzerland, possibly in 1656. He rose rapidly in the church hierarchy, and soon became a respected leader. From all accounts, he was a stern and righteous man— not unlike an Old Testament prophet—journeying from place to place, admonishing, exhorting, dutifully defending the faith.

What distressed him most was the fact that some Mennonite leaders were not enforcing the *Meidung*. One thing led to another, factions developed, and in 1693 it became obvious that the *Meidung* controversy was irreconcilable. Those who believed in the ban joined Amman's group and became known as the Amish. The others stayed within the larger Mennonite fold.

[1]For an account of the Anabaptist origins, see J. Denny Weaver, *Becoming Anabaptist: The Origin and Significance of Sixteenth-Century Anabaptism* (Scottdale, PA: Herald Press, 1987).

When the two groups came to America, the schism persisted, as it does to this day. The *Meidung* itself, moreover, remains a key concept. In fact, it would be no exaggeration to say that the *Meidung* is the heart of the Amish system of social control. Details will be discussed in a later section.

What do the present-day Amish think of Jacob Amman? Some members contend that he was overly harsh in both his views and his implementation, although others defend his actions as necessary—given the temper of the times. He is certainly not a revered leader. Indeed, many of the Old Order Amish evidence little knowledge of—or interest in—Jacob Amman.

The reason is not hard to find. Amman was a strong leader with strong convictions, qualities that the Amish tend to *deemphasize*. The Old Order Amish are devout believers in humility, brotherly love, group discussion, and consensus, and they are suspicious of those with leadership aspirations. Little wonder that their attitude toward Amman is one of ambivalence. Still, it is questionable whether the Amish would have survived as a separate group had it not been for the strong hand and unbending will of Jacob Amman.

America   Interestingly, no one knows when the first Amish came to America, or just where they settled. Both sailing lists and land records are inconclusive, although there is no record of any Amish in America during the 1600s. In the early 1700s, certain Amish names made their appearance in various Pennsylvania counties, though genealogical verification is lacking. In 1737, the ship *Charming Nancy* brought a number of families whose genealogy has been documented as Amish. The first "Amish ship," it carried a sufficient number of families to make two Pennsylvania settlements possible—in Lancaster and Berks counties.[2]

While they faced the usual hazards encountered by American colonists, the followers of Jacob Amman found an almost matchless opportunity for agricultural development. Climate, soil, rainfall, and topography were excellent. Best of all, the land was cheap and seemed to be in almost limitless supply. The Old Order Amish had come upon a farmer's dream, and they proceeded to make the most of it.

They grew and prospered, from a relatively small number of families in the 1700s to thousands in the 1800s. Indeed, the "almost limitless" supply of land in Pennsylvania eventually turned out to be anything but limitless, and in order to form new settlements the Amish were forced to migrate to other regions. Today there are settlements in no fewer than

---

[2]For a comprehensive discussion of this early American period, see John A. Hostetler, *Amish Society* (Baltimore: Johns Hopkins University Press, 1980), pp. 54–64.

twenty states. Of the more than 100,000 Old Order Amish, however, approximately 75 percent live in Ohio, Pennsylvania, and Indiana.[3]

The Old Order Amish also have a number of communities in Canada, Central America, and South America. Paradoxically, there are no Amish in Europe, their original homeland.

Although the secular and religious practices of the Amish show many similarities no matter where they live, there are also some significant regional differences. And while we will try to present a more or less generalized account, special attention will be given to the Amish of Lancaster County, Pennsylvania, one of the oldest, largest—and certainly one of the most interesting—of all the Amish groups.[*]

"... A Peculiar People"

In their olden attire and horse and buggy, the Old Older Amish appear to be driving out of yesterday. Actually, they are more than simply old-fashioned. Conservatism is part of their religion, and as such it permeates their entire life.

The followers of Jacob Amman believe in a literal interpretation of the Bible and rely heavily on the statement, "But ye are a chosen generation, a royal priesthood, an holy nation, a peculiar people" (1 Peter 2:9). And since they have been specifically chosen by God, the Amish take great pains to stay "apart" from the world at large. They do this not only by living apart, but by rejecting so many of the standard components of modern civilization: automobiles, radio and television, high school and college, movies, air conditioning, jewelry and cosmetics, life insurance, cameras, musical instruments. The list goes on and on.

This is not to say that the Old Order Amish reject all change. As will be shown later, some of the changes have been fairly far-reaching.[4] But in general, the followers of Jacob Amman resist converting to what they believe to be harmful worldly ways.

Appearance and Apparel   Sociologists often use the term *in-group* to depict those who think of themselves as a unit, in contrast to the *out-group*, or nonmembers. An in-group is generally characterized by the

---

[3]*New York Times*, August 25, 1987.

[4]Stephen Scott and Kenneth Pellman, *Living Without Electricity* (Intercourse, PA: Good Books, 1990).

[*]Readers familiar with Lancaster County will recognize the picturesque names of towns and villages in Amishland: Intercourse, Smoketown, Leola, White Horse, Compass, Bird-in-Hand, Beartow, Gap, Mascot, Paradise, and others. Despite sizable out-migration in years past, the Lancaster County Amish continue to grow. Their numbers are expected to go well over the 20,000 mark during the 1990s.

loyalty, like-mindedness, and compatibility of its constituents. Members refer to the in-group as "we," and to the out-group as "they." In the case of the Amish, wearing apparel is one of the most distinguishing features of the in-group.

Men's hats—probably the most characteristic feature of their attire—are of low crown and wide brim; smaller models are worn by the youngsters. Coats are without collars or lapels, and almost always include a vest. (An Amishman and his vest are not easily parted.) Wire hook-and-eye fasteners are used on suit coats and vests.

Amishmen's trousers deserve special mention, since (1) they never have creases or cuffs; (2) they are always worn with suspenders (belts are taboo); and (3) they are without zippered or buttoned flies. Instead, the flap or "broadfall" type is utilized.* It might also be mentioned that, with the exception of their shirts, Amish men's attire is predominantly black.

Following the biblical injunction, Amish women keep their heads covered at all times: indoors, by a small white lawn-cap; outdoors, by the familiar black bonnet. Cosmetics and makeup, of course, are prohibited at all times.

Dresses are of a solid color—blues and purples are quite common—with (variable) long skirts and aprons. In public, women also wear shawls and capes. Scott explains the latter practice as follows:

> The kerchief or cape is worn by nearly all plain women. It is also found in many surviving folk costumes of Western Europe. Its wide appeal to pious country women is no doubt based on the modesty it provides. The extra covering is seen to conceal the neckline and the form of the bosom, and provides privacy when nursing a baby.
>
> A 19th-century English woman remarked on . . . the cape, "Certainly the most ingenious device ever contrived for concealing all personal advantage."[5]

For Amish women, stockings must be black, and shoes are the black, low-heeled variety. Interestingly enough, in recent years young boys and girls have taken to wearing jogging shoes. In fact, the two most popular forms of footwear for the youngsters are jogging shoes and bare feet! For both sexes, all jewelry (including the wedding ring) is

---

[5]Stephen Scott, *Why Do They Dress That Way?* (Intercourse, PA: Good Books, 1986), p. 86.

*"When fly closures for pants were introduced in the 1820s," writes Scott, "some considered them indecent. In 1830, the *Gentlemen's Magazine of Fashion* pronounced the fly 'an indelicate and disgusting fashion.' While the larger society eventually accepted this feature, many plain people did not." Among the plain people were the Old Order Amish. See Stephen Scott, *Why Do They Dress That Way?* (Intercourse, PA: Good Books, 1986), p. 114.

taboo, since whatever is worn is presumed to be functional.* An ornamental exception might be the Amishman's beard, though this does have recognition value: prior to marriage young men are clean-shaven, while married men are required to let their beards grow. Mustaches—which in the European period were associated with the military—are completely taboo.

Amish males wear their hair long, unparted, in a Dutch bob, with the necessary trimming done at home. Amish females also have their own special hairdo, both cutting and curling being forbidden. (Shaving their legs and plucking their eyebrows are also taboo.) Their hair braiding is distinctively Amish, however, and a classroom of twenty Amish girls—all with identical hair styles—is an unusual sight for an outsider to behold!

The Old Order Amish are quite cognizant of the fact that they look different, and they have no intention of changing. On the contrary, their "difference" makes them feel close to one another and accentuates the in-group feeling.

Some observers believe that, since the Amish are thrifty, they deliberately utilize clothing that never goes out of style. This is not the reason, however. True, the followers of Jacob Amman are indeed thrifty. With the exception of shoes, stockings, and hats, they make nearly all of their own clothing. They also wear their clothes until they are literally worn out. But the basic reason they will not change styles is that they consider such change to be worldly—and worldliness has negative connotations.

Stephen Scott, an authority on the subject, writes that

> The plain people . . . feel the world is controlled by Satan and the forces of evil. And so, they reason, conformity to the fads and fashions of popular society indicates identity with the world's system.
>
> The plain people insist that the church, guided by the Word of God and not the dictates of fashion, should decide what a Christian should wear. They point out that the fashion centers have not been known for their righteousness. Economically, they judge the fashion industry to be a deceitful, greedy force. Keeping up with the latest styles is seen as wasteful, planned obsolescence.[6]

Scott notes also that the basic guidelines for the plain people in matters of dress and appearance stem from the Bible:

---

[6]Ibid., p. 6.

*The Amish sometimes appear inconsistent in their prohibitions. Thus, wristwatches are forbidden while pocket watches are permitted. Sometimes there is a good reason for the seeming inconsistency, and the Amish are well aware of the explanation. At other times, the answer would likely be, "It has always been so."

From [biblical] verses the plain people learn that their dress should be modest, simple, and economical, and that jewelry and elaborate hairdo are inappropriate for the Christian. By a lack of emphasis on external beauty, the plain people believe the inner virtue of the heart can better shine through. They also think that if one's mind is not preoccupied with beautifying one's body, a person can be free to do the Lord's work.[7]

General Life-Style   It was Thorstein Veblen, one of the early giants of sociology, who first used the term *conspicuous consumption*, by which he meant the tendency to gain attention through the overt display of one's wealth. But whereas such display might be expected on the part of many Americans, it has no place in the Amish community. Their homes, for example, some of which have surprisingly modern features, would never contain elaborate furniture, fancy wallpaper, or Oriental rugs. Clothes, as we have seen, are plain and functional, and neither sex will wear adornments of any kind.

With their emphasis on humility, it is understandable that the Old Order Amish would dislike all types of public recognition. Pride, in fact, is considered a cardinal sin. As a consequence, actions that are more or less commonplace in society at large are seldom encountered in Amishland. Boasting is rare. Having one's portrait painted or picture taken is prohibited; indeed, cameras are completely taboo. Such behavior would be considered a sign of self-aggrandizement.*

Bicycles, motorcycles, and automobiles are strictly *verboten* in the Lancaster County settlement, and any adult who bought one would be subjected to severe group pressures. The automobile is the best-known case in point, and—as will be shown—the Amish life-style is strongly influenced by their being a horse-type rather than an automobile-type culture.

It should be kept in mind that the Old Order Amish are a slow-tempo community. They value such traits as obedience, modesty, and submission, rather than mobility and competitiveness.[8] The hustle and bustle that characterize so much of society at large will not be found in Amishland. It would be rather unusual to see an adult Amish person in a hurry!

In their business ventures, the Amish follow a fairly conservative

---

[7]Ibid., p. 15.

[8]For a discussion of Amish personality, see Hostetler, *Amish Society*, pp. 185–189, and pp. 333ff.; and Donald Kraybill, *The Riddle of Amish Culture* (Baltimore: Johns Hopkins University Press, 1989), pp. 24–45.

*For readers who appreciate a mystery, here is one with no immediate answer. The followers of Jacob Amman do not own cameras, and are dead set against having their pictures taken. Yet, on the basis of postcards, brochures, pamphlets, newspapers, magazines, and books, the Amish may well be the most photographed group in America!

route. They have no interest in stocks, bonds, or other forms of "speculation." They are staunch believers in private enterprise, however, and will take out mortgages, borrow money from banks, and utilize checking accounts. Banks consider them excellent customers and excellent credit risks.

The followers of Jacob Amman have no strong interest in politics. Although they do vote—in local more than in national elections—voter turnout is relatively low. Hostetler reports that when they register, most do so as Republicans.[9] The Amish themselves have never held a major office of any kind, for a good reason: the church would not permit it.

The Old Order Amish tend to reject various forms of commercial insurance, including life insurance. However, they do have a fairly comprehensive network of mutual-aid organizations and self-help programs, some of which involve monetary assessments. A sick farmer can count on his fields being tended, and even harvested, by his neighbors. Should an Amish family's barn burn down, up to a hundred neighbors will gather, and in a day or two, raise a new barn. Amish barn raisings have attracted nationwide publicity.

Readers will be interested to learn that the Amish have even rejected social security benefits. In the mid-1950s, they sent a delegation to Washington bearing a petition signed by some 14,000 members. The petition stated that they were quite willing to make social security *payments*. What they were asking Congress for was special legislation exempting them from social security *benefits*.

Knowing that "most people come to Washington to get something," Congress was flabbergasted at the request. The law was eventually changed, and today Amish farmers neither make payments nor receive benefits of any kind, including retirement, disability, and Medicare.*

Actually, there was a good deal of logic behind the Amish offer. In the Amish community there are no rest homes, convalescent homes, or homes for the aged. Each family takes care of its own aged and infirm members, and no Amish person has ever been on welfare. Leaders were afraid that once social security checks started to arrive, the entire self-help program would be undermined, with a corresponding weakening of both family and community.

It is this system of intrafamily support, group solidarity, mutual aid—and, of course, faith in God—that prompts the followers of Jacob Amman

---

[9]Hostetler, *Amish Society*, p. 253.

*In certain instances, Amish are required to make social security payments. An Amish person who works for a non-Amish employer will have social security automatically deducted from his or her paycheck. Also, an Amish employer who hires a non-Amish employee must pay the employee's social security tax. There are other examples. In no case, however, will an Amish person accept any of the benefits.

to reject insurance. When trouble strikes, they know that help is no further away than their Amish neighbors. At one time, they were even reluctant to patronize doctors and hospitals, and some Amish are still reluctant to do so. Most members, however, now utilize medical facilities when the situation calls for it. The majority of Amish women, though, have their babies at home, delivered by an authorized midwife.[10]

It should be mentioned, in connection with medicine and health, that the Old Order Amish are conservative in death as well as in life. Their funerals are plain: no flowers, no metal caskets, no music, no decorations, no mourning bands, no crepe. Most districts permit embalming, but a few do not. There are no Amish undertakers, however, and even funeral parlors are taboo. The wooden coffin is made by an Amish carpenter, services are held at home, and an Amish bishop presides. The olden custom of holding a wake—sitting up all night around the body of the deceased—is still practiced in most areas.

One unusual custom—not found outside of Amishland—is the following, reported by Scott:

> In many Amish communities, it is a common practice to hold two funeral services simultaneously for the same person. Usually one service is held in the house, and another in the barn or another farm building. This is necessary because of the large number of people who attend—over a thousand in some cases.[11]

Amish cemeteries are startlingly plain. There are no flowers, no decorations, no elaborate tombstones, and no mausoleums. In fact, there is not even a caretaker, so that the graves sometimes have a run-down look. In general, the only man-made signs are small, uniform headstones, with the name and dates of the deceased—no scrolls, epitaphs, or other inscriptions. Most Amish cemeteries are off the beaten track. For the most part, they are—or were—part of an Amish farmer's land, and there is no charge for the use of burial lots.

As might be imagined, the entire cost of an Amish funeral and burial is only a fraction of that normally spent by the "English" (non-Amish).

The Amish Farmstead

Amish life—literally as well as figuratively—revolves around the home. Most inhabitants of Amishland are born at home, they work at or near

---

[10]See Penny Armstrong and Sheryl Feldman, *A Midwife's Story* (New York: Arbor House, 1986). See also, Carol Morello, "Embattled Midwife to the Amish," *Philadelphia Inquirer*, July 23, 1989.

[11]Stephen Scott, *The Amish Wedding and Other Special Occasions of the Old Order Communities* (Intercourse, PA: Good Books, 1988), p. 103.

home, and they socialize at home. Most of their clothing is homemade, and nearly all of their meals are eaten at home. Church services are held at one home or another. The Old Order Amish also marry at home, and—as a most fitting finale—their funeral services are held at home.

"Home," however, has a special meaning, for the followers of Jacob Amman are predominantly a rural people, and their traditional dwelling can best be described as a farmstead. Indeed, for most of the Amish in the United States, farm and home tend to be synonymous, a feeling that complements their religious philosophy.

Amish farms are acknowledged to be among the best in the world. In addition to fairly extensive crop acreage, their holdings often consist of large, well-kept houses and barns, stables, springhouses, silos, sheds, and storehouses. And, since the Amish community maintains no homes for the aged, a farmstead may include two, three, or even four generations. Additions are made to the farmhouse as needed. The presence of so many oldsters on the farm, of course, serves as a self-perpetuating conservative influence. At any rate, it is little wonder that some of the larger Amish farms have the appearance of miniature villages.

It is difficult for an outsider to understand an Amish person's relation to the soil. As Hostetler puts it:

> Soil for the Amish has a spiritual significance. . . . They hold that man's first duty is to dress the garden. That is, he is to till it, manage it. . . .
>
> Second, man is to keep the garden, protect it from harm through the use of his labor and oversight. Ownership is God's, while man's function is looking after it on behalf of God. . . . His stewardship is continuous, ending in a day of reckoning when man will be called to give an account.[12]

The followers of Jacob Amman believe not only that God meant them to till the soil, but that He intended them to till it in a certain way. This way is sometimes confusing to outsiders.

Basic to the Amish agricultural system is the fact that they do not employ tractors in the field. Whereas such a handicap might seem almost insurmountable to other farmers, the Amish try to turn it to their advantage. True, by using a team of horses instead of a tractor, the Amish farmer spends more time in covering less ground. However, he does not mind hard work. He has ample free labor in the form of his sons. He saves money by not having to buy and replace tractors. And his horses supply him with a rich source of natural fertilizer. As one Amish farmer is reported to have said, "When you put gasoline in a tractor, all you get out is smoke!"

Aside from tractors, the Amish do use a variety of up-to-date farm machinery: sprayers, cultivators, binders, balers, and haymaking equip-

---

[12]Hostetler, *Amish Society*, p. 117.

ment. Gasoline engines are permitted, and often a stationary tractor is used as a source of power.

Agricultural failure is infrequent, for the Amish farmer is a master of his trade. He understands the soil, his crops, and his dairy herds, and he loves his work. His farm products are choice, and he is able to sell them for top dollar. And while he may buy food on the open market, much of what he and his family eat is homegrown. In view of present-day food prices, this is a real advantage. Farming also supplies the Amishman with one of his chief topics of conversation.

Level of Aspiration   While farming is their chief occupation, not all Amish are farmers, though most would certainly like to be. Huntington writes as follows on the subject:

> Although there is considerable range in [Amish] family income, and some families have a higher status than others, there are no class distinctions within the community. . . . In each Amish settlement of any size there are Amishmen who own small businesses that are related to farming and the Amish way of life.
>
> Thus there will be a blacksmith, a harness maker, a buggy shop, a shop for adapting tractor-drawn farm equipment to horse-drawn, and specialized carpenters who do cabinet work and make Amish coffins.
>
> The Amish build and remodel their own homes and barns with the help of Amish construction crews. There are Amishmen who can draw up plans, lay brick, and install plumbing. . . . [However,] farming continues to be the preferred occupation.[13]

It should be mentioned, incidentally, that the Amish religion forbids any member from joining a union. In some settlements, therefore, "small factories have been built to take advantage of the cheap (non-union), skilled, reliable labor [the Amish] supply."[14]

In many of the above instances the jobs are only temporary, to be held until the Amishman can procure a suitable farm of his own. In many other cases, however, the jobs become more or less permanent. This is especially true in the Lancaster Country area, where there has been a serious "land squeeze" for some time. Farmland has become so expensive and so difficult to obtain that an increasing number of Amishmen have opened a variety of shops, businesses, and cottage industries.

Kraybill reports that 30 percent of the married Amish men in Lancaster County today are in jobs other than farming, although many of these

---

[13]Gertrude Enders Huntington, "The Amish Family," in Charles Mindel, Robert Habenstein, and Roosevelt Wright, eds., *Ethnic Families in America* (New York: Elsevier, 1988), p. 381.
[14]Ibid., p. 394.

jobs are indirectly related to the farm economy.[15] (Married women do not normally work outside the home.) The percentage of nonfarming Amishmen in other parts of the country—or in other parts of the state, for that matter—would be smaller than this figure.

But the question that must be asked is this: Does not the emphasis on farming and farm-related occupations have a stultifying effect on those whose aptitudes and talents lie elsewhere? After all, an impressive array of occupations is closed to the followers of Jacob Amman: medicine, law, dentistry, higher education, optometry, veterinary medicine, banking, finance, the military and the police, acting, music, professional athletics, politics and government work, corporate positions, and so on. The list is indeed a mighty one.

The stultifying effect, however, while it undoubtedly exists in individual cases, has thus far not been a serious problem. The explanation hinges on what sociologists call *level of aspiration*. That is, in society at large there is often a gap between what a person wants to be (aspiration level) and what he or she actually is (achievement level). If the gap is substantial, the person may have an adjustment problem.

But such problems have been minimal among the Old Order Amish, for they believe that by working the soil or engaging in farm-related pursuits they are following the path that God intended. In an occupational sense, therefore, the level of aspiration is much the same throughout the Amish community.

The level of aspiration explanation makes sense as long as the Amish remain wedded to the soil, which on a nationwide basis they have every intention of doing. But what happens if and when the "land squeeze" becomes widespread? Members will have little choice but to reach out to nonfarm pursuits. This has already happened in certain areas, and may cause a rash of internal problems. The matter will be explored in the concluding section.

Amish Homes   It is not easy to describe the typical Amish home of the 1990s. In addition to the usual regional and district variations, the "generational" factor must be considered. Homes of the younger Amish may be noticeably different from those of their parents' generation.

Like the farm, the traditional Amish home is well kept and well run. It is plain, lacking in many of the modern conveniences, in good repair, and solid as an oak. (It needs to be, for untold generations of the same family will live there.)

Most of these houses are fairly large, for several reasons. The Amish have a high birthrate, and at any given time there are likely to be a

[15]Kraybill, *Riddle of Amish Culture*, p. 197. See also Rebecca Rubin, "Time of Change," *Philadelphia Inquirer*, August 26, 1989.

number of children living at home. Also, Amish farmers tend to retire early in life, and they usually turn the house over to one of their sons while they themselves live in the adjoining *Grossdawdy House*. And finally, as will be shown later, the Old Order Amish have no church buildings. Their home is their church, and services are held on a rotating basis. Houses, therefore, must be large enough to seat the congregation.

In the traditional Amish home, rooms are large, particularly the kitchen, where huge quantities of food are cooked and served. (There is no dining room.) Throughout the house, furnishings tend to be functional, though not drab. The Amish religion does not forbid the use of color. Walls are often light blue, dishes purple. Articles such as bed coverings and towels can be almost any color. Outside the house, there is likely to be a lawn and a flower garden. Fences, walls, posts, and landmarks may also be brightly colored.

Although they love colors, the followers of Jacob Amman do not believe in mixing them. Wearing apparel, fences, posts, buggies—all are of solid colors only. Plaids, stripes, and prints are considered too fancy. For this reason, contrary to popular impression, the Amish never put hex signs on their barns.

Newer Amish houses differ from the traditional variety in a number of ways. They tend to be smaller, and many do not have a "farmhouse" appearance at all. In fact, except for such items as no electrical wiring and the lack of curtains, they often look much like non-Amish houses. In the matter of modern appliances and equipment, the differences between "traditional" and "new" are even more significant.

The Amish have never permitted their members to use electricity furnished by public power lines. The church has been unyielding on this point, and the prohibition has served to restrict the kinds of devices and appliances available to members. Over the years, however, the followers of Jacob Amman have come up with some rather interesting alternatives: bottled gas, batteries, small generators, air pressure, gasoline motors, hydraulic power. The net result has been a variety of modern devices that have become available to the Amish, not only in their homes, but in their barns, workshops, stores, and offices.[16]

In addition to a fashionable exterior, for example, the contemporary Amish home in Lancaster County is likely to have modern plumbing and bathroom facilities, attractive flooring and cabinet work, and a moderately up-to-date kitchen. The latter would include a washing machine, stove, and refrigerator, all powered by one of the nonelectrical sources mentioned above.

---

[16]See the discussion in Kraybill, Ibid., pp. 150–164.

The Pace of Change How significant are the foregoing changes? There is no denying that the Lancaster County Amish have experienced some meaningful alterations, both in their home life and in their employment. Although the reasons may be complicated, many of the changes and modifications have acted as a safety valve; that is, they have given members some necessary leeway, denial of which might have caused internal dissension.

At the same time, the above-mentioned modernization should not obscure the larger picture: *resistance to change* is still one of the hallmarks of Amish society. A substantial majority of all Amish remain in farming and farm-related occupations. Amishland remains a basically agricultural community.

Amish homes in the Lancaster area, furthermore, though surprisingly modern in certain respects, are without electricity. There are no light bulbs, illumination being provided by oil lamps or gas-pressured lanterns. And the list of prohibitions remains long: dishwashers, clothes dryers, microwaves, blenders, freezers, central heating, vacuum cleaners, air conditioning, power mowers, bicycles, toasters, hair dryers, radios, television—all are taboo.[17]

There is little indication, therefore, that change in the Amish life-style will get out of hand. The "land squeeze," forcing more of the Amish into nonfarm occupations, will doubtless continue, but only in certain areas. Regional differences in conservatism may undergo modification. The Lancaster County settlement, for instance, was at one time among the more conservative groups, but this is no longer true. In terms of both their population growth and their own distinctive quality of life, however, they continue to thrive.

Leisure and Recreation

The followers of Jacob Amman work hard; indeed, it is difficult to see how any group could work harder. Recreation and leisure are another matter, however, for in these spheres they have somewhat restricted options. There are a number of reasons for this.

To begin with, the typical Amish farmer and his wife have a limited amount of leisure time. For the husband, the prohibition on tractors means that fieldwork is laborious and time-consuming. And since his wife is denied the use of so many electrical appliances, a number of her routine chores—particularly food preparation—must be done largely by hand.

[17]Ibid.

Also, the Amish do not have a wide range of interests. Except for necessary business trips, they tend to stay away from cities. They feel that city life epitomizes worldliness, and worldliness is linked with wickedness. But this means that the Old Order Amish effectively cut themselves off from much of the cultural life of America. They do not attend operas, ballets, or concerts. They do not patronize movies or stage shows. They do not go to art exhibits. Generally speaking, they seldom dine out—nor do they go to bars or nightclubs. Attendance at sporting events is strictly *verboten*.

At home, the followers of Jacob Amman are similarly restricted in their choice of activities. They do not have television, radio, or stereo. They do not dance, play cards, or attend cocktail parties. They have no pianos or other musical instruments. They are not particularly interested in popular magazines or novels. They are not even permitted that great American invention, the telephone!*

The Amish community does not celebrate most American holidays. Memorial Day, Halloween, Labor Day, Veteran's Day, Lincoln's and Washington's birthdays, the Fourth of July—all are ignored. Christmas and Easter are celebrated, although the emphasis is religious rather than secular. Christmas does not involve a Christmas tree, lights, mistletoe, decorations, Christmas cards, or Santa Claus. All work is suspended, however, and the children are given presents.

The Ban on Autos   Another restrictive factor—one of the most striking, in terms of leisure and recreation—is the Amish ban on automobile ownership. The ban is unequivocal, although it is permissible to ride in someone else's car. It is also acceptable to take a bus or taxicab.

Several reasons have been suggested for the ownership ban. It has been pointed out that horses are mentioned in the Bible. It is said that automobiles—and their maintenance—are expensive compared to the horse and buggy. The matter of fertilizer (or lack of it) has already been mentioned. But while these factors may be contributory, they do not comprise the real reason. The real reason is that the Old Order Amish feel that automobile ownership would disrupt their entire way of life.

When automobiles first became popular in the 1920s, they were expensive and unreliable. They were, nevertheless, a major invention, and represented a sharp break with the more traditional forms of transportation. Accordingly, they were rejected by both the Amish and the majority of Mennonites. But whereas most Mennonite groups eventually lifted the ban, the Amish community refused to budge, a position they have held to this day.

*Although they are permitted to use pay telephones, which abound in Amishland. Also, depending on the district, phones may be found in Amish shops.

Scott writes as follows on the matter:

> The various groups that retain horse-drawn vehicles believe it is very important to maintain a close-knit family, church, and community structure. It is felt that the auto is a disintegrating force on these institutions. With fast, easy transportation readily available, family members are apt to be away from home more often than not, and the church community is likely to become very scattered.
>
> The auto tends to draw people to the city, and the plain people feel that this is no place for a Christian to be. . . . Also, cars are often the objects of pride and ostentation, whereas humility is a central theme in Old Order doctrine.[18]

The followers of Jacob Amman have come under heavy pressure to permit the ownership of automobiles. Horseshoes make grooves in the road, and in a number of areas grooved roads are commonplace. More important, modern highways are dangerous, and buggies have been smashed by oncoming cars, especially at night. State laws require lights on moving vehicles, and the Amish have had to install night lights, powered by under-the-seat batteries. Pressures for automobile ownership have become so great that occasionally an Amish family will leave the church and join the Beachy Amish, a more liberal (but much smaller) group that permits its members to own and drive automobiles.

For years, some observers have predicted that it would only be a matter of time before the followers of Jacob Amman converted to autos, but the predictions have not come true. They probably never will either, and the reason is based on a long-recognized sociological principle.

Many years ago, W. I. Thomas—one of the founding fathers of sociology—hit upon the concept *definition of the situation*. Stated simply, this means that a social situation is whatever it is defined to be by the participants. In Thomas's own words, "What men define as real is real in its consequences." The point is that the Old Order Amish have defined the automobile as a threat to their social equilibrium, and they are acting accordingly.

Both individually and collectively, the Amish are wedded to the soil, to the church community, and to the horse and buggy. The automobile would represent a far-reaching and detrimental change. True, the followers of Jacob Amman may be wrong in their judgment. The auto might not bring with it the feared aftereffects. But that is irrelevant. The Amish have already defined the situation, and they can hardly change the definition without also changing their entire social perspective.

---

[18]Stephen Scott, *Plain Buggies: Amish, Mennonite, and Brethren Horse-Drawn Transportation* (Intercourse, PA: Good Books, 1981), p. 6.

Relative Deprivation   The automobile aside, there does appear to be an imbalance in Amishland; that is, there seems to be an overabundance of work and a scarcity of leisure and recreation. As a consequence, are the Amish not disgruntled? Have they no desire to lead fuller lives?

The answer is no. A large majority of Amish people have no desire whatsoever to lead any other kind of life. They do engage in leisure activities, but even if they did not, it is doubtful whether their outlook would be appreciably dampened. The fact is that they believe whole-heartedly in the simple, uncomplicated, slow-paced way of life, and neither hard work nor the lack of many conveniences disturbs them.

One of the reasons for this can be explained by *relative deprivation*, another concept widely employed by sociologists. According to this concept, people feel aggrieved not because of what they are deprived of in any absolute sense, but *because of what they are deprived of in terms of their reference group.*

An employee who receives a $3,000 raise would probably be satisfied if it were known that the amount was as high or higher than that received by others in the department. But if the employee discovered that most of the others had received larger increases, his or her morale would suffer accordingly. Similarly, students are generally satisfied with a B grade—until they learn that the majority of the class received As, with B being the lowest grade given.

Applied to the Amish community, relative deprivation explains a great deal. Most Amish are early risers, day in and day out. They work exceptionally hard, yet are not permitted to own such things as automobiles, television, and air conditioning. But the point is, the entire reference group—all of Amishland—is experiencing the same set of restrictions. A feeling of relative deprivation, therefore, is lacking.

The followers of Jacob Amman are anything but disgruntled. They lack certain conveniences, true, but they all accept this as the will of God. They work hard, but since they generally love their work they do not consider this a burden. As a matter of fact, an Amish family has little trouble operating a 150- or 200-acre farm. The difficulty is not in running a large farm, but in finding a farm large enough to keep the family busy!

The Positive Side   Thus far, we have discussed the negative side of Amish recreation—things they do not do. But what *do* they do in this connection? Much of their social activity revolves around their home and their religion. Socializing—usually men with men and women with women—takes place both before and after church services. On Sunday evenings, the young people hold "singings," social gatherings that serve as a kind of adjunct to dating and courtship. Certain religious holidays afford opportunities for further socializing, and—as will be shown later—weddings are gala occasions.

Just plain visiting is one of the principal forms of entertainment in Amishland. Church services are held every other week, and on alternate Sundays many families visit (or are visited by) relatives or friends. In spite of some acknowledged restrictions, Amish life is far from somber.

The followers of Jacob Amman are also fond of outings and picnics, and from the amount of food consumed on these occasions, eating should perhaps be classed as a recreational activity! The Amish have a special place in their hearts for animals of all kinds, and it is quite common to see an Amish family enjoying a day at a zoo.

Within their own homes, the Amish do some reading, though they are not a bookish group. They read the Bible, the *Ausbund* (the Amish hymnal), and *Martyrs Mirror,* the story of early Anabaptist persecutions. Farm journals are fairly common, and many families subscribe to local papers. Interestingly enough, there is one Amish newspaper, *The Budget*, put out by a non-Amish publisher.

The Old Order Amish occasionally play games, such as chess and checkers, and the youngsters engage in a variety of sports. Some men chew tobacco, and many districts—including those in Lancaster County—now permit smoking. And while drinking is frowned upon, individual Amishmen are sometimes known to "take a nip." Generally speaking, the followers of Jacob Amman evidence a certain degree of tolerance toward drinking, at least on the part of the men.

Religious Customs

Although outsiders are often unaware of it, the Old Order Amish have neither churches nor any kind of central church organization. They have no paid clergy, no missionaries, and no Sunday schools. Yet they are one of the most devout groups in America, and their decentralized church structure—which is simplicity itself—has been remarkably successful.

The Amish are organized into church districts, each district covering a certain geographical area and including a certain number of families. Membership varies, depending on region, but most districts in the United States probably average between 150 and 200 members, including children. When the figure exceeds this number the district usually divides—a fairly frequent occurrence, since the followers of Jacob Amman have always had a high birthrate.

Held in Amish homes on a rotating basis, the Sunday morning service lasts about three hours. Men and women sit separately, with men occupying the first few rows and women at the rear. (Each district has a set of benches, which are hauled to the designated house ahead of time.) The sermons—almost entirely in German—are quite lengthy, and it is not uncommon to see members start to squirm after the first hour or so, especially since the benches have no backs.

Inasmuch as the Old Order Amish do not permit musical instruments, it is sometimes thought that they prohibit singing, but this is not so. Hymns are an integral part of their Sunday service; in fact, their hymnbook—the *Ausbund*—was first published in 1564 and is the oldest hymnal used by any Protestant group. The hymns themselves—140 in number and written for the most part by Anabaptist prisoners—tell of great suffering and steadfastness. The amazing thing is that the tunes are handed down orally from one generation to the next, for the *Ausbund* has no written notes, only words.

The Clergy   Each Amish district is normally presided over by four clergymen: a bishop, two preachers, and a deacon. The bishop (*Volle Diener,* minister with full powers) is the spiritual head of the district. One could really say "spiritual and secular head," because in Amishland the two spheres tend to blend. In any case, the *Volle Diener* is the head man. He presides at weddings, funerals, baptisms, communion services, and excommunications. He also preaches, although this is not his main job. His main job is to prescribe and enforce the rules and otherwise hold the community together. And since the rules of the church are never written, they are—in point of fact—what the bishop says they are.

The two preachers (*Diener zum Buch,* minister of the Book) assist the bishop at ceremonial affairs such as communion and baptism. But their chief duties are delivering the Sunday sermons, leading the congregation in prayer, and interpreting the Bible. The preachers must be well versed in biblical authority and must be able to stand before the congregation and deliver their sermons without notes or books of any kind.

The deacon (*Armen Diener,* minister of the poor) also assists at the Sunday services and at ceremonial affairs. His chief duties, however, have to do with the day-to-day operation of the district. For example, the deacon serves as go-between during marriage arrangements, he obtains information about reported rule infractions, he tries to settle internal difficulties, he looks after families with problems, particularly those involving widows and orphans, and so on.

It should be kept in mind that the four clergymen are not salaried. They must attend to their farms and their families like any other Amishman. And since the church has no property, no treasury, and no centralized administration, the four officers have their work cut out for them. Women, incidentally, are not eligible for the clergy.

If two or more districts are in "full fellowship" with one another—that is, if they agree on specific rules of conduct, mode of dress, allowable equipment, and so forth—they may exchange preachers on a given Sunday. If the districts are not in full fellowship, there is little or no contact between them. In some areas, such as Lancaster County, the bishops of the various districts meet twice a year to discuss church matters and iron out differences. But this is as close to a centralized church organization as the Amish ever get.

Chosen by Man and God   Old Order Amish clergy are always selected by a "combination of man and God"; that is, they are nominated by a vote of the adult congregation, but the "winner" is chosen by lot. More specifically, if a vacancy should occur in the rank of preacher, the congregation is asked to make nominations. Any member who gets at least three votes has his name entered in the lot. On the day of the selection, a number of Bibles are placed on a table, the number corresponding to the number of candidates. One of the Bibles contains a slip of paper with a biblical quotation. As the candidates walk by, each one selects a Bible, and whoever draws the Bible with the slip is the new preacher. He is thus believed to have been chosen by God.

This is the procedure followed for the selection of preachers and deacons. However, the Amish believe the bishops should have some prior experience, and when a vacancy occurs at this level, the selection is made directly by lot from among the preachers and deacons. Once selected, clergy of all ranks normally hold their positions for life. And while in many ways their jobs are thankless ones, most Amish clergymen apparently consider it an honor to have been chosen.

While all the clergy are important, there is no doubt that the bishop is the central figure, since it is he who determines the character of the district. Although outsiders may see little difference among the various Amish communities, the differences are indeed there, and the bishop is aware of them—down to the last detail. Trimming of the beard, design of women's shawls and aprons, type of hats and bonnets, gadgets on the buggy, tractor usage, house furnishings, barnyard and shop equipment— all come under the careful scrutiny of the *Volle Diener.*

It is easy to see why some Amish districts do not have full fellowship with their neighbors. In some districts, the buggies have gray tops; in others, black tops; in others, white tops; and in others, yellow tops. Districts vary in the tempo of their hymn singing. In some districts, men wear their hair at shoulder length; in others, the hair does not even cover the ears. The style of women's head coverings and the length of their skirts vary. Permissible items in the way of home furnishings also vary. And so on.

"Temporary Visitors"   The followers of Jacob Amman believe strongly that they are only temporary visitors on earth, and that their principal duty is to prepare for the next world. The present world—and all that it connotes—is bad; hence the Amish try to remain aloof from it. This explains why they insist on being "peculiar"; that is, dressing differently, acting differently, and living differently.

Like most other aspects of their lives, Amish theological beliefs are the essence of simplicity. Since they are on earth for only a short period, the Old Order Amish have little interest in improving the world or making it a better place to live in. Their entire orientation is otherworldly. They believe that the Word of God calls for self-denial and are quite content to make the necessary sacrifices. God, furthermore, is a personal, literal God, and the Bible is a literal transcription of His word. Also—and this is quite important—God is omnipotent. All things are ordered by Him, and nothing happens without His knowledge.

As for personal salvation, the Amish believe in eternal life, which involves a physical resurrection after death. The eternal life, however, may be spent in either heaven or hell, depending on how one lives during one's visit on earth. Members can expect to go to heaven if they follow the rules of the church, for by so doing they put themselves in God's hands.

Although there are no written rules, all the Amish know what is expected of them. Furthermore, there is always the Bible to turn to; in fact, a good many of their customs—including the *Meidung*—are based on specific biblical passages.

Sanctions

The term *sanctions* refers to rewards and punishments employed by a group to bring about desired behavior on the part of its members. Sanctions can thus be either positive or negative, and most groups—including the Old Order Amish—utilize both kinds. The Amish have been more successful than other groups, however, because of the nature of their religious and social organization.

Positive sanctions are quite similar to those used by other communities: membership privileges, group approval, clerical blessings, rites and rituals such as baptism and communion, opportunities for socializing, and, of course, the satisfaction of worshiping God with one's own people.

For *negative sanctions*, the followers of Jacob Amman employ a series of penalties or punishments ranging from the very mild to the very severe. The first step involves informal sanctions: gossip, ridicule, derision, and other manifestations of group disapproval. Such responses are used by groups everywhere, but each Amish community is a small, close-knit unit, and the operation of adverse opinion is particularly effective.

The next step is a formal admonition by one of the clergy. If the charge is fairly serious, the offender might be visited and admonished by both preacher and bishop. The errant member might also be asked to appear before the congregation at large—to confess his or her sin and ask for the group's forgiveness.

The *Meidung* The ultimate sanction is the imposition of the *Meidung*, also known as the "shunning" or "ban," but because of its severity, it is used only as a last resort. The followers of Jacob Amman have a strong religious orientation and a finely honed conscience—and the Amish community relies on this fact. Actions such as gossip, reprimand, and the employment of confession are usually sufficient to bring about conformity. The *Meidung* would be imposed only if a member were to leave the church, or marry an outsider, or break a major rule (such as buying an auto) without full repentance.

Although the *Meidung* is imposed by the bishop, he will not act without the unanimous support of the congregation. Generally speaking, however, the ban is total. No one in the district is permitted to associate with the errant party, including members of his or her own family. Even normal marital relations are forbidden. Should any member of the community ignore the *Meidung*, that person would also be placed under the ban. In fact, the *Meidung* is honored by all Amish districts, *including those that are not in full fellowship with the district in question.* There is no doubt that the ban is a mighty weapon. Jacob Amman intended it to be.

On the other hand, the ban is not irrevocable. If the shunned member admits the error of his or her ways—and asks forgiveness of the congregation—the *Meidung* will be lifted and the transgressor readmitted to the fold. No matter how serious the offense, the Amish never look upon someone under the ban as an enemy, but only as one who has erred. And while they are firm in their enforcement of the *Meidung*, the congregation will pray for the errant member to rectify his or her mistake.

Although imposition of the ban is infrequent, it is far from rare. Males are involved much more often than females, the young more frequently than the old. The *Meidung* would probably be imposed on young males more often were it not for the fact that baptism does not take place until the late 'teens. Prior to this time, young males are expected to be—and often are—somewhat on the wild side, and allowances are made for this fact.

Baptism changes things, of course, for this is the rite whereby the young person officially joins the church and makes the pledge of obedience. Once the pledge is made, the limits of tolerance are substantially reduced. More than one Amish youth has been subjected to the *Meidung* for behavior that, prior to baptism, had been tolerated.

Courtship and Marriage

As might be expected, Amish courtship and marriage patterns differ substantially from those of non-Amish society. Dating customs are dissimilar. There is no engagement or engagement ring. There is no fancy wedding. There is no traditional honeymoon, wherein the newlyweds have a chance to be by themselves. And both before and after marriage, woman's place is firmly in the home. There is no such thing as a women's movement in Amishland. While their connubial behavior does show some similarity to that of the larger society, the Amish tend to have their own way of doing things.

Dating Practices   Amish boys and girls are much more restricted in their courting activities than are the youth of other groups. For one thing, Amish youth work longer hours; hence they have less time for "running around."* Also, Amish youngsters have a limited number of places to meet the opposite sex. They do not attend high school or college, so they are deprived of the chief rendezvous of American youth. They do not normally frequent fast food places, shopping malls, movies, bars, dances, rock concerts, summer resorts, and other recreational catchalls. Nor are their families permitted to have automobiles, which place a further limitation on their amorous activities.

Another restrictive factor has to do with the so-called endogamous provision. Anthropologists employ the term *endogamy* to denote marriage within the tribe or other social unit, in contrast to *exogamy*, or marriage outside the group. Sociologists use the terms with reference to broad groupings such as religion, race, nationality, and social class. But in contrast to the trend in society at large—where exogamous practices seem to be on the increase—the Old Order Amish remain strictly endogamous.

Amish parents forbid their young people to date the "English" (non-Amish). In fact, the only permissible dating is either within the district or between districts that have full fellowship with one another. Endogamy among the Amish, therefore, does serve to limit the number of eligible mates. In outlying districts, this limitation may present some problems.

Despite these factors, Amish dating and courtship are at least as successful as that practiced in society at large. Since Amish youth marry at about the same age as the "English"—women between twenty-one and twenty-three, men between twenty-two and twenty-five—both sexes have a fair amount of exposure to dating. In the process, most of them seem to enjoy themselves, and nearly all of them marry.

Amish courtship activities generally revolve around the "singings" held on Sunday nights. These usually take place at the same farm where that day's church services were held. Singings are run by the young people themselves and often involve participants from other districts.

*"Running around" is an Amish expression and seems to be one of the few terms the outside society has borrowed from them.

Refreshments are served, songs are sung, and there is always a good deal of banter, joking, and light conversation. If he has a date, the boy may bring her to the singing. If he does not, he tries to get one in the course of the evening, so that he may drive her home.

Should the girl permit the boy to drive her home, a dating situation may or may not develop, just as in the outside society. Unlike the larger society, however, Amish youth place less emphasis on romantic love and physical attractiveness, favoring instead those traits that will make for a successful family and community life: willingness to work, fondness for children, reliability, good-naturedness, and the like. The couple them-selves, incidentally, tend to avoid any display of affection in public.

Once the couple decide to get married, the young man is required to visit the deacon and make his intentions known. The deacon then ap-proaches the young woman's father and requests formal permission for the marriage. Permission is usually granted, for both sets of parents are probably well aware of developments and may already have started preparations for the wedding.

Marriage   Weddings are the most gala occasions in Amishland and in Lancaster County alone there are more than a hundred of them each year.[19] Marriage is a major institution for the followers of Jacob Amman, and they go out of their way to emphasize this fact.

The announcement is first made by publishing the banns at a church service, usually two weeks before the wedding. Unless the abode is too small, the wedding is held at the home of the bride. June is not a popular month, as it comes in the midst of planting season. The large majority of Amish weddings take place in November and December, after harvest.

It might also be mentioned that most weddings are held on Tuesdays and Thursdays. Scott offers the following rather ingenious explanation:

> A full day is needed to prepare for a wedding, and making these arrange-ments on a Sunday would be considered sacrilegious. That leaves out Monday. Many weddings are held on Tuesday; but Wednesday is out because people involved in a Tuesday wedding would be cleaning up from the previous day, and those preparing for a Wednesday wedding could not attend on Tuesday.
>
> Thursday is a good day, but a wedding could not be held on Saturday because there could be no cleaning up on Sunday. As for Friday, weddings have simply never been held on that day.[20]

The ceremony itself is not elaborate, although it is rather long, as certain portions of the Old Testament are quoted verbatim. There are no

---

[19]Scott, *Amish Wedding*, p. 30.
[20]Ibid., p. 9.

bouquets or flowers of any kind. The bridal veil, maid of honor, best man, photographs, decorations, wedding march, or other music—all are missing, though there is a good deal of group singing.

The groom wears his Sunday suit, and the bride wears a white cape and white apron. (The only other time she will ever wear white is after death—when she is laid out in a casket.) At the conclusion of the ceremony, no wedding rings are exchanged, nor do the couple kiss. The bishop says simply, "Now you can go; you are married folk."

While the wedding ceremony is unpretentious, the meal that follows is a giant. Enormous quantities of food are prepared, for the entire district may be invited, plus assorted friends and relatives. It is not uncommon to find several hundred people in attendance. Some people, in fact, actually attend several weddings on the same day.[21]

At any rate, in view of the attendance—and of the fact that the Amish have healthy appetites—it is easy to visualize the feast that takes place on a wedding day. Note the following description:

> Traffic was heavy from the temporary kitchen in the basement to the eating areas. Some of the smaller items were passed up the stairs bucket-brigade style. Food for all courses was placed on the table: first, the main dish, bread filling mixed with chicken ("roast" in Amish terminology); then mashed potatoes—ten gallons would be used in all—and gravy (ten quarts).
>
> There was creamed celery—a traditional wedding dish—along with cole slaw (twenty quarts), apple sauce (fifty quarts), thirty cherry pies, four hundred doughnuts, fruit salad, tapioca pudding, and, of course, the standard bread, butter, jelly, and coffee.
>
> Jars of select celery were spaced at regular intervals on the tables, so that the leaves formed a flower-like arrangement.[22]

To help in the preparation and serving of the food, women of the district volunteer their services. Kitchens are often large enough to accommodate several cooks at a time. If not, temporary kitchens may be set up. Guests are generally served in shifts.

When the festivities are over, the bride and groom start on their "honeymoon." While for most young people the honeymoon is a vacation whose chief aim is privacy, among the Amish it is merely an extended series of visits with friends and relatives. Since most of the followers of Jacob Amman have lots of relatives, the visits often last for two or three weeks. As guests on the honeymoon circuit, the newlyweds receive a variety of wedding presents, usually in the form of practical gifts for the home.

After the honeymoon, the couple take their place in the community as

[21]Ibid., p. 13.
[22]Ibid., p. 21.

husband and wife. If it is at all possible, they will settle down to the business of farming. If it is the youngest son who has married, he and his wife may live in his parents' home, gradually taking over both farming and household duties. Even in other instances, however, the young couple will try to live close by, in a house purchased (with considerable parental help) because of its proximity to the parental homestead.

The Amish Family System

There is an old saying in the Amish community that the young people should not move farther away "than you can see the smoke from their chimney." And it is true that a large majority of the Amish were born in the same county as their parents. Rarely will the Amish sell a farm out of the family. Moreover, about the only time an Amish breadwinner will move from the area is when there is no more land available, or when he has had a deep-seated rift with the bishop. As a result, the Amish family system tends to be perpetuated generation after generation, with little change. The church not only frowns on major change, but—should young couples get ideas—parents, grandparents, and assorted relatives are usually close enough to act as restraining influences.

The Amish family system is at once simple and effective. Both husbands and wives are conscientious workers. They take pride in their endeavors. They are known to be such excellent farmers and workers that outsiders often believe them to be quite wealthy. In a monetary sense this is not so, although many Amish do possess sizeable holdings of extremely valuable land.

Since the farm is likely to be an Amish couple's daily concern, they usually have a large number of children to aid in the enterprise. As will be shown later, Amish youngsters are generally exempt from higher education, so that things like compulsory school laws and child labor laws have limited meaning. Consequently, unlike other children, Amish youngsters are considered to be economic assets. Families with ten or more children are far from uncommon; in fact, the *average number* of births per couple is around seven.

To the Old Order Amish, parenthood is quite in keeping with the nature of things. Birth control—of any kind—is held to be against God's will, and is prohibited. Thus, the followers of Jacob Amman have one of the highest rates of increase in North America. Between 1970 and 1990 in Lancaster County, both the number of districts and the Amish population more than doubled.[23]

---

[23]Kraybill, *Riddle of Amish Culture*, p. 263. The 1990 figure was extrapolated.

Role of Women   It is widely understood throughout Amishland that woman's place is in the home. Wives do not lack for kindness and respect—so long as they maintain their subordinate status. As the Amish see it, this duality is simply in keeping with God's wishes: "Man is the image and glory of God; but the woman is the glory of man" (1 Cor. 11:7).

To the outsider, it is readily apparent that the women's movement has no real place among the Old Order Amish. Men make the major decisions, both in the community and in the church. As was mentioned earlier, women are not eligible for the clergy. In addition to their usual household duties, women also perform such tasks as milking cows, mowing the lawn, gardening, and painting walls and fences. In some cases, women can be seen plowing and harvesting with a team of horses. Indications are, though, that Amish men rarely help out with household tasks such as washing dishes, preparing food, cleaning, and the like.

Although there are doubtless exceptions, Amish wives seem well adjusted to the patriarchal way of life. Their social roles are not only well defined, but are uniform throughout Amishland. Amish women realize that their "English" sisters have achieved a much greater degree of equality, yet there is little indication that they desire to change the traditional status quo. They have a substantial voice both in home management and in raising the children. They have an official vote in all church matters, including nominations for the clergy. And—perhaps most important—they have the inner comfort that comes from the knowledge that they are following God's word.

One final note. In any Amish gathering, it can be seen that men tend to associate with men, women with women. The men do not kiss their wives or utter words of endearment. From this, it might be inferred that Amish spouses have only moderate affection for one another, but this is hardly the case. What the followers of Jacob Amman object to is not affection itself but any *overt display* of affection. After all, the Amish are a conservative people, and the idea of kissing, fondling, or holding hands in public is distasteful. In private, they are doubtless as affectionate as any other group.

Family Names   The subject of Amish names is of special interest to genealogists because (1) the Amish themselves seldom marry outside the group, and (2) outsiders rarely marry into the group. And since the number of Amish families immigrating to America was small, most of the present membership can trace their genealogy back to the original families. Amish surnames are much the same today as they were in the 1700s.

Despite the many thousands of Amish in Lancaster County, a dozen or so surnames cover most of the group. In fact, four of the names— Stoltzfus, King, Fisher, and Beiler—account for nearly 60 percent of the households. (There is an oft-told story about the one-room Amish schoolhouse in which thirty-nine of the forty-eight pupils were named Stoltzfus!) Other common surnames include Lapp, Zook, Esh, Smucker, Glick, Riehl, Blank, and Petersheim. Oddly enough, there do not seem to be any Ammans among the Amish of Lancaster County—or elsewhere.

To add to the cognominal confusion, the Old Order Amish rely on the Bible for first names. For males, names like John, Amos, David, Jacob, Samuel, and Daniel are quite popular. For females, Mary, Annie, Katie, Sarah, Rebecca, and Lizzie predominate. Anyone who sends a letter to John Beiler or Mary Stoltzfus, with nothing more than a rural delivery address, is likely to create an interesting problem for the mail carrier.

Given the structure and frequency of their names, how do the Amish themselves—in referring to one another—manage to communicate? The answer is that they are ingenious in their use of nicknames and employment of other identifying features. Hostetler writes:

> Name differentiation is achieved by adopting an abbreviation, describing the physical traits of the person, noting individual preferences or habits, relating a humorous happening, or by referring to the person's occupation or place of residence.
>
> Chubby Jonas, Curly John, and Shorty Abner are indicative of physical traits. Applebutter John, Butter Abe, and Toothpick John derive from personal habits. Gravy Dan stuck with one Amishman when he poured gravy instead of cream into his coffee.
>
> Jocky Joe is a horse trader, Chicken Elam operates a chicken farm, and Chickie Dan works for him. Gap Dave, Gap Elam, and Gap Joe live near a village named Gap. When my own family moved from Pennsylvania to Iowa, my father was nicknamed "Pennsylvania Joe."
>
> Among young people, there is a great deal of nicknaming, especially among boys. Examples are Ashpile, Beanbag, Blip, Bull, Dog, Fatz, Fegs, Fuddy, Gomer, Pinky, and Yo-Yo.[24]

Ogburn's Theory of Family Functions   A number of years ago, William F. Ogburn, a sociologist interested in the study of cultural change, made an interesting observation apropos of the American family. From the colonial period to the present, he said, the family has been characterized by a progressive *loss of functions*. He went on to list the declining functions as education, religion, protection, recreation, and the economic function. The thrust of his argument was that other institutions had taken over these functions. Thus, the function of religion, once centered in the home, had been taken over by the church. Education had become

[24]Hostetler, *Amish Society*, pp. 241–44.

the province of the schools. Recreation had been usurped by commercialized ventures. The economic function had been lost because the family was no longer a producing unit—due largely to the fact that child labor laws and compulsory school laws prohibited children from working. Ogburn's conclusion was that, because of these declining functions, the American family had been weakened.

Some sociologists have accepted Ogburn's thesis, others have questioned it, and the issue is far from dead. Some feel that, while the family may have lost some functions, it has gained others.[25] The Old Order Amish add another dimension to the debate, for the functions that Ogburn claimed had disappeared from the mainstream of American family life are still being performed by the Amish family.

Economically, the Amish farm family is an effective producing unit. Education is still largely a family function, as is recreation. Even religious services are held in the home, and, of course, prayers play an integral part in the life of every Amish family.

The upshot is that in a functional sense the Amish family is a remarkably strong unit. This strength, moreover, is manifest in a number of other ways. Indeed, there is considerable evidence that the Old Order Amish maintain one of the most stable family systems in America. Their birthrate is exceptionally high and is unaffected by social or economic conditions. They have a low infant-mortality rate. Nearly everyone marries, and they seldom marry outside the group. Loss of membership is not a serious problem. Husband-wife-children units are wedded to the land and show strong family and group loyalty. Their farm-type economy has proved both durable and successful.

The Amish have no sexual problems to speak of. Illegitimacy and adultery are almost unheard of. Desertion is practically unknown, and no divorces have yet been reported.

Compared to the larger society, the Amish experience fewer problems with the young—and with the old. The youth are seldom in trouble with the law, and, as mentioned earlier, the oldsters are cared for by their own families, not public institutions. Orphans, widows, and other dependents are looked after by the community, and no Amish person has ever been on welfare.

The Amish Kin Network   One final point that should be mentioned in connection with the Amish family system is their kinship structure, for nothing like it—nothing remotely like it—exists among typical American families. After all, around one-half of American couples do not even sustain their own marriage—they separate or get divorced. Of those

---

[25]See the discussion in William Kephart and Davor Jedlicka, *The Family, Society, and the Individual* (New York: Harper & Row, 1988), pp. 7–13.

who do stay together, one or two-child families are the norm. As a consequence, the extended family—aunts, uncles, nieces, nephews, cousins—tends to be small in number and limited in function.

In Amishland, the opposite is true. The family is clearly the heart of Amish society, and their large kin network functions as a vascular support system. Here is Kraybill's account.

> After a new family "settles down" in a residence after marriage, its members typically live there for the rest of their lives. . . .
>
> A mother of six children explained that all of them live within Lancaster County, and that she delights in visiting her thirty-six grandchildren at least once a month. Those living on the other side of the house she, of course, sees daily. With families averaging nearly seven children, it is not unusual for a couple to have forty-five grandchildren.
>
> A typical child will have two dozen aunts and uncles, and as many as seventy-five first cousins. . . . Embroidered or painted rosters of the extended family hang on the walls of Amish homes—a constant reminder of the individual's notch in the family tree.[26]

Although it was reported back in the 1960s, the American record for the largest family is probably still held by an Amishman—John Eli Miller, who died at the age of ninety-five.

> He was survived by five of his seven children, 61 grandchildren, 338 great grandchildren, and six great-great grandchildren, a grand total of 410 descendants. . . . At the end of his life, the postman was bringing John Miller word of the birth of a new descendant on the average of once every ten days.
>
> What did he think about his large family? Did it worry him to see it growing so large? Indeed it did. John Miller summarized it in one simple question: "Where will they all find good farms?"[27]

Education and Socialization

It is commonly believed that the Old Order Amish are against education, but this is not true. What they are against is the kind of education that would tend to alienate their young people and threaten their agrarian, conservative way of life. In Amishland, therefore, schooling is likely to mean reading, spelling, arithmetic, penmanship, and grammar—plus elements of geography, history, and hygiene.

Today, Amish parents are more than willing to have their youngsters attend school—provided it is an Amish school—for the first eight

---

[26]Kraybill, *Riddle of Amish Culture*, p. 76.
[27]Glenn Everett, "One Man's Family," *Population Bulletin*, 17, No. 8, 1961, pp. 1ff.

grades.[28] But beyond that they balk. They feel that the years fourteen to eighteen are critical, and they object to having their teenagers exposed to high-school worldliness. Over the years, the Amish community has refused to give in on this point.

In the late 1960s, Amish parents in Wisconsin were arrested and convicted for refusing to send their children to the local high school. After a series of legal battles, the case eventually reached the Supreme Court. In a landmark decision in 1972, the Court ruled 7–0 in favor of the Amish parents. While acknowledging the state's justifiable interest in universal education, the Court declared that there were balancing factors, "such as those specifically protected by the Free Exercise Clause of the First Amendment, and the traditional interest of parents with respect to the religious upbringing of their children. . . ."

While the Amish community continues to have school problems in a few states, the 1972 Supreme Court decision has served to eliminate much of the ill feeling. Now, too, it is apparent that public opinion has swung to the side of the Amish. In Lancaster County, the Amish have worked out an accommodation with state officials on a variety of school-related matters. Any new problems will likely be handled in a similar vein.

The Amish School   Amish schools are a true reflection of the Amish people: unassuming, efficient, economical. There are no frills—no school newspaper, clubs, bands, athletic programs, dances, or class officers. The Old Order Amish have no nursery, preschool, or kindergarten programs; in fact, the large majority of their schools have but one room and one teacher. Average enrollment is about thirty.

Amish communities either build their own schools or purchase them from the state. If they are purchased, certain alterations are made, including the removal of all electrical fixtures. Amish school buildings are heated by wood or coal stoves, and generally do not have indoor toilets. But aside from differences in heating, lighting, and toilet facilities, the Amish school looks much the same as any other one-room school: blackboards, chalk, bolted desks, coat racks, posters and colorful pictures, paper and pencils, and—naturally—homemade artistry adorning the walls.

The Amish teacher, usually a young, unmarried woman, is quite different from her non-Amish counterpart. The typical American teacher is a college graduate who, by virtue of having taken specialized courses in

[28]For a classic account of the Amish educational system, see John A. Hostetler and Gertrude Enders Huntington, *Children in Amish Society: Socialization and Community Education* (New York: Holt, Rinehart and Winston, 1971).

education, has acquired a state-issued teaching certificate. The Amish teacher, by contrast, has not even been to high school, let alone college.

The followers of Jacob Amman are convinced that being a good teacher has no relationship to such things as college degrees and state-issued certificates. They feel, rather, that teaching is a kind of calling, and that the calling is a God-given attribute. The ideal Amish teacher is one who, by her very being, can convey to youngsters the Amish outlook on life. Accordingly, she should be well adjusted, religious, and totally committed to Amish principles.

While there are exceptions, naturally, most Amish teachers are dedicated individuals. Although they do not attend high school, many of them take correspondence courses. They have their own teachers' association, attend yearly conferences, and subscribe to the Amish teachers' *Bulletin*. They are often required to serve without pay as teaching assistants for a year or so before being assigned schools of their own. And when they are given their own classrooms, they are willing to work at a very low rate of pay.

It should be noted that the Amish teacher is more than "just a teacher." She is also principal, janitor, nurse, custodian, playground supervisor, and disciplinarian. Although Amish children are better behaved than most, disciplinary problems do arise, in which case the teacher applies the usual antidotes: reprimands, lectures, admonitions, keeping children after school, and having them write their "sins" on the blackboard. For serious infractions—such as willful disobedience or leaving the schoolyard without permission—most Amish teachers will not hesitate to use corporal punishment.

Values   As used by sociologists, the term *values* refers to ideals and beliefs that people feel strongly about. In fact, values are so basic to those who hold them that they tend to be accepted without question. Most people, furthermore, seem to feel more comfortable when they are in the company of those with a similar value system.

As much as anything else, it is the *totality of values* that sets one group apart from another, a point well illustrated by the Amish school. It is not simply curriculum and course content that differentiate the Amish school from the public school—it is values. Accuracy, for instance, receives much greater emphasis than speed. Memorization of facts and the learning of (Amish) principles are considered more important than analytical thinking and inquisitiveness.

Amish children receive grades—from A to F—but at the same time they are taught not to compete with one another for top marks. To the followers of Jacob Amman, talent—like so many other things in this world—is God-given; hence, it is no disgrace to be a slow learner. In their hierarchy of values, it is more important to do good and to treat others with kindness.[29]

Amish schools are as much concerned with the children's moral development as they are with their mental prowess. Values such as right–wrong, better–worse, good–bad are alluded to over and over again. It is this repeated emphasis on morality—not only by the school but by the church, the home, and the community—that serves to mold the individual's conscience. This fact was mentioned earlier and is worth repeating, for while the threat of the *Meidung* undoubtedly keeps potential wrongdoers in line, it is *conscience* that is a key element in Amish conformity.

Is the educational system of the Old Order Amish successful? Given their religious orientation and their general outlook on life, the answer would have to be yes. Here is the statement of an Amish schoolteacher with several years' experience.

> Amish schools prepare their children to be God-fearing, hard-working, self-supporting persons. They do not, however, teach them to be self-seeking, ambitious, and competitive. . . .
>
> An Amish child is not taught to have selfish needs of privacy, space, recognition and admiration, ambition and rewards that a child in large society absorbs as its birthright. . . .
>
> An Amish child has an enormous sense of security in community. . . . Leaving that security for the fleeting pleasure of higher education is not only risky but fearsome for most.[30]

Primacy of the Home   While the Amish recognize the importance of the school, there is no doubt in anyone's mind that primary responsibility for the socialization of children falls upon the parents. If a youngster has difficulty in school, it is the parents who are consulted. If a boy has trouble within the Amish community, the bishop will talk with the parents as well as with the boy. And if a young person runs afoul of the law, the congregation will sympathize with the parents.

Generally speaking, Amish child rearing embodies a mixture of permissive and restrictive philosophies. Infants are more or less pampered and are seldom alone. As soon as possible, they are fed at the family table and made to feel a part of the group. Relatives and friends shower them with attention. Children soon come to feel that they are welcome members of the community, which in fact they are.

As soon as infants learn to walk, they are subject to discipline and taught to respect authority. Although the Amish family is not authoritarian in structure, it is true that great stress is placed on obedience. This is

---

[29]See the discussion in Hostetler and Huntington, Ibid., pp. 54–96.

[30]Sara Fisher and Rachel Stahl, *The Amish School* (Intercourse, PA: Good Books, 1986), pp. 90–91.

not a contradiction. The obedience is presumed to be based on love rather than fear, on the assumption—unquestioned in Amishland—that parents know best. Spanking and other forms of corporal punishment are quite common, yet the youngsters harbor no resentment. They learn early that such actions are for their own good and are simply manifestations of parental love and wisdom.

Training at home tends to supplement that received at school. Acceptance of traditional values is encouraged, and inquisitiveness discouraged. Cooperativeness rather than competitiveness is emphasized. Children are conditioned to the view that they are all creatures of God, and that therefore they should have deep consideration for the feelings of others. They are reminded—over and over again—of the dangers and evils that lurk in the outside world.

Is the socialization process successful? Practically all observers agree that it is. Hostetler, the foremost authority on Amish life, gives much the same type of answer regarding the home as the Amish schoolteacher gave with respect to the school:

> Early in life the child learns that the Amish are "different" from other people. Thus, he must learn not only how to play the role at home and in the Amish system, but also how to conduct himself in relation to the norms of his "English" neighbors. . . .
>
> Amish children are raised so carefully within the Amish family and community that they never feel secure outside it.[31]

Amish Problems

All groups have social problems of one kind or another, and the Old Order Amish are no exception. At the same time, it is clear that the Amish do have a remarkable record in the "problems" area. Crime, corruption, poverty, divorce and desertion, alcoholism, drug addiction, wife and child abuse—such problems have a low incidence in Amishland. In fact, their low problem rate makes the followers of Jacob Amman wonder what the school controversy was all about. More than one Amish person has said, in effect, "They wanted us to send our youngsters to the consolidated public school and on to high school—but they're the ones with the problems, not us. . . ."

Human nature being what it is, the fact that the Amish have relatively few social problems does not make those that do occur any easier to solve. On the contrary, a given problem may cause more anguish in Amishland than in the larger society. At any rate, the following prob-

---

[31]Hostetler, *Amish Society*, p. 157.

lems are singled out not because they represent major disruptions, but because they are recurrent headaches that the Amish must somehow learn to live with.

The Youth Problem One of the more serious problems facing the Old Order Amish is that of their teenage youth, boys in particular. The latter will sometimes get drunk, become disrespectful, indulge in worldly activities (including buying a car), and otherwise persist in violating Amish mores. Even the girls are sometimes involved. As Kraybill puts it, "The rowdiness of Amish youth is an embarrassment to church leaders and a stigma in the larger community."[32] Accounts like the following appear from time to time in the newspaper:

> A weekend-long end-of-summer hoedown attended by about 500 young Amish in Lancaster County was broken up by police Saturday night after neighbors complained about loud rock music and underage drinking. Police from five small Lancaster County departments descended on Mill Creek at 9:30 P.M. warning the partygoers to clear out or be arrested, according to a West Lampeter police officer. "It was getting uncontrollable," he said. "We decided to shut it down." . . .
>
> Many of the Amish men arrived in automobiles, instead of the customary horse-drawn buggies, and wore modern "English clothes" rather than the dark suits and hats approved by the church. Most of the women wore the traditional Amish dresses and bonnets.
>
> The officer added that the parties were "known for underage drinking," and that there had been arrests in previous years. "This year," he said, "when we went in, the underage kids ran from us."[33]

A young man's owning a car, incidentally, is by no means uncommon, and naturally the various Amish districts are dead set against the practice. But as long as the offender is not yet baptized (hence is not a member of the church), the *Meidung* cannot be imposed.

Fortunately, once a boy is baptized, he nearly always "straightens himself out." Unfortunately, from the Amish point of view, a fair number of Amish youth leave rather than submit to the baptismal vows. Although exact figures are not available, observers estimate the attrition rate to be somewhere in the area of 20 percent. Many of those who do leave join one of the more liberal Mennonite groups.

Threat of Modernization Every decade brings a variety of new inventions and technological improvements to society at large, and the Amish must continually fight against the inroads. Automobiles, telephones, electric lights, tractors, radio and television—such things have taken

---

[32]Kraybill, *Riddle of Amish Culture*, p. 138.
[33]*Philadelphia Inquirer*, September 3, 1984.

their toll on the followers of Jacob Amman. Every Amish community knows of adult members who have left the fold because of what they felt were unnecessarily strict rules.

In several cases, *entire congregations* have seceded. Thus in 1927, an Amish bishop, Moses M. Beachy, led a movement away from the main body. As mentioned earlier, members of this group—known today as the Beachy or Church Amish—are permitted to own automobiles and certain other modern conveniences. In 1966, a group known as the New Order Amish began to form. The New Order have installed telephones, permit the use of electricity, and utilize tractor-drawn farm machinery.

If, as is so often the case, history repeats itself, the Old Order Amish will probably experience further schisms and secessions in the decades to come.

Annoyance of Tourism   The Amish are a folk society whose way of life hinges on remaining apart from the outside world. The influx of tourism into Amishland, therefore, represents an increasingly irritating problem. By bus, train, plane, and private automobile, visitors are now cascading into certain Amish communities.

The Lancaster County group has been especially hard hit since they are only an hour or two from Wilmington, Baltimore, Washington, Philadelphia, and New York. It is estimated that some 5 million tourists now visit Lancaster County each year, roughly 350 visitors for every Amish man, woman, and child.[34]

Motels, guest houses, restaurants, farmers' markets, shopping centers, country stores, handicraft outlets, antiques, souvenir and novelty shops, discount operations, buggy rides—the number and variety of such enterprises seems endless. The tourists themselves spend hundreds of millions of dollars annually, a very small fraction of which goes to the Amish.

Bus tours—as many as fifty a day—are especially obnoxious to the Amish community. Run by professional tour guides, the vehicles clog the narrow roads, block the horses and buggies, park in front of the schools and farms, and otherwise upset the daily routine. Also, the Old Order Amish are forbidden to have their pictures taken, but camera-wielding tourists often seem to laugh at the proscription.

The mid-1980s were especially trying for the Amish because of the motion picture *Witness*. Filmed over a ten-week period in Lancaster County, the picture purports to show various episodes in the life-style of the Old Order Amish. The Amish themselves objected strongly to the film, feeling that it was an invasion of both their privacy and their religion. Nevertheless, the film was not only completed but proved to be

---

[34]Kraybill, *Riddle of Amish Culture*, p. 228.

immensely popular at the box office. How many viewers were prompted to visit Amishland firsthand will never be known, but the number must have been substantial.

Some Amish have left the area for quieter pastures, although in recent years the exodus has largely stopped. Instead, hundreds of craft shops and produce stands, run by the Amish, now dot the landscape. Some observers feel that large-scale tourism has tended to reinforce cultural identity among the Amish, but this is debatable. In any case, the Amish of Lancaster County are one of the largest tourist attractions in America, and the situation is not likely to change. In most other areas, fortunately, tourism is not nearly so pressing.

Government Intervention   As the nation grows, the web of government becomes more complicated, laws proliferate, bureaucracy increases, and the Amish, no less than other citizens, are confronted with a maze of regulations. The followers of Jacob Amman must now have their children vaccinated and inoculated. Amish dairy farmers have been forced to have their milk inspected according to government regulations. And, though outsiders may or may not be aware of it, the Amish must pay state and federal income taxes, property taxes, and sales taxes.

As has been mentioned, at one time or another the Old Order Amish have also had run-ins with government agencies regarding such issues as compulsory education, building codes, social security and medicare, safety devices on buggies, zoning regulations, unemployment insurance, and military conscription.

The last issue—involving draft laws and compulsory military service—deserves special mention, for the Amish are pacifists in a literal sense. They will not fight *under any condition*. As Huntington points out, "All forms of retaliation to hostility are forbidden. An Amishman may not physically defend himself or his family even when attacked. He is taught to follow the New Testament of the Sermon on the Mount."[35]

It follows, of course, that the Old Order Amish will not serve in the armed forces or otherwise fight for their country. And because of their stand, they had some altercations with the authorities during both world wars. Generally, though, their position has been respected by the government. If they were to be drafted today, Amish youth would be allowed to perform alternative service as conscientious objectors.

When all is said and done, nevertheless, there is no doubt that the followers of Jacob Amman often find government regulations both burdensome and obstructive. As the record shows, they have had more than their share of bureaucratic grief. And while they have thus far been

[35]Huntington, "Amish Family," p. 382.

able to hold their own, the Amish community never knows when trouble will strike again.

Vanishing Farmland: The Number-One Problem?   Many observers feel that the scarcity of farmland is the biggest problem facing the Amish today. Although there is no real shortage of land in the United States, *good farmland* is extremely scarce in some Amish communities. The reasons are rather obvious. The Old Order Amish are increasing much faster than the population at large, and since most Amish turn to farming, the supply of arable land in a given community tends to become exhausted.

As a further aggravation, the Amish must often bid for land not only against other farmers but against industrial and commercial developers. In Lancaster County, for instance, the price of land has become astronomical, with some tracts selling for as high as $7,000 and $8,000 an acre.

From the Amish point of view, what is the answer?

Aside from subdividing their farmland among one or more of their sons—clearly a limited solution—the followers of Jacob Amman have only two realistic choices. They can either relocate, or they can turn to nonfarming occupations. During earlier periods, a number of Lancaster County Amish did indeed migrate to other areas, but in the last decade or so the exodus has stopped. Instead, the Amish have turned increasingly to other occupations. At the present time, to repeat, an estimated 30 percent of married Amish men work in jobs other than farming.

Does this nonfarming trend pose any real danger to the Amish way of life? At a "Coping with Modernity" conference held in Pennsylvania in the late 1980s, more than one authority voiced genuine concern. In fact, both the Lancaster and Philadelphia papers carried similar headlines: "Off-Farm Jobs Threatening Amish Life."[36] Headlines aside, however, what does the future hold? In view of the various problems discussed in the preceding pages, is life in Amishland really threatened?

The Future

To begin with—and speaking generally—the followers of Jacob Amman are very good in the "problem-solving" area. Some critics have argued that the Amish will not survive in their present form, that they will be gobbled up by high-powered, industrialized society. The Amish, however, have outlasted their critics and in all likelihood will continue to do so.

[36]*Lancaster Intelligencer Journal*, July 25, 1987; *Philadelphia Inquirer*, July 26, 1987.

The aforementioned social problems, while certainly real enough, are somewhat deceptive. The youth problem is actually not so serious as it sounds. True, more than a few of their young people misbehave, and a number even defect to other groups—*but this process serves as another safety valve.* The Amish know full well that their rules are strict, and that certain individuals will be unable to conform. But by giving their young people a certain amount of leeway prior to baptism, it is felt that those who do join the church will prove to be loyal and conscientious members.

In practice, the safety-valve theory seems to work, since—overall—a small percentage of baptized members actually leave the fold. As a matter of record, the Amish population has shown spectacular growth: 5,000 in 1900; 33,000 in 1950; well over 100,000 today.

Tourism seems to be more of a chronic irritation than a major problem. And one way or another, the Old Order Amish have learned to live with it. In fact—ironically enough—while most of the tourist dollars go to the non-Amish, tourism does provide the Amish community with some monetary income.

Problems such as government intervention and the threat of modernization are evidently being taken in stride. On the latter point, Huntington makes some pointed observations.

> . . . Movies are forbidden but offer little threat to the Amish community because there is no interest in them; they are too far from the individual's experience and value system to do more than elicit passing curiosity.
>
> In many ways the Amish culture is oral rather then literary. They are not really threatened by the printed word, by radio, or even by television. Consistent with the oral tradition, the Amish stress shared knowledge and the importance of meaningful social interaction.
>
> They are so far outside the mainstream of American culture that they have little shared knowledge with the average American, and little reason to interact socially with him. . . .[37]

It is true that the vanishing farmland has more or less forced some Amish men to take other jobs, and this transposition should not be minimized. It is important, however, to look at the *nature* of these jobs. In Lancaster County, for instance, the Amish have not sought blanket entry into the outside job market. On the contrary, their choice of occupations has been highly selective.

As Kraybill points out, many of the men work in craft shops located on or adjacent to the farm. Married women who work—quilting, baking, craftwork—do so at home.[38] Amish men operate a wide array of shops and small businesses: cabinetry, plumbing, construction, hardware,

---

[37]Huntington, "Amish Family," p. 396.
[38]See Kraybill, *Riddle of Amish Culture*, pp. 197–198.

butchering, machinery repair, masonry, upholstery, furniture, and a variety of retail stores. However, they generally reject factory work as being a bad influence. Indeed, more than 75 percent of those who work away from home are either self-employed or work for an Amish employer.[39]

The same author goes on to conclude that although a third of the Lancaster County Amish have left the farm,

> . . . they have not embraced modern work. Nonfarm work is, by and large, local, family-oriented, small-scale, and nestled in ethnic networks. The Amish have retained personal craftsmanship and job satisfaction, as well as a high degree of identity with, and control over, their products. Moreover, they also control the time, speed, and other conditions of their work. . . .[40]

Conclusion All things considered, the Amish would seem to have a promising future in America. They have handled their problems inimitably and, on the whole, successfully. In the process, they have managed to solidify their identity. Outlook on life, relation to God and the universe, theology, sex roles, clothing styles, love of the soil, separatism, frugality, humility, pacifism, industriousness, attitude toward education—in brief, the basic ingredients of "Amishness"—are much the same today as they always have been.

In the past, the Old Order Amish have sometimes been misunderstood, hassled, fined, and even jailed. Today, conversely, they tend to benefit from public opinion. Tourism has brought millions of Americans to the various Amish communities. And as people have come to see and learn about the Amish firsthand, they have also come to respect the Amish way of life. Consequently, in disputes with the government, an Amish community can often count on valuable public support.

As they look ahead, the Amish are quite optimistic, both in a secular and a sacred sense. The latter, of course, is the critical component, for the followers of Jacob Amman have placed themselves in God's hands—permanently—and they have absolutely no doubts about their future.

SELECTED READINGS

Armstrong, Penny, and Feldman, Sheryl. *A Midwife's Story.* New York: Arbor House, 1986.

[39]Ibid., pp. 199–205.
[40]Ibid., p. 211.

Bryer, Kathleen B. "The Amish Way of Death: A Study of Family Support Systems." *American Psychologist*, 34 (March 1979): 255–61.

The Budget. Sugarcreek, Ohio. (Weekly newspaper published for Amish readers.)

Enninger, Werner. "Coping with Modernity." *Brethren Life and Thought*, 33 (Summer 1988): 154–70.

Fisher, Sara, and Stahl, Rachel. *The Amish School*. Intercourse, PA: Good Books, 1986.

Good, Merle. *Who Are the Amish?* Intercourse, PA: Good Books, 1985.

Hostetler, John A. *Amish Society*. Baltimore: Johns Hopkins University Press, 1980.

———, and Huntington, Gertrude Enders. *Children in Amish Society: Socialization and Community Education*. New York: Holt, Rinehart and Winston, 1971.

Huntington, Gertrude Enders. "The Amish Family." In *Ethnic Families in America*, ed. by Charles Mindel, Robert Habenstein, and Roosevelt Wright, pp. 367–399. New York: Elsevier, 1988.

Kollmorgen, Walter. *Culture of a Contemporary Community: The Old Order Amish of Lancaster County, Pa.* Washington, DC: U.S. Department of Agriculture, 1942.

Kraybill, Donald. *The Riddle of Amish Culture*. Baltimore: Johns Hopkins University Press, 1989.

Kuvlesky, William P. "Some Amish Move a Lot: The Old Order Amish in Texas," paper presented at the 1987 meetings of the Southern Association of Agricultural Scientists, Nashville, Tennessee.

Luthy, David. *The Amish in America: Settlements That Failed, 1840–1960*. Aylmer, Ontario: Pathway Publishers, 1986.

Morello, Carol. "Embattled Midwife to the Amish." *Philadelphia Inquirer*, July 23, 1989.

Schreiber, William. *Our Amish Neighbors*. Chicago: University of Chicago Press, 1972.

Scott, Stephen. *Plain Buggies: Amish, Mennonite, and Brethren Horse-Drawn Transportation*. Intercourse, PA: Good Books, 1981.

———. *Why Do They Dress That Way?* Intercourse, PA: Good Books, 1986.

———. *The Amish Wedding and Other Special Occasions of the Old Order Communities*. Intercourse, PA: Good Books, 1988.

Seitz, Ruth and Blair. *Amish Country*. New York: Crescent, 1987.

Smith, Elmer. *The Amish People*. New York: Exposition Press, 1958.

Smucker, Mervin R. "How Amish Children View Themselves and Their Families: The Effectiveness of Amish Socialization." *Brethren Life and Thought*, 33 (Summer 1988): 218–36.

Weaver, J. Denny. *Becoming Anabaptist: The Origin and Significance of Sixteenth-Century Anabaptism*. Scottdale, PA: Herald Press, 1987.

CHAPTER TWO

THE ONEIDA COMMUNITY

Most readers are familiar with the term *culture,* which refers to the lifestyle of a people—their customs, attitudes, values, and shared understandings that bind them together as a society. Less familiar, probably, is the concept of *subculture.* Yet, as the term suggests, a subculture is a "culture within a culture." In a true subculture, the shared beliefs and values may have more influence on members' behavior than does the larger society. Voluntary subcultures, furthermore, are often formed because of dissatisfaction with society at large.

Such subcultures often develop around a *charismatic leader,* an individual with unusual personal magnetism. John Humphrey Noyes, founder of the Oneida Community, was a person who exuded infectious optimism. He was an astute judge of character. He could "read" his followers with uncanny accuracy, knowing when to praise and when to blame. He knew when—and to whom—to delegate authority. And he always knew the mood and temperament of his community.

On the one hand, as will be shown, Noyes was an original thinker, a sound judge of human nature, and an exceedingly versatile individual. On the other hand, he was capricious, unpredictable, and at times given to making errors in judgment. Little wonder that social historians have been hard pressed to depict the "real" John Humphrey Noyes.

Background

Unlike most of the other leaders discussed in the present volume, John Humphrey Noyes was of upper-class origin. His mother, Polly Hayes, was a cousin of Rutherford B. Hayes, the nineteenth president of the United States. His father was John Noyes, a United States congressman from Vermont and a successful businessman.

Not much is known about the boyhood of John Humphrey Noyes. One of eight children, he was born in 1811 at Brattleboro, Vermont. In 1821, his family moved to Putney, a small town ten miles to the north. Redhaired, freckled, and somewhat self-conscious about his appearance, he was noticeably shy around girls. With members of his own sex, however, he showed clear evidence of leadership. He entered Dartmouth at fifteen, a typical college age at that time, and was eventually elected to Phi Beta Kappa.

Upon graduation, Noyes worked as an apprentice in a New Hampshire law firm. However, it soon became obvious that he was not cut out to be a barrister, and he returned home to Putney. Up to that time, he certainly had no thoughts of founding a subculture, and it is doubtful whether he had ever heard of a place called Oneida.

The early 1830s found the country caught up in a frenzy of religious rejuvenation, and, as luck would have it, a four-day revival was held in Putney in September 1831. Noyes attended, listened—and succumbed completely. To those who knew him, he suddenly seemed to come alive with ideas, spiritual enlightenment, and visions of eternal truth. Although religion had not heretofore been a major part of his life, it was obvious that he had found his calling. Henceforth he would devote himself to disseminating God's word. A few weeks later he enrolled in theological seminary—first at Andover, then at Yale.

At Yale, Noyes acquired the reputation of being a radical, and although he was granted his license to preach in 1833, he was not a success. At one point, for example, he declared himself to be without sin—for which heresy he was called before the theological faculty. He refused to recant, whereupon his preaching license was revoked.

Putney

Jobless, penniless, and now looked upon as a religious oddity, John Humphrey Noyes did not appear to have much of a future, but there were several things in his favor. He was only twenty-three years old. He had an inner flame that was inextinguishable. He was already making a few converts, and soon he would make more. In an oft-quoted statement, he said, "I have taken away their license to sin, and they keep on sinning. So, though they have taken away my license to preach, I shall keep on preaching." Events were to prove the statement more prophetic than Noyes realized.

For the next few years he traveled through New York and New England, living on a shoestring and spreading the doctrine of Perfectionism: man could be without sin. Although the concept did not originate with him, Noyes's brand of Perfectionism was genuinely new. And while, over the years, he added a number of additions and refinements, his basic theological postulate remained unchanged: Christ had already returned to earth—in A.D. 70—so that redemption or liberation from sin was an accomplished fact. Given the proper environment, therefore, man could lead a perfect, or sinless, life.

This was a radical notion, of course, and while he made some head-way in spreading the gospel of Perfectionism, the existing churches turned a deaf ear to his teachings. Noyes returned home in 1836, so-bered by his experience. He would spend the next dozen years in Put-ney, incorporating Perfectionism into the most radical social experiment America had ever seen.

Things started off innocently enough. Noyes's first converts in Putney were members of his own family: his sisters, Charlotte and Harriet, his brother, George, and his mother. (His father rejected the whole idea.) Other converts trickled in, one here, one there. In 1838, he married Harriet Holton, granddaughter of the lieutenant governor of Vermont. She not only was a convert but remained a loyal Perfectionist all her life. By 1844, however, adult membership was still only about two dozen, although there were other small groups of followers scattered through-out New England.

During the early years, the Putney Perfectionists were not a commu-nal organization. Members lived in individual houses and worked at individual jobs. They had resources; in fact, they were incorporated for $38,000, the money coming largely from the estate of Noyes's father. But even before they adopted the communal style of life, one thing was clear: the Putneyites were not a democracy. John Humphrey Noyes was both the leader and the binding force. And while he often gave the impression of operating through discussion and persuasion rather than by proclamation, there was no doubt in anyone's mind—including his own—about who made the rules.

Finally, in 1844, the Putney Perfectionists adopted economic commu-nism as a way of life. They commenced to share their work, their food, their living quarters, and their resources. Their children began to attend a communal school. And once every day, for a protracted period, they met together for Bible reading, theological discussion, and a sharing of religious experiences.

In 1846, the group began to share spouses.

Coitus Reservatus   Following his marriage to Harriet Holton in 1838, Noyes fathered five children in six years. Unfortunately, all but one were stillborn, a fact that was to have utmost significance. The Perfectionist leader grieved deeply, not only for the lost children but for their mother. Was this to be woman's lot in life, to bear children year after year, whether or not they were wanted? To suffer, to mourn, to be kept out of the mainstream of daily activity—all because of nature's imperious call? He thought not, but what could be done about it?

The Shakers had solved the problem—to their own satisfaction, at least—by practicing celibacy. Noyes rejected this rather drastic solution, although he realized that, whatever the answer was, it would have to include some sort of birth control. He finally hit upon the novel idea of *coitus reservatus*, or, as he called it, male continence. It was not necessary, he said, for a man to reach ejaculation during the sex act. With a little practice, he could enjoy sex relations without attaining the climax that might lead to conception.

In his widely-quoted pamphlet *Male Continence*, Noyes had this to say:

> Now we insist that this whole process, up to the very moment of emission, is *voluntary*, entirely under the control of the moral faculty, and *can be stopped at any point*.
>
> In other words, the *motions* can be controlled or stopped at will, and it is only the *final crisis of emission* that is automatic or uncontrollable. . . . If you say that this is impossible, I answer that I *know* it is possible—nay, that it is easy. (pp. 7–8)

As it turned out, Noyes's contention was correct, at least insofar as the Perfectionists were concerned. Throughout the whole of the group's existence, *coitus reservatus* was used—and used successfully.

Exodus   As might have been predicted, once the Perfectionists began the practice of spouse sharing, the word soon spread. Actually, there was never any attempt—then or later—to keep the matter a secret. In his numerous sojourns and talks, Noyes often alluded to the fact that his brand of communism involved sexual as well as economic sharing.

Nevertheless, to the citizens of Putney, right was right, and wrong was wrong—and sex outside of marriage was wrong. It was the 1840s (not the 1990s!), and marriage meant one man and one woman, joined in the sight of God and legally recorded in the town-hall registry. The followers of John Humphrey Noyes, quite obviously, were not only living in sin but were more or less flaunting the practice. The following bizarre episode, for example, is cited by Whitworth:

> In June 1847, Noyes "miraculously" cured Harriet Hall, an associate of the group, who had been an invalid for some years, and had been given up by her doctors as suffering from an incurable, and certainly unusual, combination of dropsy and tuberculosis.
>
> Subsequently, the sectarians cited this case as the most convincing proof of Noyes' spiritual powers. However, the gratitude of Mr. Hall, who had always been ambivalent about the sect, was insufficiently deep to withstand Noyes' admission that sexual intercourse had been part of the treatment. Accordingly, he lodged a complaint with the State Attorney at Brattleboro.[1]

One thing led to another. Finally, irate citizens met in protest and demanded action. In October 1847—amidst rumors of mob violence—John

---

[1]John Whitworth, *God's Blueprints: A Sociological Study of Three Utopian Sects* (London and Boston: Routledge & Kegan Paul, 1975), p. 116.

Humphrey Noyes was indicted by a grand jury on grounds of adultery. He was released, pending trial, on $2,000 bail. Had the trial been held, the Perfectionist leader would almost surely have been found guilty. However, after much soul-searching and discussion—and upon the advice of his lawyer—Noyes fled to New York. As he explained it later, the reason for his flight from Vermont was not to escape justice, but to save his followers and others from the mob violence which was clearly imminent. Oddly enough, though he probably caused more shock and outrage than any other religious leader of his time (with the probable exception of Joseph Smith, founder of the Mormons), John Humphrey Noyes was never to stand trial for his unorthodox—and illegal—practices.

Oneida

All during his stay in Putney, Noyes had made periodic forays into the hinterland to gain converts. His various publications had helped to spread the word. By 1847, when the Perfectionists' sexual system became operative, the popular press was also giving John Humphrey Noyes and his followers a good deal of publicity. When Noyes left Putney, therefore, other Perfectionist centers—rather loosely organized— were available to him. One such spot was a fairly large tract of land along Oneida Creek in New York State.

Formerly a reservation belonging to the Oneida Indians and now the site of a sawmill, the property was owned by Jonathan Burt, an ardent follower of Noyes. Burt had come upon hard times and was quite willing to turn over his land to the Perfectionist cause. Noyes was attracted to the site and wasted no time in reassembling the little flock of Putneyites. Burt and his associates stayed on. Other small groups of followers joined them. They cleared land, made their own implements and furniture, and held discussions. Working as farmers, they were able to buy up adjoining properties. Before long, their Oneida holdings totaled nearly six hundred acres. And in spite of adverse conditions, membership continued to grow. By the end of the first year, 1848, there were eighty-seven persons living in the Community. A year later, the number had more than doubled!

From the very beginning, the mission of the group was made crystal clear. With the help of Almighty God, as expressed through the person of John Humphrey Noyes, they were going to create a heaven on earth. There was never any doubt about their utopian goal. Nor was there any doubt about how they were going to attain it.

The Mansion House   During their first winter at Oneida, the little group of Perfectionists lived in the existing dwellings: Jonathan Burt's homestead plus some abandoned Indian cabins. Top priority, however, was given to the construction of a communal home. John Humphrey Noyes believed that, in actual day-to-day living, true communism could best be achieved by having all members live under one roof. This was the way the Perfectionists lived throughout the rest of their existence.

In the summer of 1849, the first communal home was built. No one knows how it got the name Mansion House, but it was a wooden affair and was constructed by the entire Community. Membership grew so rapidly, though, that in 1862 the wooden structure was replaced by a brick building. In subsequent years, wings were added as needed, and the building still stands in its entirety. Noyes helped in the planning of both the original and the present building, and both were exceptionally well thought out.

Although most adults had small rooms of their own, the building as a whole was designed to encourage a feeling of togetherness rather than separateness. To this end, *group facilities* predominated: a communal dining room, library, concert hall, recreation area, picnic grounds, and the like. It was in the Big Hall of the Mansion House that the regular evening meetings were held, and it was here that Noyes gave most of his widely quoted home talks.

Over the years, the Perfectionists developed a lively interest in the performing arts, and—although most of the talent was homegrown—they were able to organize such activities as symphony concerts, choral recitals, and Shakespearian plays. Occasionally, outside artists were invited to perform, but on a day-to-day basis the Community was more or less a closed group, with members seldom straying far from home.

Sociologically speaking, the Perfectionists' reference behavior related entirely to the group. The larger community, figuratively and literally, was considered to be "outside" and was usually referred to as "the World." It was this system of *integral closure,* sustained over several decades, that served as a primary solidifying force. And, of course, it was the Mansion House that made the system operable.

Primary-Group Interaction

All of us have certain emotional needs: to talk, to be listened to, to socialize, to share experiences, to exchange banter, to elicit sympathy and understanding, and so on. These needs, for most people, are best satisfied within the dimensions of a small, face-to-face group, such as the family, the clique, the friendship circle. Sociologists refer to such groups, therefore, as *primary groups.* By contrast, *secondary groups*—such as the large corporation, the business firm, or the government bureau—are characterized by an impersonality of association. For the most part, members tend not to relate to one another in an emotionally meaningful way.

With several hundred people living under one roof, the Oneidans had an interesting problem in human relations: how to enjoy the benefits of primary-group association in an organization that had already grown to secondary-group size? They had the advantage, naturally, of believing both in John Humphrey Noyes and in the tenets of Perfectionism, but these convictions alone would hardly account for the operational smoothness that prevailed.

Their success is explained by the fact that they worked out an amazingly effective system of interpersonal relationships. If it weren't that the discipline of sociology had not yet been envisioned, one would have thought that the Oneida Community had somehow gained access to a text in introductory sociology!

Practically everything the Perfectionists did was designed to play down the "I" in favor of the "we." Members ate together at a common dining table, worked together at common tasks, and played together in a variety of recreational pursuits. They shared their property. They shared their sexual partners. And they shared their children.

In their day-to-day activities, they were ever on guard against things that might become "antigroup." Thus, tea, coffee, and alcoholic beverages were taboo. At the dining table, pork products, including bacon and sausage, were never served; in fact, meat of any kind appeared infrequently. The Perfectionists reasoned that proclivities such as coffee drinking and meat eating might become habitual and hence distractive. By the same token, dancing was encouraged since it was a group activity, while smoking was prohibited because it was too individualistic.

From an outsider's view, some of the prohibitions seem excessive. An interviewer was told, for example, of an episode involving all the girl children. There were several large dolls which, like other material things in the Community, were shared. Around 1850, some kind soul thought it would be better if each of the little girls had a doll of her own, and this plan was put into effect. Unfortunately, it developed that the youngsters spent too much time with their dolls and not enough on household chores. Accordingly, on a specified date, all the girls joined hands in a circle around the stove, and one by one were persuaded to throw their dolls into the fire. From that time on, dolls were never allowed in the nursery.

Often overlooked is the fact that the religious practices of the Oneidans also served to accentuate primary-group association. It is true that the Perfectionists dispensed with most of the formal aspects of religion. They maintained no church or chapel, held no prayer services, had no paid clergy. Neither baptismal nor communion services were utilized. Since there was no marriage, there were no weddings. Death was played down,

and there were no formal funeral arrangements. Christmas was not celebrated as a religious holiday, although in deference to outsiders, no work
was performed on that day.

At the same time, religion was a central part of the Oneidans' daily
lives. This was the whole point. Rather than have special religious celebrations or special days set aside for worship, the Perfectionists believed
that every day should involve religious awareness. They were avid readers of the Bible and loved to discuss the various parables. They believed
in Perfectionism. And they believed that by listening to John Humphrey
Noyes—and following his teachings—they were listening to the voice of
God.

The Big Hall   Every night of their lives, the Oneidans met in the Big
Hall to combine the sacred and the secular. Women brought their sewing
and knitting, and both sexes sat in groups around small tables. The
program was conducted from in front of the stage by one of the senior
members. A hymn was sung, passages from the Bible were read, and if
he was present, Noyes would give one of his home talks. The talks
themselves, involving as they did the secular application of Perfectionist
theology, were one of the highlights of the evening—so much so that if
Noyes were traveling, the talk would be read by someone else. Also
included in the nightly program were news and announcements, lectures, dancing, comments and suggestions by members of the audience,
business reports, and so forth. The evening meetings can thus be seen as
another means of promoting group solidarity. According to the weekly
Oneida Circular of July 17, 1863, the meetings were "the most cherished
part of our daily lives."

Noyes, incidentally, was no prude. He enjoyed entertainment and
activities of all kinds, and encouraged his followers to do the same. Even
on this point, however, he insisted on *group* involvement: a glee club
rather than a soloist, a band or orchestra rather than a recital, a play or
an operetta rather than a monologue, and so on.

Although by modern standards such entertainment might seem rather
tame, there is no doubt that the system worked. The Oneidans were
clearly successful in their efforts to establish a primary rather than a
secondary-group atmosphere. They were also successful at preventing
the development of a *culte du moi* in favor of an integrated and sustained
we-feeling. Both in their conversation and their publications, it was "the
family" this and "the family" that.

One of the oft-told stories of the Community pertains to the time a
visitor was shown through the Mansion House. "What is the fragrance I
smell here in this house?" the stranger asked. The guide replied, "It
must be the odor of crushed selfishness."

Decision Making

All organizations have a power structure and a decision-making process, and the Oneida Community was no exception. However, the Perfectionists had a special problem since (1) they were all housed under one roof, and (2) they were attempting to combine the social and the economic. They solved the problem by employing a combination of the democratic and the autocratic.

Committee Work   In keeping with their emphasis on group solidarity, the followers of John Humphrey Noyes might have been expected to arrive at decisions on a democratic basis. And in one sense, there was ample opportunity for discussion. The Community *Handbook*, for example, states:

> In determining any course of action or policy, *unanimity* is always sought by committees, by the Business Board, and by the Community. All consider themselves as one party, and intend to act together or not at all. . . . If there are serious objections to any proposed measure, action is delayed until the objections are removed. The majority never go ahead leaving a grumbling minority behind. (p. 17)

True enough, but what these lines refer to were the day-to-day operational decisions. Major decisions, as well as Perfectionist doctrine and Community policy, were made by Noyes.

On operational matters, members were indeed encouraged to speak out at the evening meetings. Moreover, there were a sufficient number of committees and departments to enable everyone to have a real voice in the day-to-day management of the Community. In this respect, the trouble was not that members had insufficient authority, but that they had too much. There were no less than twenty-one standing committees and forty-eight different departments. Such things as heating, clothing, patent rights, photographs, haircutting, fruit preserving, furniture, music, dentistry, bedding, and painting all involved a committee or a department. There was even a department for "incidentals"!

The committees and committee heads met; departments and department heads met; the business board met. The Community itself met nightly. In a given thirty-day period, there were probably more managerial discussions in the Oneida Community than in any organization of comparable size in the United States.

The upshot was that the Perfectionists wasted too much time thrashing out details and inaugurating meaningless change. In fact, change was almost a fetish with them. They changed the work schedule, the meal schedule, and the number of meals per day, discussing endlessly which foods to serve and which to prohibit. (The debate over whether to serve tea, for example, took several years. They finally decided to permit only a brew made from strawberry leaves.) The prohibition against smoking was also years in the making. The Perfectionists liked to change their jobs and their way of doing things. For some reason, they even had a habit of changing their rooms.

A revealing statement on the matter of change appears in the *Circular* of April 25, 1864.

> It is a point of belief with us that when one keeps constantly in a rut, he is especially exposed to attacks of evil. The devil knows just where to find him! But inspiration will continually lead us into new channels by which we shall dodge the adversary.

The Central Members   Noyes was the acknowledged leader of the Community, ruling benevolently but firmly and basing his authority on divine inspiration. As his son Pierrepont put it, "The Community believed that his inspiration came down what he called the 'link and chain'—from God to Christ; from Christ to Paul; from Paul to John Humphrey Noyes; and by him made available to the Community."[2]

On their part, the Perfectionists were quite content with the arrangement. They acknowledged that Noyes was God's representative on earth. As a matter of fact, such acknowledgment was one of the preconditions for membership.

Nevertheless, Noyes was away a good part of the time, and in his absence important decisions had to be made—on some basis other than the twenty-one committees and forty-eight departments. The system employed was the utilization of "central members." These were a dozen or so men and women who more or less served as Noyes's deputies. They were all older, dedicated individuals, many of whom had been with John Humphrey Noyes at Putney.

This, then, was the leadership process. Noyes made the major decisions, aided and abetted by the central members. These decisions encompassed economic policy, sexual matters, relations with the outside, admission of new members, childbearing and child rearing, and, of course, Perfectionist doctrine. Day-to-day operational details were handled by committees and departments, in consultation with the general membership.

The Oneida Community was hardly a model of functional efficiency. The Shakers, communistic in form, were much better organized. Yet the Perfectionists' system worked. Up to the very end, the Community func-

---

[2]Pierrepont B. Noyes, *My Father's House: An Oneida Boyhood* (Gloucester, MA: Peter Smith, 1966), pp. 132–33.

tioned with scarcely a major quarrel. What they lost in operational efficiency, they gained in their primary-group associations and in their feelings of closeness to one another.

Role of Women

Because there were a number of divergent forces at work, the role of
women must have presented something of a problem for the Perfectionists. On the one hand, they believed in equality. Concepts of rank and
privilege were foreign to them. They were communists, and they were
proud of it. On the other hand, in society at large, women held a clearly
inferior position. They were generally excluded from higher education,
from the professions, and from public office. All but the most routine
jobs were closed to them. When the Oneida Community was founded in
the spring of 1848, a wife had no legal control over her own personal
property, and the right to vote was more than seventy years away. Indeed, the first Women's Rights Convention—at Seneca Falls, New
York—had not yet been held.

To complicate matters, John Humphrey Noyes—in this sense, at
least—was a product of his times, for he, too, believed in man's innate
superiority over woman. As Foster aptly points out, "Although Noyes
emphasized the necessity of a reciprocal relationship of mutual respect
between the sexes, he made it clear that man's primacy over woman was
part of the very nature of the universe."[3]

The Perfectionists solved their problem by way of a compromise. They
refused to acknowledge that, inherently, women were the equal of men.
But as far as the allocation of jobs was concerned, the Community was far
ahead of the World. The Oneida *Handbook* makes the following statement:

> Communism emancipates a woman from the slavery and corroding cares
> of a mere wife and mother; stimulates her to seek the improvement of
> mind and heart that will make her worthy of a higher place than ordinary
> society can give her. . . .
> Gradually, the Community women have risen to a position where, in
> mind and in heart, they have all and more than all that is claimed by the
> women who are so loudly asserting their rights. And through it all, they
> have not ceased to love and honor the truth that "the man is the head of
> the woman," and that woman's God-given right is to be "the glory of
> man." (p. 26)

---

[3]Lawrence Foster, *Religion and Sexuality: Three American Communal Experiments of the Nineteenth Century* (New York: Oxford University Press, 1981), p. 105.

In practice, the Oneida women did women's work, but they also handled jobs that were normally reserved for men. They did the cooking, washing, sewing, mending, and nursing, and were responsible for child care, but they also worked in various business and industrial departments. They held jobs in the library and on the Community newspaper. In a number of other areas, they worked side by side with the men. And they were well represented on the various committees, including that of the central members. As one of the female interviewees remarked:

> Most people have overlooked the fact that Father Noyes delegated a lot more responsibility to the women here than they ever would have received on the outside. Every committee had women on it. It made a difference, too. All the old folks will tell you it made both men and women respect each other.

There were a number of so-called adult educational programs within the Community, and women as well as men were encouraged to take part. Subject matter included mathematics, science, music, and foreign languages. At one time, the Perfectionists even discussed plans for the establishment of a university. And while the plans never materialized, there was no doubt that women would have been admitted to the same courses as men. The point is worth mentioning because at the time, in 1866, only Oberlin College in all the United States admitted women.

The New Attire   Male members of the Oneida Community dressed much like anybody else, but visitors were caught off guard when they first saw the women's attire. It was John Humphrey Noyes, never the one to accept a conventional practice if he could find an "improvement," who first pointed to the impracticality of the standard female attire. "Woman's dress is a standing lie," he wrote in the first annual report of the Community in 1848. "It proclaims that she is not a two-legged animal, but something like a churn, standing on castors!"

He went on to suggest a change: "The dress of children—frock and pantalettes—is in good taste, not perverted by the dictates of shame, and well adapted to free motion." Accordingly, three of the women embarked upon a daring stylistic venture. Following Noyes's suggestion, they proceeded to cut their skirts down to knee length and to use the cut-off material to fashion pantalettes, which reached to the ankle. After a demonstration and discussion at one of the evening meetings, the new garb was adopted forthwith. Thereafter, it was the only attire worn by the women of the Community.

In addition to short skirts and pantalettes, the Oneida women bobbed their hair. Their reasoning was that long hair took too long to fix and was not functional. The new style was quite satisfactory, although some outsiders thought the coiffure too "brazen." Oddly enough, although the

Oneida women first bobbed their hair in 1848, the custom was not introduced to the outside world until 1922 (by dancer Irene Castle).

According to comments made in interviews, the distinctive appearance of the Oneida women was another factor that served to strengthen
their we-feeling.

> Your asking of sociological questions about what held the Community
> together reminds me of something my aunt used to tell me. The Oneidans
> kept pretty much to themselves, but during the summer months they
> permitted visitors. Some Sunday afternoons, whole trainloads of visitors
> would come. They were served, picnic-style, on the lawn of the Mansion
> House. I think they were charged a dollar for the whole thing.
>
> Of course, the visitors couldn't get over the way the Oneida women
> dressed, and they kept staring. My aunt always felt that the way outsiders
> looked at them and talked about them had a lot to do with their feeling of
> closeness.

Membership and Secession

All groups face the problem of numbers. Some, like the Amish and
Mormons, show fantastic rates of growth. Others, like the Shakers and
the Father Divine Movement, lose members so rapidly that survival
becomes a problem. The Oneida Community fell between these two
extremes. Once they were fully established, their numbers remained
fairly constant. Dissolution—in 1881—had nothing to do with loss of
membership. In fact, the Perfectionists had much more trouble keeping
people out than keeping them in.

What was the total membership of the Community? It depends on
what is meant by "total." Available records indicate that at any given
time, there were around three hundred members. When deaths and
secessions are taken into consideration, total all-time membership was
probably in the area of five hundred. There were roughly equal numbers
of males and females, although there were somewhat more females at
the older age levels.

At one time or another, there were seven branches, all under the
leadership of John Humphrey Noyes. In addition to the main group at
Oneida, there were smaller branches at Willow Place, New York; Cambridge, Vermont; Newark, New Jersey; Wallingford, Connecticut; New
York City; and Putney, Vermont (reopened four years after Noyes departed). The branch at Wallingford, Connecticut—with about forty-five
members—survived until the very end.

Except during the early Putney period, the Perfectionists did little or
no active proselytizing. Yet they had no difficulty in attracting members.
In some years, they received as many as two hundred applications. Over

and over again, the *Oneida Daily Journal* reported requests for membership (evidently more male than female), but in most cases the applications were turned down.

The reason for the steady stream of membership applications is not hard to find. The Oneidans were a successful group—and word of their success traveled fast. Their own publications, as well as the popular press, afforded them wide coverage. Noyes himself journeyed and lectured extensively. And, of course, visitors to the Community could not help but be impressed by what they saw. (The total number of visitors must have been staggering. The *Circular* reports that on one day—July 4, 1863—between 1,500 and 2,000 persons visited the Community.)[4]

Applicants who were admitted were carefully screened, and once accepted they went through a probationary period for a year or so. The idea was to determine not only whether the newcomers could adjust to Community life, but whether they possessed the necessary devoutness. Over the years, most new members adjusted very well. Educational and recreational programs abounded, work was not excessive, and relations both within the Community and between the Community and the outside world were generally pleasant.

It should be pointed out that, unlike the Shakers or the Father Divine Movement, the Oneida Community was not primarily of lower- or working-class origin. They had more than their share of skilled artisans and (especially in later years) professionals. Carden points out that when the Community was first starting, Noyes carefully selected—from among the ranks of enthusiastic Perfectionists—

> those who were deeply committed to his teachings and also were responsible, talented craftsmen and farmers. They could provide for almost all of life's material necessities. . . . They also brought their savings. Few arrived empty-handed. One suspects that Noyes shrewdly selected at least some of them for their wealth.
>
> By 1857, the members had invested almost $108,000 in the Community and its branches. Without this large capital investment, Oneida would almost certainly have perished, as did such little-known New York experiments as the Bloomfield Association, the Ontario Union, the Moorhouse Union, and the Jefferson County Phalanx.[5]

After the Perfectionists were on a solid footing, their ranks came to include any number of lawyers, dentists, doctors, teachers, engineers, accountants, ministers, and business managers. Also, many of the chil-

---

[4]Constance Noyes Robertson, ed., *Oneida Community: An Autobiography, 1851–1876* (Syracuse, NY: Syracuse University Press, 1970), p. 71.

[5]Maren Lockwood Carden, *Oneida: Utopian Community to Modern Corporation* (Baltimore: Johns Hopkins University Press, 1969), pp. 37–39.

dren born in the Community eventually went on to college and professional school.

Secession   While most of those who joined Oneida were satisfied with their decision, some were not. Each year a few individuals left—for a variety of reasons. Some were unable to adjust to the sharing of sexual partners. Others became discontented with the economic philosophy. Still others found themselves disturbed by Noyes's brand of Perfectionism.

In isolated cases, individuals joined for the wrong reason and soon became disillusioned. For example, from time to time Noyes would renounce orthodox medical treatment in favor of faith cures. (He himself was alleged to have cured a woman who was both crippled and blind.) Those whose hopes for a miracle cure were not fulfilled were natural candidates for secession.

In general, those who left the group were likely to be from the more recent additions. Veteran members seldom withdrew. The actual number of seceders is not known, but the figure was probably not high. Those who left were permitted to take with them whatever property they had brought, and those who had nothing were given a hundred dollars.

Unlike the Shakers, the Oneidans were not plagued with legal suits based on property rights. And unlike the Mormons, the Perfectionists seldom had to contend with apostates who spread untrue stories. In all the many decades of their existence, there were only two embarrassing experiences. One member, William Mills—for reasons that will be explained later—was asked to leave, refused, and had to be forcibly evicted. Another member, the highly unstable Charles Guiteau, left the Community in 1867 after a short stay. Fourteen years later, Oneidans were dismayed to learn that the same Charles Guiteau had assassinated President Garfield. (Guiteau himself was subsequently hanged.)

By and large, however, those who left did so with good will. A number of them actually came back and rejoined the Community. For the fact was that, on a day-to-day basis, the Oneidans were a happy group—more so, perhaps, than almost any of the other groups discussed in this book.

Even those who eventually voted to disband the Community had kind words and pleasant memories. The following remarks occurred during a personal interview:

> I was too young to remember much. But as I grew older and asked my relatives about the Community days, their faces would light up. My own folks were "come outers"; that is, they thought the thing had gone on long enough and weren't too sorry when the group broke up. But even they

loved to talk about the "old days" and how much they missed them. They were wonderful people and they had wonderful times.

Mutual Criticism

One unusual technique used by the Perfectionists had an important bearing on high morale—and low secession. The technique was known as *mutual criticism,* and it deserves special mention for it was used by no other group. Mutual criticism apparently originated during Noyes's seminary days, when a group of students would meet regularly for the purpose of assessing one another's faults. The criticisms were carried on in a friendly but forthright manner, and all the participants—including Noyes—were pleased with the results. Response was so gratifying that Noyes instituted the practice at Putney. It was continued at Oneida and remained in effect throughout the whole of the Community's existence.

The technique of mutual criticism changed over the years. Sometimes the person involved simply stood up at the evening meeting and was criticized by each member of the group. As membership grew, however, the system proved unwieldy, and committees were appointed to conduct the criticism. Frequently Noyes added his own comments. But irrespective of the method, the goal remained the same: to bring about self-improvement through the testimony of impartial witnesses.

For certain members, understandably, criticism was traumatic. It is not easy for sensitive persons to listen to their own faults examined in public. A few Perfectionists, in fact, left the Community rather than submit to what they felt was unwarranted censure. The large majority, however, looked upon the criticism not as a personal attack but as an impersonal expression of group opinion, an expression aimed at maximizing group morale.

Initially, mutual criticism involved those who were believed to be failing in the spiritual realm, or whose individuality was too pronounced. After the "treatment," they were expected to show some improvement. As Estlake, one of the Perfectionists, put it: "Mutual criticism is to the Community what ballast is to a ship."[6]

The following brief account appeared July 18, 1866, in the *Circular:*

> During the evening meeting, Meroa K. was criticized. Much dissatisfaction was expressed with her present unimproving and disobedient state. It was thought that if there was not a thorough change in her spirit she would have to be invited to leave the Community.

---

[6]Allan Estlake, *The Oneida Community: A Record of an Attempt to Carry out the Principles of Christian Unselfishness and Scientific Race-Improvement* (London: George Redway, 1900), p. 58.

She is inefficient in business, is gross in her alimentiveness, and spends a great deal of time in reading novels and newspaper stories. A committee was appointed to talk with her and find out what her real character and purpose are, and determine what course shall be taken with her.

As time went on, however, the technique of mutual criticism came to be employed whenever a member genuinely desired self-improvement. In this instance, the person would volunteer, and although no records were kept, mutual criticism evidently grew in popularity to the point where most sessions were voluntary. But voluntary or otherwise, the technique was effective. Most Oneidans benefited. The following remarks appeared during 1871–1872 in the *Circular:*

> I feel as though I had been washed . . . through the advice and criticism given. I would call the truth the soap; the critics the scrubbers; Christ's spirit the water.

*   *   *   *   *

> Criticism is administered in faithfulness and love without regard to persons. I look upon the criticism I have received since I came here as the greatest blessings that have been conferred upon me.[7]

It should be mentioned that all the Perfectionists were subject to mutual criticism, including the central members. The only exception was John Humphrey Noyes, who was never criticized by the Community. On occasion, however, he did undergo self-criticism.

Excesses   The Oneidans had a habit of going to extremes, and their application of mutual criticism was a case in point. So enamored were they of the technique that sometimes whole departments were criticized. Thus on October 29, 1866, the Community's newspaper, the *Oneida Community Daily,* reported that "in the evening meeting we had a faithful and sincere criticism of the *Journal,* which we hope will result in its improvement."

Even children were occasionally involved in mutual criticism. The *Circular* of May 13, 1872, cites the case of a nine-year-old boy

> whose spirit and manners had given offense for some time, and he was advised to offer himself for Criticism. He was old enough to know that it would do him good, and he had grace enough to want to improve, so he offered himself. The children were very sincere. Every one of them had something to say about the boy's selfish, inharmonious ways. Even youngsters of six or seven had been outraged in their sense of what is right and

---

[7]Quoted in Harriet Worden, *Old Mansion House Memories* (Kenwood, Oneida, NY: privately printed, 1950), pp. 15–16.

wrong. There was no malice in what the children said. They are too ingenuous to hold a grudge.

The Perfectionists also employed criticism as a cure for various aches and illnesses. Called "krinopathy," the criticism cure was widely used in both children and adults. The *Circular* of December 4, 1863, reports:

> It is a common custom here for every one who may be attacked with any disorder to send for a committee of six or eight persons, in whose faith and spiritual judgment he has confidence, to come and criticize him. The result, when administered sincerely, is almost universally to throw the patient into a sweat, or to bring on a reaction of his life against disease, breaking it up and restoring him soon to usual health.

Another statement in the *Circular* (June 4, 1853) simply informs readers that "S. P., having a bad cold and symptoms of a run of fever, tried the criticism cure and was immediately relieved." Krinopathy was also used for more serious illnesses.

Perhaps the most bizarre feature of mutual criticism was the fact that death did not necessarily put a stop to the process! Deceased members whose diaries or letters were found to be incriminating might find themselves being subjected *in absentia* to a "rousing criticism."

Aside from excesses such as the above—and these were the exception rather than the rule—there is no doubt that mutual criticism was beneficial. It enhanced both individual morale and group cohesion. By its very nature, of course, most criticism was negative: it was aimed at revealing a person's faults. Noyes recognized this fact, and sporadic attempts were made at introducing "commendatory criticism," but the idea never took hold.

Economic Communism

One of the principal features of the Oneida Community was their total adherence to economic communism. From beginning to end, they rejected all forms of personal wealth and private property. They never once had second thoughts about the correctness of their economic path.

Everything was jointly owned, including such things as clothes and children's toys. Pierrepont Noyes writes:

> Throughout my childhood, the private ownership of anything seemed to me a crude artificiality to which an unenlightened Outside still clung. . . .
> For instance, we were keen for our favorite sleds, but it never occurred to

me that I could possess a sled to the exclusion of the other boys. So it was with all Children's House property.[8]

On the subject of clothes, the same author states, "Going-away clothes for grown folks, as for children, were common property. Any man or woman preparing for a trip was fitted out with one of the suits kept in stock for that purpose."[9]

How did the Oneidans make out financially, in view of the fact that they were operating a communist economy in a capitalist society? The answer is, very well. Very well indeed, as we shall see. There are, however, some qualifications.

For the first ten years or so, the Community had more than their share of economic woes. Almost everything they tried seemed to fail. They started in agriculture, but although they had a number of experienced farmers in their midst, they somehow could not compete successfully in the open market. They next tried light manufacturing, turning out such products as outdoor furniture, baskets, slippers, and bags, to no avail. Then came commercialism, and the Perfectionists set about "peddling" such wares as silk thread, pins and needles, and preserved fruits and vegetables. Again they lost money.

A few of the lines showed a small profit, but overall, expenditures outstripped profits year after year. At one time, members agreed to sell their watches in order to reduce losses. In fact, if it had not been for the $108,000 brought in by those who joined the Community, the Oneidans would have gone bankrupt. They were losing an average of $4,000 a year.

They failed for several reasons. In some of their endeavors they lacked experience. In others, they had some unfortunate setbacks, such as a fire which destroyed supplies of goods. But the chief reason for their failure was that they were spread too thin: seven different branches in four different states. Accordingly, Noyes decided to retrench. All the branches were phased out except Oneida and Wallingford—with the bulk of the economic operation remaining at Oneida. As it turned out, this was a wise move. But there was a wiser one just around the corner.

Traps   In 1848, shortly after their founding, the Community admitted to membership one Sewell Newhouse. A north woods hunter and trapper, Newhouse was a lengendary figure even before he joined the Perfectionists. More or less a loner, he knew every foot of the wilderness surrounding Oneida Lake. And he knew hunting and trapping. Around Oneida, his fame equaled that of Davy Crockett.

---

[8]Noyes, *My Father's House*, pp. 126–27.
[9]Ibid.

Aided by his prodigious strength, Newhouse made his own traps by using a blacksmith's forge, anvil, and hand punch. He made an excellent product and had no trouble selling his traps to local woodsmen. He had no real desire to make money or establish a business, however, and between sessions of trap making, he would invariably disappear into the north woods for a prolonged period.

Pierrepont Noyes says about Sewell Newhouse:

> Why he joined, even more why the Community let him join, is a mystery to me. Behind his gnarled face was a gnarled character. Perhaps his wife, whom I remember as a very religious woman, persuaded him and persuaded the community.
>
> When, as a boy, I knew him, he was in his sixties. His face was grim, his whiskers gray, and he moved with a shuffling gait that I associated with the Indians who stole through the forests.
>
> He still seemed a woodsman, something of a hero to a boy. For years he had been allowed to make trapping expeditions to the north woods each winter, and his book, *The Trapper's Guide,* was read and reread to help boys' trapping and excite their imagination for Indian scouting in the local woods.[10]

Why Newhouse joined may have been a mystery, but his effect on the Community was indelible. At first, no one thought of using the traps as a basic Community product. Among other things, their manufacture involved a secret process of spring tempering, which Newhouse was reluctant to reveal. Under Noyes's patient prodding, however, Sewell Newhouse finally relented, and by the late 1850s the Oneida Community was turning out traps by the hundreds.

Demand for the product grew rapidly. To meet the orders that were pouring in, the Oneidans were forced to use assembly-line methods. In fact, whenever there was a deadline on a large order, the entire Community—including the children—would pitch in. And even this was not enough. By 1860, the Newhouse trap not only had become standard in the United States and Canada but was being used all over the world. Many professional trappers would use no other brand.

By this time, of course, the Perfectionists could not possibly handle all the orders themselves. They began to hire outside workers, the number eventually reaching several hundred. The trap factory, located near the Mansion House, developed into a typical industrial plant of the period. By the late 1860s, the Community was turning out close to 300,000 traps

---

[10]Pierrepont B. Noyes, *A Goodly Heritage* (New York: Holt, Rinehart and Winston, 1958), pp. 120–21.

a year. During one record-breaking period, they actually manufactured over 22,000 traps in a single week.[11]

Interestingly enough, once they had "turned the corner" with the trap business, their other products—canned vegetables and preserved fruit, bags, silk thread—proved to be valuable sidelines. So, too, did their tourist business. As the fame of the Perfectionists grew, the number of visitors—with their admission fees—also grew.

Later on, in 1877, the Community began the manufacture of silverware. Although there were some ups and downs, this business also proved successful. In 1881, when the Community disbanded, the industrial component was perpetuated under the name of Oneida Ltd. These silversmiths have grown and prospered, and their products are in wide use today.

It is often said that John Humphrey Noyes was the indispensable man insofar as the Perfectionists were concerned, an assertion which is doubtless true. Without him, there would have been no Community, and after he was gone the Community fell apart. But one question remains. How successful would Noyes have been if it hadn't been for a crusty old woodsman named Sewell Newhouse?*

Self-sufficiency and Ethnocentrism   Once trap making had made their economic base secure, the Perfectionist brand of communism worked rather well. The Oneidans built their own home; made all their own clothes, including shoes; did their own laundry; raised their own food; and provided their own services. They did all these things, furthermore, at a remarkably low cost. The *Community's Annual Reports* indicate that the yearly expenditure for food was $24.00 per person, while the corresponding figure for clothing was $10.50![12]

Like the Old Order Amish, the Oneida "family" performed functions that were disappearing from society at large. They provided their own recreation and their own religious services. They ran their own school, and—even though they practiced faith healing and krinopathy occasionally—they had their own doctors and dentists. The Perfectionists also had their own "social security benefits," which included child care, full employment, old-age assistance, and the like.

Functionally, economically, and socially, the Oneida Perfectionists

---

[11]According to the *Oneida Community Daily Journal* of November 5, 1866, if it hadn't been for a mechanical defect, they would have been able to turn out 80,000 traps that week!

[12]*Bible Communism: A Compilation from the Annual Reports of the Oneida Association* (Brooklyn, NY: Oneida Circular, 1853), p. 16.

*A "Newhouse/Oneida" bear trap (11" by 36") was advertised in the October 1989 *Shotgun News* for $350.

were close to being a self-sufficient community. This self-sufficiency not only enhanced their in-group solidarity but gave rise to ethnocentric feelings. Sociologically, *ethnocentrism* is the belief that one's own group—with its values, beliefs, and ways of doing things—is superior to other groups. The Oneidans were building the best traps. They were making money. Visitors were flocking to their doors, and there was a steady stream of new applications. Little wonder that John Humphrey Noyes and his followers felt that their way of life was superior to that found on the outside. As one of the members put it, "It was never, in our minds, an experiment. We believed we were living under a system which the whole world would sooner or later adopt."[13]

Working Arrangements   On a typical work day, Community members would rise between five and seven-thirty and proceed to the dining hall. Following breakfast, there was a short period of Bible reading, after which members would go to their assigned jobs in the trap factory, the mill, the farm, or elsewhere. A square board with pegs—each peg containing a member's name—was located near the library, and at a glance it was possible to tell each person's whereabouts. Dining hours changed over the years, but the Oneidans came to prefer a two-meal-a-day schedule, with dinner being served from three to four. After dinner there were adult classes in French, algebra, science, and other subjects, followed by the evening meeting. By nine or ten o'clock, most of the Community had retired.

While they were working, the Perfectionists liked to combine the social and the economic. Men and women worked side by side, and there was incessant talking and laughing. During an interview, one former member made the following comments:

> As children, we loved to visit the various departments they used to have: the laundry, the kitchen, the fruit cellar, the bakery, the dairy, the tailor shop. The thing is that small groups of people worked side by side in most of these places, and they were able to talk with each other as they worked. It was this sort of thing, year after year, that gave rise to a kindred spirit.

While a certain amount of inefficiency was acknowledged, it should not be thought that the Perfectionists were idlers whose chief preoccupation was socializing. On the contrary, they were good workers. Their methods simply did not include regimentation, time clocks, quotas, and the like. As Robertson puts it, "From the beginning, the Community believed in work; not legally—that is, work forced upon the worker as a duty—but work freely chosen, as they said 'under inspiration.' "[14]

---

[13]The statement was made by Pierrepont Noyes's mother-in-law, and is quoted in *My Father's House*, pp. 17–18.

[14]Robertson, *Oneida Community*, p. 47.

When there was work to be done, the Oneidans did it—without coercion. For the smaller projects, one of their most effective innovations was a cooperative enterprise known as the bee.

> The bee was an ordinance exactly suited to Community life. One would be announced at dinner or perhaps on the bulletin board: "A bee in the kitchen to pare apples"; or "A bee to pick strawberries at five o'clock tomorrow morning"; or "A bee in the Upper Sitting Room to sew bags."[15]

For the larger tasks—a building project, an influx of visitors, an important industrial order—a much larger proportion of the membership would turn out. All of the above, of course, was in addition to the daily work assignments. Generally speaking, while the Perfectionists never claimed to be a model of economic efficiency, their system worked.

The economic aspects of the Community have been discussed in some detail since most of the other sixty-odd communist experiments then underway in America failed because of economic difficulties. The followers of John Humphrey Noyes succeeded. Despite the fact that the accumulation of material wealth was not their primary concern, the Oneida Community—at the time it disbanded—was worth some $600,000. In 1881, this was no small amount.

Level of Living   On a day-to-day basis, the Perfectionists did not bask in luxury, but neither did they lead a Spartan existence. They ate well, in spite of their dietary prohibitions. They were amply clothed, although, like the Amish, there was no conspicuous consumption. If a man needed a suit, he would go to the Community tailor and—in accordance with a budgetary allotment—get measured for a new one. The same procedure was followed for other needs.

Members could, if they wished, travel or visit on the outside, but few availed themselves of the opportunity. There were too many attractions at home: recreation and entertainment, adult education, a well-stocked library, social and sexual privileges, opportunities for self-expression in the musical and performing arts, physical comforts (the Mansion House even included a Turkish bath)—all this in addition to the spiritual enlightenment provided by John Humphrey Noyes.

Even in the matter of work assignments, the Oneidans were given every consideration. There was no such thing as demeaning labor. Members were respected for the spirit with which they did their work rather than for the work itself. Menial tasks, such as cleaning and mending, were generally rotated. Special skills and abilities, on the other hand, were amply rewarded. Those with writing aptitude were assigned to the Community newspaper, those with a love for children worked in the children's department, and so on.

[15]Ibid., p. 103.

Complex Marriage

The world remembers the followers of John Humphrey Noyes not for their social or economic system, but for their practice of complex marriage. Right or wrong, just as the term "Mormon" brings to mind polygamy, so the term "Oneida" conjures up thoughts of the "advanced" sexual practices of the Community. It was Noyes himself who coined the phrase "free love," although because of adverse implications the phraseology was discarded in favor of "complex marriage."

According to Noyes, it was natural for all men to love all women, and for all women to love all men. He felt that any social institution which flouted this truism was harmful to the human spirit. Romantic love—or "special love," as the Oneidans called it—was harmful because it was a selfish act. Monogamous marriage was harmful because it excluded others from sharing in connubial affection. The answer, obviously, was group marriage, and throughout the whole of their existence, this was what the Oneidans practiced.

Noyes's views on matrimony were also based on biblical interpretation. In the *Bible Argument*, published by the Oneida Community, the following statement appears:

> In the kingdom of heaven, the institution of marriage—which assigns the exclusive possession of one woman to one man—does not exist (Matt. 22:23–30).
>
> In the kingdom of heaven, the intimate union, which in the world is limited to pairs, extends through the whole body of believers. . . . (John 17:21). The new commandment is that we love one another, not by pairs, as in the World, but en masse.[16]

Over and over again, on both secular and religious grounds, John Humphrey Noyes criticized monogamy and extolled the virtues of group marriage.

> The human heart is capable of loving any number of times and any number of persons. This is the law of nature. There is no occasion to find fault with it. Variety is in the nature of things, as beautiful and as useful in love as in eating and drinking. . . . We need love as much as we need food and clothing, and God knows it; and if we trust Him for those things, why not for love?[17]

Although he did not say it in so many words, Noyes hoped that the sharing of partners would serve as yet another element in the establishment of group solidarity. That he was able to succeed in this realm—

---

[16]Quoted in ibid., p. 267.
[17]Quoted in Robert Parker, *A Yankee Saint: John Humphrey Noyes and the Oneida Community* (New York: Putnam, 1935), pp. 182–83

despite the fact that the bulk of his followers had Puritan backgrounds—attests to his leadership capacity.

The system of complex marriage was relatively uncomplicated. Sexual relations were easy to arrange inasmuch as all the men and women lived in the Mansion House. If a man desired sexual intercourse with a particular woman, he simply asked her. If she consented, he would go to her room at bedtime and stay overnight. Once in a while, because of a shortage of single rooms, these arrangements were not practicable, in which case the couple could use one of the "social" rooms set aside for that purpose.

Sexual Regulations   Sex is never a simple matter (among humans, at least), and from the very beginning, complex marriage was ringed with prohibitions and restrictions. Other modifications arose over the years. By the early 1860s, a fairly elaborate set of regulations was in force, so that throughout most of the Community's existence, sexual relations were not nearly so "free" and all-encompassing as outsiders believed.

As early as Putney, Noyes taught that sex was not to be considered a "wifely duty"; that is, something accepted by the female to satisfy the male. Later on, the notion was stated in more positive terms, as in the following excerpt from the *Handbook:*

> The liberty of monogamous marriage, as commonly understood, is the liberty of a man to sleep habitually with a woman, liberty to please himself alone in his dealings with her, liberty to expose her to childbearing without care or consultation.
>
> The term Free Love, as understood by the Oneida Community, does *not* mean any such freedom of sexual proceedings. The theory of sexual interchange which governs all the general measures of the Community is that which in ordinary society governs the proceedings in *courtship.*
>
> It is the theory that love *after* marriage should be what it is *before* marriage—a glowing attraction on both sides, and not the odious obligation of one party, and the sensual recklessness of the other. (p. 42)

Noyes went to great pains in his discourses to separate the "amative" from the "propagative" functions of sex. It was only when the two were separated, he said, that the true goals of Perfectionism could be attained. In practice, this meant that men could have sexual intercourse up to, but not including, ejaculation. (Women, of course, could achieve sexual climax at any time.)

There were two exceptions to the nonejaculatory rule: (1) when the man was having intercourse with a woman who was past menopause, and (2) when a child was desired. Authorization for childbearing involved a special procedure and will be discussed in the following section. However, by permitting men to achieve ejaculation only with postmenopausal women, the Perfectionists not only were employing a novel method of birth control—effective, as it turned out—but were using an ingenious method of providing older women with sexual partners.

The *Handbook* also points up the desirability of courtship, and there is no doubt that in the Oneida Community sustained courtship was the order of the day. Men were eager to win the women's favor, so they acted accordingly. And the women evidently found it refreshing to be wooed by the men. Pierrepont Noyes catches the full flavor of the relationship in the following passage:

> There has survived in my memory an impression, a dim recognition, that the relation between our grown folks had a quality intimate and personal, a quality that made life romantic. Unquestionably, the sexual relations of the members under the Community system inspired a lively interest in each other, but I believe that the opportunity for romantic friendship also played a part in rendering life more colorful than elsewhere.
>
> Even elderly people, whose physical passions had burned low, preserved the fine essence of earlier associations; child as I was, I sensed a spirit of high romance surrounding them, a vivid, youthful interest in life that looked from their eyes and spoke in their voices and manners.[18]

As in society at large, the men were apparently more enthusiastic than the women, at least in a strictly sexual connotation. The practice of having the man ask the woman for sexual relations, therefore, was soon replaced by a new system.

Use of a Go-between   Under the new system, the man would make his request known to a central member—usually an older woman—who in turn would pass on the request. In practice, the use of a go-between served a number of purposes. It spared the women—it was they who suggested the system—the embarrassment of having to voice a direct refusal or conjure up an excuse. As one of the interviewees said: "Sex relations in the Community were always voluntary. There was never any hint at coercion. But after they started using a go-between, it made things easier for everybody."

Employment of a go-between also gave the Community a measure of control over the sexual system. For example, the Perfectionists were ever on guard against two of their members falling in love—special love, as they called it. So if a particular couple were having too-frequent relations, the go-between would simply disallow further meetings between them. In the matter of procreation, too, it was important that the Community be able to establish paternity. And while this was not always possible, the go-between greatly facilitated the identification process.

[18]Noyes, *My Father's House*, p. 131.

It should be mentioned that the Oneidans considered sex to be a private matter. Aside from the particular go-between involved, "who was having relations with whom" never became common knowledge. Indeed, the subject itself was taboo. Public displays of affection, vulgarity of any kind, sexual discussions or innuendoes, immodest behavior— all were forbidden. During the many decades of their existence, the Perfectionists had but one unpleasant experience along these lines.

William Mills was accepted into the Community during the early 1860s. A rather vulgar person, it soon became obvious that he was a misfit. The women would have nothing to do with him. As a consequence, he started to cultivate the friendship of teenage girls. Breaking the Perfectionist taboo, Mills would discuss sexual matters openly with them, asking them about their amours and boasting of his own. The situation soon became intolerable, and he was asked to leave. He refused. The central members were in a quandary: from time to time others had been requested to leave, but none had ever refused. After several discussions, it was decided—in an almost literal sense—to take the bull by the horns. According to Robert Parker:

> Mills found himself, one winter night, suddenly, unceremoniously, and horizontally propelled through an open window, and shot—harmlessly but ignominiously—into the depths of a snowdrift. It was the first and only forcible expulsion in the history of the community.[19]

Taken collectively, the regulations concerning sex were designed to permit maximum freedom for the individual without jeopardizing the harmony of the group as a whole. This involved a delicate balance of rights and responsibilities, and Noyes was well aware of this fact. He strove mightily to keep sex "within bounds," and whenever there were excesses he moved to correct them.

To take one example, the original procedure had been for the man to go to the woman's room and remain all night. Some of the women evidently complained that the practice was too "tiring," and Noyes saw to it that a change was made. Henceforth, the man would stay for an hour or so and then return to his own room. This was the procedure followed throughout most of the Community's existence.

Along these same lines, the Perfectionist leader constantly inveighed against the so-called fatiguing aspects of sexual intercourse. Instead of advocating *coitus reservatus*, for instance, he could have endorsed *coitus interruptus*—both being equally effective as birth-control techniques. But Noyes was convinced that ejaculation had a debilitating effect on the male; hence he preached against its danger.

He was also against *coitus interruptus* on theological grounds, since the practice is condemned in the Bible. That is, when Onan had intercourse with his deceased brother's wife, he refused to ejaculate in natural fashion. Instead, he "spilled it on the ground, lest that he should give seed to his brother. And the thing which he did displeased the Lord" (Gen. 38:9–10).

Additionally, Noyes totally rejected all forms of contraception. For reasons best known to himself, he looked upon them as "machinations of the French" and refused even to consider them. To be acceptable, birth control had to include a strong element of (male) self-control.

Interestingly enough—and in spite of some rather questionable logic— John Humphrey Noyes's ideas about sex and birth control proved workable. His goal was to provide complex marriage with a spiritual base, and he apparently succeeded. Throughout the whole of the Community's existence, there were no elopements, no orgies, no exhibitionism. Nor was there any instance of homosexuality, sadism, masochism, or any other sexual activity that would have been considered reprehensible by the standards then current.

Ascending Fellowship   Complex marriage did pose one problem that Noyes went to great pains to solve: how to keep the older members of the Community from being bypassed in favor of the younger members. True, it was only with postmenopausal women that men were allowed to achieve ejaculation, but this restriction provided an inadequate answer to the problem. The real answer was to be found in the principle of ascending fellowship.

According to this principle, members were ranked from least to most perfect. Any follower who wished to improve, therefore, was advised to associate with someone higher on the spiritual scale. (Noyes taught that a high-ranking person would not in any way be downgraded by associating with a person of lower rank.) Since it took time and experience to achieve high spiritual rank, those at the upper end of the scale were nearly always the older, more mature members. It was these older Perfectionists rather than the younger members who were thus held up as the desirable partners.

The Oneida *Handbook* contains the following explanation:

> According to the Principle of Ascending Fellowship, it is regarded as better—in the early stages of passional experience—for the young of both sexes to associate in love with persons older than themselves, and if possible with those who are spiritual and have been some time in the school of self-control—and who are thus able to make love safe and edifying.
>
> This is only another form of the popular principle of contrasts. It is well understood by physiologists that it is undesirable for persons of similar

character and temperament to mate together. Communists have discovered that it is undesirable for two inexperienced and unspiritual persons to rush into fellowship with each other; that it is better for both to associate with persons of mature character and sound sense. (p. 39)

There is no doubt that age was shown great respect in the Community. This is the way Noyes wanted it, and this is the way it was. In addition, the fact that younger men were encouraged to have sexual relations with older women served to strengthen the birth-control measures that were used.

Complex Marriage: Unanswered Questions

Although the foregoing pages give the broad outlines of the sexual system employed by the Perfectionists, a number of questions remain unanswered. To what extent did the women refuse sexual requests? Was a go-between really used, or was this a formality that was easily bypassed? Did women as well as men initiate sexual requests? Was not the factor of jealousy a problem? Did members have difficulty adjusting sexually to a large number of different partners? Researchers have attempted to find answers to these questions, but they have had only limited success. One of the interviewees made the following points:

> I grant the questions are of sociological interest, but look at it from our view. If somebody came to you and asked questions concerning the sex life of your parents and grandparents, you'd have a tough time answering. The same with us. When the old Community broke up, there was a natural reluctance to discuss sex. Former members didn't discuss their own sex lives, and naturally their children and grandchildren didn't pry.

One of the officers of Oneida Ltd. supplied the following information. During the decades of the Community's existence, many of the Oneidans were in the habit of keeping diaries. (Diary keeping was evidently much more common in the nineteenth century than it is today.) Some of the Perfectionists also accumulated bundles of personal letters. After the Community broke up, and as the members died over the years, the question arose as to what to do with all these documents.

Since so much of the material was of a personal and sexual nature, since names were named, and inasmuch as a number of the children and grandchildren were still living, it was decided to store all the old diaries, letters, and other personal documents in the vaults of Oneida Ltd. Several years ago, this officer received permission to examine the material in order to see what should be done with it.

I went through some of the stuff—old diaries and things—and a lot of it was awfully personal. Names and specific happenings were mentioned— that kind of thing. Anyway, I reported these facts to the company, and it was decided that all the material should be destroyed.

So one morning we got a truck—and believe me, there was so much stuff that we needed a truck—loaded all the material on, and took it out to the dump and burned it. We felt that divulging the contents wouldn't have done ourselves or anybody else any good.

While there is little doubt that the burned material would have shed much light on the sexual behavior of the Perfectionists, the action taken by the company is understandable. Oneida Ltd. is not in business to further the cause of sociological research, and regardless of how much the material might have benefited social scientists, there was always the possibility that the contents would have proved embarrassing to the company or to some of the direct descendants.

The diary-burning episode has been mentioned in some detail in order to show how difficult it is to answer sexual questions of the kind posed earlier. The interview information presented here should be thought of as a series of clues rather than as a set of definitive answers.

To what extent did the Oneida women refuse sexual requests? The company official who had examined some of the to-be-burned material reported that there was nothing therein to suggest a high refusal rate. Another male respondent stated that he had been informed by an old Community member that the man "had never been refused." One female interviewee felt that refusal was a problem "in some instances." Most of those interviewed, however, had no specific information to offer. The overall impression given is that female refusal was not a major problem, although the issue probably arose from time to time.

Was a go-between really used, or was this a formality that was easily bypassed? None of those interviewed had any direct evidence to offer. All that can be said is that there were no *reported* instances where the rule was broken. Since the matter was never raised by the Oneidans themselves, it is doubtful whether a real issue was involved. Given the religious orientation and esprit de corps of the members, there is every reason to suppose that the stipulated procedure was followed.

Did the Oneida women, as well as the men, initiate sexual requests? This question drew a generally nagative answer from all the respondents. Several said they knew of some coquetry on the part of certain women, but they had never heard of anything more direct. Two of the older female respondents stated that there was one known case where a woman went to a man and asked to have a child by him. In this instance, however, the implication is not clear, since the Perfectionists differentiated sharply between amative and procreative aspects of sex. All reports considered, it appears that the Oneida women were no more disposed to assume the role of active partner than were women in society at large.

Was male jealousy a problem? Apparently not; at least, none of the interviewees knew of any major flare-ups. One respondent said:

> I don't think it was much of a problem. Certainly the old folks, when they talked about the Community, never made any issue of it. Their religious teachings emphasized spiritual equality, and their whole way of life was aimed at stamping out feelings of jealousy.
>
> Also, with so many women to choose from, why would a man experience feelings of jealousy? Once in a while a man and woman would be suspected of falling in love—"special love" they call it—but it happened infrequently. When it did, the couple were separated. One would be sent to Wallingford, Connecticut—we had a small branch there.

Noyes himself constantly preached against the dangers of male jealousy. On one occasion, he remarked, "No matter what his other qualifications may be, if a man cannot love a woman and be happy seeing her loved by others, he is a selfish man, and his place is with the potsherds of the earth."[20] On another occasion—referring to a man who was becoming romantically involved with a particular woman—he said, "You do not love her, you love happiness."[21]

It is likely that male jealousy was at most a minor problem, though it did receive a certain amount of attention. Female jealousy was evidently no problem at all. It was not mentioned by any of those interviewed, nor, so far as could be ascertained, was the matter ever raised during the Community's existence.

Did the members of the Community have difficulty in adjusting sexually to a large number of different partners? The Oneidans were encouraged to have sex with a variety of partners but were not supposed to become emotionally involved with any of them. Respondents had little or nothing to report on this matter—which is unfortunate, since the question is an intriguing one.

The Eugenics Program

Since John Humphrey Noyes had so many other "advanced" ideas about life on earth, it was predictable that he would not overlook the subject of children. His views on the matter, however, shocked even those who were used to his radicalism, and little wonder! Not since Plato's *Republic*

---

[20]W. T. Hedden, "Communism in New York, 1848–1879," *The American Scholar,* 14 (Summer 1945): 287.

[21]Quoted in Raymond Lee Muncy, *Sex and Marriage in Utopian Communities* (Bloomington: Indiana University Press, 1973), p. 176.

had such utopian concepts been expounded. Noyes's plans, moreover—unlike those of the Greek philosopher—were more than just words on paper. He both preached them and put them into practice.

It will be remembered that Noyes introduced *coitus reservatus,* or male continence, to spare the Oneida women from being plagued with unwanted children—as they were in the world at large. He also felt that the Oneidans needed time to prove themselves—in both a financial and social sense—before children were permitted. Accordingly, when the Community was founded, the Perfectionist leader announced that there would be no children until further notice. As it turned out, "further notice" stretched for a period of twenty years (1848–1868), during which time the prohibition remained in effect.

By the late 1860s, however, it was evident to both John Humphrey Noyes and the general membership that the ban should be lifted. There was much discussion within the Community, and the Perfectionists wondered when the announcement would be made and what form it would take. On his part, Noyes had given the matter a great deal of thought. He was ready to lift the ban on children, but he was not ready to endorse a system of uncontrolled births such as that found in the outside world.

John Humphrey Noyes read widely on the subject of propagation. He studied Francis Galton's works on hereditary improvement. He read Charles Darwin's *On the Origin of Species.* And the more he thought about it, the more he became convinced that a scientific breeding program could be adapted to the needs of the Oneida Community. Although the word "eugenics" was unknown—it was coined by Galton in 1883—eugenics was precisely what Noyes had in mind. In 1869, the Perfectionists embarked on their program, the first systematic attempt at eugenics in human history.

Stirpiculture   Noyes called his program "stirpiculture" (from the Latin *stirps,* meaning root, stock, or lineage), and from its inception there was no doubt about the goals, methods, or enthusiasm involved. The goal was crystal clear: biological improvement of the Oneida Community. In the words of the *Circular:*

> Why should not beauty and noble grace of person and every other desirable quality of men and women, internal and external, be propagated and intensified beyond all former precedent by the application of the same scientific principles of breeding that produce such desirable results in the case of sheep, cattle, and horses?[22]

The methods were also made explicit: only certain persons would be permitted to become parents. The selection would be made by a

---

[22]Quoted in Robertson, *Oneida Community,* p. 341.

stirpiculture committee, headed by Noyes, and the committee's decision would be final. There would be no appeal. And even though this meant that the majority of Oneidans might never become parents, there was no objection from the membership. On the contrary, the Perfectionists endorsed every facet of the program.

At the start of the eugenics program, fifty-three women and thirty-eight men were chosen to be parents (stirpicults). Over the years others were added, so that eventually about one hundred members took part in the experiment. Approximately 80 percent of those who took part actually achieved parenthood. During the decade or so that the program was in effect, sixty-two children were born, including four stillbirths.

There were also a dozen or so accidental conceptions. Despite their pledge, a few of the "unchosen" individuals did their best to achieve parenthood—with some success. For instance, there was a passage in one of the burned diaries in which a man—referring to his sexual encounter with a particular woman—said, "She tried to make me lose control." In general, though, both the men and women who were bypassed seem to have accepted their lot willingly enough.

The precise method of selection used by the stirpiculture committee was never revealed. Throughout most of its existence the committee was composed of central members, and presumably they judged applicants on the basis of physical and mental qualities. Most of the candidates applied as couples, although on occasion the committee suggested certain combinations.

While it was never explicitly stated, John Humphrey Noyes was undoubtedly the chief figure in the stirpiculture process. The concept was his, the committee was his, and it was he who served as chief judge and policy maker. The records show, for example, that the fathers were much older than the mothers, a fact which reflects the principle of ascending fellowship. Noyes felt strongly that the qualities necessary for fatherhood could only be acquired through age and experience. And while this was an erroneous, Lamarckian view, it was adhered to. In fact, a number of men in their sixties were chosen as stirpicults. Noyes himself fathered at least ten of the children, so that evidently he was not averse to self-selection. The principle of ascending fellowship was less applicable to women, naturally, because of the menopause factor.

What were the results of the stirpiculture program? Was it successful? Were the offspring really superior? Most observers thought so. During the entire program, no defective children were ever born, no mothers ever lost. As compared to children on the outside, the Oneida youngsters had a markedly lower death rate. A number of them went on to achieve eminence in the business and professional worlds. Several wrote books. And nearly all of them, in turn, had children who were a credit to the Community. How much of the program's success was due to the eugenic factor will never be known, since the children presumably had a favorable environment *as well as* sound heredity.

Perhaps the only disappointing feature of the stirpiculture program was that so few children were born. In view of the high birthrate that prevailed in society at large, the fact that the stirpicults produced only fifty-eight live children is difficult to understand. *Coitus reservatus*, practiced by the Oneida males for so many years, may have had an unaccountable effect on their fertility, although this is probably a far-fetched explanation.

The most likely answer is that John Humphrey Noyes was fearful of the effects of multiple childbirth on the health of women. His own wife, in the pre-Oneida period, had had four stillbirths, and his entire outlook on life had been shaped by her experience. Nearly all the female stirpicults, for example, were authorized to have but one child. A handful had two children, and only two women had three. If there were other reasons for the Perfectionists' low birthrate, they have not come to light.

Child Rearing

According to Noyes's teachings, all adults were supposed to love all children and vice versa, and the entire program of Community child rearing was based on this philosophy. Excessive love between children and their own parents was called "stickiness" and was strongly discouraged.

In practice, Oneida children were anything but neglected. For the first fifteen months they were under the care of their own mothers. After that, the youngsters were moved to the Children's House, where they were raised communally. There they were taught to treat all Community adults as they would their own parents, and there they received their formal education. There too they were introduced to John Humphrey Noyes's brand of Perfectionism.

A fair amount of published material exists on the Community child-rearing program. Evidence indicates that the program was patently successful. The following question-and-answer session—although totally fictitious—is based on factual information. The answers are those a Community spokesman might have given, say, in the 1870s.

Q.   Where do the Oneida children live?
A.   In the Children's House. Originally this was a separate building. However, in 1870 a south wing was added to the Mansion House, and the children have been there ever since.
Q.   Do the youngsters have their own facilities?
A.   Yes. The south wing was designed with this in mind. The children have their own nursery, sleeping quarters, schoolrooms, playrooms, and so forth.

Q. Who is in charge of the children?

A. I suppose you could say the whole Community. But if you mean who is in charge of the Children's House, there are a dozen or more adults whose full-time job is looking after the youngsters.

Q. Are all these adults women?

A. No. Most of them are, but we do believe in having a show of male authority.

Q. What about the children's education?

A. They are taught the same subjects as other children. But they also receive an equal amount of on-the-job training in the various departments. And when we have a bee, they often join in like everybody else.

Q. Do you use outside teachers?

A. No, we have our own.

Q. Do the children like school?

A. Do children anywhere?

Q. How is their religious instruction handled?

A. They meet for an hour a day—in prayer, Bible reading, discussions of Perfectionism, confession of faults, and so forth.

Q. How do the children like this type of training? Is it effective?

A. The only thing they like about it is when the hour is over! At the same time, whether they like it or not, we think it is effective.

Q. Do they have their own dining facilities?

A. No. We believe in bringing them into the life of the Community as early as possible. After the age of two, they eat in the regular dining room. And after the age of ten, they are permitted to sit at the same tables as adults.

Q. Do the youngsters know who their real parents are?

A. Of course.

Q. Whose name do they take?

A. Their fathers'.

Q. Are they permitted to associate with their parents?

A. Oh, yes. They spend a certain amount of time with their parents every week. However, we try to get the children to think of all Oneida adults as their parents.

Q. Doesn't this work a hardship on the children? Isn't there a natural desire to establish a bond of personal affection?

A. Perhaps so. It depends on how a child is conditioned. We think that under our system, a young person gets more love and understanding than on the outside.

Q. It's hard to believe the Oneida youngsters don't yearn for their own parents.

A. Well, one little girl did. She would stand outside her mother's window and call to her, even though her mother wasn't supposed to answer. That was an exceptional case, however.

Q. And you contend that under the Perfectionist system, the children are happy?

A. We do. But why not ask them?

Q. Do you not have problems of discipline?

A.   Of course, and both the adults and the children spend a good deal of time discussing the matter. On the whole—since we're a tightly knit group—we probably have fewer disciplinary problems than they do on the outside.

Q.   There are reports that Oneida children are afraid of visitors. . . .

A.   As a matter of fact, some of the younger children are. They usually grow out of it, but we're not entirely satisfied with that end of it.

Q.   Are the adult members of the Community happy at being separated from their children?

A.   Well, they knew the rules when they joined. However, they are not really separated. They have the love of their children and the pleasure of their company, without the day-to-day burden that plagues most parents.

Q.   Is there any likelihood that the Perfectionists will ever change their system of child rearing?

A.   None whatsoever. As far as we're concerned, the system has proved itself. It's here to stay.

The End of the Road

All good things must come to an end—or at least, so it must have seemed to the Oneidans by the late 1870s. John Humphrey Noyes had been expounding his Perfectionist views for almost fifty years. Communal living—at both Putney and Oneida—had been successfully practiced for more than forty years. There was no doubt that, sociologically, the Perfectionists had established a genuine subculture. But now the currents were going against them. There was no single reason. The causes ran together like foam on the ocean. Nevertheless, the tide was inexorable.

Outside Pressures   By and large, outsiders who lived in the vicinity of Oneida were favorably disposed toward the Community. The Perfectionists were known to be honest, industrious, and law-abiding. Moreover, as time went on, Oneida was recognized as a growing source of employment. Unfortunately, as their fame grew, so did their "notoriety." Free love, complex marriage, scientific breeding—such things were more than nineteenth-century America could accept. And so the pressures grew—from isolated editorials and sermons in the 1860s to a concentrated barrage in the 1870s. Two of the attackers, in particular, are worthy of mention.

Anthony Comstock, self-appointed watchdog of American morals, was in a special position to hurt the Oneidans. A member of Congress from New York, he sponsored the omnibus state law forbidding immoral works. He also organized the New York Society for the Suppression of Vice. Most important, in 1873 he persuaded Congress to enact a federal obscenity bill which, among other things, forbade the dissemination of all literature dealing with birth control. As fanatical a reformer as the country had ever seen, Comstock succeeded in tarring the Perfectionists with the brush of vice and obscenity. His followers found the Community an easy—and rather defenseless—target.

Less well known than Comstock, but even more effective, was Professor John Mears of Hamilton College. Whereas Comstock was against "obscenity" in any form, Mears's sole obsession was the Oneida Community. Week after week he wrote to the newspapers, gave public talks, and preached Sunday sermons—all against the "debaucheries" being practiced by John Humphrey Noyes and his followers. Typical of his newspaper pieces was the following:

> Here in the heart of the Empire State is an institution avowedly at war with the foundation principles of our domestic and civil order, a set of men banded together for the purpose of practicing shameful immoralities, and leading the young of both sexes who unfortunately happen to come under their care into impure and shocking practices. . . .
>
> The people of Illinois could not endure the immorality of the Mormons, but drove them from Nauvoo in 1846, and compelled them to take refuge a thousand miles from the outskirts of civilization. Thus was polygamy treated; while the far more corrupt concubinage of the Oneida Community luxuriates in the heart of New York State, is visited by throngs of the curious, by picnic parties organized for this purpose, and even by Sunday School excursions.[23]

Methodists, Presbyterians, Baptists, Congregationalists—all took up the cry. Committees were appointed, conferences held, legal action demanded. Anthony Comstock's help was solicited. And while some editorials were fair, others joined in the diatribe against the Oneidans. Meanwhile, back at the Community . . .

Internal Pressures   All was not well. Dissent was not only in the air; it was stalking the corridors and invading the rooms. Behind closed doors, small groups of Perfectionists voiced their complaints. And while there is no doubt that outside pressures were a contributing factor, it was the internal dissension which really destroyed the Community.

To begin with, the nature of Perfectionism was changing. The deeply religious orientation gave way to an emphasis on social science, then in its infancy. Bible reading and sermons were superseded by talks on self-improvement and social engineering. Noyes himself seems to have initiated the trend, announcing in the *Circular* that that publication would no longer be a "strictly religious" paper.[24] While there were some in the Community who went along with the change, others—particularly

[23]Quoted in Parker, *Yankee Saint*, p. 268.
[24]Ibid., p. 274.

those in the older age groups—felt that the whole basis of their life was being violated.

Problems, too, were arising with the young people. Three in particular are worthy of mention: (1) Acceptance of John Humphrey Noyes as the ultimate authority came to be resented, especially by those who went to college and returned to live in the Community. Not unnaturally, they demanded a larger role in the decision-making process. (2) The principle of ascending fellowship began to be questioned. Young men and women objected to being paired off sexually with the older members. And (3) those who failed to qualify for parenthood under the stirpiculture program took umbrage at the fact.

The Townerites   At the evening meeting of April 21, 1874, Noyes made an important announcement. (How important, even he did not realize.) Twelve new members—remnants of the defunct Free Love Society of Cleveland—were being admitted into the Community. Their leader was a minister-turned-lawyer, James W. Towner.

A man of some talent, Towner became a divisive force almost immediately. Those with complaints—a growing number, it seems—found him a ready listener. And although a majority of the Perfectionists remained loyal to John Humphrey Noyes, Towner succeeded in winning over a fair minority of the membership. In retrospect, he seems to have been a "shrewd operator" who was out to gain control of the Community for his own ends. While he failed in the attempt, he succeeded in dividing the Oneidans into two factions, Noyesites and Townerites.

The Townerites complained that Noyes was too autocratic, and they wanted an equal voice. While the entire story is much too long to relate here, an important part centered on a strictly sexual matter.[25]

According to the principle of ascending fellowship, young people were required to have their first sexual encounter with the older, more spiritual members of the Community. Noyes evidently reserved for himself the right to initiate the young girls, although as he grew older he sometimes delegated the authority to one of the central members. However, the Townerites questioned his authority to make the decision, and the controversy became bitter.

Although Noyes exercised the rights of "first husband" for many years, he did so only with girls who had reached menarche (first menstruation). The catch was that some of the girls reached menarche at a very early age—as low as ten in some instances, with a range of ten to

---

[25]For an excellent analysis of the controversy, see Constance Noyes Robertson, *Oneida Community: The Breakup, 1876–1881* (Syracuse, NY: Syracuse University Press, 1972).

eighteen, and an average age of thirteen.[26] The Perfectionist leader's exercise of first husband rights, therefore, provided the Townerites with a powerful weapon. If legal charges were brought, Noyes could be accused of statutory rape; in fact, Towner was rumored to be gathering evidence against the Perfectionist leader. Towner denied the allegation, but the argument continued.

Lack of Leadership   Where was John Humphrey Noyes all this time? As Comstock and Mears mounted their attacks, as internal dissension accelerated, as Towner succeeded in tearing the Community apart— what was the Perfectionist leader doing? Unbelievable as it may seem, the answer is: nothing. After battling all his life for what he believed in, John Humphrey Noyes—for no known reason—seemed to give up. He left the Community for extended periods of time, and even when he was there he seemed to withdraw more and more from a position of active leadership. Little by little, the central members were permitted to make both operational and policy decisions. Unfortunately, they were not qualified to do so.

The Perfectionist leader not only withdrew from Community life, but the decisions he did make were disastrous. He permitted Towner to join, probably the worst decision of his entire career. He changed the Community's focus from the sacred to the secular—another misjudgment. And he made no provision for succession of leadership, other than to recommend his son Theodore for the job—still another bad decision. It was not only Noyes's spirit that waned, but his judgment as well.

The Breakup   In 1877, Noyes resigned. One of his last acts was to appoint a committee to succeed him, headed by Theodore, who actually directed the Community for the next few years. But the group was too far gone to be saved by anyone—least of all by Theodore.

On June 22, 1879, John Humphrey Noyes left the Oneida Community, never to return. He left secretly in the middle of the night, aided by a few close friends. And he left for the same reason that he had fled Putney thirty-two years earlier: to escape the law.

Noyes felt that Mears or the Townerites were about to bring charges against him on grounds of statutory rape, and in view of his vulnerability he decided to leave New York State. Actually, he may have been overcautious. The Townerites could hardly have brought charges inasmuch as they were guilty of the same offense. And since Mears was exceedingly unpopular in the Community, he could hardly have gath-

---

[26]Ely van de Warker, "A Gynecological Study of the Oneida Community," *American Journal of Obstetrics and Diseases of Women and Children*, 17 (August 1884): 795.

ered the necessary evidence. Nevertheless, Noyes left for Canada where—through emissaries—he kept in touch with Oneida.

In August, he sent word to the Community recommending that they abandon the practice of complex marriage. The recommendation satisfied both the Noyesites and the Townerites and passed without a dissenting voice. Shortly thereafter, a large number of monogamous marriages took place within the Community. Where it was possible, mothers married the fathers of their children. In the case of some of the younger women, Noyes more or less arranged the marriages.

For a while, the Oneidans continued to live communally, but it was clear to both insiders and outsiders that the end was imminent. Dissension prevailed. The aging Noyes remained more or less isolated in Canada. No new leader appeared. During 1880, plans for dissolution were discussed and approved, and on January 1, 1881, the Oneida Community officially ceased to exist.

The Aftermath

Although the group dissolved itself, it did not—in a literal sense—go out of business. For in spite of the wrangling and dissension mentioned above, the economic side of the Community held up surprisingly well: its net worth was $600,000. At the time of dissolution, a joint-stock company was formed—Oneida Ltd.—and the stock was apportioned among the members.

Like most business organizations, Oneida Ltd. has had its ups and downs. On the whole, however, the company has grown and prospered. For the first fifty years or so, the enterprise was managed—in whole or in part—by Pierrepont Noyes, a son of John Humphrey and an extremely able businessman. It was under his direction that the company phased out the traps and concentrated on silverware.

In 1960, P. T. Noyes—son of Pierrepont and grandson of John Humphrey—took over the presidency. And in 1967, the company was accepted for listing on the New York Stock Exchange with the simple designation "Oneida." During the late 1970s, the company diversified: copper wire and cooking utensils were added to the silverware lines. Today, Oneida Ltd. is a worldwide organization with thousands of employees.

What about the other phases of Community life following the breakup? A few members left the area entirely, never to return. A handful of the older members went to Canada, where they could be near their former leader. Towner's influence declined sharply, and a year after the breakup he and some twenty-five of his followers left for California. Many of them prospered, although they made no attempt to live communally. Towner eventually became a county court judge.

John Humphrey Noyes stayed in Canada with a few of the faithful. Most of his time was spent in Bible reading and—most likely— reminiscing. He died in 1886, at the age of seventy-four. He was buried at Oneida in the Community cemetery, his simple headstone indentical to all the others.

Most of the ex-Perfectionists remained in the Oneida area. Some stayed on in the Mansion House, in private apartments. Others moved to nearby houses. The majority of the men retained their positions with Oneida Ltd., many becoming officers, a pattern that has persisted down to the present. The Mansion House, over the years, served as a kind of social headquarters for the Oneidans and their descendants. While the social function today is minimal—an occasional wedding, a funeral, an anniversary celebration—the building is still in excellent condition. It contains apartments, a dining hall, a library, a museum, and—if one knows where to look—some fascinating memories.

The Oneida Community: A Contemporary Assessment

Was Oneida a success or a failure, a rewarding venture or a waste of time? Was John Humphrey Noyes a genius, an egomaniac, or simply a religious eccentric? Writers collided over these questions a hundred years ago—when the Community was still in existence—and there is still disagreement. Perhaps there always will be.

In a sociological sense, the Perfectionists were anything but failures. They not only lived together, communally, for many decades, but developed an economic base that was strong enough to spawn a multimillion-dollar corporation. Furthermore, they were able to provide society at large with a genuinely new perspective.

As used by both anthropologists and sociologists, *cultural relativism* is the doctrine "which holds that no judgments of comparative value or worth can be made about different culture patterns, because each has its own integrity and rationale for its own members. The doctrine also applies to differing moral standards within a culture, or to subcultures within the larger culture."[27] As a distinct subculture, the Oneida Community provides a good example of the significance of cultural relativism. That is, when the Community was flourishing, most Americans did not agree with the Perfectionist value system. Noyes's brand of commu-

---

[27]Melvin Tumin, *Patterns of Society* (Boston: Little, Brown, 1973), p. 417.

nism, after all, had limited appeal. At the same time, it drove home to many Americans—firsthand—*the realization that there were viable life-styles other than their own.*

This lesson is not lost even today. Students who read about the Oneida Perfectionists surely have a keener awareness of a completely different way of life. Most of us show little willingness to relinquish personal property, renounce conjugal love, or reject parenthood. Yet if one gives some serious thought to the Oneidans, their life-style becomes—if not attractive—at least understandable. Through understanding comes tolerance, the great lesson of cultural relativism.

SELECTED READINGS

Burridge, Kenelm. *New Haven, New Earth: A Study of Millenarian Activities.* New York: Schocken, 1969.

Carden, Maren Lockwood. *Oneida: Utopian Community to Modern Corporation.* Baltimore: Johns Hopkins University Press, 1969.

Cross, Whitney R. *The Burned-over District: The Social and Intellectual History of Enthusiastic Religion in Western New York, 1800–1850.* Ithaca, NY: Cornell University Press, 1950.

Dalsimer, Marlyn Hartzell. *Women and Family in the Oneida Community, 1837–1881.* Ph.D. diss., New York University, 1975.

Estlake, Allan. *The Oneida Community: A Record of an Attempt to Carry out the Principles of Christian Unselfishness and Scientific Race-Improvement.* London: George Redway, 1900.

Fogarty, Robert. "Oneida: A Utopian Search for Religious Security," *Labor History,* 14 (Spring 1973): 202–227.

Foster, Lawrence. *Religion and Sexuality: Three American Communal Experiments of the Nineteenth Century.* New York: Oxford University Press, 1981.

Handbook of the Oneida Community. Oneida, NY: Office of the Oneida Circular, 1875.

Hayden, Dolores. *Seven American Utopias: The Architecture of Communitarian Socialism, 1790–1975.* Cambridge, MA: MIT Press, 1976.

Kephart, William M. "Experimental Family Organization: An Historico-Cultural Report on the Oneida Community." *Marriage and Family Living,* 25 (August 1963): 261–271.

———. "The Oneida Community." In Kephart, *The Family, Society, and the Individual,* pp. 121–40. Boston: Houghton Mifflin, 1981.

Levine, Murray, and Bunker, Barbara Benedict. *Mutual Criticism.* Syracuse, NY: Syracuse University Press, 1975.

Muncy, Raymond Lee. *Sex and Marriage in Utopian Communities.* Bloomington: Indiana University Press, 1973.

Nordhoff, Charles. *The Communistic Societies of the United States.* New York: Dover, 1966.

Noyes, Corinna Ackley. *Days of My Youth*. Oneida, NY: Oneida Ltd, 1960.

Noyes, George Wallingford. *John Humphrey Noyes: The Putney Community*. Oneida, NY., 1931.

Noyes, Hilda H., and Noyes, George W. "The Oneida Community Experiment in Stirpiculture." *Eugenics, and the Family*, 1 (1923): 374–386.

———. *Essay on Scientific Propagation*. Oneida, NY: Oneida Community, 1873.

———. *Male Continence*. Oneida, NY: Office of the Oneida Circular, 1872.

Noyes, Pierrepont B. *A Goodly Heritage*. New York: Holt, Rinehart and Winston, 1958.

———. *My Fathers House: An Oneida Boyhood*. Gloucester, MA: Peter Smith, 1966.

Parker, Robert. *A Yankee Saint: John Humphrey Noyes and the Oneida Community*. New York: Putnam, 1935.

Robertson, Constance Noyes (ed.). *Oneida Community: An Autobiography, 1851–1876*. Syracuse, NY: Syracuse University Press, 1970.

———. *Oneida Community Profiles*. Syracuse, NY: Syracuse University Press, 1977.

Thomas, Robert. *The Man Who Would Be Perfect: John Humphrey Noyes and the Utopian Impulse*. Philadelphia: University of Pennsylvania Press, 1977.

Wagner, Jon (ed.). *Sex Roles in Contemporary American Communes*. Bloomington: Indiana University Press, 1982.

Walters, Ronald G. *American Reformers, 1815–1860*. New York: Hill & Wang, 1978.

CHAPTER THREE
THE GYPSIES

Of all the groups discussed in the present volume, the Gypsies are the most "extraordinary." Even for experienced observers, their culture patterns are difficult to grasp. For the fact of the matter is that the Gypsies have a life-style that comes close to defying comprehension. On the dust jacket of Peter Maas's controversial and widely read *King of the Gypsies*, for example, the following blurb appears:

> There are perhaps a million or more Gypsies in the United States—nobody knows exactly how many, not even the government. They no longer live in horse-drawn caravans on dusty roads; they live in cities, drive cars, have telephones and credit cards. Yet they do not go to school, neither read nor write, don't pay taxes, and keep themselves going by means of time-honored ruses and arrangements. Gypsies themselves recognize the contrast they make, and they are proud of it.[1]

Given the nature of modern journalism, can this statement be true? The answer is not a simple one, and each of the above points requires some explanation.

It is true that no one knows how many Gypsies there are in the United States, although the million figure commonly reported in the press may be too high. More reliable estimates place the figure closer to 500,000.[2] If the latter figure is correct, it would mean that only two other countries in the world have larger Gypsy populations: Yugoslavia (750,000), and Romania (680,000).[3]

Although 500,000 seems a reasonable estimate, it is unlikely that the real figure will ever be known. Gypsies move about so much, have so many different names and aliases, and are generally so secretive that it is often difficult to pinpoint the numbers for a given city let alone for the nation at large.

---

[1]Peter Maas, *King of the Gypsies*, (New York: Viking, 1975).

[2]See Ian F. Hancock, "Gypsies," in Stephan Thernstrom, ed., *Harvard Encyclopedia of American Ethnic Groups*, (Cambridge, MA: Harvard University Press, 1980), p. 441.

[3]See William Lockwood, "Balkan Gypsies: An Introduction," in Joanne Grumet, ed., *Papers from the Fourth and Fifth Annual Meetings, Gypsy Lore Society, North American Chapter* (New York: Gypsy Lore Society, 1985), pp. 91–99.

Gypsies live in cities and drive cars? Indeed they do. They are not likely to be found on farms or in the suburbs. They will not be found on the water. They are urban dwellers—towns and cities—and they reside in nearly all fifty states. At the same time, Gypsies are, and always have been great travelers. They may be the greatest travelers the world has ever known. (In England, the terms "Gypsy" and "Traveler" are often used interchangeably.) As we shall see, traveling serves as an integral part of the Gypsy life-style.

As for cars, Gypsies not only drive them but sometimes make their living repairing them. The days of horse-drawn wagons and caravans have long since gone, but Gypsies—as is their wont—have adapted remarkably well to motorized transportation. Indeed, despite the fact that they are a low-income group, Gypsies often drive Cadillacs.

Gypsies do not go to school? Not very often—and not for very long. They feel that formal education is not germane to their way of life and that the American school system would tend to "de-Gypsyize" their youngsters. Both claims are at least partially true, and the subject will be discussed in a later section.

Gypsies neither read nor write? True. A large portion of them are functionally illiterate. They cannot even read or write their own language, Romany, for it is a spoken rather than a written tongue. The literacy situation is improving, but so far progress has been slow. In spite of their self-imposed linguistic handicap, however, Gypsies have made a remarkable adaptation to their environment.

Gypsies do not pay taxes? Some observers would reply: "Not if they can help it." And it is true that many Gypsies do not pay property taxes because they have no taxable property. They often prefer to rent rather than to buy a dwelling place. Also, many Gypsies work irregularly and have low-paying jobs, so that their income taxes would be negligible. A fair number are on welfare. On the other hand, at least some Gypsies are moving into white-collar occupations, and their tax payments are probably commensurate with those of other white-collar workers.

The Internal Revenue Service, however, has had difficulty taxing even substantial Gypsy holdings, as this recent account indicates:

> . . . The Police found more than $1.5 million in cash when they raided two Gypsy homes [in Spokane, Washington, during a search for stolen goods]. The IRS claimed the money, contending that the Gypsies had not paid federal taxes on it. Immediately afterward, Internal Revenue agreed to return $519,000 leaving about $1 million in dispute.

The Gypsies sued in U.S. District Court, contending that the seizure was illegal. In the Tax Court they challenged the way the IRS calculated the tax. The Gypsies said the money was a community fund belonging to the entire Gypsy nation and was being held by the Gypsy leaders. (In an out of court settlement, the IRS agreed to return all but about $350,0000.)[4]

Gypsies keep themselves going by means of time-honored ruses and arrangements? A complicated question, surely, but then the Gypsies are a complicated people. As is true of all ethnic groups, there are honest Gypsies and there are dishonest Gypsies. Unfortunately, however, many Gypsies continue to believe that all *gadje** (non-Gypsies) are fair game. And more than occasionally this belief does culminate in ruses and petty swindles.

At the same time, Gypsy attitudes toward the *gadje* have been shaped in part by the *gadje* themselves. As will be shown, Gypsies have not been met with open arms by the various host countries. On the contrary, they have experienced near-universal prejudice and discrimination. Social distance studies in several countries, including the United States, simply confirm the obvious; namely, that Gypsies rank at the absolute bottom of the status scale.[5]

Through it all, the Gypsies have survived. Gypsies always survive. If they haven't exactly flourished, they have in many ways given a very good account of themselves. It is not easy to be a Gypsy. As one writer put it: "Only the fit need apply."[6] It is hoped that in the following pages the full implications of this statement will become clear.

Who Are the Gypsies?

Like so many other aspects of their life, Gypsy origins are draped in mystery. The word "Gypsy" derives from "Egyptian," for the Gypsies were mistakenly thought to have originated in Egypt. This was a belief that they themselves did little to discourage. In fact, some Gypsies still believe in their Egyptian roots, although it has now been rather well established that their original homeland was India. (Romany, the Gypsy language, has it roots in Sanskrit.)

Exactly when the Gypsies left India—or what their status was—is still being debated. They have been variously described as being descended from the Criminal and Wandering Tribes, as being deported prisoners of war, and as being "a loose federation of nomadic tribes, possibly outside

---

[4]"IRS Will Return Most of the Gypsies' Cash Cache," *Insight* (November 9, 1987), p. 47.

[5]Cited in Matt Salo and Sheila Salo, *The Kalderasha in Eastern Canada*, (Ottawa: National Museums of Canada, 1977), p. 17.

[6]Rena C. Gropper, *Gypsies in the City*, (Princeton, NJ: Darwin, 1975), p. 189.

*Interestingly enough, the Gypsy language has not been standardized. Consequently, most of their terms have a variety of spellings. In the present account, spelling has been adapted to fit the pronunciation.

the Indian caste system entirely."[7] Rishi contends that "the majority of Gypsies, before migrating from India, formed a vital part of the upper strata of the Indian population, such as the Rajputs, Kshatriyas, and Jats."[8]

Whatever their class or caste origins, it seems likely that the proto-Gypsies left India at different times—and from different areas—perhaps during the first few centuries A.D.[9] By the fifth century, they seem to have settled in and around Persia and Syria. And although their early migration patterns are anything but clear, Gypsies were reported in Southeastern Europe (Greece, Hungary, Romania, Serbia) by the 1300s, and in Western Europe (France, Germany, Italy, Holland, Switzerland, Spain) by the 1400s.[10] Today there are Gypsies in practically every European country. They are also well established in North Africa, the Near East, South America, the United States, and Canada.

The term "Gypsy," incidentally, is not a Romany term. Gypsies refer to themselves as "Rom." (In the present account, the two terms will be used interchangeably.) And while there is much physical variation, the Rom tend to have dark hair, dark eyes, and medium to dark complexions. On the whole, they are of average or a little below average height. Several writers have noticed that Gypsies tend to become obese as they age.

(Some groups who are often thought of as Gypsies are not in fact true Gypsies, or Rom. These would include the Tinkers of Ireland and Scotland, and the Taters of Norway.[11] The Irish Tinkers, for example, are of Celtic origin, and they speak Shelte, a Celtic dialect.[12] In the present account, we are concerned only with the Rom.)

As they spread throughout Europe, Gypsies came to be—above all else—travelers. "A Gypsy who does not keep on the move," wrote Block just prior to World War II, "is not a Gypsy."[13] Actually, there have always been a fair number of sedentary Gypsies, or *Sinte*. Lockwood reports that in Yugoslavia there is currently a community of some 40,000 Gypsies.[14]

---

[7]Donald Kenrick and Grattan Puxon, *The Destiny of Europe's Gypsies*, (New York: Basic Books, 1972), pp. 13–14.

[8]P. W. R. Rishi, "Roma Preserves Hindu Mythology," *Roma* (January 1977): 13.

[9]See the discussion in T. A. Acton, "The Social Construction of the Ethnic Identity of Commercial Nomadic Groups," in Grumet, ed., *Papers*, pp. 5–23.

[10]See Gropper, *Gypsies in the City*, pp. 1–16.

[11]Frederik Barth, "The Social Organization of a Parish Group in Norway," in Farnham Rehfisch, ed., *Gypsies, Tinkers, and Other Travelers* (New York: Academic Press, 1975), pp. 285–99.

[12]For an interesting discussion, see George Gmelch, *The Irish Tinkers* (Prospect Heights, IL: Waveland Press, 1985).

[13]Martin Block, *Gypsies: Their Life and Their Customs* (New York: Appleton-Century, 1939), p. 1.

[14]Lockwood, "Balkan Gypsies: An Introduction," in Grumet, ed., *Papers*, p. 92.

Nevertheless, *Sinte* or no *Sinte*, it was the horse-drawn wagons and gaily decorated caravans that seemed to strike a responsive chord in people of all ages. Jan Yoors, author of one of the most widely read books on Gypsy life, ran away as a young boy and lived for many years with a Gypsy group.[15] Webb, another writer, states that

> for as long as I can remember, Gypsies have fascinated me. These dark-skinned strangers, indifferent to the rest of the world, mysterious in their comings and goings, traveling the roads with parades of highly colored raggedness, fired my imagination. I was curious about them and wanted to know more. But nobody, it seemed, could tell me more.[16]

The Rom themselves seemed captivated by the caravan style of life. Indeed, some still talk about the good old (premotorized) days. Whether, in fact, caravan life was all that good can be debated. Yoors himself writes as follows:

> One year, for the first time, I stayed with the Rom throughout the winter. Lying half awake in the cold stillness of the long nights in Pulika's huge wagon, I heard the snapping noise of the nails in the boards as they creaked under the effect of the severe frost. The windows had been covered up with boards, old overcoats and army blankets, straw or pieces of tar paper, but the wind blasted through cracks too many to fill.
>
> The dogs whimpered all night. The drinking water froze in the buckets, and washing in the morning became an ordeal. Hands chapped, lips cracked and bled. The men ceased to shave. The small children cried bitterly when they were put outside and chased away from the wagons near which they had wanted to relieve themselves. Clothes could not be washed. The air inside the wagons was thick and unbreathable, mixed with the coal fumes from the red-hot stove, from which small children had to be kept away.
>
> During the winter months, not enough dead wood could be gathered outside to keep the fires going all day and part of the night, so the Rom were forced to buy, beg, or steal coal.[17]

No combination of elements, however, could dampen the Gypsy spirit—or their fondness for bright colors, especially greens, yellows, and reds. As one effervescent Gypsy put it, "I wear bright beads and bright colors because we're a bright race. We don't like anything drab."[18]

The Gypsy Paradox With their unusual life-style, there is no doubt that Gypsies have held a real fascination for the *gadje*, almost irrespective of the country involved. Novels, plays, operettas, movies, and

[15]Jan Yoors, *The Gypsies* (New York: Simon and Schuster, 1967).

[16]G. E. C. Webb, *Gypsies: The Secret People* (London: Herbert Jenkins, 1960), p. 9.

[17]Yoors, *Gypsies*, p. 86.

[18]Jeremy Sandford, *Gypsies* (London: Secker & Warburg, 1973), p. 13.

songs have portrayed—and sometimes glorified—the romantic wanderings of the Gypsy vagabond. Popular pieces like "Gypsy Love Song" and "Play Gypsy, Dance Gypsy" have become part of the worldwide musical repertoire.

Yet side by side with the attraction and fascination has come harassment and persecution. This is the Gypsy paradox: attraction on the one hand, persecution on the other. The climax of persecution came during World War II, when the Nazis murdered between 250,000 and 600,000 Rom.

Despite worldwide persecution, however, the Gypsies have managed to survive. Gypsies always survive. As Gropper puts it:

> For 500 years Gypsies have succeeded in being themselves against all odds, fiercely maintaining their identity in spite of persecution, prejudice, hatred, and cultural forces compelling them to change. We may have something to learn from them on how to survive in a drastically changing world.[19]

The Modern Period   Following World War II, urbanization and industrialization—together with population expansion—literally cramped the Gypsies' life-style. There was less and less room on the modern highway for horse-drawn caravans. Camping sites became harder to find, and the open countryside seemed to shrink. But—as always—the Gypsies adapted. Travel continued, albeit on a reduced scale. Caravans and wagons were replaced by automobiles, trucks, campers, and trailers. Somehow, by one method or another, the Rom managed to get by. And they did so without sacrificing their group identity or their freedom.

Their identity was not maintained without a price, however, for prejudice and harassment continued. Gypsy nomads were often hounded from one locale to another. The *Sinte* or sedentary Rom—whose proportion tended to increase—were also met by hostility and discrimination. "No Gypsies Allowed" signs came more and more to be posted in public places.

The issue was hardly one-sided. From the view of local authorities, Gypsies were using community services without paying their share of the taxes. Indeed, they were often not paying any taxes at all. Additionally, the Rom were dirty, they would not use indoor toilets, they lied, they cheated, and they stole. Sometimes the charges were true; often they were unfounded.

Fortunately, the Gypsies also had friends and supporters, and in a number of countries efforts were made to set up camping sites, establish housing facilities, provide legal assistance, and otherwise improve the

---

[19]Gropper, *Gypsies in the City*, p. 1.

lot of the Rom. By the 1970s, a number of national and international committees and councils had been organized—with Gypsy representation. The purpose of these groups has been not only to protect the interests of the Rom but to dispel stereotypes, combat false portrayals in the media, and act as a clearinghouse for information about Gypsies.

When all is said and done, however, there is no doubt that the Rom continue to have problems. According to Dodds, the idea of their having a carefree, romantic life is a myth. In reality, "the Gypsy's life is one of perpetual insecurity."[20]

And yet, contrast the foregoing statement with the following, by Clebert: "Gypsies themselves are Lords of the Earth. . . . All real Gypsies are united in their love of freedom, and in their eternal flight from the bonds of civilization, in their desire to be their own masters, and in their contempt for what we pompously call the 'consequences.' "[21]

Which of the two views is correct? Perhaps both are. In some ways, the Rom do indeed have a difficult life. Their relationship with the *gadje* often takes on the appearance of an interminable contest. At the same time, Gypsies show little inclination to assimilate. They are demonstrably proud that they are Gypsies, an attitude that is unlikely to change.

How many Gypsies are there in the world today? Estimates vary from 5 to 10 million, with the latter figure probably being closer to the truth. (More than half are in Eastern Europe.) There is a general—though not unanimous—agreement that the Rom are divided into four tribes or nations (*natsiyi*): the Lowara, Machwaya, Kalderasha, and Churara. While there are linguistic and cultural differences among the four *natsiyi*, surprisingly little has been written on this score.

The United States   The first Gypsies to come to what is now the United States arrived in Virginia, Georgia, New Jersey, and Louisiana during the 1600s, although their fate remains unknown.[22] It is known that these early arrivals had been deported from various European countries—hardly an auspicious beginning. Significant numbers of the Rom, however, did not enter the United States until the 1880s and after.[23]

Up until the 1930s, the Rom followed their traditional traveling and camping patterns, replete with horse-drawn vehicles and colorful caravans. By the 1930s, though—as was true in Europe—the caravan had generally given way to motorized transportation.

The Depression of the 1930s saw another significant event insofar as the Gypsies were concerned: the election of Franklin Roosevelt and the

[20]Norman Dodds, *Gypsies, Didikois, and Other Travelers* (London: Johnson, 1976), p. 16.
[21]Jean-Paul Clebert, *The Gypsies* (London: Vista, 1963), pp. xvii–xix.
[22]Hancock, "Gypsies," p. 441.
[23]Gropper, *Gypsies in the City*, p. 18.

introduction of large-scale relief and welfare programs. To take advantage of the situation, the Rom began to flock to the large cities, such as Chicago and New York.[24]

The extent to which they stayed in the cities—and later in the smaller towns—depended on such things as economic opportunities, welfare practices, and degree of police harassment. And since all three of these factors changed from time to time, the Gypsy population in a given city often fluctuated. Nevertheless, the Rom were in the cities to stay, and today there are a reported 10,000 in Chicago and 15,000 in Los Angeles. While they reside in nearly all the states, the largest Gypsy concentrations are to be found in New York, Virginia, Illinois, Texas, Massachusetts, and on the Pacific Coast.[25] Although Romany practices in other countries will be alluded to from time to time, our primary concern in the following pages will be with the American Gypsies.

Difficulties in Studying the Rom

> If you ask a dozen Gypsies the same question, you will probably get a dozen different answers. If you ask one Gypsy the same question a dozen times, you will still probably get a dozen different answers.
>
> —*Anonymous*

Although there are many versions, this adage contains more than a little truth. Gypsies live—and always have lived—in alien cultures. The boundaries between Rom and *gadje* are sharp, and the Rom have every intention of maintaining the sharpness. Deception, avoidance, misrepresentation, and lying are part of the Gypsies' arsenal, and they have had hundreds of years to perfect and embellish their defenses. In many ways, investigating the Rom is like trying to penetrate a secret society.

Perhaps the most formidable obstacle the researcher has to face is the avoidance syndrome. The Rom ordinarily do not mingle with the *gadje;* in fact, except for a possible visit to a fortune-teller, most Americans never come into contact with a Gypsy. Almost certainly they never see the inside of a Romany dwelling. Researchers face much the same problem. The fact that researchers are accredited university personnel means little to the Rom. Generally speaking, Gypsies have no intention of divulging their life-style and customs to social scientists or to anybody else.

Fortunately, we have some excellent American field studies, such as those by Anne Sutherland[26] and Rena C. Gropper.[27] Both of these investi-

---

[24]Ibid., p. 20.
[25]Hancock, "Gypsies," p. 441.
[26]Anne Sutherland, *Gypsies: The Hidden Americans* (New York: Free Press, 1975).
[27]Gropper, *Gypsies in the City.*

gators are not only trained observers but spent several years among the Rom, learning the language and achieving a fair degree of acceptance. Yet even they experienced difficulties! Sutherland writes that

> the first Gypsy I met was a young woman of my own age who smiled at me, talking soothingly and ingratiatingly, but when I asked to speak with her father, she lunged at me, grabbing my face with her fingernails, screaming and cursing, "WHAT DO YOU WANT?"
> The second Gypsy I talked with vehemently denied that he was a Gypsy (what better technique for not answering questions), and the third feigned imbecility, mumbling to herself and staring wildly into space. . . .
> It soon became clear that these are people who, through centuries of experience in avoiding the prying questions of curious outsiders, have perfected their techniques of evasion to an effortless art. They delight in deceiving the *gadje*, mostly for a good reason, but sometimes just for the fun of it or to keep in practice![28]

Although avoidance and deception serve as major impediments in studying the Rom, there are other difficulties involved—difficulties that make it hard to *generalize* about Gypsy life. To begin with, all four *natsiyi* or tribes are represented in the United States. Customs and practices that apply to one group might or might not apply to the others. (Actually, the Kalderasha and the Machwaya are by far the most numerous of the *natsiyi* in the United States, and most of the American studies have been done on these two groups. Little is known about the Churara, and there are relatively few Lowara in this country.)

Practices of the Rom also vary depending on their mobility patterns. Some Gypsies have lived in the same domicile for many years. Others move about constantly. Still others travel as the mood strikes them. And customs and life-style vary somewhat from one group to another.

Even if all Rom followed similar travel practices, their social structure would be difficult to analyze. Gypsies live in extended families (*familiyi*), which form part of a larger kinship or cognatic group called the *vitsa*. (The *vitsi*, in turn, are affiliated with one of the four tribes, or *natsiyi*: Lowara, Machwaya, Kalderasha, and Churara.) The point is that many Gypsy customs may vary from one *familia* to the next, and from one *vitsa* to the next, making it hard, again, to generalize.

One final factor complicates the study of American Rom: their customs often depend on their country of origin. The Romnichals (English Gypsies), for instance, differ from the Boyash (Romanian), and both groups are culturally different from the Arxentina (Gypsies from Argentina and Brazil).[29]

---

[28]Sutherland, *Hidden Americans*, p. 21.
[29]See the discussion in Marcel Cortiade, "Distance between Romani Dialects," *Newsletter of the Gypsy Lore Society, North American Chapter*, 8 (Spring 1985): 1ff.

In brief, American Rom do not present a uniform culture pattern. Because of their kinship structure, their social and economic organization, their geographical mobility, and their nationality differences, it would be difficult to generalize about Gypsies even if they were cooperative—which they are not. (And even the "cooperative" Gypsies pose a problem for the researcher. The Rom often have a working knowledge of their own particular group—but no other. Very few Gypsies have anything like a broad view or a historical picture of their own people.)

Marimé

Central to any understanding of the Rom is their concept of *marimé*. It is *marimé* that is the key to their avoidance of the *gadje*, and it is *marimé* that serves as a powerful instrument of social control.

Marimé means defilement or pollution, and as used by the Gypsies it is both an object and a concept. And since there is really no comparable term used by non-Gypsies, it is sometimes difficult for the latter to comprehend the meaning. "*Marimé*," writes Miller, "extends to all areas of Rom life, underwriting a hygienic attitude toward the world. . . . Lines are drawn between Gypsy and non-Gypsy, the clean and the unclean, health and disease, the good and the bad, all of which are made obvious and visible through the offices of ritual avoidance."[30]

The most striking aspects of *marimé* have to do with the demarcation of the human body. The upper parts, particularly the head and the mouth, are looked upon as pure and clean. The lower portions, especially the genital and anal regions, are considered *marimé*. As the Rom see it, the upper and lower halves of the body must not "mix" in any way, and objects that come into contact with one half most not come into contact with the other.

There are countless examples of this hygienic-ritualistic separation. Ronald Lee, who is himself a Gypsy, writes that

> you can't wash clothes, dishes, and babies in the same pan, and every Gypsy has his own eating utensils, towels, and soap. Other dishes and utensils are set aside for guests, and still others for pregnant women. Certain towels are for the face, and others for the nether regions—and there are different colored soaps in the sink, each with an allotted function.[31]

Marimé apparently originated in the early caravan period, when—for hygienic purposes—it was imperative that certain areas of the camp be

---

[30]Carol Miller, "American Rom and the Ideology of Defilement," in Rehfisch, *Gypsies*, p. 41.

[31]Ronald Lee, *Goddam Gypsy: An Autobiographical Novel* (Montreal: Tundra, 1971), pp. 29–30.

set aside for cooking, cleaning, washing, taking care of body functions, and the like. Also, within the close confines of the wagons and tents, it was important that rules pertaining to sex be carefully spelled out and enforced. As is so often the case, however, over the years the various hygienic and sexual taboos proliferated. Miller notes, for example, that at the present time:

> Items that come into contact with the upper portions of the body are separately maintained and washed in running water or special basins. These items would include soap, towels, razors and combs, clothes, pillows, furniture like the backs of chairs, and the tops of tables, tablecloths, aprons, sinks, utensils, and, of course, food itself, which is prepared, served, and eaten with the greatest consideration for ritual quality. . . .
>
> Any contact between the lower half of the body, particularly the genitals, which are conceptually the ultimate source of *marimé*, and the upper body is forbidden. The inward character of the genitals, especially the female genitalia—which are associated with the mysteries of blood and birth— make them consummately impure. Items that have contact with this area are carefully segregated because they contain a dangerous threat to the status of pure items and surfaces. The most dreadful contact, of course, would be between the genitals and the oral cavity.[32]

Gropper states that "a woman is *marimé* during and after childbirth, and during her monthly period. . . . A *marimé* woman may not cook or serve food to men. She may not step over anything belonging to a man or allow her skirts to touch his things. Women's clothing must be washed separately from men's."[33]

Even such a natural phenomenon as urination may cause difficulties for the Rom. "One old lady called off a visit to a friend because she was indisposed and felt it would be too embarrassing to urinate frequently. Men often go outside to urinate rather than do so in their own homes, especially if guests are present."[34]

Interestingly and—given their conception of *marimé*—quite logically, Gypsy women attach shame to the legs rather than the breasts. Sutherland points out that it is shameful for a woman to have too much leg exposed, and that women who wear short skirts are expected to cover them with a sweater when they sit. On the other hand:

> Women use their brassieres as their pocketbooks, and it is quite common for a man, whether he be the husband, son, father, or unrelated, to reach

[32]Miller, "American Rom," p. 42. See also Elwood Trigg, *Gypsy Demons and Divinities* (Secaucus, NJ: Citadel, 1973), p. 64.
[33]Gropper, *Gypsies in the City*, pp. 92–93.
[34]Sutherland, *Hidden Americans*, p. 266.

into her brassiere to get cigarettes or money. When women greet each other after a certain absence, they squeeze each other's breasts. They will also squeeze the breasts to show appreciation of a witty story or joke.[35]

Marimé vs. Melalo   Mention should be made of the distinction between *marimé* and *melalo*. *Marimé* is pollution or defilement, as just described. *Melalo* simply means dirty, or as Lee describes it, "dirty with honest dirt."[36] Someone who has not had a bath would be *melalo*, but not *marimé*. Hands that are dirty because of manual labor would be *melalo* rather than *marimé*—although they would be *marimé* if they had touched the genitals.

(In actual practice, Gypsies tend to wash their hands many times a day—because they may have touched any number of objects or organs that are *marimé*. Miller states that "a working Rom also washes his face and hands whenever he feels his luck leaving him during the day; he washes again upon returning from his work.")[37]

The distinction between *marimé* and *melalo* explains why a Gypsy domicile often appears dirty to a non-Gypsy—and vice versa. Some Romany dwelling places, for example, are anything but spic and span. Food scraps, cigarette butts, paper, wrappings—all may be thrown on the floor, presumably to be swept out later. Such a condition is not *marimé* so long as the proper rules of body hygiene, food preparation, and so forth are followed. As one writer puts it: "Americans tend to be shocked at visible dirt, but Gypsies abhor invisible pollution."[38]

The *Gadje:* Definition of the Situation   Not all of the *natsiyi* follow the same rules and procedures regarding *marimé*. There are also some variations among family groups within the same *natsia*. (The Salos note that families who follow a strict observance pattern have a higher status than those who tend to be lax.)[39] But there is one point on which all true Rom are agreed: the *gadje* are *marimé*. Miller writes as follows:

> The *gadje* are conceived as a different race whose main value is economic, and whose *raison d'être* is to trouble the Rom. The major offense of the *gadje*, the one offense that the Rom can never forgive, is their propensity to defilement. *Gadje* confuse the critical distinction between the pure and the impure. They are observed in situations which the Rom regard as compro-

---

[35]Ibid., p. 264.
[36]Lee, *Goddam Gypsy*, p. 244.
[37]Miller, "American Rom," p. 47.
[38]Gropper, *Gypsies in the City*, p. 91.
[39]Salo and Salo, *Kalderasha*, p. 115.

mising: forgetting to wash in public bathrooms; eating with the fork that they rescued from the floor of the restaurant; washing face towels and tablecloths with underwear at the laundromat; relaxing with their feet resting on the top of the table.

Because they do not protect the upper half of the body, the *gadje* are construed as *marimé* all over, head to foot. This condition, according to Rom belief, invites and spreads contagious disease. Rom tend to think of all illness and physical disability as communicable, and treat them accordingly.[40]

Since the *gadje* are *marimé*, relations with them are severely limited. In fact, Sutherland states that "interaction with the *gadje* is restricted to economic exploitation and political manipulation. Social relations in the sense of friendship, mutual aid, and equality are not appropriate."[41] The same author goes on to say that

not only the person of non-Gypsies but items that come into contact with them are *marimé*. Any time a Rom is forced to use *gadje* places or to be in contact with large numbers of *gadje* (for example, in a job, hospital, welfare office, school), he is in constant danger of pollution. Public toilets are particularly *marimé* places, and some Rom go to the extent of using paper towels to turn faucets and open doors.[42]

The reader may recall that in the chapter on the Amish the concept *definition of the situation* was used; that is, "What men define as real is real in its consequences." And just as the Amish have defined the automobile as a threat to their social equilibrium, so the Gypsies have defined the *gadje* as *marimé*.

Barrier to Assimilation   Do not the various rules and prohibitions involved in *marimé* impose a hardship on the Rom? In one sense, the answer is yes. The urban world, the Gypsies' major habitat, is seen as "pervasively *marimé*, filled with items and surfaces that are subject to use and reuse by careless *gadje*, polluted, diseased, and therefore dangerous."[43] To avoid the danger, Gypsies must take any number of daily precautions—and there is no doubt that these precautions are time-consuming and burdensome. Little wonder, as Miller points out, that "the home is the final bastion of defense against defilement, and the only place that the Rom feel altogether at ease."[44]

At the same time, *marimé* serves as an extremely effective *barrier to assimilation*. As used by sociologists, the term *assimilation* refers to the

[40]Miller, "American Rom," pp. 45–46.
[41]Sutherland, *Hidden Americans*, p. 258.
[42]Ibid., p. 259.
[43]Miller, "American Rom," p. 47.
[44]Ibid.

absorption of one population group by another, where the end result is a blending of culture traits. The so-called melting pot in America has boiled unevenly, some groups being assimilated much faster than others. The Gypsies, of course, would fall at the lower end of any assimilation scale—which is just where they want to be. As the Rom see it, assimilation would be tantamount to group extinction.

Nowhere is this resistance to assimilation more apparent than in their attitude toward the *gadje*. The belief that the *gadje* are *marimé* not only serves as a barrier to assimilation but acts as an ever-present sustainer of pride and self-respect. In fact, so pervasive is their negative attitude toward the *gadje* that Gypsies will not assimilate even after death! Nemeth's analysis of cemetery plots and tombstones revealed that the Rom attempt "to maintain distance in the graveyard between themselves and non-Gypsies, and between themselves and outcasts from their own society."[45]

Some Gypsiologists, however, believe that the rules pertaining to *marimé* are softening. The Salos, in their study of Canadian Rom, found this to be the case.[46] In most areas of the United States, however, *marimé* still seems to be a potent force. When an older Gypsy woman was asked whether she felt that *marimé* was weakening, she shrugged and said, "Maybe. I hope not. Some of the young kids don't know it, but it's what holds us together."

Family and Social Organization

Gypsies maintain a rather complicated form of social organization, and it is sometimes difficult to unravel the various kinship and community networks. It will simplify matters, however, if two points are kept in mind:

1. Gypsies are not loners. Their lives are spent in the company of other Gypsies. In fact, the term "individual Gypsy" is almost a play on words. In most of their communities, there are no single-person households, and no households of childless newlywed couples.[47]

2. The Rom are living in an alien culture, and they have no intention of assimilating. They are keenly aware of their position, and they are determined to keep an ever-clear line between the *gadje* and themselves. Their social organization is designed *to enhance the process of boundary maintenance.*

[45]David Nemeth, "Gypsy Taskmasters, Gentile Slaves," in Matt T. Salo, ed., *The American Kalderasha: Gypsies in the New World* (Hackettstown, NJ: Gypsy Lore Society, 1981), p. 31.
[46]Salo and Salo, *Kalderasha*, pp. 128–29.
[47]Ibid., p. 39.

The *Familia*   The heart of Gypsy culture is the *familia*. As Yoors points out: "The inner cohesion and solidarity of the Gypsy community lies in the strong family ties—which are their basic and only constant unit."[48]

The *familia*, however, is much larger and more complex than the American nuclear family. Whereas the latter is generally thought of as a husband-wife-children unit, the *familia* includes spouses, unmarried children, married sons and their wives and children, plus other assorted relatives and adopted youngsters. And since Gypsy couples often have six or more children, the *familia* may easily total thirty to forty members.[49] By the same token, since in many ways the Gypsy world is a man's world, the male head of the *familia* may wield considerable power.

The *familia*, then, appears to be an extended family, but it is actually more than that: it is a *functional extended family.* Members live together (or close by); they often work together; they trust and protect one another; they celebrate holidays together; they take care of the sick and the aged; they bury the dead. The *familia*, in brief, is close to being a self-sufficient unit. One of the few functions it does not perform is that of matrimony, since marriages between first cousins are frowned upon.

Although the Rom believe in private property and free enterprise, ownership is often thought of in terms of the *familia* rather than the individual. Traditionally, as Clebert notes, "the essential nucleus of the Gypsy organization is the family. Authority is held by the father. . . . [P]roperty belongs to the family and not to the individual. But the family is not limited to the father, mother, and children. It includes aunts, uncles, and cousins."[50]

The *familia* is particularly effective as a *supportive institution.* Whether the problem is economic, social, political, or medical, the various family members unite in their efforts to provide aid. Should a police official, social worker, inspector, tax collector, or any other unwelcome *gadjo* appear on the scene, the intruder will be met with formidable—and generally effective—opposition. Should a family member fall ill, the *familia* will spare no expense in obtaining professional help, especially if it is a serious illness.

As hospital personnel can attest, a full-blown *familia* on the premises creates something of a problem. The Salos write that "illness, especially a terminal illness, requires the supportive presence at the hospital of the entire extended family. Hospitals often balk at the consequent waiting-room crowds."[51]

The very structure of the *familia*, of course, creates some problems—

---

[48]Yoors, *Gypsies*, p. 5.
[49]For an interesting account of the *familia*, see Gropper, *Gypsies in the City*, pp. 60–66.
[50]Clebert, *Gypsies*, p. 129.
[51]Salo and Salo, *Kalderasha*, p. 19.

housing and otherwise. Landlords do not take kindly to rentals involving a dozen or more persons. Noise, sanitation disposal, complaints by neighbors—all must be reckoned with. Also, by virtue of its size the *familia* is cumbersome. It is one thing for a Gypsy couple to pack up and move; it is quite another for a large *familia* to "hit the road." And since the Rom obviously like to travel, the extended family presents a mobility problem.

The *familia* has functional as well as structural problems. Disagreements and conflicts are bound to occur. Jealousies do arise. Living arrangements are sometimes felt to be unsatisfactory. In her study of Philadelphia Gypsies, Coker found that

> there is constant slandering; rumors are started, and attacks and counterattacks are made. Most of the rumors involve sex. Some reflect on the morals of young girls, implying that they are dating non-Gypsy men, or, as a particularly vicious accusation, that they are going out with Negroes.[52]

Despite the problems involved, the Rom show few signs of abandoning the *familia*. On the contrary, they seem to thrive on it. In some cases, the size of the extended family has been reduced. In others, the married sons may form their own households. Nevertheless, the *familia* continues to be the center of the Gypsy world. As long as the *gadje* are seen in an adversary context, the *familia* will remain the Gypsies' principal bastion of security.

The *Vitsa* Whereas the *familia* can be thought of as an extended family, the *vitsa* is a cognatic kin group made up of a number of *familiyi*. Some Gypsiologists refer to the *vitsa* as a clan or a band, but the important point is that the Rom think of it as a *unit of identity*. Members of the highly publicized Bimbalesti *vitsa*, for example, would identify with one another—feel a kindred relationship—even though they might all come together very infrequently.

Vitsi vary in size from a few *familiyi* to a hundred or more households. Members of a smaller *vitsa* may live near one another and operate as a functioning group. The Rom have large families, however, and most *vitsi* tend to grow. The majority of American *vitsi*, therefore, function as a group on only two occasions: at a Gypsy trial (*kris romani*) and at a death feast (*pomana*), especially where the deceased has been a respected elder.[53]

After a certain point, a *vitsa* may simply become too large, whereupon a split often takes place, usually along sibling or cousin lines. Sutherland cites the Minesti as an example of a large *vitsa* that has recently divided

---

[52]Gulbun Coker, "Romany Rye in Philadelphia: A Sequel," *Southwestern Journal of Anthropology*, 22 (1966): 98. See also Gropper, *Gypsies in the City*, pp. 60–66.

[53]Sutherland, *Hidden Americans*, pp. 82–83.

into several smaller *vitsi*.[54] The head of the *vitsa*, incidentally, is generally a respected male elder, although leadership problems do arise—and may be another reason for a *vitsa* to split.

Gypsies identify themselves—and other Rom—by their *vitsa* affiliation and by the liberal use of nicknames. However, they also have one or more names that are used in dealing with the *gadje*. These "*gadje*" names, according to Clark, are often popular American names such as John, George, and Miller.

> The *gadjo* may find a John George, George John, Miller John, John Miller, Miller George, and George Miller. He may even find a Gypsy named Johnny John or Miller Miller. But he probably won't find the John George Miller he is looking for unless the man wants to be found.
>
> The Rom deny that this is done deliberately to confuse the *gadje*. With a broad smile, a Gypsy explained that these were just nice names and everybody liked them.[55]

Arranged Marriages and the Bride Price

Gypsies are one of the few groups in America who follow the olden custom of arranged marriages.* Indeed, such marriages seem to be a cornerstone of the Rom the world over. Matrimony is important to Gypsies, and they are reluctant to place their young people in Cupid's hands. This is not to say that the young are forced into marriage. Although Romany marriages may be arranged, the parents do not arbitrarily impose their will. However, parents do play a major role in the mate selection process, and the arrangements for the bride price, or *daro*, are entirely in their hands.

It must be kept in mind that Gypsy culture stresses the importance of group rather than individual activity. And as Gropper observes, "Marriage for the Rom is quite definitely more than a union of husband and wife; it involves a lifetime alliance between two extended families."[56]

Arranged marriages normally include a *daro*, a payment by the groom's family to the bride's family. The actual figure varies from less than $1,000 to $10,000 or more. The higher the status of the young woman's *familia*, and the greater her personal attractiveness, the higher will be the asking price.

Although a *daro* of several thousand dollars is quite common, part of

---

[54]Ibid., p. 194.

[55]Marie Wynne Clark, "Vanishing Vagabonds: The American Gypsies," *Texas Quarterly*, 10 (Summer 1967): 208.

[56]Gropper, *Gypsies in the City*, p. 86.

*Another such group is the Hasidim, covered in Chapter 8.

the money is spent on the wedding festivities. The money is also used to pay for the bride's trousseau, to furnish the couple with household equipment, and so on. Additionally, part of the money may be returned to the groom's father, "as a sign of good will."[57]

Weddings themselves are private in that they involve neither religious nor civil officiants. They are, in a very real sense, *Gypsy weddings,* and are usually held in a rented hall. The festivities—involving ample food and drink—are fairly elaborate, and while formal invitations are not issued, all Gypsies in the community are welcome.[58]

The *daro* has traditionally served as a protection for the young wife. That is, if she should be mistreated by her husband or his *familia,* she can return home—whereupon the money might have to be forfeited.

Whether Gypsy wives are abused more than other wives is doubtful, but it is true that both sexes marry at a relatively young age. Marriages of eleven- and twelve-year-olds are known to occur, although the desired age range is between twelve and sixteen, and "not over 18 for a first marriage."[59] It seems likely, therefore, that many Gypsies are marrying under the legal age, although this fact would cause them no undue worry. The Rom are not overly concerned about marriage and divorce records, birth certificates, and other vital statistics.

While any two Rom can marry, most marriages involve partners from the same *natsia.* Young people are also encouraged to marry within the *vitsa,* provided the relationship is not that of first cousin or closer. The Rom feel that by having their youth marry someone in the same *vitsa*—a second cousin, for example—the prospects for a happy marriage will be increased. *Vitsa* members not only have blood ties, but follow the same customs, have the same *marimé* proscriptions, and so forth.

The *Bori*   After the wedding, it is customary for the young wife to live with her husband's *familia.* She is now known as a *bori* and comes under the supervision of her mother-in-law.

> The groom now has a wife who caters to his needs and whom he orders about, so his mother and sisters may devote less time to him. The bride, on the other hand, is now a *bori,* to be ordered around by all. She is expected to be the first one to awake in the morning and the last one to go to bed.
>
> She should do much of the housework as well as work as a fortune-teller, giving her earnings to her husband and mother-in-law. She should eat sparingly and only after everyone else has finished. She must ask

---

[57]Sutherland, *Hidden Americans,* p. 232.
[58]Gropper, *Gypsies in the City,* p. 158.
[59]Sutherland, *Hidden Americans,* p. 223.

neither for clothing nor for an opportunity to go out. She should be grate-
ful if she gets either.[60]

It should be mentioned that contrary to the American culture pattern,
Gypsy girls tend to be *older* than the boys they marry. As Sutherland
explains, "It is important that the girl be older than the boy, since after
marriage she must be able to perform her duties as a *bori* and make
money for her husband; however, her husband need not take many
responsibilities until he is fully mature."[61]

Despite the age difference, there is no doubt that many a *bori* has
experienced genuine difficulties in adapting to her new role. More than
occasionally, she simply gives up and returns to her own *familia*. In many
instances, of course, the *bori* is treated well—as it is to everyone's advantage to have a smooth-running household.

The *bori*, naturally, is expected to bear children—lots of them. Birth-
control measures apparently are not utilized. On the contrary, childless
marriages are looked upon as a great misfortune. Clebert states that
according to Gypsy tradition, female sterility was believed to be caused
by having coitus with a vampire.[62] At any rate, Andersen states that

> the *bori* becomes a full-fledged woman when she bears her first child.
> Women I talked with in Philadelphia who are recently married, await the
> births of children eagerly, for they are aware of the improved status it will
> bring them. . . .
>
> The *bori* then becomes a *romni*, a Gypsy woman and wife. Her ties to her
> husband's extended family then become very strong, for if she decides to
> end the marriage for some reason and return to her parent's home, she
> may not be permitted to take the child with her.[63]

Once in a great while sex roles are reversed, and the boy lives with the
girl's *familia*. This situation might occur because the boy was unable to
meet the bride price, or because he possessed some undesirable physical
or mental trait. Such a person is called a "house Rom," and because he is
under the domination of his parents-in-law he loses the respect of the
other men in the community[64]

Changes in the System   Although arranged marriages and the *daro* remain integral parts of Gypsy culture, the system may not be so rigid as it
once was. Like society at large, the Gypsy world is witnessing increased
freedom on the part of its young people. The Salos note, for example,

---

[60]Gropper, *Gypsies in the City*, p. 162.
[61]Sutherland, *Hidden Americans*, p. 223.
[62]Clebert, *Gypsies*, p. 161.
[63]Ruth E. Andersen, "Symbolism, Symbiosis, and Survival: Roles of Young Women of the
Kalderasha in Philadelphia," in Salo, ed., *American Kalderasha*, pp. 16–17.
[64]Sutherland, *Hidden Americans*, p. 175.

that at one time young Gypsies were not permitted to date without chaperones being present, a custom that is now often disregarded.

Parents are paying more heed to their children's wishes, and romantic love seems to be gaining in popularity. John Marks concludes that "parents still arrange the marriage, but now some young people fall in love whereas they used to marry without ever seeing each other beforehand."[65] Premarital chastity on the part of the young woman, however, has always been highly regarded—and it remains so.

Elopements are reported to be increasing, and some of the young men "are willing to defend their wives against their mothers."[66] Some adults are openly critical of the traditional marriage system, although others stoutly defend it. Thus far, the number of families that have actually dispensed with the *daro* is relatively small.

The "Passing" Question   In spite of the above changes, there is one Gypsy custom that has remained unaltered: the prohibition against marriages with the *gadje*. Because the *gadje* are *marimé*, intermarriage with them is also *marimé*. To repeat, this is the Gypsy *definition of the situation*, and they show no signs of relenting on the issue.

Despite the prohibition, such marriages do take place—much to the chagrin of the Gypsy community. When they do occur, it is usually a marriage between a Gypsy man and a *gadji* (non-Gypsy woman). The frequency of such marriages is a matter of debate. In her study of Barvale, California, Sutherland found that Rom-*gadje* marriages comprised only 5.5 percent of all Gypsy marriages.[67]

Lauwagie maintains, however, that the Rom-*gadje* intermarriage rate must be fairly high, and that significant numbers of Gypsies are "passing"; that is, becoming part of the larger community. She argues that the Rom have a substantially higher birthrate than non-Gypsies, and that if a significant number of them did not pass every year, the Gypsy population would be much larger than it is at present.[68]

Economic Organization

Gypsies are not the world's best workers. They have traditionally been involved in marginal and irregular occupations: horse trading, scrap metal, fortune-telling, blacktopping (repairing driveways), auto-body re-

---

[65]Quoted in ibid., p. 219.

[66]Gropper, *Gypsies in the City,* p. 163.

[67]Sutherland, *Hidden Americans,* p. 248.

[68]Beverly Nagel Lauwagie, "Ethnic Boundaries in Modern States: *Romano Lavo-Lil* Revisited," *American Journal of Sociology,* 85 (September 1979): 310–37.

pair, and carnival work. Clebert adds the phrase "musicians and mounte-banks,"[69] and Block contends that begging and stealing are among their principal occupations.[70]

Actually, as Hancock notes, the American Rom are to be found in a variety of pursuits, including "real estate, office work, acting, and teaching."[71] Nevertheless, as a group, Gypsies have not been noticeably successful in climbing the socioeconomic ladder, and it is doubtful whether this type of success has much appeal for them.

The Rom are quite willing to use banks, credit cards, charge accounts, and other appurtenances of a competitive economic system, but as a group they are loath to become involved in what they perceive to be the "rat race." Indeed, many Gypsies are quite adept at staying out of the race.

In his Chicago study, Polster found that the Gypsy men did not have steady jobs but worked only when they felt like it.[72] In their Canadian investigation, the Salos concluded that the Rom saw work as a necessity and not as a goal or way of life.[73] The same writers go on to say that

> although the Gypsy is ingenious in adapting occupationally, the true commitment of each man is to earn the respect of his people. The pursuit of social prestige among his fellow Rom makes up a significant portion of his life. The Rom must be free to visit, gossip, politick, arrange marriages, and to undertake journeys connected with these activities. The earning of a livelihood is a secondary though necessary activity.[74]

It should be mentioned that the Rom face a number of economic and occupational handicaps. Many of their traditional pursuits have dried up. Horse trading has long been defunct. Metalwork, a traditional Gypsy standby (Kalderash actually means "coppersmith"), has largely been taken over by factory methods. Carnival work has been steadily reduced.

The Rom are also penalized by the lack of education, since all of the professional occupations require college and graduate training. And finally, a number of jobs—plumber, nurse, certain kinds of hotel and restaurant work—are off limits to the Rom because of their *marimé* proscriptions.

All things considered, the wonder of it all is not that Gypsies have failed to climb the economic ladder, but that they have adapted as well as they have. In fact, one could argue—as one writer does—that the Rom

[69]Clebert, *Gypsies*, p. 96.

[70]Block, *Gypsies*, p. 142.

[71]Hancock, "Gypsies," p. 442.

[72]Gary Polster, "The Gypsies of Bunniton (South Chicago)," *Journal of Gypsy Lore Society* (January–April 1970): 142.

[73]Salo and Salo, *Kalderasha*, p. 73.

[74]Ibid., p. 93.

"fill a gap, albeit marginal, in the *gadje* system of production. They perform needed tasks, such as repair of shopping carts and seal-coating of driveways, that under usual economic conditions are too irregular or unprofitable to be attractive to larger, *gadje* economic enterprises."[75]

The *Kumpania*   It is important to note that the Rom produce none of their own material needs. These must be procured from the *gadje*. And the procurement is often psychologically as well as materially rewarding:

> Economic relationships of Rom with *gadje* are ideally exploitative. *Gadje* are by definition ignorant and foolish. The Rom value governing these relationships may be defined as "living by one's wits." The psychological satisfaction of "putting one over" on the *gadje* is often, at least in anecdotal retrospect, valued even more highly than the actual profit made.[76]

According to Sutherland, "The *gadje* are the source of all livelihood, and with few exceptions the Rom establish relations with them only because of some economic or political motive."[77] The same author points out that *economic relations among Gypsies* are based on mutual aid, and that they consider it immoral to earn money from other Gypsies. The only legitimate source of income is the *gadje*, and "skill in extracting money from them is highly valued in Rom society."[78]

The economic unit in this "extraction" process is not the *familia* or the *vitsa*, but the *kumpania*, a unionlike organization composed of all male Gypsies living in a particular town or city. An effective *kumpania* would determine the number of blacktopping businesses or fortune-telling establishments to be permitted in the area, whether licensing or political protection was necessary, and so on. Such a *kumpania* would have the power to keep out unaffiliated *familia*. A loose *kumpania* would lack such power. *Familia* could come and go at will, making for an untenable social and economic situation.[79]

The *kumpania* takes on added meaning when seen from the vantage point of Gypsy culture. As part of their effort to maintain a sharp boundary between themselves and the *gadje*, the Rom avoid working with non-Gpysies. If necessary, they will accept employment in a factory or commercial establishment, but this is not their normal practice. Typically, Gypsies operate in terms of *wortacha*, small work units consisting of adult members of the same sex. Thus, two or three men might engage in blacktopping or

[75]Beverly Nagel Lauwagie, "Explaining Gypsy Persistence: A Comparison of the Reactive Ethnicity and the Ecological Competition Perspectives," in Grumet, ed., *Papers*, p. 135.

[76]Matt T. Salo, "Kalderasha Economic Organization," in Salo, ed., *American Kalderasha*, p. 73.

[77]Sutherland, *Hidden Americans*, p. 65.

[78]Ibid.

[79]See Sutherland, *Hidden Americans*, pp. 34–35.

auto-body maintenance. Women might work in small-sized groups doing door-to-door selling or fortune-telling.

Welfare Practices   A number of Gypsiologists have commented on the ability of the Rom to extract money via the welfare route. In Sutherland's study, for instance, virtually all the Rom in Barvale, California, were receiving some sort of aid from the Welfare Department.[80]

> The Rom believe that acquiring welfare entails the same kinds of skills that other occupations require; that is, the ability to understand, convince, flatter, cajole, pressure, and manipulate the social worker. Welfare is not considered a hand-out; it is money that they convince the *gadje* to give them. . . .
>
> They do not consider themselves a depressed minority having to beg for charity from the middle-class majority. On the contrary, welfare is to them an incredible stroke of luck, yet further proof of the gullibility of the *gadje*.[81]

There is evidently some geographic variation in welfare practices, however, for none of the Gypsies in Coker's Philadelphia study were reported to be on welfare.[82] Similarly, in his article in the *Harvard Encyclopedia of Ethnic Groups*, Hancock makes no mention of Gypsy welfare proclivities.[83]

Quasi-Legal and Illegal Activities

Although most of the economic activities of the Rom are legal in nature, some are quasi-legal while others are clearly illegal. Blacktopping and sealing of driveways, for instance, are perfectly legal operations. But when the asphalt is laid at only one-third of the required thickness, and when the sealer has been surreptitiously diluted, the legality becomes questionable. Similarly, auto-body repair is legal, but if instead of actually removing the dents a thick coating of "paint and putty" is used, the practice is obviously unethical.

Fortune-Telling   Fortune-telling is a special case, for if there is one field that has been monopolized by the Rom it is certainly fortune-telling. Indeed, the terms "Gypsy" and "fortune-teller" seem to go hand in hand—and with good reason, as the following account by Andersen indicates:

> The little girl is expected to be a fortune-teller or reader and advisor, as early as thirteen or fourteen, and as a child she is trained for this profes-

[80]Ibid., p. 83.
[81]Ibid., p. 78.
[82]Coker, "Romany Rye," p. 89.
[83]Hancock, "Gypsies," pp. 440–445.

sion. Fortune-telling as a means of livelihood is a tradition among Gypsy women, and many little girls observe their mothers, aunts, and other female relatives performing within this tradition every day.

They are taught that they have a natural gift for the practice, that they received this gift from God, and that as fortune-tellers they will be performing a type of psychological counseling service for non-Gypsies.[84]

Fortune-telling is not a difficult occupation to learn, overhead expenses are negligible, and—depending on the location—business may be good. Clark cites the old Gypsy saying: "A fortune cannot be true unless silver changes hands."[85] And there have always been enough *gadje* who believe in this aphorism to make crystal gazing, palmistry, and card reading profitable ventures. Fees typically range from $2 to $5 per session, with a surprising number of repeat customers. Most of the latter are reportedly drawn from the lower socioeconomic ranks. As Bercovici puts it: "The Gypsy fortune-teller is the psychoanalyst of the poor."[86]

The *Bujo* On occasion, Gypsy fortune-tellers have been accused—and convicted—of flimflam, or *bujo*. The *bujo* is nothing more than a swindle, whereby a gullible customer is cheated out of a goodly portion of his or her savings. One common ruse is called "switch the bag." In this instance, a bag of fake money or cut-up paper is substituted for a bag of real cash—which the customer had brought to the fortune-telling parlor in order to have the evil spirits or curse removed. (In Romany, *bujo* means "bag.")

According to the New York police, *bujo* swindles in excess of $100,000 have occurred. And according to Mitchell, there are some Gypsy fortune-tellers "with a hundred or more arrests on their record."[87] Obviously, these are unusual cases; in fact, many Rom frown on the *bujo* because it causes bad community relations and is likely to bring police action.

At the same time, the *bujo* has occurred often enough to cause many areas to outlaw fortune-telling. Major cities like New York and Philadelphia, as well as most Canadian regions, have banned fortune-telling. Some observers feel that the illegalization of fortune-telling may be the Gypsies' biggest problem. (Interestingly enough, in 1985, the California Supreme Court, overruling a lower court decision, found that an ordinance prohibiting fortune-telling for profit violated the constitutional right to free speech. The suit was brought by a *romni*, and the ramifica-

---

[84]Andersen, "Symbolism," in Salo, ed., *American Kalderasha*, p. 14.

[85]Clark, "Vanishing Vagabonds," p. 205.

[86]Konrad Bercovici, *Gypsies: Their Life, Lore, and Legends* (New York: Greenwich House, 1983), p. 236.

[87]Joseph Mitchell, "The Beautiful Flower: Daniel J. Campion," *The New Yorker*, June 4, 1955, p. 46.

tions are as yet unknown. It is quite possible, however, that the case will eventually reach the United States Supreme Court.)

Legalities aside, the Rom continue to ply their trade, even though they are somewhat restricted in many areas. They often pose as "readers" and "advisors" rather than as seers. And this, in turn, may necessitate a measure of police "cooperation." But by one method or another, the Gypsies survive. Gypsies always survive.

Other Illegal Activities   What about other types of crime—robbery, burglary, rape, murder, and so on—are the Gypsies not involved in these, also? The answer is yes and no. They are seldom involved in crimes of violence, such as assault, mugging, rape, and murder. Stealing is another matter, however, and the police are likely to have strong feelings on the subject. Because Gypsies tend to commit crimes in novel ways, some twenty police officers across the United States have become specialists in Gypsy crime. Penn cites the following as examples of Gypsy criminal ingenuity:

> In some thefts, several Gypsies unfold sheets to block witnesses' view of the gang member who is taking cash or goods, or use other tactics to distract onlookers. A gang . . . of Gypsies flew to California from Illinois last March to loot food stores. At a Santa Ana supermarket, part of the gang searched for the store's cash while others attempted to distract employees with mind-numbing requests.
>
> "They asked if they could get beer without yeast," says . . . a deputy district attorney in Santa Ana. "They said they wanted 50 chickens to be stuffed with steaks."
>
> Last Spring, a Gypsy gang looted a jewelry store in a Chicago suburb. When two policemen showed up to arrest them, "one of the women lifted her dress over her head. . . . While the cops stared at her, her companions had time to flee."[88]

The blunt fact is that law enforcement officers who come in contact with them believe that an undue proportion of American Gypsies are engaged in theft. District attorneys and prosecutors are likely to take a similarly dim view of the Rom, for it is both difficult and exasperating to try to send Gypsies to jail. To the Rom, time spent in prison means breaking a variety of *marimé* proscriptions. Consequently, an individual Gypsy will go to almost any length to avoid an actual jail sentence. Zucchino writes as follows on this point:

> Prosecuting a Gypsy is a process as transient and bewildering as the Gypsy culture itself. Convictions and jail sentences are rare. In most cases, the several thousand Gypsies prosecuted in this country each year

[88]Stanley Penn, *Wall Street Journal*, December 15, 1988.

for burglary or theft jump bail or pay fines, according to national police estimates. . . .

Here the law enforcement system, splintered into thousands of local police agencies, is paralyzed by Gypsy transience. Here a court system based on due process provides time to post bond and disappear. . . .

"You end up taking their bail money and getting rid of them. Basically, you're sicking them on some other county," said a former district attorney. "That sounds bad, but the aggravation, the sheer frustration, is just unbelievable."[89]

Life-Style

Although it is difficult to generalize about the life-style of any people, the Rom do have certain culture traits that set them apart from other groups. At or near the top of the list—and a trait that has been alluded to several times in the present account—is the Gypsies' indomitable love of freedom.

The Rom do not like to be tied down—by schools, businesses, material possessions, community affairs, financial obligations, or any other social or economic encumbrance. Their life-style not only reflects this predilection, but they are quite proud of it. Writers both Gypsy and non-Gypsy have commented on the matter. Ronald Lee, a Gypsy, says:

> The Gypsy is invisible and he has many weapons. You have a name but he has two: one you will never know and one he is always changing. Today he is Tom Jones, yesterday he was William Stanley, and tomorrow he might be Adam Strong.
>
> He can melt away at a moment's notice, which is his way of dealing with bill collectors. You cannot do this, for you have a name, an identity in the community, and a job which ties you down. You are a prisoner of your society, but he, existing beyond the pale of public morality, has only his wits, his cunning, his skills, and his faith in a just God.[90]

Gypsies also associate freedom with fresh air and sunshine, a belief that goes back to the days of the caravan. In this earlier period, the Rom linked illness and diseases with closed spaces. Fresh air was believed to be a cure-all. Clebert reports that at one time a Gypsy would not die in bed but would be moved outdoors so as not to pollute the home.[91]

Along with their love of freedom is the Gypsy tendency to live in the present rather than to plan for tomorrow. Perhaps the two traits go

---

[89]David Zucchino, "Officials Say Gypsies Live by Their Own Rules," *Philadelphia Inquirer,* February 1, 1982, pp. 1–2A.

[90]Ronald Lee, "Gypsies in Canada," *Journal of Gypsy Lore Society* (January–April 1967): 38–39.

[91]Clebert, *Gypsies,* p. 187.

together; that is, it may be that "freedom" is reduced by the necessity to plan ahead. Webb writes that "the Rom live only for today. Why should a man hurry? Who knows what the morrow may bring? . . . Today is a happy time, and men grow old quickly enough. Why wish away life by looking for tomorrow?"[92]

Travel and Mobility   Nowhere is the Gypsy love of freedom more apparent than in their fondness for travel. As Lee points out, the Rom may no longer be nomads, but they remain a highly mobile people.[93] One important reason for their mobility is the economic factor. While many Rom have a home base, job opportunities may arise elsewhere. Roofing, auto-body repair, carnival work, summer harvesting—all may require periodic travel. In at least some cases, overseas journeys are involved. The Salos report that

> the dispersion of the Rom, coupled with an efficient system of communication provided by the *gadje*, allows them to be aware of economic conditions far afield. Some of the Canadian Gypsies have contacts in or first-hand knowledge of conditions in Ireland, Wales, England, Belgium, France, Yugoslavia, Greece, U.S. (including Hawaii), Mexico, Australia, and South Africa.[94]

The Rom also travel for social reasons: to visit friends and family, to find a *bori* (bride), to celebrate Gypsy holidays, to attend weddings and death feasts. Illness is a special category, and Gypsies will travel long distances to be with a sick relative.

Predictably, the Rom frequently travel for tactical reasons: to avoid the police, social workers, school authorities, landlords, and the like. This sort of travel—coupled with their aforementioned name changes— makes it exceedingly difficult for the authorities to track down and identify "wanted" Gypsies. In fact, during their travels the Rom often pass themselves off as non-Gypsies. Silverman writes that

> Gypsies deliberately conceal their ethnicity to avoid confrontations with and harassment by truant officers, landlords, the police, and the welfare department. They pass as Puerto Ricans, Mexicans, Armenians, Greeks, Arabs, and other local ethnics in order to obtain jobs, housing, and welfare. Gypsies usually report themselves as members of other groups to census takers, causing Gypsy census statistics to be extremely unreliable. Gypsies have developed these skills so well that many Americans are unaware that there are any Gypsies in America.[95]

---

[92]Webb, *Secret People*, p. 123.
[93]Lee, "Gypsies in Canada," p. 37.
[94]Salo and Salo, *Kalderasha*, p. 76.
[95]Carol Silverman, "Everyday Drama: Impression Management of Urban Gypsies," in Matt T. Salo, ed., *Urban Anthropology, Special Issue*, 11, No. 3–4 (Fall–Winter 1982): 382.

A final reason for travel—and an important one—is simply that Gypsies like to move about. It makes them feel better, both physically and mentally. Sutherland notes that the Rom associate traveling with health and good luck, "whereas settling down is associated with sickness and bad luck. . . . Barvale Rom all agreed that when they were traveling all the time they were healthy and never needed doctors, but now that they live in houses they are subjected to many *gadje* diseases."[96]

The Life-Cycle   Gypsy children arrive in large numbers, and they are welcomed not only by their *familia* but by the entire Gypsy community. Although they are supposed to show respect for their parents, youngsters are pampered. As John Kearney points out, the maxim "Children should be seen and not heard" was surely never coined by a Gypsy.[97] Corporal punishment is used sparingly—and reluctantly. A Romany child is the center of attention, at least until the next one comes along.

In many ways, Gypsy children are treated like miniature adults—with many of the same rights. Their wishes are respected in much the same manner as those of adults.[98] Subservience and timidity are not highly regarded by the Rom—and children are encouraged to speak up.

Gypsy children also spend much more time in adult company than do their non-Gypsy counterparts. This would almost have to be the case, since the Rom do not have much faith in formal education. While some government-funded Gypsy schools have been set up in various parts of the country, the Gypsy child's real training comes either at home or in what has been called "participatory education."[99] From the age of eight or nine, boys accompany their fathers on various work assignments, while the girls engage in household activities and start to observe fortune-telling routines.[100]

Although aggressiveness in children may be encouraged, adolescents—boys in particular—often need no encouragement. Like teenagers the world over, Romany youth do cause problems. They misbehave, they are disrespectful, they sometimes mingle with the *gadje*. In fact, Clark believes that a major problem in the Gypsy world right now is their adolescents, "who want to be teen-agers first, and Gypsies second."[101] In most cases, however, maturity seems to serve as a panacea—with no harmful aftereffects.

In Gypsy culture, both sexes tend to achieve higher status as they get

[96]Sutherland, *Hidden Americans*, pp. 51–52.
[97]John Kearney, "Education and the Kalderasha," in Salo, ed., *American Kalderasha*, p. 48.
[98]Gropper, *Gypsies in the City*, p. 130.
[99]Barbara Adams, Judith Okely, David Morgan, and David Smith, *Gypsies and Government Policy in England* (London: Heinemann, 1975), p. 136.
[100]Gropper, *Gypsies in the City*, p. 138.
[101]Clark, "Vanishing Vagabonds," p. 165.

older. A young man marries, matures, and has children. And as his children grow, "so does his status." When he is ready and able to marry his youngsters off, his position in the community is generally secure.

As he grows older, he will be expected to solve family problems and settle altercations. He also acts as a repository for Gypsy traditions and culture. He will spend increasing time and energy "on the affairs of the band rather than on those of his own immediate family. He is becoming an Old One and a Big Man."[102]

A parallel sequence is followed in the case of the Gypsy female. As a young girl she is expected to assist in the housework. Later on—when she marries and becomes a *bori*—she is under the domination of her mother-in-law. But as she ages and has children of her own, she achieves a measure of independence and her status rises accordingly.

In many Gypsy communities, it is the woman rather than the man who deals with outsiders—school officials, social workers, and the like. And if she is successful in this regard, her position in the community becomes one of respect. She, too, is looked upon as a repository of wisdom, especially when it comes to dealing with the *gadje.*

Both sexes look forward to becoming parents, and both look forward to having grandchildren. The latter, it is said signify true independence, for now the Old Ones have both their children and their children's children to look after them.

Sex Roles   The Rom have sharply defined sex roles. Indeed, one Gypsiologist states that "the male-female division is the most fundamental in Rom society."[103] The sex roles, furthermore, are characterized by separateness. Whether the occasion is a Gypsy function or simply day-to-day activity within the *familia,* men tend to gather on one side of the room, women on the other. The Rom are great talkers, but unless a special situation arises, the conversation will probably not be a mixed one.[104]

This separateness extends even to the marital sphere. Except for having a sex partner and someone besides his mother to cater to his needs, the groom's life-style changes very little.

> Gypsy marriage is not predicated on romantic love, and the Rom frown on any display of affection between husband and wife. The husband wants the wife to perform services for him, but he continues to spend much of his time with his brothers and cousins. Husband and wife rarely go out together.[105]

[102]Gropper, *Gypsies in the City,* p. 165.
[103]Sutherland, *Hidden Americans,* pp. 149ff.
[104]Ibid.
[105]Gropper, *Gypsies in the City,* p. 88.

Occupationally, also, sex roles tend to be definitive. Women tell fortunes; men are responsible for the physical layout of the fortune-telling parlor. Women cook and take care of the household chores. Men are responsible for the acquisition and maintenance of transportation facilities. In many areas, the women bring in more money than the men. In fact, Mitchell claims that, economically, one Gypsy woman is worth ten men.[106] And while this may be an exaggeration, the women's income seems to be steadier and more reliable than the men's It is the men, nevertheless, who normally hold the positions of power in the *familia*, the *vitsa*, and the *kumpania*.

Social Control

Romania—not an easy term to define—refers to the Gypsy way of life and their view of the world. It embraces their moral codes, traditions, customs, rituals, and rules of behavior. In brief, as Hancock puts it, *romania* is what the Gypsies consider to be right and acceptable.[107] It is the glue that holds their society together.

Romania is not a set of written rules, however. It is, rather, a built-in aspect of Gypsy culture. And because it is not a written code, the Rom face two problems: (1) Who determines what is and what is not *romania?* and (2) How to handle those who knowingly or unknowingly fail to comply? These questions raise the whole issue of social control.

As used by sociologists, *social control* refers to the methods employed to "keep people in line." *Informal control* includes the application of gossip, ridicule, reprimand, and scorn. *Formal control* refers simply to the use of law, backed by physical force. Sociologically, informal control is considered more important than formal, and the Gypsies are a good case in point. The Rom have dispensed almost entirely with formal controls and rely largely on the informal variety.

Gossip, ridicule, and wisecracks, for example, are highly effective because the Rom are a closed society. Individual members cannot escape into anonymity—as is often the case in society at large. In any Gypsy community, therefore, reports and rumors of aberrant behavior lose no time in making the rounds.

Leadership: The *Rom Baro*   In most groups, leadership serves as an important instrument of social control, but in this respect Gypsies are not so fortunate. The Rom are not known for their leadership qualities. For one thing, Gypsy leadership is a function of age; that is, the older

[106]Mitchell, "Beautiful Flower," p. 54.
[107]Hancock, "Gypsies," p. 443.

one gets, the greater knowledge one has of *romania*—and knowledge of *romania* is a recognized source of power. Almost by definition, then, the Rom seldom have any young leaders.

Another drawback is the tendency for Gypsy leadership to be fragmented. Theoretically at least, each *familia*, each *vitsa*, and each *kumpania* has its own leader. And while there is some overlap—and some real harmony—there is also much bickering and infighting, especially when different *natsiyi* are involved.

Leadership starts in the *familia*, where the head is known as a *phuro*. As the *phuro* ages and as his *familia* grows in size and strength, his standing in the community—and his power—increase accordingly. Should his judgment prove sound, should he show genuine interest in the various members of his *familia*, and should he prove effective in his dealings with the *gadje*, the *phuro* might become the leader of the *vitsa* or of a *kumpania*. He would then be known as a *Rom Baro* or "Big Man."

The Big Man has a dual function: to provide help and services for his followers, and to serve as a liaison with the non-Gypsy community, especially in a political sense. A Big Man rules by persuasion and discussion rather than by coercion, and should his persuasive powers fail he may be replaced. Also, should he be convicted of a crime, his tenure as a *Rom Baro* may be terminated.

Although there are any number of Big Men in the Gypsy world, there really is no "King of the Gypsies," even though certain individuals often make the claim in order to ingratiate themselves with local authorities. For example, Silverman writes that the "status of King or Queen is invoked when securing hospital rooms or visiting privileges in funeral homes. One informant said, 'Any Gypsy who enters a hospital is automatically a King. They get better treatment. . . . There's no such animal in the Gypsy race as a King. But you go to the newspaper morgues in New York and get old papers, and every time a Gypsy died he was King. There has got to be 1,000 Kings.' "[108]

The same writer goes on to report the following eye-catching case:

> Gypsies deliberately tend to perpetuate the stereotype of the King in order to inflate the power and romanticism of the Gypsies. The King is presented as the rightful and respected representative of the Gypsy people whenever there is some advantage in appearing as a unified, organized, and stratified society. For example, John Ellis of Portland was invited to Ronald Reagan's inauguration because he was "King of the Western North American Gypsies." He said he would use the opportunity to ask Reagan to place

[108]Carol Silverman, "Negotiating 'Gypsiness': Strategy in Context," *Journal of American Folk-Lore*, 101 (July/Sept. 1988): 261–275.

Gypsies on the same level as other minorities and make available grants and funds.[109]

The most famous (or infamous) Gypsy leader in modern times was Tene Bimbo, *Rom Baro* of the Bimbulesti *vitsa*. Tene Bimbo pursued power from coast to coast, and in the process he was reportedly arrested 140 times—for everything from petty larceny to murder! "If there are any charges that have not been brought against Tene Bimbo," one newspaper reported, "it is probably just an oversight."[110]

Tene Bimbo died in 1969 at the age of eight-five, and there has been no *Rom Baro* like him since that time—and there probably never will be. Although his descendants speak fondly of him, and liken him to a modern Robin Hood, most Gypsies are glad that he is no longer on the scene. They feel that he brought unwanted notoriety to the Rom and was responsible for a distorted view of the Gypsy world. (Peter Maas's *King of the Gypsies*, mentioned earlier, was based on the struggle for power that erupted after Tene Bimbo's death.)

Marimé **as Social Control**   Although Gypsy leadership may or may not be an effective source of social control, *marimé* has traditionally been a powerful instrument. Indeed, it may just be the most important factor in keeping the Rom in line. The reason is not hard to find, for *marimé* is more than a simple declaration that a person or thing is polluted. A Gypsy who has been declared *marimé* is ostracized by the entire group. Other Rom will have nothing to do with him or her.

It cannot be emphasized too strongly that within the confines of their own society, Gypsies are gregarious. They are never really alone. Practically all of their waking moments are spent in the company of other Rom. Talking, laughing, working, arguing, gossiping, and, most important perhaps, eating—all are considered group activities. To be declared *marimé*, therefore, effectively cuts a Gypsy off from the very roots of his existence. He brings shame not only upon himself but upon his family.

Sutherland writes that *marimé* "in the sense of being rejected from social intercourse with other Rom is the ultimate punishment in the Gypsy society, just as death is the ultimate punishment in other societies. For the period it lasts, *marimé* is social death."[111] A permanent *marimé* sentence is not only the most severe form of Gypsy punishment, but if there is no way to win reinstatement, the person involved may actually prefer to end his life by suicide.[112]

---

[109]Ibid.
[110]Cited in Maas, *King of the Gypsies*, p. 4.
[111]Sutherland, *Hidden Americans*, p. 98.
[112]Gropper, *Gypsies in the City*, p. 100.

The *Kris Romani* Fortunately for the Rom, *marimé* need not be permanent. Accused Gypsies have the right to a trial in order to determine whether they are guilty as charged. The trial is known as a *kris romani*. As used by the Rom, the term also refers to their system of law and justice, for they do not generally utilize American courts.

The *kris romani* consists of a jury of adult Gypsies, presided over by an impartial judge. Certain judges, or *krisatora*, are known for their wisdom and objectivity and are in great demand. No judge, however, will accept a case unless the litigants agree beforehand to abide by the verdict. In addition to allegations involving *marimé*, *kris* cases include disputes over the bride price, divorce suits, feuds between *vitsi*, allegations of cheating, and so on.

A *kris* is convened only for serious reasons, since Gypsy trials are time-consuming—and expensive. Personnel may come from other parts of the country, and it may be necessary to use a rented hall. In a lengthy trial, "courtroom" supplies may include food and liquor, payment for which must be made by the guilty party.[113]

Because of these factors, a *kris romani* is not likely to be held until all other attempts at adjudication have failed. Ordinary disputes, for example, may be settled by the *Rom Baro* or by informal debate. And even if these efforts should fail, a *divano*—a public discussion by concerned adults—can be requested.

Is the *kris romani* an effective instrument of social control? It is hard to say. In most cases, probably yes—but there is a built-in weakness to the system. Presumably the disputants agree beforehand to abide by the decision. If they do not, theoretically at least they have no recourse but to leave the Gypsy world. In the last analysis, however, what can really be done with Gypsies who refuse to obey their own laws? As Acton observes, "It is difficult today for any Gypsy group larger than the extended family to exert effective sanctions on their members."[114] Yoors puts it as follows:

> The *kris*, or collective will of the Rom, is a structure in flux. . . . The effectiveness of the pronouncements of the judges depends essentially on the *acceptance of their decisions by the majority of the Rom*. There is no direct element of coercion to enforce the rule of law. The Rom have no police force, no jails, no executioners.[115]

---

[113]See the discussion in ibid., pp. 81–102.

[114]Thomas Acton, *Gypsy Politics and Social Change* (London and Boston: Routledge & Kegan Paul, 1974), p. 99

[115]Yoors, *Gypsies*, p. 174. (Italics added.)

Prejudice and Discrimination

Prejudice and discrimination are realities that virtually all Gypsies must learn to face—and live with. The sad fact is that the Rom have been persecuted in practically every country they have ever inhabited. As was mentioned, the Nazis murdered hundreds of thousands during World War II. Entire *vitsi* were wiped out. Furthermore, Kenrick and Puxon note that during the many months of the Nuremberg war crimes trial, not a single Gypsy was every called as a witness![116] Nor was any monetary restitution ever made to the surviving Romany groups.

In 1979, President Carter formed the *U.S. Holocaust Memorial Council;* its purpose was to establish a lasting memorial to all those who suffered and died in Hitler's death camps. There are no Gypsies on the sixty-five-member council. In a report from the commission to President Carter

> the word Gypsy appears just once, along with Poles, Soviet prisoners of war, Frenchmen, Serbs and Slavs as "others," in an appendix. The total number of Romani dead is now estimated to be some 600,000. While this amounts to a tenth of the number of Jewish victims, in terms of the genocide of an entire people, the proportions are nevertheless similar. . . .[117]

Apparently, in today's Germany, some Gypsies find it advantageous to pass as Jews. One Gypsy musician, unable to find work, "changed his name, Kroner, to Rosenberg. . . . With a new Jewish name, he was highly employable." [Kroner-Rosenberg commented], "the German conscience is very selective. . . ."[118]

Although the wholesale slaughter ceased with the downfall of Hitler, Gypsy problems continue in both Western and Eastern Europe. About three-quarters of the European Gypsy population currently reside in Communist—or formerly Communist—countries.

The Gypsy underclass in Communist countries are an impediment to achieving the Marxist ideal of a classless society. Recent statistics extracted from Hungary's official press reveal the plight of the 500,000 or so Gypsies in that country:

> . . . 75 percent of Hungarian Gypsies live at or below subsistence level. (Approximately 35,000 still live in earthen huts.) Those who work—15 percent are unemployed—almost invariably take the lowest paying jobs. . . .

[116]Kenrick and Puxon, *Destiny of Europe's Gypsies*, p. 189.

[117]Ian F. Hancock, *The Pariah Syndrome: An Account of Gypsy Slavery and Persecution* (Ann Arbor: Karoma Publishers, 1988), p. 81.

[118]Jeremy Marre and Hannah Charlton, *Beats of the Heart* (New York: Pantheon Books, 1985), p. 196.

Despite official literacy campaigns, an estimated 40 percent of Gypsies do not complete elementary school.
    . . . Half the children under state care are Gypsies, many of them veteran criminals. According to statistics compiled by Hungary's National Police, the proportion of Gypsies among apprehended criminals is twice as high as the group's share of the general population.[119]

American Gypsies, too, continue to face prejudice and discrimination. Some large cities—like New York and Chicago—have special police assigned to the Rom. In smaller towns, sheriffs will often escort Gypsies to the county line, glad to be rid of them. A recent issue of the *Police Chief* contains an article advising the police on how to keep their districts free of Gypsies.[120] Hancock reports that

various states have also directed laws against Gypsies. As recently as 1976, a family was expelled from the state of Maryland, where the law requires Gypsies to pay a licensing fee of $1,000 before establishing homes or engaging in business, and there is a bounty of $10 on the head of any Gypsy arrested who has not paid this fee.
    In New Hampshire in 1977, two families were legally evicted from the state without being charged with any crime, solely for reasons of their ethnic identity.[121]

Why does the persecution continue? Some observers contend that it is a matter of ethnic prejudice, similar to that experienced by African-Americans, Chicanos, and certain immigrant groups. Others, however, simply feel that the Rom are perceived as nonproductive troublemakers. As one police offical put it, "they're nothing but economic parasites." The truth of the matter can be debated, but that is beside the point. If people *perceive* of Gypsies as nonproductive dissidents, then unfortunately for all concerned, prejudice and discrimination might be looked upon as justifiable retaliation.

Adaptability: The Gypsy Trademark

It is doubtful whether the Rom spend much time thinking about the causes of discrimination. Being realists, they expect it. And being Gypsies, they learn to live with it. In fact, being Gypsies, they learn to live with a great many things they do not like or agree with. This, indeed, is the Gypsies' trademark: adaptability.
    In addition to coping with discrimination, Gypsies have also had to

---

[119]"Gypsy Underclass a Hungarian Dilemma," *Insight* (July 27, 1987), p. 7.
[120]Hancock, "Gypsies," p. 44.
[121]Ibid.

adapt to a vast panorama of social change. Times change, customs change, governments change—sometimes it seems that nothing is permanent—but whatever the transformation, the Rom seem to make the necessary adjustments. *They adapt without losing their cultural identity.*

Examples of their adaptation are numerous. Gypsies have never had their own religion. In all their wanderings and migrations, they have simply adapted to the religion—or religions—of the host country. The same is largely true of clothing styles, although as Polster observes, Gypsy women often do wear colorful outfits.[122] And aside from a seeming fondness for spicy dishes, the Rom adapt to the foods and cuisine of the country or area they are living in.

During the days of the caravan, Gypsy nomads camped outside the towns and cities—off the beaten track. When changing conditions forced them from the road, they took to the cities, where they have adapted rather well. Today, most of the American Rom are to be found in urban areas.

When horses were replaced by mechanized transportation, the Rom adapted. Instead of being horse traders, they learned auto-body repair and motor maintenance. When metalworking—long a Gypsy specialty—was superseded by factory-type technology, the Rom turned to roofing and blacktopping. When fortune-telling became illegal in various places, Gypsies became "readers" and "advisors." And when these latter efforts were challenged, the Rom resorted to bribery and police "cooperation."

Gypsies make no claim to being quality workers, or even to being industrious. But both in America and elsewhere they are versatile. *They adapt.* As one Gypsy remarked to Adams and her colleagues, "Put me down anywhere in the world, and I'll make a living."[123]

It should also be mentioned that some Gypsies manage to do well even when they are not "making a living." Despite their literacy handicap, and despite their unfamiliarity with (and distain for) documentary records, they have learned to adapt to the welfare bureaucracy with—in many cases—remarkable results.

The Future

What does the future hold for the American Rom? Not even a Gypsy with a crystal ball can tell. It is possible, nevertheless, to make some educated guesses.

To begin with, it is likely that Gypsy activism will increase—somewhat. On the international scene, meetings such as the World Romany Con-

---

[122]Polster, "Gypsies of Bunniton," p. 139.
[123]Adams et al., *Gypsies and Government Policy*, p. 132.

gress have had some success in focusing attention on Gypsy problems. In the United States, the American Gypsy Organization and other groups have also been established. Such organizations cannot help but have a positive effect on Gypsy-*gadje* relations.[124]

At the same time, there are inherent limits to Gypsy activism. The American Rom are a low-profile group. It is often difficult to find them, let alone activate them! They have traditionally resorted to travel and avoidance rather than organization and demonstration. Mass protest, for example—often used by other minorities—would hardly strike a responsive chord in most Gypsy communities. (Stranger things have happened, of course. Hoffman reports that in 1978, "British Gypsies threatened to block highways unless they received better treatment from local authorities."[125] Whether American Rom would employ such tactics is problematical.)

Looking ahead, it is likely that the widespread illiteracy that has characterized the Rom will be reduced—somewhat. Schools for Gypsy youngsters have been set up in California, Washington, D.C., Philadelphia, Chicago, Seattle, and Camden, New Jersey, and the trend may continue. As Hancock points out, however, failures have thus far outnumbered successes, and "the majority of Gypsies remain opposed to schooling of any kind."[126]

Assuming that their illiteracy rate is reduced, the position of the Rom in the American job market should also improve—somewhat. Even now, there are Gypsies to be found in white-collar and professional positions. Their number is relatively small, however, for the Rom have scarcely penetrated the realm of college and graduate education.

Still looking ahead, relations between the Rom and the *gadje* may improve—somewhat. In many ways, American Gypsies have cut themselves off from the economic rewards of the larger society. To partake of these rewards they will probably have to change their attitude toward the *gadje*, and the extent to which they will do this can only be conjectured.

The Rom may also soften the rules pertaining to *marimé*—somewhat. In certain Gypsy communities, these rules have already been softened, and if the trend continues, improvements in the relations with the larger society may be one of the by-products. At the same time, most Rom know full well that the concept of *marimé* lies at the heart of the Gypsy world. Without *marimé*, social control would be difficult to maintain. Whether any further erosion of the rules will occur, therefore, remains to be seen.

---

[124]See Hancock, "Gypsies," pp. 444–45.
[125]Paul Hoffman, "Here Come the Gypsies: Call Them Citizens," *New York Times*, April 30, 1978, Section E, p. 8.
[126]Hancock, "Gypsies," p. 444.

To sum up, it would appear that any changes in the Gypsy way of life, or in *romania*, will be moderate rather than drastic. The Rom are keenly aware of what they are and who they are—and they are proud of it. And while they may make some changes that will improve their adaptation to the larger society, it is unlikely that they will become a functioning part of that society. They will not assimilate. They will not give up their unique identity. They will not renounce their culture. Thus, in all probability they will continue to feel the twin prongs of discrimination and harassment, albeit on a reduced scale.

Exactly how much change the Rom will allow—or what form these changes will take—is debatable. But one thing seems certain: the Gypsies will survive. Gypsies always survive.

SELECTED READINGS

Andersen, Ruth E. "Symbolism, Symbiosis, and Survival: Role of Young Women of the Kalderasha in Philadelphia." In *The American Kalderasha: Gypsies in the New World*, ed. by Matt T. Salo, pp. 11–28. Hackettstown, NJ: Gypsy Lore Society, 1981.

Beck, Sam. "The Romanian Gypsy Problem." In *Papers from the Fourth and Fifth Annual Meetings, Gypsy Lore Society, North American Chapter*, ed. by Joanne Grumet, pp. 100–109. New York: Gypsy Lore Society, 1985.

Clark, Marie Wynne. "Vanishing Vagabonds: The American Gypsies." *Texas Quarterly*, 10 (Summer 1967): 204–10.

Clebert, Jean-Paul. *The Gypsies*. London: Vista, 1963.

Cortiade, Marcel. "Distance between Romani Dialects." *Newsletter of the Gypsy Lore Society, North American Chapter*, 8 (Spring 1985): pp. 1ff.

Dodds, Norman. *Gypsies, Didikois, and Other Travelers*. London: Johnson, 1976.

Friedman, Victor A. "Problems in the Codification of a Standard Romani Literary Language." In *Papers from the Fourth and Fifth Annual Meetings, Gypsy Lore Society, North American Chapter*, ed. by Joanne Grumet, pp. 55–75. New York: Gypsy Lore Society, 1985.

Gmelch, George. *The Irish Tinkers*. Prospect Heights, IL: Waveland Press, 1985.

Gropper, Rena C. *Gypsies in the City*. Princeton, NJ: Darwin, 1975.

Hancock, Ian F. "Gypsies." In *Harvard Encyclopedia of American Ethnic Groups*, ed. by Stephan Thernstrom, pp. 440–45. Cambridge, MA: Harvard University Press, 1980.

———. *The Pariah Syndrome: An Account of Gypsy Slavery and Persecution*. Ann Arbor: Karoma Publishers, 1988.

Kearney, John. "Education and the Kalderasha." In *The American Kalderasha: Gypsies in the New World*, ed. by Matt T. Salo, pp. 43–54. Hackettstown, NJ: Gypsy Lore Society, 1981.

Lee, Ronald. *Goddam Gypsy: An Autobiographical Novel*. Montreal: Tundra, 1971.

Lockwood, William G. "Balkan Gypsies: An Introduction." In *Papers from the Fourth and Fifth Annual Meetings, Gypsy Lore Society, North American Chapter*, ed. by Joanne Grumet, pp. 91–99. New York: Gypsy Lore Society, 1985.

Maas, Peter. *King of the Gypsies*. New York: Viking, 1975.

Marre, Jeremy, and Charlton, Hannah. *Beats of the Heart*. New York: Pantheon Books, 1985.

Nemeth, David. "Gypsy Taskmasters, Gentile Slaves." In *The American Kalderasha: Gypsies in the New World*, ed. by Matt T. Salo, pp. 29–41. Hackettstown, NJ: Gypsy Lore Society, 1981.

Okely, Judith. *The Traveler-Gypsies*. New York: Cambridge University Press, 1982.

Pippin, Roland N. "Community in Defiance of the Proscenium." In *The American Kalderasha: Gypsies in the New World*, ed. by Matt T. Salo, pp. 99–133. Hackettstown, NJ: Gypsy Lore Society, 1981.

Polster, Gary. "The Gypsies of Bunniton (South Chicago)." *Journal of Gypsy Lore Society* (January–April 1970): 136–51.

Rehfisch, Farnham, ed. *Gypsies, Tinkers, and Other Travelers*. New York: Academic Press, 1975.

Salo, Matt, and Salo, Sheila. *The Kalderasha in Eastern Canada*. Ottawa: National Museums of Canada, 1977.

Salo, Matt. T., ed., *The American Kalderasha: Gypsies in the New World*. Hackettstown, NJ: Gypsy Lore Society, 1981.

Silverman, Carol. "Everyday Drama: Impression Management of Urban Gypsies." In Matt T. Salo, ed., *Urban Anthropology, Special Issue*, 11, No. 3–4 (Fall–Winter 1982): 377–398.

Sutherland, Anne. *Gypsies: The Hidden Americans*. New York: Free Press, 1975.

Tong, Diane. "Romani as Symbol: Sociolinguistic Strategies of the Gypsies of Thessaloniki." In *Papers from the Fourth and Fifth Annual Meetings, Gypsy Lore Society, North American Chapter*, ed. by Joanne Grumet, pp. 179–187. New York: Gypsy Lore Society, 1985.

Yoors, Jan. *The Gypsies*. New York: Simon and Schuster, 1967.

———. *The Gypsies of Spain*. New York: Macmillan, 1974.

CHAPTER FOUR

THE SHAKERS

Although her actual birth record has never been discovered, Shaker tradition has it that Ann Lee was born in Manchester, England, on February 29, 1736. (That she was supposedly born during Leap Year may or may not be a coincidence.) She came from a working-class family, and while much of her background remains obscure, there is no doubt that Ann Lee was one of the "common folk." She had no education of any kind, and at an early age was forced to work at menial jobs. From all indications, her working-class origins and bleak childhood were instrumental in shaping both the Shaker economy and the Shaker philosophy.[1]

When she was twenty-two, the turning point came in Ann Lee's life, although neither she nor anyone else realized it at the time. She became acquainted with James and Jane Wardley, leaders of a radical religious sect. Originally Quakers, the Wardleys had "seen the light" and broken away from the Society of Friends.

It is difficult to describe a religious meeting of the Wardley group, but it must have been a sight to behold. Starting with a silent meditation so typical of the Quakers, the Wardleyites would suddenly erupt into a paroxysm of shouting, shaking, and talking with the Lord. Because of these "agitations of the body," the group came to be called by a variety of names: jumpers, shiverers, Shaking Quakers, and eventually Shakers.

These early Shakers retained some of their Quaker practices—such as simplicity of dress and pacifism—but they had no definitive theology or philosophy. And while Ann Lee was welcomed, she had no immediate impact on the group. In 1762, however, an event took place that was to have a lasting effect on both Ann Lee and the Shakers. She married one Abraham Stanley. (Being illiterate, both signed the marriage registry with an X.)

Concupiscence Exactly why the marriage took place is not known, for the couple were obviously not suited to one another. Ann had grave difficulties during childbirth. She had four children, all of whom died in

---

[1]For a good account of Shaker history and life-styles see Priscilla J. Brewer, *Shaker Communities, Shaker Lives* (Hanover: University Press of New England, 1986).

early infancy. For the last child, forceps were employed, and Ann Lee's life was in real danger. Although she survived, she was convinced that children signified trouble.

Ann Lee interpreted the childbirth catastrophe as a sign of God's displeasure. In her view, she had given way to temptations of the flesh—not once, but several times. And on each occasion she had been punished severely. Thus, it was "concupiscence," or sexual desire, which was the root of all evil, and unless a person could repress this desire, he or she would have to answer for the consequences. Since sex and marriage were strongly intertwined, *marriage per se must be wrong.*

Soon Ann started to avoid her husband. By her own confession, she began to regard her bed "as if it had been made of embers." She also took a more active interest in the Wardley group, speaking out against sins of the flesh. And while not all her colleagues agreed with her, she eventually won them over. Before long, the Shakers were not only condemning all carnal practices but were criticizing the established church for permitting such activities.

The townspeople were quick to react. Allegations of sorcery, heresy, and blasphemy were made, and on several occasions angry mobs attacked Ann Lee. Once she was imprisoned for "disturbing the congregation" of Christ Church, Manchester. Shaker tradition has it that she was treated cruelly, locked in a small cell for two weeks, and left without food. She would have died except for one of her ardent disciples who, during the night, managed to insert a small pipe into the keyhole of her cell, through which he fed her milk and wine. Although the prison story is doubtless an exaggeration, it does show the reverence with which Ann Lee had come to be regarded by the Wardleyites.

Mother Ann   Predictably, Ann Lee soon found herself the Shaker leader, saint, and martyr all in one. The Wardleys had felt for some time that the second coming of Christ was imminent, and that it would be in the form of a woman. After Ann Lee's prison experience, they were sure that "she was the one." From that day on, she was known as Mother Ann Lee and invested with a messiahship, a belief that the Shakers hold to this day. In fact, while the term "Shakers" is accepted by them, the official name of the organization is the United Society of Believers in Christ's Second Appearing, or Believers for short.

What kind of person was Ann Lee that she could command such devotion and reverence on the part of her followers? Physically, she was a short, thickset woman with brown hair, blue eyes, and a fair complexion. According to her followers, she had a dignified beauty that inspired trust. By all accounts, she was a dedicated, unselfish, thoughtful, and totally fearless individual.

As with so many other leaders discussed in the present volume, however, verbal descriptions are grossly inadequate. Ann Lee had a genuinely charismatic bearing, a compelling inner force that made itself felt whenever she was among her followers. In some indefinable way, she was able to make them feel that they were in the presence of a heavenly person.

Beginnings in America

A few months after her release from prison, Mother Ann Lee had a divine revelation in which she was not only directed to go to America but was assured that in the New World the Believers would prosper and grow. Revelation aside, it was becoming apparent that the Shakers had little future in England or on the Continent. Their physical gyrations and their renunciation of sex had brought them little except physical abuse and legal prosecution. Accordingly, they made plans for their overseas voyage, and in May 1774 Ann Lee and eight of her followers set sail for New York. Oddly enough, the Wardleys did not accompany her. Odder still—and for reasons best known to himself—her husband did!

Arriving in August, the little band of Believers soon established themselves at Niskayuna, a native American–named tract of land just outside Albany. They put up buildings, cleared land, planted crops, and brought in money through blacksmithing, shoemaking, and weaving. But in a spiritual sense, progress was discouragingly slow. Records indicate that by 1779 they had gained but a single convert. Abraham Stanley, moreover, seems to have vanished from the scene.

Some of the group became disconsolate over the failure of Shakerism to make much headway, but Mother Ann preached patience. When the time was right, she would say, new converts would "come like doves." Sure enough, before many months had passed, converts did indeed come streaming in. The most important convert was Joseph Meachem, a Baptist minister and one of the most influential members of the clergy in the area. Meachem not only became an eloquent supporter of Mother Ann, but ultimately proved to be one of the two or three most influential figures in the history of Shakerdom.

Sex-Role Behavior   In spite of her success, Ann Lee faced two difficulties sometimes overlooked by historians. The first pertains to what sociologists call *sex-role behavior*. Role, sociologically speaking, refers to what individuals do and are expected to do by virtue of the positions they occupy in their society. Thus, police officers have a set of behavioral responses that accord with their law-enforcement positions, nurses have their own set, and so on. Role responses constitute learned behavior, and it is on the basis of this behavior that both the participant and society are able to interact with reasonable smoothness.

In the 1700s, sex-role behavior was sharply defined. Men and women had quite different roles, particularly in the occupational sphere, and there was little overlapping. The professions, for example—medicine, dentistry, law, higher education, the clergy—were male provinces, and any female who sought admittance was suspect. For all intents and purposes, the clergy was entirely male, and the fact that Ann Lee was not only the head of her church but believed to be the incarnation of Christ was a handicap of major proportion.

The second difficulty faced by Mother Ann was the fact that her position on sex and marriage was not popular. True, she was preaching in a period close to Puritanism, yet the Shaker doctrine was an extreme one even for that day and age. That Ann Lee was able to win adherents in spite of the celibacy rule is a further tribute to her spiritual and charismatic powers.

Persecution and Prosecution

It should be kept in mind that the decade 1774–1784 virtually coincided with the revolutionary war. And the Shakers—recently arrived from England—were naturally suspected of being British sympathizers. It was almost inevitable that the followers of Ann Lee would run afoul of the law, and in 1780 the inevitable happened. Among those jailed were Mother Ann Lee, Joseph Meachem, William Lee, Mary Partington, John Hocknell, and James Whittaker.

Joseph Meachem has already been mentioned. William Lee was Ann Lee's brother. The Hocknells and Partingtons were the only members of the original group to come from the moneyed class; in fact, John Hocknell had supplied most of the capital for the Shakers' passage to America and for the land at Niskayuna. And it was James Whittaker who had reportedly kept Ann Lee from starving to death in an English jail by feeding her through the keyhole. Thus, virtually the entire Shaker leadership was in jail because of alleged British sympathies.

Even after they were released from prison, unruly mobs showered the Believers with indignities and abuse. Fines, expulsions, jail sentences, beatings, clubbings—at times it must have seemed as though God had deserted them. James Whittaker was beaten and left for dead. William Lee had his skull badly fractured by a rock. Mother Ann was stoned and severely mauled on several occasions. And while all three managed to survive, the fact that they died at a relatively young age is attributed to their recurrent exposure to hostile mobs.

The Death of Mother Ann   In September 1783, Ann Lee and her lieutenants returned to Niskayuna, after having been on the road for more than two years. In most respects, their trip had been successful. They had spread the Shaker faith to those who had never heard it before. They had gained a great many converts. They had laid the specific groundwork for at least a half-dozen Shaker societies. By their devotion to principle and refusal to yield to pressure, they earned the sympathy and respect of many Americans who otherwise disagreed with their position.

On the negative side, however, it was obvious that the sojourn had taken its toll. The first to succumb was William Lee, who died only ten months after the return to Niskayuna. He was a strapping young man who had served as a kind of bodyguard to his sister, but the ravages of mob action had taken their toll. His death visibly affected Mother Ann, also in declining health. Two months later, on September 8, 1784, Ann Lee died, although she was only forty-eight years old. Apparently she had had premonitions, because a few days before her death she was heard to remark, "I see Brother William coming, in a golden chariot, to take me home."

Thus ended the short but very remarkable career of a very remarkable person. Through the quiet force of her own personality, she was able to transform a tiny band of ineffectual ecstatics into a respected and rapidly growing religious body. And while the United Society of Believers in Christ's Second Appearing was not to become one of the major religious organizations, it was to have a prolonged and interesting history. Indeed, the Shakers were to become one of the largest, longest-lasting, and the most successful of all the communist groups in America.

The Attractions of Shaker Life

For the next seventy-five years or so, the Believers grew and prospered, eventually expanding into nineteen different societies in eight states—with a reported all-time membership of some 17,000. This figure is especially noteworthy when one considers that most other experimental groups of the period—New Harmony, Brook Farm, the Fourierists, and others—fell by the wayside after a few short years.

Shaker societies imposed strict rules on their members: confession of sins, rejection of marriage, celibacy, manual labor, separation from the world, and total renunciation of private property in favor of a communist economy. Taken collectively, these factors would seem to weigh against a growth in membership. Yet in practice, there was a very pronounced growth. Why?

Although a combination of factors was involved, one sociological concept should be mentioned at this point in the Shaker story. This concept is *manifest vs. latent function,* first proposed by Robert Merton. According to Merton, many social processes and institutions have a dual function: a conscious, deliberate, or "manifest" function, and an unconscious, unrealized, or "latent" function.

College fraternities and sororities, for example, have the manifest function of providing food, housing, and camaraderie for interested students. But there is also a latent function: the conferring of social status upon those invited to membership. And so it was with the Shakers. Men and women joined manifestly because they believed in the religious orientation of the group, but in a latent sense, the Shaker community provided them with certain rewards not otherwise attainable.

To begin with, there is no denying the fact that some people joined because of an unhappy married life. Today, couples who are dissatisfied have easy recourse to the divorce courts, but it was not always so. In many of the colonies, there was simply no provision for divorce. Even where it was permitted, divorce was a rare occurrence because it was socially unacceptable. For unhappy spouses, therefore, the United Society offered a legitimate way out. A couple could join one of the many Shaker communities, and by following the rules—one of which was that the sexes be segregated—could start a whole new way of life.

But was not sexual abstinence an excessively high price to pay? This is a difficult question, and about all that can be said is that most of the converts were in the middle and older age groups, whose sexual ardor had perhaps been dimmed. Also, for some women, socialized to accept the mores of the time, the sex factor was probably not of major importance. In the eighteenth and nineteenth centuries, sexual gratification was considered more of a male than a female prerogative. The percentage of women who thought of marriage in sexual terms can only be conjectured.

It may be, additionally, that those with relatively high sex drives—whether male or female—did not join the Shakers in any great number. In any case, membership lists have always shown a preponderance of females over males, the actual ratio being approximately two to one.

Shakerdom also provided a haven for those women whose husbands had died and who had no real means of support. This was especially true for women with small children. Life insurance was virtually unknown in this period, and jobs for women were severely limited, both in number and kind. Social welfare programs, furthermore—Medicare, social security, family aid, and the like—were to be hallmarks of the twentieth century, not the nineteenth. At any rate, widows often had a hard time of it—another reason why converts to Shakerdom were so often women.

A widow who joined, incidentally, retained her married name. But a married woman, according to Muncy, "relinquished her husband's name and resumed her maiden name in order to eradicate, as much as possible, all traces of the marriage."[2]

It was not only widows, of course, who were attracted to the economic security provided by the Believers. Some Americans were just not suited to the demands of capitalism. By virtue of such factors as temperament, ability, or outlook on life, they simply had no desire to engage in the day-to-day challenge of a competitive system. Such individuals found a more relaxed atmosphere and a more secure way of life within the confines of a communist organization.

Sociality   A few years ago an interviewer, in talking to one of the older Shaker women, asked the question, "What was there about the Shaker way of life that attracted so many people?" And she replied, almost without thinking: "Well, you knew everybody cared about you. There was good feeling all around—lots of people to be with and talk to. It was a very pleasant association."

Shakers were rarely alone. Brewer describes the living arrangements in a typical family dwelling at New Lebanon in 1832:

> . . .[Sixteen] "retiring rooms" were shared by eighty-one Believers in the Family, or about five people to a room. The arrangement of members within the dwelling is interesting because it provides a unique perspective of the relationships that developed within the Shaker Family structure.
>
> Room #1 housed the two Family Deacons, aged fifty-eight and thirty-two, and their counterparts, the Deaconesses, aged fifty-four and twenty-eight, lived across the hall in Room #2. Four "aged brethren" (older than seventy) lived in Room #3 across the hall from nine "aged sisters" who shared Room #4. The two Elders (ages seventy-one and fifty-five), and the two Eldresses (ages sixty-eight and fifty-three), occupied the Rooms #5 and #6. Rooms #7 and #8 were shared by five middle-aged Brethren and seven middle-aged Sisters.
>
> On the floor above, ages were generally more mixed, with a few teenagers scattered in each room under the supervision of one or two middle-aged members. Interestingly, it appears that occupation within the community may have had some influence in this arrangement, because two physicians were among the tenants of Room #7 and at least four woodworkers were among the occupants of #15. . . .[3]

Emotionality and Hyperactivity   Another reason for the Shaker success with converts was that some Americans genuinely embraced the emotionality and hyperactivity that were the hallmarks of the United Soci-

[2]Raymond L. Muncy, *Sex and Marriage in Utopian Communities* (Bloomington: Indiana University Press, 1973), p. 20.

[3]Brewer, *Shaker Communities, Shaker Lives*, p. 69.

ety's brand of worship. Throughout most of their existence, the Believers engaged in some rather frenzied behavior. And while most of their day-to-day routine was marked by order, steadfastness, and laborious attention to the details of community living, their religious services were something else. More about their Sunday worship will be discussed later, but Foster's comments on the subject are most revealing:

> Shaker revivalistic activities were another factor attracting individuals. . . . Among the types of behavior described in Shaker sources were shaking and trembling, shouting, leaping, singing, dancing, speaking in strange tongues, whirling, stamping, rolling on the floor, crying out against sin and carnal nature, and trance. . . .
>
> Many of these activities seemed to be clearly beyond any conscious human agency, and thus were seen as manifestations of the supernatural. . . . Believers saw them as a sign of God's continuing workings in human history and the existence of an authority going beyond the purely man-made.[4]

Christ on Earth   There were some Americans who also concluded that Mother Ann was indeed the incarnation of Christ. She was a remarkable woman and—in her own way—an inspirational leader. Shaker literature has attributed a number of miracles to her, and as time went on it was more or less natural that the legends would grow. Her gift of healing included mending broken bones and crippled joints, curing infections and sores, obliterating cancer, healing lameness, and so on. For those who believed in these miracles, it is easy to see why the United Society came to be accepted as the one true faith.

These, then, were the attractions of Shakerdom. They have been mentioned in some detail since *the only way* the Society could grow was by conversion. Being a celibate group, their birthrate was zero. Conversions were their life blood, and for many decades the blood flowed smoothly and with amazing vitality.

Expansion

James Whittaker succeeded Ann Lee as head of the Shakers, and upon Whittaker's death in 1786, Joseph Meachem assumed the leadership. Again, it was a matter of the right person in the right place at the right time. For by now, what the Believers needed above all else was someone to systematize, organize, and set the stage for expansion. Joseph Meachem was that person.

Father Joseph was a brilliant organizer, and one of his first acts was to ap-

---

[4]Lawrence Foster, *Religion and Sexuality: Three American Communal Experiments of the Nineteenth Century* (New York: Oxford University Press, 1981), p. 29.

point Lucy Wright to the headship "in the female line." She was an exceptionally intelligent woman and a sound leader in her own right. These two guided the Society for ten years, and following Joseph Meachem's death in 1796, Mother Lucy continued in the top position for another twenty-five years. Joseph Meachem and Lucy Wright were the first of the American-born Shaker leaders. They were also probably the greatest.

After the head community was established at New Lebanon, New York, the United Society of Believers grew—both numerically and geographically—for many decades. Some of the settlements were founded and developed with little difficulty. Others, however, were faced with the most deplorable conditions: persecutions and mob violence, topographical handicaps, attacks by native Americans, inadequate medical facilities, and other perils associated with a frontier environment. Considering the poor roads of the period, Shaker expansionism seems even more impressive. Most of their communities were hundreds of miles from one another.

Following, in chronological order, are the dates, locations, and membership estimates of the various Shaker societies.[5]

Date	Location	Total Membership
1787	New Lebanon, N.Y.	3,202
1787	Niskayuna (Watervliet), N.Y.	2,668
1790	Hancock, Mass.	548
1792	Canterbury, N.H.	746
1792	Enfield, Conn.	739
1792	Tyringham, Mass.	241
1793	Alfred, Maine	241
1793	Enfield, N.H.	511
1793	Harvard, Mass.	500
1793	Shirley, Mass.	369
1794	Sabbathday Lake, Maine	202
1806	Union Village, Ohio	3,873
1806	Watervliet (Dayton), Ohio	127
1809	Pleasant Hill, Ky.	800
1810	South Union, Ky.	676
1811	West Union (Burso), Ind.	350
1822	North Union, Ohio	407
1825	Whitewater, Ohio	491
1826	Groveland, N.Y.	793

[5]See Charles Nordhoff, *The Communistic Societies of the United States* (New York: Dover, 1966); Marguerite Fellows Melcher, *The Shaker Adventure* (Cleveland: Western Reserve Press, 1968); Edward Andrews, *The People Called Shakers* (New York: Oxford University Press, 1953). Membership figures are very rough approximations and are based on records of the Western Reserve Historical Society, cited by Andrews, pp. 290–91.

Like the Divinites, who will be discussed in Chapter 6, the Believers were reluctant to disclose their membership numbers. And as Whitworth points out, "they justified this reluctance by biblical reference."[6] Nevertheless, in addition to the locations listed in the table on the preceding page there were at least a dozen other branches and short-lived communities in states as far south as Georgia and Florida. It is certain, therefore, that the membership figure of 17,000, given in standard reference works, is a gross underestimation. In fact, on the basis of documentary records at the Shaker Museum and Library, Sabbathday Lake, Maine, total membership appears to have been about 64,000.[7]

The Believers worked hard at gaining converts, despite the fact that their own societies were strictly separatist. According to Whitworth: "The Shakers sought converts enthusiastically and ardently. Each accession of new members vindicated the utopianism of the sect, and the establishment of each new society was seen as a distinct step towards the conversion of the earth into the Kingdom of God."[8]

Economic Organization

For the United Society of Believers in Christ's Second Appearing, economic communism was a natural outgrowth of their religious philosophy. Their reasoning was that in order to practice celibacy, they had to live apart from the world. And to live apart successfully, it was necessary to abolish private property.

Some Shaker leaders also felt that Christian virtues such as humility and charity were best exemplified through common ownership. Throughout Shakerdom, at least, there would be no rich, no poor; no masters, no slaves; no bosses, no underlings. Such a system, admittedly, constituted what sociologists call an *ideal type;* that is, a hypothetical situation where all the preconceived criteria are met or where everything goes according to plan. The ideal type has value in that it enables the sociologist to compare the actual situation with the conceptualized ideal. In this sense, the Believers came reasonably close to attaining their ideal.

Manual Labor   In both theory and practice, manual labor held an exalted position in the Shaker scheme of things. Exalted. No other word will do. "Put your hands to work and your hearts to God," Ann Lee had

---

[6]John Whitworth, *God's Blueprints: A Sociological Study of Three Utopian Sects* (London and Boston: Routledge & Kegan Paul, 1975), p. 37.
[7]Written communication from the Director.
[8]Whitworth, *God's Blueprints,* p. 37.

been fond of saying, and the Shakers used these words as the corner-stone of their economy.

With the exception of the aged and the infirm, every adult was expected to work at some manual task. This applied to the leaders as well as to the group at large. Ann Lee had worked as a mill hand, James Whittaker was a skilled weaver, Joseph Meachem was a farmer, and so on. Shakers held that this was the natural order of things and pointed out that Jesus had been a carpenter, Paul a sailmaker, and Peter a fisherman.

Believers felt strongly that manual labor was not something imposed on individuals. It was, rather, a feeling that came from within, and took the form of a moral commitment. Thus, while there were men and women in charge of the various trades and departments—orchard dea-con, cabinet deacon, herb deaconess, and so forth—their job was not to boss or supervise but rather to handle paper work, allocate supplies, and otherwise handle administrative matters.

Work: A Cultural Theme   Non-Shakers often have difficulty in under-standing just what made the Believers so industrious, since there were no apparent work pressures of any kind. Similarly, some of those who joined the United Society expecting their duties would be easy—the so-called Winter Shakers—could not adjust to the energetic work pattern and soon resigned from the organization. Work was indeed one of the *cultural themes* of the Believers, as the following expressions—all by Mother Ann Lee—indicate:

You must not lose one minute of time, for you have none to spare.
The devil tempts others, but an idle person tempts the devil.
The people of God do not sell their farms to pay their debts, but they put their hands to work and keep their farms.

As Henri Desroche puts it, Ann Lee looked upon idle conversation

as time lost from work. Laziness, play, and self-indulgence were taboo. The Shakers lived standing up. Their furniture will long testify to this inspiration. From the tone of these moral warnings, one concludes that Shaker economic efficiency was closely tied to their idea of salvation: there are no idlers in heaven.[9]

The same inner commitment that prompted the Believers to work hard was also responsible for the exceptional quality of their labor. Whether the product was a chair, a table, or a broom, the buyer could be assured of the finest craft. Shaker-made furniture was of top-grain

---

[9]Henri Desroche, *The American Shakers: From Neo-Christianity to Presocialism* (Amherst: University of Massachusetts Press, 1971), p. 228.

wood, properly cured, functionally designed, joined and fitted to perfection, and constructed for long, tough usage. It was not simply work but *quality work* that constituted the Shaker trademark. Even in selling fruits and vegetables, choice quality was maintained. If a buyer bought a basket of apples, he or she knew that each layer would be uniform, with no "plugs" hidden underneath.

Which particular occupation a person followed was left pretty much a matter of individual choice. A number of Believers were skilled at more than one trade and divided their efforts as needed. The total list of skilled roles filled by Shakers approximated that of society at large: carpenter, cabinetmaker, farmer, blacksmith, weaver, metalworker, mechanic, and so forth.

Division of Labor   Division of labor in the various Shaker communities—retrospectively, at least—can be seen as something of a paradox. On the one hand, women and children were integral parts of the occupational structure. All youths, in fact, were required to learn a trade. Likewise, all the Shaker women worked, and any number of them achieved positions of real leadership.

On the other hand, there is no gainsaying the fact that, positions of leadership notwithstanding, women did "women's work" and men did "men's work"—much as in society at large. Thus, women did most of the domestic chores: food preparation, cooking, sewing and mending, housekeeping, and nursing. Men worked the farms, cut the lumber, made the furniture, engaged in metalwork, and the like.

In all likelihood, one of the reasons that the male-female division of labor followed that of society at large was the Shaker insistence on separation of the sexes. To have assigned jobs without regard to gender, and at the same time to have maintained strict sexual segregation, might well have created insurmountable problems.

There is also some evidence that Shakers considered labor as separate but equal, with the more physically demanding occupations the province of men. In a letter written to Mother Lucy Wright shortly before his death, Joseph Meachem said: "Thou, tho' of the weaker sex, . . . will be the elder or first born after my departure."[10]

Functionalism   It goes almost without saying that not all Shaker craftspeople were of equal skill. As in the world at large, some were better than others. The same applied to the various Shaker societies—some were more efficient than others. Throughout the whole of Shakerdom, however, the basic motif was functionalism. Frills, scrolls, refinements, ornaments, elaborations—such things had no place in the United Society.

---

[10]Brewer, *Shaker Communities, Shaker Lives*, p. 28.

To be right, a chair had to be light, strong, durable, easy to clean, and comfortable. Building such a chair along straight, simple lines was the mark of Shaker genius. As a former member put it, "Bureaus, chests, and tables were all made with simple, straight lines, but with fine workmanship. There was nothing slipshod about the Shakers. You could depend on it—everything about them, from their religion to the things they produced, was genuine."[11]

Shaker furniture has an esthetic quality all its own: the lines invariably are right, and the viewer perceives them as such. It is interesting that whereas Shaker religion has left no real mark on the world, Shaker furniture has become appreciated as a distinctive art form.

In today's market, authentic Shaker chairs, tables, cabinets, and other items bring exorbitant prices. For example, Donegan reported the following in 1989:

> The most desirable examples of Shaker furniture now sell (at auction) in the $100,000 range, and some private asking prices are reportedly as high as $140,000–$150,000. At auctions during the last year and a half, pieces fetching record prices included a simple tall revolving chair that sold for $88,000, a long trestle table that brought $94,600, and a chest of six small drawers over six large drawers that went for $99,000.[12]

Shaker Inventions   The Believers are also credited with a number of inventions, such as the circular saw, brimstone match, screw propeller, cut nail, clothespin, flat broom, pea sheller, threshing machine, revolving oven, and a variety of machines for turning broom handles, cutting leather, and printing labels. Oddly enough—with few exceptions—the Shakers did not patent their inventions, believing that such a practice was monopolistic.

No Shaker ever received money for his or her work. This rule extended to church officials as well as to regular members. On the other hand, no Believer was ever in need. When someone wanted a pair of shoes or a new shirt or dress, he or she simply went to the common store and signed for them. At mealtime, members went to the common dining room, where they could eat their fill.

There is no doubt that a fair degree of ethnocentrism pervaded the various Shaker communities. Members were convinced that Mother Ann had pointed the way, and that their life-style was superior to any other. As a group, they showed little inclination to mingle with the outside. As will be shown later, however, the trustees carried on a fairly extensive economic interrelationship.

---

[11]Sylvia Minott Spencer, "My Memories of the Shakers," *The Shaker Quarterly*, 10 (Winter 1970): 126–33. See also June Sprigg, *By Shaker Hands* (New York: Knopf, 1975).
[12]Frank Donegan, "Shaker Chic," *Americana*, 16 (January/February 1989): 66.

Assessing the Shaker Economy

In the last analysis, of course, the question that must be asked of any economic experiment is, does it work? Applied to the Believers, this was a doubly important question, for they were attempting to operate a collectivist economy in the midst of a capitalist system.

Simple questions, alas, do not always have simple answers—and this is certainly true of the issue at hand. The United Society did succeed in working out a rather effective social system. Their day-to-day activities went smoothly, there was a minimum of internal discord, and—considering the size of the various Shaker communities—social cohesion was consistently strong. In assessing their economic efficiency, however, a number of complicating factors arise.

For one thing, it is difficult to tell whether the success of the Shaker economy was due to the socialist factor or to plain hard work. With their zeal and dedication, would not the Believers have been equally successful as a corporate enterprise?

How much of their economic success was due to their religious zeal, and to the fact that their economy and their religion were intertwined? And how much was due to the succession of forceful leaders: Ann Lee, James Whittaker, Joseph Meachem, Lucy Wright, Richard McNemar, and Frederick Evans?

The extent to which these factors were interrelated will probably never be known. However, there is no denying that the collectivist factor, per se, did contribute to their economic viability. Their ready supply of labor, their self-sufficiency, and their ability to deal profitably with the outside world—these were all positive features. And finally, of course, the fact that they paid no salaries and had no stockholders meant that all profit could be reinvested in the society.

It seems likely, therefore, that up to the Civil War, at least, the success of the Shaker economy was due at least in part to the socialist aspects. This was the opinion of most writers of the period.

Lawsuits   The early days of Shakerdom were marked by hostility and persecution. As time went on, however, and the United Society acquired a reputation for honesty, hard work, and devoutness, much of the ill will abated. In place of the persecutions, unfortunately, a new threat arose: the lawsuit, usually brought in the guise of economic recovery.

When a person joined the Shakers, he or she signed a covenant relinquishing all his or her property and permitting the Society to make use of it as they saw fit. Any time a member wished to withdraw, he or she was not only permitted to do so but would have his or her original property returned. If the person had joined empty-handed—as many of the Winter Shakers had—he or she would be given a liberal monetary allowance.

Upon withdrawing, however, some individuals insisted that they be remunerated for their services during the period of their membership. This the Believers refused to do, and in consequence a number of bitter lawsuits were fought. Some of the suits were simply brought by profiteers; others were brought by those who felt they had a just and moral claim. In general, though, the suits were unsuccessful, and the courts sided with the United Society.

Nevertheless, the cases did provoke bitterness, and the allegations often made front-page headlines. Furthermore, the suits were so numerous that handling them became one of the trustees' recognized duties. Eventually, the wording of the covenant was tightened and made into a binding contract. The remarkable thing was that although the trustees were not lawyers, few of the legal challenges to the Society were successful.

Social Organization

Unlike most of the other communist experiments in the United States, the Shaker venture involved large numbers of men and women spread over many states. At its peak, the United Society of Believers in Christ's Second Appearing owned more than a 100,000 acres of land and hundreds of buildings. Caring for these vast holdings was no easy task, but the Shakers managed their affairs with a minimum of bureaucratic involvement. Mistakes were made—some of them serious—yet the Believers must be given a high rating for overall efficiency.

Each of the nineteen Shaker societies was divided into "families" of approximately a hundred members. The families—a rather ironic term—lived separately, worked separately, and were administered separately. Thus, at Niskayuna there were four families; at Hancock and Union Village, six; at New Lebanon and Pleasant Hill, eight; and so on. Although the various families and societies were socially and economically independent of one another, it was commonplace for one group to help another, particularly in time of trouble.

(Not all Shakers lived in families. Some were permitted to follow the gospel in their own homes and were known as First Order, or Novitiate, Shakers. Exactly how many First Order Shakers there were is unknown, since membership lists contained only those who had been "gathered" into one of the families.)

Each family was ordinarily governed by two male elders and two female elders, and their rule was absolute—subject only to the approval of church headquarters at New Lebanon. The elders were responsible for both the spiritual and temporal order of things within their family. They heard confessions, conducted meetings, enforced rules of conduct, served as preachers, acted as missionaries, and admitted (or rejected) new applicants.

The elders were also responsible for economic policy, work assignments, and financial transactions with the outside world. On such matters, however, they customarily appointed assistants in the form of deacons and trustees. The deacons were in charge of the various workshops and food-production centers, while the trustees carried on the business activities with the outside world. It is evident from the following account that the trustees had to perform a unique balancing act:

> Being a trustee was a delicate job. If a trustee committed the serious sin of incurring debts for the community, or if he committed the no-less-serious sin of becoming too important on his job, he was recalled and replaced. Among the Shakers, a job like this was not an enviable one. . . . It was also the only post in the Shaker hierarchy which women did not hold along with the men.[13]

The elders themselves were appointed, or approved, by the church headquarters at New Lebanon, although it was customary for a family to accept an appointed elder by acclamation. Acclamation or no acclamation, however, the United Society of Believers was anything but a democracy. There was no vote. There were no elections. There was no appeal. The family elders, or ministry, were housed in separate quarters, and their decisions were final—albeit on policy matters they normally consulted with New Lebanon.

The central ministry at New Lebanon was also composed of two male elders and two female elders, with the head elder being the official head of the church. This group was self-perpetuating: they not only appointed their own successors, but the head of the church could claim a mantle of divine authority straight back to Mother Ann Lee. The central ministry determined overall church guidelines, printed and distributed rules of conduct, kept its hand on the pulse of the various societies and families, and otherwise molded the disparate Shaker elements into a unified body.

One might think that, with their near-absolute powers, the various ministries would use their position to become oppressively dictatorial. But while there may have been some despotic characters, they seem to have been few and far between. The nature of the Shaker faith—with its stress on humility, confession of sins, and service to God—was such as to preempt the unjust use of authority.

The elders, deacons, and trustees were devout, responsive individuals

---

[13]Desroche, *American Shakers*, pp. 215–16.

who nearly always inspired the trust of their followers. And since they had to work at a manual trade in addition to their ministerial duties, their record becomes all the more impressive.

The general membership included persons from all walks of life: doctors, lawyers, farmers, unskilled workers, merchants, artisans. For the most part, though, converts were drawn from the working class rather than from the upper socioeconomic levels. Most of the major religious bodies were represented—Baptists, Methodists, Adventists, Presbyterians, Jews, although there is no record of any Roman Catholic having joined. African-Americans could—and did—belong, and the same was true of the foreign-born. All ages were represented, from the very young to the very old, although in later years the bulk of the membership was composed of middle-aged and older people.

At all times, membership in the United Society was voluntary. Shakers believed firmly that any member who wanted to should be permitted to resign. And while some individuals did not find the austerity to their liking, the number of apostates was not excessive. One reason for this was the fact that all applicants were carefully screened and instructed by the elders and, upon acceptance, underwent a period of probation.

Separation of the Sexes

It must be kept in mind that another of the Society's *cultural themes* was their total renouncement of sex and marriage. Indeed, Believers were quite fond of proclaiming the "joys of celibacy." They looked upon such joys as a mandate from heaven and acted accordingly. As Muncy puts it, "The theme of celibacy filled the Shaker hymnals."[14]

All this fervor notwithstanding, segregation of the sexes was not left to the members' discretion. Printed rules emanated from the ministry at New Lebanon and were carefully enforced by the elders of the various families. It would not be much of an exaggeration to say that never in history were men and women so systematically precluded from physical contact with one another. It was not simply sex that was prohibited, but *physical contact of any kind.*

Men and women ("brothers and sisters") slept in different rooms on different sides of the house. They ate at different tables in the common dining room. They were not permitted to pass one another on the stairs, and—as if this were not enough—many of the dwellings included separate doorways. Even the halls were made purposely wide so that the sexes would not brush by one another. To repeat, all physical contact was prohibited, including shaking hands, touching, and "sisters mend-

---

[14]Muncy, *Sex and Marriage*, p. 36.

ing or setting buttons on the brethren's clothes while they have them on."

Men and women were not permitted to be alone together without a third adult present, a rule that applied both to business and social occasions. Wherever possible, all association of the sexes was done in groups. Moreover, brothers and sisters were not even allowed to *work together in groups* without special permission of the elders.

The children's order was also run along sexually segregated lines. Boys and girls lived in separate quarters and were permitted no physical contact with one another. Boys were generally under the supervision of the brothers, girls under the sisters. It was thus possible for a young child raised in a Shaker family to live virtually his or her entire life without once touching a member of the opposite sex.

While all families were strict with regard to segregation of the sexes, some apparently went to extremes; for example, the elders would spy through shuttered windows or make surprise visits to the dwelling quarters. One of the largest Shaker societies, at Pleasant Hill, Kentucky, went so far as to have watchtowers on the roof!

In general, though, relations between the sexes were not marred by incidents. There was little tension, unpleasantness, or antagonism. On the contrary, men and women lived together harmoniously, with a security that comes from inner peace. For example, each brother was assigned a sister, who looked after his clothes, took care of his laundry and mending, and otherwise kept a "general sisterly oversight over his habits and temporal needs." In return, the brother performed menial tasks for the sister, particularly those involving heavy manual labor.

Special mention should also be made of the "union meetings" between men and women. The meetings were held three or four times a week in one of the brethren's rooms, a half-dozen or so of the sisters sitting in a row facing an equal number of brothers. The two rows were a few feet apart, permitting each sister to converse with her counterpart.

The pairs were presumably matched (by the elders) on the basis of age and interests. The ensuing conversation might relate to aspects of Shaker economy, theology, or similar topics. Although the talks were required to be on an impersonal basis, the participants employed levity, humor, and other techniques used by people everywhere. Occasionally the get-together developed into a songfest. The principle of the union meeting, however, was to encourage a positive relationship between the sexes rather than the strictly negative one that might arise from forced segregation.

Despite strict segregation of the sexes, a few "backsliders" were able to find time alone. Several cases of fornication have been documented, at least one resulting in a pregnancy. Reports that "backsliders" regretted their decisions bolstered Shaker convictions that theirs was the "right way." Brewer refers to the following account, from an elder's journal, written after he had visited two couples who had left the Society to marry:

> . . . their hell has already begun, for they reflect on themselves for the sad condition in which they have plunged themselves, & they accuse John . . . of being the instigator of the whole plan. They shed a flood of tears when too late. John was more braced for a time, but he finally burst forth in torrents. Poor Mary . . . could hardly find words to express how awful it felt to her to lose her state of innocency which she had been brought up in. She said if someone would dig a hole in the ground & bury her therein it would be a heaven to her!!!![15]

A Typical Shaker Day

Days began early in the United Society—four-thirty A.M. in the summer and around five during the winter. At the sound of the morning bell, Believers would arise and kneel in silent prayer. Then the beds were stripped, the bedding placed neatly on the chairs, and the chairs hung on the ever-present pegs that bordered the walls. The allotted time for this activity was fifteen minutes, after which the designated sisters would clean the rooms, make the beds, and replace the chairs.

While other sisters prepared breakfast and set the dining-room tables, the brothers performed the morning chores: they brought in the wood, started the fire, fed the livestock, milked the cows, and arranged the day's work.

Breakfast was served at six-thirty, and as with all meals, the brothers and sisters gathered beforehand in separate rooms for a period of quiet prayer. Then, led by the elders, they entered the dining room through separate doors—brothers on the left, sisters on the right. After taking their places at separate tables, the entire congregation knelt for a moment of grace. The food was then served.

Each table seated from four to eight adults—children were served separately—and the bill of fare was ample if not fancy. Dietary matters varied from one society to the next, but in general the Believers preferred dairy products and vegetables to meat. In some societies, meat was not served at all, and pork was forbidden throughout Shakerdom.

More important than dietary rules, however—which were fairly liberal—were the rules of conduct that governed dining behavior. Good posture was required at all meals; elders were to be served first; members were permitted as many helpings as they wanted, but all food taken was to be eaten, nothing was to be wasted; knives and forks

[15]Brewer, *Shaker Communities, Shaker Lives*, p. 140.

were to be placed in a specified position when the meal was finished; food was not to be taken from the table; meat cut from the platter was to be cut square and of equal part "lean, fat, and bones."

Perhaps most unusual was the rule that forbade all conversation at mealtime. The prohibition was in force throughout all Shaker societies, and if the idea of silent meals seems rather dismal to most of us, all that can be said is that, in the religious atmosphere that prevailed, the Believers apparently took the custom in stride. The practice of silent meals does not seem to have been overly punitive.

After breakfast, each Shaker, including the elders, proceeded to his or her specific work task. Many of the jobs, particularly in the female realm, were rotated. But irrespective of the job, Believers were excellent workers.

Foster states that "Shakers always appeared busy doing something, but the work was done at a relaxed pace, and the range of assignments was varied and flexible within the overall structure of the needs of each community."[16]

The bell for the midday meal sounded a little before noon, and the earlier ritual was repeated. Afternoons were devoted to regular work activity, followed by supper at six. Most evenings were taken up by planned activity of some sort: general meetings, religious services, singing and dancing sessions, union meetings, and so on. Bedtime was usually between nine and nine-thirty.

Although the Shakers did not all wear similar apparel—as do the Amish—their clothing styles were more or less prescribed. Despite some changes over the years, typical attire for men included broad-brimmed hats, plain shirts buttoned at the throat and worn without neckties, vests and long coats, and dark trousers.

Women wore loose bodices with ankle-length skirts. Aprons were required, as were capes and Shaker bonnets. More than one observer commented on the fact that female attire was deliberately formless, so as not to arouse feelings of lust on the part of the men. By the same token, while both sexes were permitted the use of color, only subdued shades were authorized.

"Entertainment" for the Believers was rather limited because of their lack of contact with the outside world. Except in a real emergency, members of the Society would not even call in an outside doctor, preferring instead to treat their sick brothers or sisters with herbs, extracts, and whatever Shaker assistance was available. For most members, the only prolonged exposure to the outside world came during their journeys to other Shaker communities. Visiting of this type was one of the high points of their year.

By worldly standards, the United Society of Believers in Christ's Second

---

[16]Foster, *Religion and Sexuality*, p. 59.

Appearing was anything but a joyous organization. Daily living was a serious undertaking. The Believers had a regimented existence and a restricted range of opportunities. Their list of prohibitions was a formidable one: no sex, no marriage, no money, no private property; no conversation at mealtime; no outside contacts, and a minimum of entertainment; few visits and fewer visitors. Even household pets were prohibited, because it was feared they would somehow arouse maternal feelings on the part of the young girls. The only pets permitted were cats, used to control rodents.

Order   Rosabeth Kanter, an authority on the subject, believes that *order* is a common characteristic of utopian communities. She states that "in contradistinction to the larger society, which is seen as chaotic and uncoordinated, utopian communities are characterized by conscious planning and coordination. . . . Events follow a pattern. . . . A utopian often desires meaning and control, order and purpose, and he seeks these ends explicitly through his community."[17]

The Shakers were a good case in point, for in their societies order and purpose were combined to produce a definitive life-style. Their buildings, for example, were severely furnished: no rugs, no pictures, no photographs, no ornamentation. Such things were considered dirt catchers, and as the Believers were fond of saying, there is "no dirt in heaven." (It was hardly an accident that one of the very first Shaker industries involved broom making!) Furniture was sparse, since most cabinets and drawers were built into the walls. Here is Marguerite Melcher's perceptive account:

> Cleanliness and order were bywords in any region where Shakers lived. Their houses were so constructed and so furnished that whatever dirt might collect was plainly visible. There were no elaborate moldings in the rooms, no pictures on the walls, no ornamentation on the furniture. The handmade rugs on the floors were removable and washable, the windows were uncurtained.
>
> Around the walls of every room were flat narrow boards in which were set rows of wooden pegs to hold chairs when the floors were cleared for sweeping. Each outside door had its footscraper. Each stove had its dustpan and brush beside it.
>
> The word *orderliness* was coupled with that of cleanliness. Shaker buildings were planned for orderly communal living. Most of the rooms had built-in cabinets and drawers, designed to hold the necessary tools or supplies. There were drawers of all sizes and shapes: drawers for seeds and seed bags in the seed sorting room; drawers for herbs in the herb shop; drawers in the retiring rooms.

[17]Rosabeth Moss Kanter, *Commitment and Community: Communes and Utopias in Sociological Perspective* (Cambridge, MA: Harvard University Press, 1973), p. 39.

The cobblers' shops had racks on the walls to hold lasts of shoes, for each Shaker brother or sister had his or her own last. Although the Believers never tried to make life easy for themselves on the spiritual plane, they spared no pains to provide the best facilities for shop and household.[18]

The Sabbath   Sunday was a special day throughout the United Society. Although it was a holy day, with no work being performed, it was not—as in so many Christian groups—a solemn day. On the contrary, for Shakers of all ages it was a time of spiritual uplift, rejoicing, singing, and dancing. It was as though the quiet, the reserve, the temporal subjugation—traits in evidence six days a week—were released on the seventh day in an outpouring of spiritual ecstasy.

The dances themselves—or "marches," as they were called—ranged from mildly exuberant to highly explosive. On the mild side were rhythmic exercises in which the participants would march "with their hands held out in front of the body, and with elbows bent, moving the hands up and down with a sort of swinging motion, as though gathering up something in the arms. This motion signified 'gathering in the good.' They also believed in 'shaking out the evil.' "[19]

The following account by an ex-Shaker gives some idea of what the more volatile dances were like:

> In the height of their ecstasy, Shakers were constrained to worship God in the dance. . . .
>
> The *rolling exercise* consisted in being cast down in a violent manner, doubled with the head and feet together, and rolled over and over, like a wheel—or stretched, in a prostrate manner, turning like a log. . . .
>
> Still more mortifying were the *jerks*. The exercise began in the head, which would fly backward and forward and from side to side, with a quick jolt, . . . limbs and trunk twitching in every direction. And how such could escape injury was no small wonder to spectators.
>
> The last grade of mortification was the *barks*. These frequently accompanied the jerks . . . and one would take the position of a canine, move about on all fours, growl, snap the teeth, and bark.[20]

There is also some rather convincing evidence that in certain instances both Shaker men and women indulged in naked dancing and naked flagellation.[21] No sexual overtones were involved, however, and in any case such behavior was clearly the exception.[22]

---

[18]Melcher, *Shaker Adventure*, pp. 156–57.
[19]Spencer, "My Memories of the Shakers," pp. 126–33.
[20]Desroche, *American Shakers*, pp. 118–19.
[21]Thomas Brown, *An Account of the People Called Shakers: Their Faith, Doctrines, and Practice* (Troy, NY: Parker & Bliss, 1812), pp. 322–23, 334–36. Cited in Foster, *Religion and Sexuality*, pp. 42–43.
[22]Ibid.

Overview   In spite of these extreme forms of behavior—many of which reportedly occurred during the early, formative years of the Society—the Shakers lived a serious life, a life without frills, adornments, or luxuries of any kind. It was also a peaceful, contented life, and this fact puzzled outsiders. But it was clear that the followers of Ann Lee had an inner serenity that was hard to disturb, one they would not have found in society at large.

Understandably, outsiders had mixed feelings about the United Society. On the one hand, the Shakers were resented because they led an "unnatural" life, and because they would not vote, participate in public life, or bear arms for their country. On the other hand, they were genuinely admired for their honesty, their spiritual devoutness, and their capacity for hard work. As the nineteenth century wore on, the Believers came to be treated as respected members of the larger community.

Children: The Unsuccessful Venture

There is no doubt at all that children were one of the less successful Shaker ventures. While no children were ever born into the United Society, youngsters of every age were accepted, either as orphans or as children whose parents had converted. When they reached twenty-one, they were given the choice of staying in the Society or leaving. And a large majority chose to leave. Results were so poor that after the Civil War more and more Shaker societies stopped accepting children altogether.

The following abstract, taken from the journal entry of a Kentucky Shaker Society in 1867, contains an all-too-familiar story:

> Gone at last! Achille L'Hotte left clandestinely today, being the last one of eighteen boys brought from the orphan asylum at New Orleans in 1843. Three of the youths died here. All the rest chose the world. Achille, the last to go, is 34 years old.
>
> The oldest of the lot was only 12 years of age, the youngest 8. They are all gone and out of sight in 24 years. It becomes a question whether we should be taking in destitute children. Certainly there cannot be much gain if not one in 20 remains true to the good cause. We now have between 30 and 40. Shall not one be saved?[23]

Diaries and journals indicate that Shakers, for whatever reason, simply did not enjoy teaching. This may well have had a negative effect on their students. Typical Shaker teachers were young, usually in their early twenties. Brewer cites the following poem written by a young man, released from a teaching assignment after only three months:

[23]Julia Neal, *The Kentucky Shakers* (Lexington: Kentucky University Press, 1977), p. 81.

> I'm now released from the boys
> And from a deal of din and noise
> And John is left to rule the roost
> Without a second mate to boost
> My elders gave me a good name
> So I do leave devoid of shame
> Ha ha he he how glad I be
> I've no more boys to trouble me[24]

Eventually the Shakers came to accept only adults. But the question remains: why did they fail with the children? The reasons are not fully understood. The youngsters were given the best of care and were treated with kindness. Corporal punishment was frowned upon. In the 1800s, the idea of public education took hold in the United States, and the Believers followed suit with schools of their own. Their youngsters were taught the three *R*s in sexually segregated classes. There was typically a winter term for boys and a summer term for girls.

In day-to-day living, Shaker children followed much the same routine as the adults. Each youngster was taught one or more manual skills. Pride in workmanship was instilled at an early age. Cleanliness was stressed. The sexes were kept strictly apart. Dietary rules and regular dining procedures were observed. Even the clothing was identical with that of the adults; visitors often commented that the children looked like miniature Shakers. And, of course, permeating virtually every aspect of their lives was the inculcation of the religious values laid down by Mother Ann Lee.

Inasmuch as the children were more than adequately cared for, why did so many of them renounce Shakerism? While the answers can be challenged, the fact seems to be that the Believers were a special kind of people. It was not everybody who could renounce normal marital and familial relationships. For an adult to *choose* this way of life was one thing. But for the average person—especially the average young person—a regimented life without romantic love, sex, or children must have seemed a grim prospect.

Educational Policy   Another factor that must have discouraged young people from remaining in the Shaker fold was the negative attitude of the Believers toward education. Although the Shakers themselves tended to gloss over the matter, they were distrustful of most intellectual and artistic pursuits.

Ann Lee said, "Put your hands to work and your hearts to God," a principle that the Believers have followed to the present. But she made no mention of the mind, and the omission also became part of Shaker

---

[24]Brewer, *Shaker Communities, Shaker Lives*, p. 77.

policy. Education, as carried out in the Society's schools, did not go much beyond the basics of English, arithmetic, and geography. Subjects such as science, literature, foreign language, history, and the fine arts had little place in the Shaker scheme of things.

It is true that young people in the United Society were given training that many outside youth never received. In addition to learning a manual or domestic skill, Shaker boys and girls were given extensive instruction in religion and the Bible. They were taught humility, honesty, kindness, punctuality, and sincerity. They were cautioned against the evils of the flesh. They were encouraged to promote the happiness of other people and to avoid contention. In brief, as the elders saw it, they were given training in the development of character and moral responsibility.

But for the young boy or girl with real intellectual curiosity—with some feeling for the world of the mind—the United Society must have been a bleak environment. Books, magazines and journals, philosophical debates, abstract ideas, political discussions—all were discouraged. Of higher education there was none. No Shaker youth ever went to college. None ever became a doctor or lawyer.* None ever held a significant public office. None ever achieved fame in the natural or physical sciences.

In the arts, the situation was much the same. Poetry, drama, literature, sculpture, painting, symphonic and operatic music—all were missing in Shaker culture. For a youngster with talent along these lines, the path cleared by Mother Ann was painfully narrow.

Reference-Group Behavior   Sociologically speaking, a *reference group* is one that people look to for standards of behavior and appropriate conduct, one that can bestow or withhold approval. It is the group against which a person measures himself or herself. For adult Shakers, their own Society was their reference group, and they behaved accordingly.

But for the youth who were taken into the Society, it was a vastly different story. These youngsters did not choose Shakerism. They did not *voluntarily* look upon the Shaker community as a reference group, and hence they were not overly influenced by reference-group acceptability. While they were largely kept apart from the outside world, they were certainly not immune to its influences.

A young man or woman with normal sexual desires, or with more than a modicum of intellectual or artistic ability, must have found it difficult to remain within the Shaker fold. One would predict that when they were given the choice at age twenty-one of staying or leaving, they

*As stated earlier, the Believers did have some doctors, lawyers, and clergy in their midst. However, these were people who converted to Shakerism after they had achieved professional status.

would leave. And in practice, as has been mentioned, this is exactly what happened.

Shaker Theology

The theological doctrine of the United Society of Believers in Christ's Second Appearing was neither complex nor extensive. But it was radical, particularly by nineteenth-century standards. The Shakers rejected such concepts as the Trinity, damnation, the immaculate conception, resurrection of the body, and atonement. For the most part, they believed in a literal interpretation of the Bible—but they also believed that there were revelations later than the Bible.

In rejecting the Trinity, they held that God is made up of dual elements, male and female, and that this bisexuality is reflected throughout nature. Even angels were believed to have a male and female counterpart, and the same was true of Adam. Christ was considered to be a spirit, appearing first in the person of Jesus and—much later—in the person of Mother Ann. This male-female duality constituted another definition of the situation, and, in both a secular and a religious sense, the concept permeated the entire Shaker organization.

The Believers were convinced that the primitive, or pentecostal, church—with emphasis on common property, pacifism, separatism, and celibacy—was based on the right principles, but that later denominations and sects had strayed from the proper path. Violation of celibacy was a good case in point.

The Shakers' position, one from which they would never swerve, was that sin came into the world because of the action of Adam and Eve in the Garden of Eden. This "action," of course, was the sex act and was in direct disobedience of God. Henceforth, it was only by overcoming physical nature and conquering the desires of the flesh that men and women could achieve salvation. And since the Shakers had succeeded in this struggle, they felt that they alone, among the world's peoples, were carrying out God's will.

With regard to the elimination of the human race—a phenomenon that would surely occur if Shaker dogma prevailed—no serious problem was involved. The Believers thought the millennium was at hand, and consequently there was no real reason for the continuance of the human race. In the new order of things, spirituality would take the place of sensuality.

Interestingly, and perhaps contradictorily, the Shakers did not feel that human nature was basically sinful. They believed in Adam's sin in the Garden of Eden, but they also felt that the Lord was too just to penalize all people because of the mistakes of one. In like fashion, they refused to categorize marriage on the part of the world's peoples as sinful. They did feel, however, that non-Shakers were of a lower spiritual order.

Spiritualism   The Shakers were among the forerunners of modern spiritualism, the belief that the living could communicate with the dead. Members of the United Society were quite explicit on this point. They contended that they were able to talk—face to face—with their recently departed brethren, as well as with others "born before the Flood."

Communication with the spirit world varied from one Shaker community to the next and also seems to have varied over time, with the 1830s and 1840s being a particularly "vibrant" period. For a while, the religious services were so animated that the elders closed them to visitors. It is easy to see why.

Since the Believers had little entertainment, their religious services tended to take up the slack. After a greeting and some prayers by the elders, the sisters and brothers would form two large circles, one within the other. Although the sexes never touched each other at any time, the participants would group and regroup themselves in a variety of intricate patterns—all the while singing, chanting, and clapping hands.

At a certain point in the proceedings, a marked change would sweep over the dancers. A mood of expectancy would prevail. Suddenly there would be a loud "whoosh!" from the group, signifying that the devil was making his appearance. Then, in unison, those present would stamp their feet, shouting and chanting, "Stomp the devil!"

Next, two or three of the sisters would whirl round and round to cries of "Shake! Shake! Shake! Christ is with you!" When the whirlers sank to the floor from dizziness or exhaustion, their places would be taken by others. Midway in the sequence of shaking, jumping, shouting, clapping, and stamping, someone would hold up a hand and announce that Mother Ann was present—with gifts of fruit for everybody. One by one, each member would come forward and receive his or her basket, then go through the motions of peeling and eating the contents.

Then one of the elders would proclaim that Mother Ann had a message: some nearby native American chiefs were on their way to join the meeting. Whereupon the group would start to chant in a strange tongue and point to the door, waiting for the appearance of the native Americans.

Hardly was this ritual finished when the brothers and sisters would form parallel rows and begin another sequence of dances and gyrations. This time the native Americans were reported appearing at the windows, and there was an outpouring of joyous clapping. Then another "whoosh!" and some more stomping. The devil was loose again.

On and on and on the dances went, sometimes long past the curfew. While there was some variation from one service to the next, spiritual manifestations were more or less taken for granted. Mother Ann Lee was the most frequent visitor, although native Americans—for whom the Shakers seemed to have a spiritual affinity—were a close second. Other frequent guests included Alexander the Great, Napoleon, George Washington, and Benjamin Franklin.

The visions, hallucinations, messages, apparitions, and communications seemed endless. It was as though the followers of Mother Ann, by ecstatically embracing the spirit world, were able to work off all their worldly inhibitions.

After 1850, spiritualism in the United Society apparently died down— at least there is less of it reported. More than a trace remained for many decades, however, and the Believers never formally renounced the practice. As for the dances, they remained the vibratory signature of the Society for as long as the brothers and sisters had the vitality to stomp the devil.

Decline of the Order

The Shakers reached their peak around the time of the Civil War. Thereafter, membership declined, slowly at first, then faster and faster. By the mid-1870s, the Society was forced to advertise in the papers for new members. The following ad, for instance, appeared in several New York newspapers during 1874:

> MEN, WOMEN, AND CHILDREN CAN FIND A COMFORTABLE HOME FOR LIFE, WHERE WANT NEVER COMES, WITH THE SHAKERS, BY EMBRACING THE TRUE FAITH AND LIVING PURE LIVES. PARTICULARS CAN BE LEARNED BY WRITING TO THE SHAKERS, MT. LEBANON, NY.[25]

By the end of the century, whole Shaker communities were folding. By 1925, most of the remaining groups had dissolved. And by 1950, the end seemed clearly in sight, with only a scattering of hardy souls remaining.

What had happened to this once strong and spirited group? In Andrews's words, what was it that had brought about the "decline of the order"?[26] The answers are not hard to find.

To begin with, it was obvious that even before the Civil War, the American economy was changing. The old handicraft system, which was perfect for the Shakers, was being supplanted by the factory system. In spite of their emphasis on quality—or perhaps because of it—the Shakers could not compete with modern assembly-line methods. As was mentioned, Ann Lee had been fond of saying, "Put your hands to work

---

[25]Quoted in Whitworth, *God's Blueprints*, p. 75.
[26]Andrews, *The People Called Shakers*, pp. 224ff.

and your hearts to God," but she had had no inkling of the tremendous impact of the modern factory.

Transportation and communication were also affecting the life-style of the Society. With the advent of the railroad—and later the automobile— it became harder and harder for the Believers to maintain their separatism. The younger members, in particular, found it difficult to resist the various attractions of the outside world. By 1900, it was apparent to both Shaker and non-Shaker that the era of isolation had run its course.

Leadership in the Society was likewise undergoing change. The original heads—Ann Lee, James Whittaker, Joseph Meachem, and Lucy Wright—were men and women of courage, wisdom, and foresight. Later on, able leadership was provided by men such as Richard McNemar and Frederick Evans. But as time went on, it seemed that too often the ministry was unable to cope with the problems of a changing society. This was true in both the sacred and the secular spheres.

In the sacred sphere, church leadership was unable either to provide the spiritual guidance necessary to keep Shaker youth within the fold, or to gain a sufficient number of adult converts to make up for the loss of the children.

In the secular sphere, there were too many examples of economic mismanagement. Some of the trustees were clearly unsuited to their jobs. The Shaker group at Enfield, New Hampshire, lost $20,000 because of poor business practices. At Union Village, Ohio, the Society lost $40,000 when one of the trustees absconded with the money. The Shaker branch at South Union, Kentucky, lost over $100,000 because of difficulties stemming from the Civil War. And so it went. A number of the Societies also lost money because of costly lawsuits. These sums, of course, represent nineteenth-century dollars, not figures adjusted to current dollars.

Another factor that led to the decline of the order was the changing attitude toward sex in society at large. It was one thing to preach against evils of the flesh in the 1700s and early 1800s, when America was still living in the backwash of Puritanism. But by the 1900s, it was evident that fewer and fewer people thought of sex as sin. And with the emergence of more realistic attitudes toward sex, the Shaker position became correspondingly weaker.

Social welfare practices were also changing. Increasingly, various government agencies began to provide assistance for the sick, the widowed, the aged, and the orphaned. And as the whole concept of welfare came to be looked upon as a government obligation, the role of the United Society as a haven for the needy declined.

In a way, Shakerism has always contained the seeds of its own destruction. After all, in the interest of growth—or even survival—celibacy is a self-defeating doctrine. It may represent human subjugation of the flesh, but the end product, biologically speaking, is stagnation. True, the celibate orders of the Roman Catholic Church may continue to flourish, but they represent only a small percentage of the membership. With the Believers, the *entire organization* was involved. And when the rate of conversions declined, the end was just a matter of time.

One final reason for the demise of the Society should be mentioned: the loss of a certain vitality or spirit. The early Shakers were reasonably young men and women who believed in their cause with a zeal bordering on fanaticism. Their dedication, spirit, and pride were unmistakable. But over the decades, something seemed to happen. Desroche gets to the heart of the matter in the following passage:

> The characteristic Shaker dance rituals were slowly modified and eventually abandoned. Instrumental music and more conservative songs displaced the early chants and folk spirituals. The forces of religious ardor, holding compact the life of the sect, were wearing themselves out.[27]

The Shaker Heritage

What exactly is the Shaker heritage? In their two hundred years of existence, what have they done to make us remember them? There is no right-or-wrong answer to these questions. In some ways, the Shaker venture was an obvious failure; in others, it was a marked success. Where the balance lies depends in part on the personality of the assessor.

On the negative side, the Believers certainly failed in their primary objective—the establishment of a utopia, a heaven on earth. As a matter of record, they failed in both the secular and spiritual spheres. In a secular sense, Shakerdom simply did not flourish, and nothing can change this fact. Starting around the time of the Civil War, the movement declined inexorably.

Spiritually, the Believers' mark on the world is so faint as to be indiscernible. Their theology is virtually unknown today, their spiritualism is an embarrassment which is best forgotten, and their dancing or marching belongs, perhaps, in a similar category. In brief, for all their efforts and their sincerity, the Shakers have had virtually no impact on modern religious thought.

On the other hand, there is no doubt that the Believers made some significant cultural contributions to Americana. Their inventions—circular saw, screw propeller, flat broom, clothespin, brimstone match—have already been mentioned. Of equal importance was their stylistic

---

[27]Desroche, *American Shakers*, pp. 116–17.

contribution to American furniture. Tables, chairs, cabinets—all bear the functional worklike imprint of the United Society. And in the musical sphere, as Patterson reminds us, the Shakers contributed a substantial number of folk songs and spirituals.[28]

Perhaps more than any other group, the Shakers were able to link their name with *quality*. Their fruits and vegetables were top-grade. Their seeds and herbs were the best. Their furniture was fantastically sturdy. Even their buildings were seemingly indestructible. Many are still in use today, having been purchased by outside organizations following the demise of the various Shaker settlements. The buildings are used for schools, museums, state institutions, Catholic orders, and private residences, and most of them are in remarkably good condition, despite their age.

Their hoped-for utopia failed to materialize, yet the Shakers were successful in eliminating many of the social problems that plagued society at large. Poverty and unemployment, crime and delinquency, alcoholism and drug addiction—all were absent in the United Society. This was no small accomplishment, surely, since American society is still beset by these same problems. The point is that the Shakers were able to demonstrate to the world that communal living and separatism could be made to work.

Another contribution of current significance was their insistence on equal treatment for all members. Old, young, rich, poor, black, white, native-born, foreign-born—nobody felt left out in Shakerdom. All were treated as equals. And if this practice was not followed in the larger society, the latter at least had the benefit of a working example.

The Believers were also able to demonstrate the combined traits of courage and devotion, an amalgam that must have perplexed many of those on the outside. For despite long and harsh treatment, the followers of Ann Lee never once faltered in their beliefs. In the end, it was the outsiders who gave up and stopped the persecution.

Finally, of course, the United Society demonstrated to the world at large the magnitude of their self-restraint. As the contents of the present volume amply attest, America has seen any number of groups with unusual marital and sexual practices. But for an entire organization to abstain from sex on a permanent basis was all but incomprehensible to outsiders. Yet the Shakers not only abstained but gloried in the abstention. As they were fond of proclaiming, "He who conquereth himself is greater than he who conquereth a city."

All things considered, the United Society of Believers in Christ's Second Appearing added a new and interesting dimension to American culture. There has never been another group like them. If a society is

---

[28]Daniel W. Patterson, *The Shaker Spiritual* (Princeton: Princeton University Press, 1979).

enriched by its cultural diversity, then we must give the Shakers a strong plus for their contribution. Whether they can continue as a viable group will be discussed in the following section. But if they do not—a very real possibility—it is probable that we shall never see their likes again.

The Present Scene

What is the present status of the United Society of Believers in Christ's Second Appearing? Are they surviving? Growing? Are new members still being accepted? Or is it too late for a spiritual and secular resurgence?

In a physical sense, there is no doubt that the Society survives today. Several settlements remain, with dozens of buildings. Both buildings and furnishings are in excellent condition. Most of these settlements, however (Hancock, Massachusetts; Pleasant Hill, Kentucky; Mount Lebanon, New York; Canterbury, New Hampshire) are neither run nor maintained by Believers. They are actually *former* settlements, and are maintained by historical societies.

Nevertheless, readers will be interested to learn that, in spite of monumental odds, one "family" of Shakers still exists—at Sabbathday Lake, Maine. There are nine members, seven women and two men. (There are also two Shaker women who live at the Canterbury, New Hampshire, museum.) Predictably, most of the members are quite elderly, though several of the Sabbathday Lake group are under forty.[29]

It is difficult to characterize the present-day Sabbathday Lake community. On the one hand, the buildings and grounds are in splendid condition. New members are invited to "try the life," and one individual began a Novitiate as recently as mid-1989. Furthermore, in recent years the Society has prepared and transported weekly shipments of food to Friendship House, a shelter for the homeless in Portland, twenty miles away.[30]

On the other hand, rather obviously, membership—numerically speaking—is precarious. Since the mid-1950s, a mere handful of applicants have been accepted, and not all of these have remained. The *Shaker Quarterly* has not been published for some time.

While they do maintain a small charitable operation, the Sabbathday Lake group is not really a functional society. Indeed, their principal *raison d'etre* is tourism, with thousands of visitors taking the guided

---

[29]Current figures are based on correspondence with Leonard L. Brooks, Director of the Sabbathday Lake Shaker Museum and Library, during the summer of 1989.

[30]Cynthia Bourgeaul, "Shaker Mission to Portland," *Down East* (December 1988) pp. 9–10.

tour every year. In brief, with a seeming lack of function and only a trickle of new members, prospects for a revival do not appear to be overly bright.

What the future actually holds, of course, no one can say. Only time will tell whether the United Society of Believers in Christ's Second Appearing will indeed die out—after more than two hundred remarkable years. Members themselves, however, seem to have little doubt about their survival. They believe that prospects for Shakerism, by definition, are bright. Sister Mildred Barker, leader of the Sabbathday Lake group prior to her death in 1990, proclaimed that "It is God's work, and God will take care of it."

SELECTED READINGS

Ald, Roy. *The Youth Communes*. New York: Tower Publications, 1971.

Andrews, Edward. *The People Called Shakers*. New York: Oxford University Press, 1953.

Brewer, Priscilla J. *Shaker Communities, Shaker Lives*. Hanover: University Press of New England, 1986.

Desroche, Henri. *The American Shakers: From Neo-Christianity to Presocialism*. Amherst: University of Massachusetts Press, 1971.

Donegan, Frank. "Shaker Chic," *Americana*, 16 (January/February 1989): 66.

Foster, Lawrence. *Religion and Sexuality: Three American Communal Experiments of the Nineteenth Century*. New York: Oxford University Press, 1981.

Gross, Harriet, and Sussman, Marvin, eds. "Alternatives to Traditional Family Living," Special Issue of *Marriage and Family Review*, 5, No. 2 (Summer 1982).

Hayden, Delores. *Seven American Utopias: The Architecture of Communitarian Socialism, 1790–1975*. Cambridge, MA: MIT Press, 1976.

Johnson, Theodore E. "The Diary of a Maine Shaker Boy: Delmer Wilson." *The Shaker Quarterly*, 8 (Spring 1968): 3–22.

Kanter, Rosabeth Moss. *Commitment and Community: Communes and Utopias in Sociological Perspective*. Cambridge, MA: Harvard University Press, 1973.

Kolken, Diana van. *Introducing the Shakers*. Bowling Green, Ohio: Gabriel's Horn Publishing Co., 1985.

Mac-Hir Hutton, Daniel. *Old Shakertown and the Shakers*. Rev. ed. Harrodsburg, Kentucky: Harrodsburg Herald Press, 1987.

Matthaei, Julie A. *An Economic History of Women in America: Women's Work, the Sexual Division of Labor, and the Development of Capitalism*. New York: Schocken Books, 1982.

Melcher, Marguerite Fellows. *The Shaker Adventure*. Cleveland: Western Reserve Press, 1968.

Melton, J. Gordon. *The Encyclopedia of American Religions*. 2 vols. Wilmington, NC: Consortium Books, 1979.

Mindel, Charles, and Habenstein, Robert. *Ethnic Families in America*. New York: Elsevier, 1983.

Muncy, Raymond L. *Sex and Marriage in Utopian Communities*. Bloomington: Indiana University Press, 1973.

Neal, Julia. *The Kentucky Shakers*. Lexington: Kentucky University Press, 1977.

Newman, Cathy. "The Shakers' Brief Eternity." *National Geographic* (September 1989).

Nordhoff, Charles. *The Communistic Societies of the United States*. New York: Dover, 1966.

Patterson, Daniel W. *The Shaker Spiritual*. Princeton: Princeton University Press, 1979.

Pike, Kermit J. *A Guide to Shaker Manuscripts in the Library of the Western Reserve Historical Society*. Cleveland: Western Reserve Historical Society, 1974.

Richmond, Mary L. *Shaker Literature: A Bibliography*, 2 vols. Hanover, NH: University Press of New England, 1977.

Scott, Donald, and Wishy, Bernard, eds. *America's Families: A Documentary History*. New York: Harper & Row, 1982.

Wagner, Jon, ed. *Sex Roles in Contemporary American Communes*. Bloomington: Indiana University Press, 1982.

Whitworth, John. *God's Blueprints: A Sociological Study of Three Utopian Sects*. London and Boston: Routledge & Kegan Paul, 1975.

Zablocki, Benjamin. *The Joyful Community*. Baltimore: Penguin Books, 1971; Chicago: University of Chicago Press, 1980.

CHAPTER FIVE

THE HASIDIM

Emma Lazarus, the Jewish poet, wrote these words engraved on the pedestal of the Statue of Liberty:

> Give me your tired, your poor,
> Your huddled masses yearning to breathe free
> The wretched refuse of your teeming shore,
> Send these, the homeless, tempest-tossed, to me;
> I lift my lamp beside the golden door.

And the immigrants came, from every part of the world, bringing with them unique ethnic identities and established cultural patterns. Few cities in the world are as cosmopolitan as New York City. In the years since the great mass migrations to the United States, through "diffusion"—a type of cultural exchange—a local character has emerged, often identifiable as a "New Yorker."

One group of late arrivals, however, the Hasidic Jews—most of whom arrived after World War II—show no signs of assimilation with the larger community. Life in the Williamsburg, Boro Park, and Crown Heights districts of Brooklyn and in the New Square Community of Rockland County is, for nearly 200,000 Hasidic Jews, much as it was in their communities of Eastern and Central Europe two hundred years ago.*

Hasidim are easy to spot on the streets of New York. The men, in their traditional dark hats and suits, all with white shirts, wear their clothing like uniforms. Hasidim (literally, "pious ones") have resisted assimila-

---

*Hasidim constitute a small fraction of Orthodox Jewry. Orthodox Jews adhere strictly to ancient law and tradition. They reject the argument of Reform Jews that the Bible and other Jewish writings contain historically and culturally conditioned interpretations of Jewish law that may be legitimately abandoned.

The focus of this chapter is on the beliefs and life-styles of Hasidic Jews. Space precludes in-depth comparisons between Hasidim and other branches of Judaism.

Hasidim are often referred to as ultraconservative Orthodox Jews. While there is a shared tradition and argot (special language) between Hasidim and other branches of Judaism, Hasidim emphasize emotional worship, rejection of traditional Talmudic scholarship, mysticism, reincarnation from Saints, divine ordination, the concept of a human soul, withdrawal from the world, proselytizing—not generally encouraged by Jews—and rejection of secular education. These topics are expatiated in this chapter.

tion by drawing cultural boundaries between themselves and the rest of society. By adhering to a strict dress code, maintaining the Yiddish language, and resisting anglicization of their names, they make the statement: We are Jews and proud of it!

To understand the Hasidim and the microcosm they have created within the borders of one of the world's busiest cities, it is necessary to survey the group's history.

Rabbi Israel Baal Shem Tov—the Besht

During the 1740s and 1750s in Podolia, a southeastern province of Poland, a charismatic rabbi, Israel Baal Shem Tov, began teaching that men, through inner piety and sincerity, could receive redemption from God. The Besht (an acronym for Baal Shem Tov) deemphasized Talmudic scholarship in favor of an emotional relationship with God that all religious men, even the uneducated, could achieve. Baal Shem Tov taught that God's love could be found in the outpouring of the soul in prayer, rather than through intellectual powers. Women were not expected to have the same emotional intensity as men in their relationship with God.

During the Besht's lifetime, many Jews in the eastern provinces of Poland had been victims of pogroms, civil wars, peasant revolts, and Cossack raids. Most of these Jews had difficulty obeying the *mitzvahs* (divine commandments). "They toiled from early morning until nightfall in the fields, in their homes or on the streets, and were so burdened by their search for daily bread that they had little time to taste the sweetness of the Lord in prayer or in the study of His Torah."[1]

The *misnagdim* (rabbinical scholars of the day) did not take into account the plight of the masses, and were unrelenting in their reproach, constantly upbraiding them for minor sins. It is little wonder that the Besht, who taught that singing, dancing, and vibrant prayer outweighed slight transgressions, found a following. At the time of his death in 1760, it is estimated that he had 10,000 followers.

Rabbi Dov Baer

Dov Baer, a disciple of the Besht, and his successor, was a gifted Talmudic scholar. Physically frail, he did not travel among the people as the

---

[1] Mendel Bodek and Samuel H. Dresner, " 'Devekut'—The Essence of Hasidism," *Judaism: A Quarterly Journal* 36, (Winter 1987), p. 104.

Besht had done. But from his home in central Poland, Dov Baer attracted many distinguished, and often wealthy, religious intellectuals, and the movement spread.

Rabbi Dov Baer was successful in systematizing the teachings of the Besht and synthesizing them with sixteenth-century cabalist philosophy. Cabalism (Jewish mysticism) is inextricably tied to the Hasidic belief system. For example, Orthodox Jews have always believed that the 613 *mitzvahs* are associated with the solar system and the human body. The 365 prohibitive commandments (thou shalt nots) are associated with the days of the year, and the 248 positive commandments (thou shalts) are associated with the parts of the human body.

Cabalists believed the *mitzvahs* were linked to the human soul as well. Consequently, following any specific commandment has a positive effect on the solar system, the body, the soul, or any combination of the three, while a violation of the law has a negative effect on the corresponding entity or entities.

During the lifetime of the Besht, established Jewish authorities did little to curb the Hasidic movement, other than to denounce its teachings as heretical. Talmudic scholars thought the movement would die with the death of its founder. As Hasidism grew under the leadership of Dov Baer, however, the concern of the entrenched rabbinate increased. In 1772, the year Dov Baer died, rabbinical authorities placed a ban on Hasidism. In her book, *Holy Days*, Harris reprinted the following letter circulated by the *misnagdim:*

> (The Hasidim) meet together in separate groups and deviate in their prayers from the text valid for the whole people. . . . They are the same who in the middle of . . . prayer, interject obnoxious alien words (that is, Yiddish) in a loud voice, conduct themselves like madmen, and explain their behavior by saying that in their thoughts they soar in the most far-off worlds. . . .
>
> The study of Torah is neglected by them entirely and they do not hesitate constantly to emphasize that one should devote oneself as little as possible to learning and not grieve too much over a sin committed. . . . Every day is for them a holiday. . . . When they pray according to falsified texts they raise such a din that the walls quake. . . . And they turn over like wheels, with the head below and the legs above. . . .[2]

The term "Holy Roller" has always been applied to emotional Protestant sects. It is apparent, however, that the established rabbinate in Europe thought of Hasidim as Jewish Holy Rollers.

---

[2]Lis Harris, *Holy Days: The World of a Hasidic Family* (New York: Summit Books, 1985), p. 86–7.

The Tzaddikim

After the death of Dov Baer, the Hasidim were unable to choose a successor. Hundreds of *tzaddikim* (righteous men), followers of the Besht and Dov Baer, moved to every part of Eastern Europe and proceeded to establish communities. The *tzaddikim* were accorded the title *rebbe* (master)— not to be confused with the title *rabbi*, a lesser master or teacher. A *rebbe* assumed the name of his village. For example, the *rebbe* from Lubavitch, Russia, became the Lubavitcher Rebbe; the *rebbe* from Belz in Galicia became known as the Belzer Rebbe.

These *rebbes* were believed to have special powers, and their congregations grew. Seeking divine intervention, troubled Jews looked to them on all matters of importance. Hasidic legends are rife with accounts of miracles associated with or performed by these holy men. A letter exists in the Besht's own hand, written in 1750, describing how his soul encountered the Messiah while on a journey to heaven. Many of the *rebbes* strengthened their authority by claiming reincarnation from Jewish saints.

On one Yom Kippur, an Apter Rebbe told his flock that he had been a high priest in Jerusalem in a previous life. The followers of a Stoliner Rebbe were convinced that the soul of King David had passed to their leader. A Satmarer Rebbe told an audience that he had participated in the Exodus and saw the tablets destroyed. He further astounded his followers by announcing that in his third reincarnation he had, in 586 B.C., seen the Temple of Jerusalem destroyed. When asked if he had been the prophet Jeremiah, he did not issue a denial.

Because *rebbes* are thought to possess a higher soul than ordinary men, it is also believed they possess "holy seed." This concept of a hereditary, holy gift allows a *rebbe* to pass his status on to a son. If a *rebbe* is without a son or his son is deemed unsuitable for leadership, the community will choose a son-in-law, nephew, or close disciple as *rebbe* on the death of the elder *rebbe*.

Raphael Mahler writes that with *tzaddikism*, the nature of Hasidism changed:

> What had begun as a prehumanist regeneration of religion in the form of a democratic folk religion, developed towards a mass religion permeated with magic, superstition, and idolatrous adulation of the all-powerful *Tzaddik*, the "Eye of God" on earth. . . . Opposition to the misnagdim on the grounds that they held themselves above the people, was succeeded by worship of the *Tzaddikim*, who exercised unlimited power over their congregations to an extent never attained by even the most brilliant learned men. The doctrine that the rabbi's office was a sacred rank to be bequeathed from father to son, caused the number of *Tzaddik* dynasties to

multiply and branch out as fathers passed both their glory and their material assets on to their sons.[3]

The End in Europe—a Beginning in America

Hitler's final solution, ridding the world of "undesirables" such as Jews and Gypsies, decimated the Hasidic populations in Europe. After World War II, the countries of Western Europe, beset by the ravages of war, were unable to accommodate large numbers of refugees. The few small Hasidic enclaves that remain in Europe are in Belgium and England.

Remnants of the European communities had two clear choices following the war, Palestine or the United States. Palestine, still under British mandate, was rife with hostility. Most Hasidim had seen enough of death and destruction and chose resettlement in New York City, the largest Jewish population center in the non-Communist world.

The Hasidim who emigrated to the United States were not without misgivings. The *rebbes* and their flocks feared "assimilation"—a pattern of intergroup relations in which a minority group is absorbed into the majority population and eventually disappears as a distinct group. The United States was known to them as the great "melting pot," defined by historian Frederick Turner as a crucible in which immigrants were Americanized, liberated, and fused into a mixed race. Many Hasidim feared that the religious and political freedoms of the United States would finish the job that Hitler could not finish in the ovens of Auschwitz.

The Chosen People

Fundamental to all Jews is the belief that they are God's chosen people. The Torah (Divine Purpose) was given to them by God at Sinai because they, separate from the peoples of all other nations, had souls capable of bearing the burden. Acceptance of the Torah created an irrevocable covenant with God. Obeying the Torah would ultimately allow the Jews to reclaim the holy land, bless them with peace in this world, and eternal life in the next.

The ethnocentric attitude that they alone are capable of upholding the Torah solidifies the Hasidic belief that all other groups are inferior. The Yiddish term *goyim* (singular *goy*, adjective *goyish*) refers to all non-Jews. Anything immoral such as crime, sexual promiscuity, and drug use are

---

[3]Raphael Mahler, "A Marxist View of Hasidism," in *Social Foundations of Judaism*, eds. Calvin Goldscheider and Jacob Neusner. (Englewood Cliffs, NJ: Prentice-Hall, 1990), p. 80.

considered *goyish* problems, which the intrinsically superior Hasid must avoid.

Hasidim mistrust *goyim*, define them as contaminating, and avoid them whenever possible. Total avoidance, however, is impossible. Hasidim are dependent on non-Jews for jobs, use their professional services, and seek advantage with their politicians. Nevertheless, relationships rarely transcend the boundaries of defined necessity, and few real friendships develop between *goy* and Hasid. The *rebbe*, the family, the community are all that is important to Hasidim, and it is a simple matter to lock the *goyim* out of their lives.

The *Mitzvahs*   The 613 *mitzvahs*, Old Testament commandments, and laws subsequently developed from rabbinical interpretations of these commandments govern every aspect of Hasidic existence. Knowing and understanding these laws constitute, in the main, the whole of Hasidic scholarship. Marriage, business practices, property rights, sexual conduct, even minutia such as not wearing cloth made of a linen and wool blend are covered by the *mitzvahs*. The *mitzvahs* are never questioned; they were God-sent, not man made. Hasidim are tradition bound, and this bondage has led to a body of ritual and ceremony so rich that only a small portion of the whole can be covered in the present account.

The Shabbes   Early Friday afternoons, the sidewalks of New York's Hasidic communities are filled with women as they search the *kosher* (ritually correct) shops for the foods they will serve on the Shabbes (Sabbath). By late afternoon the women are gone, home preparing the Shabbes meals in advance, so they too can observe the days of rest and worship. Later in the afternoon the streets fill with Hasidic men, fresh from a *mikvah* (ritual bath), bent on being home before sundown, the beginning of Shabbes. Hasidim are expected to be in their homes, or if visiting, in their host's home, in time to observe Shabbes traditions. If away from home on a Friday, a good Hasid will allow plenty of time for travel, rather than risk violating the rule.

Harris describes prohibitions against work on the Shabbes "mind-boggling," and lists only a few of the "don'ts" that must be observed:

> . . . cooking; baking; washing laundry; chopping; knitting; crocheting; sewing; embroidering; pasting; drawing; painting; typing; writing; fishing; hunting; cutting hair (or cutting anything else, with the exception of food); building or repairing anything; gardening; carrying or pushing anything further than six feet in public; riding in cars, planes, trains, or buses; boating; buying or selling; horseback riding; playing a musical instrument; switching on an electrical apparatus. . . . [4] (Most Hasidic families cover the

[4]Harris, *Holy Days*, p. 63–4.

important light switches in their homes to prevent someone from acciden-
tally turning them off.)

Shabbes meals are important ritual events, steeped in tradition. Before
each of the three Shabbes meals (Friday evening, Saturday morning, and
Saturday just before dusk), the head of the household reads prayers and
performs the *kiddush* ceremony—a special prayer of sanctification. The
meals are as lavish as the household can afford, and the evening meal is
replete with a variety of liquors, wines, and sometimes beer. Singing and
storytelling, the recounting of religious wisdom and martyrdom, often
associated with a *rebbe,* are the highlights of Shabbes evenings.

The three Shabbes meals are repeated at the *shul* (synagogue) at the
rebbe's tish (table), where the men meet, pray ecstatically, and share
sustenance with their *rebbe.* Close relatives, worthy disciples (usually
older men), and wealthy benefactors are seated at the table with the
master. Behind the table are younger men and boys, sometimes two
hundred to three hundred deep, trying to squeeze as close to the *rebbe* as
they can. The *rebbe's* prayers are thought to have priority in heaven, and
if a Hasid's prayers are said near the *rebbe,* those prayers might reach
heaven with his.

The meal is served in courses: soup, fish, meat or chicken with vegetables, and a fruit compote. The *rebbe* takes a portion of each course before
it is passed to the seated men at his table. The meal is a symbolic sharing
in that the men, expected to have eaten their fill at home, take very small
portions of each course. After those at the table are served, the dishes
are passed back to the congregants. It is believed that the holy spirit of
the *rebbe* is passed through his food, and the assembled scramble for a
share of each course, if only for crumbs.

The Shabbes ends an hour after sundown on Saturday. To elevate the
spirits of the family, saddened at the passing of God's special days, a
plaited candle is lit, wine is drunk, a spice box is passed, and a benedic-
tion said.

Holidays   Every day is a holy day for the Hasidic Jew. Men are expected
to pray spontaneously, publicly, every day. The center of activity in every
Hasidic community is the Bes Hamedresh, a place for prayer and religious studies that contains a library and Torah scrolls. Each morning
Hasidic men meet to pray at the Bes Hamedresh. Rocking from the heels
to the balls of his feet, each man has his unique prayer style, similar to
but different from others. The oxymoron "trained-spontaneity" may be
applicable, as the men exhibit consistent prayer habits from day to day.

There are no major Hasidic holidays, only days of special observance.
It is as important to keep the *mitzvahs* of everyday living as it is to
observe holiday commandments. But Hasidim do look forward with

excitement to certain holidays and to the traditions associated with them.

Rosh Hashanah, the Day of Judgment, and Yom Kippur, the Day of Atonement, are celebrated from mid-September to early October. These holidays are sometimes called the Days of Awe; awesome because it is a period when God judges all of humanity. It is believed that God opens three books on Rosh Hashanah: the book of the righteous, the book of the wicked, and the book of those in between. Those deemed righteous will be granted a good future life, the wicked are condemned to death, and for those in between, judgment is deferred until Yom Kippur. The days between Rosh Hashanah and Yom Kippur are meant for prayer and soul cleansing before God makes his final judgment.

Bar Mitzvah: **A Rite of Passage**   A "rite of passage" is community recognition that an individual has moved from one stage of life to another. In the case of older people, for example, a retirement party has come to signal the end of regular employment and the entrance into a life-style with a different set of roles and expectations for the retiree.

Age thirteen denotes an important "rite of passage" for the Jewish male. In this instance, *bar mitzvah* signals the end of childhood and the beginning of manhood. With *bar mitzvah*, a boy becomes fully a man of Israel, with all the expectations associated with a man of that status. Minor violations of the law, sometimes winked at before *bar mitzvah*, are no longer appropriate. Serious *davening* (prayer) and strict adherence to Torah and scholarship are expected of an adult.

Hasidic celebrations of *bar mitzvah*, perhaps surprisingly, are usually not as elaborate as those of other Jews. At his *bar mitzvah*, a boy is given his *tefillin*—two leather cases, containing verses from Exodus and Deuteronomy, which are strapped to the left arm and forehead during the morning prayer. For most Hasidim, *bar mitzvah* is a family celebration, which does not require a rented hall, a caterer, and large outlays of cash.

Education

A Hasidic boy's religious socialization begins in earnest during the months preceding his third birthday. On that day the *rebbe* gives the boy his first haircut, using a pair of gold scissors. All the child's hair is cut except for the *peyes* (sidelocks), which he will wear for the rest of his life. The *rebbe* then questions the child, asking if he knows his "aleph-bes" (ABCs). The child, coached for months by his father, nods, and after the *rebbe* prompts, "aleph," the child completes the alphabet. To the cheers of family and friends, the *rebbe* pronounces the boy ready for learning.

Cakes and whiskey are passed around, and the traditional toast *L'chaim* (to life) is extended to everyone.

Hasidim recognize that English is important to group survival within the context of the larger culture, but it is not taught to children until they are deemed ready for it—after Yiddish is mastered. In many homes, nursery schools, and kindergartens, only Yiddish is spoken. Children are reprimanded for using English words and phrases that creep into their vocabularies and are told to speak only *sheyna Yiddish* (beautiful Yiddish). A common language, like common dress, is an important factor in separating the Hasidic "us" from the rest of the world "them."

This does not mean that Hasidim are unwilling to borrow educational practices from the larger culture, when viewed as appropriate. Robert Kamen, in his study of the educational system in the Bobover community, noted this interesting adaptation:

> American nursery rhymes [are used], such as "Twinkle, twinkle little star," as vehicles for moral and ethical lessons. The songs, of course, are translated into Yiddish and key words are changed to correspond with the intended theme. For instance, the last line of "Twinkle, twinkle," will be sung, "If you say Shema each day everything will be okay." The Shema is a fundamental prayer recited in the morning and evening. . . .[5]

In Europe, girls received no formal education beyond the primary grades. They were trained at home, by their mothers' sides, to become wives and homemakers. Boys could attend *yeshivas* (rabbinical seminaries), but enrollment in these institutions was restricted to the sons of the wealthy who could afford to pay their own way, and to a few gifted youngsters who could be supported by the community.

In the United States, law generally requires education until a boy or girl is sixteen years old. The law does not require that the sexes receive the same education, however. Children are segregated by sex in Hasidic schools from pre-kindergarten through high school. Hasidic boys are expected to uphold the Torah and to become religious scholars. Girls are expected to know the Bible, dietary laws, and the significance of holidays. Heavy scholarship is not expected of them.

In order to receive funding from municipal, state, and federal agencies, Hasidim have had to incorporate secular education, through the twelfth grade, into their curricula. Offerings such as mathematics, science, history, and geography are referred to as English studies and are taught only in the afternoon sessions. Parents and children alike define most English studies as a waste of time. Kamen got this typical response from a fourteen-year-old Bobover boy:

[5]Robert Mark Kamen, *Growing Up Hasidic*, (New York: AMS Press, 1985), p. 48.

Learning English and division, subtraction, addition. These things are important. You need to know these things. But theories? Triangles? Protractors? History? What am I going to do with such things? We're not public school guys. We get up at six to learn two hours before eating even! It's crazy to think we have so much strength to sit and learn Torah all day and then this. I'm a Hasid; what I have to know I know from Torah and the Rebbe. For a job I'll need English and math, but not the other things they make you learn. It's useless.[6]

By the time a boy is fifteen, he follows a strict routine: he meets with fellow students at the *yeshiva* at a little after six in the morning. After two hours of study he goes to the *mikvah* and washes up before prayers. Following breakfast in the *yeshiva* dining hall, serious studies and lectures begin. After lunch, the English courses are taught. After supper at home, the boy returns to the *yeshiva* for several more hours of religious study with his peers. An adolescent's learning is taken seriously by his parents. The youngster who spends more time at home with his family than at the *yeshiva* is suspect, and such behavior reflects poorly on the family.

The Hasidic socialization process is powerful and the norms of the community are thoroughly internalized. Few young men resent the protracted hours spent studying religious books and in prayer. In fact, most are eager to accept the community-defined need for rigorous religious training.

The first two grades in Hasidic schools are "age-graded," similar to most American schools. Beyond the second year, however, placement depends on achievement. Boys who show exceptional comprehension of Torah are placed with older students. Those who do not are placed with groups who share like educational development. Placement by ability rather than age does not appear to be socially or emotionally disruptive to the Hasidic child.

Kamen suggests that the Hasidic curriculum is less threatening than that taught in the public schools because of the nature of the subject matter, the Torah:

> Every Sabbath, a different section of Torah is recited. . . . When the last section is read [at the end of the year], . . . the reading begins anew on the following Sabbath. . . . What differentiates one group from another is the depth of commentary on a particular parsha (weekly section), rather than the introduction of continuously new subject matter. The same topics appear year after year, from the first grade on. Only emphases and interpretations vary, and these according to teacher and individual student.[7]

[6]Ibid., p. 112.
[7]Ibid., p. 56–7.

Emphasis in the *yeshiva* is on effort, not result. A pious student with academic limitations who tries his best is accorded higher status than an able student who fails to work to the maximum of his capabilities. Conformity to *yeshiva* rules and an appropriate level of piety are effected through "informal social control." A boy's peers are quick to criticize and bring into line a fellow student who is not conforming to expectations. But conformity is not all that is expected—it must be conformity with conviction.

Courtship and Marriage

Hasidic men usually marry in their early twenties, women in their late teens. It is common for young men to display a nonchalance toward courting, contending that they still have much Talmudic learning to complete. Couples may meet in a variety of ways, and anyone can act as a *shadchen* (matchmaker). Matches are usually suggested by a young man's father, close friend, or trusted rabbi, however. If a match outside the community is recommended, the girl will ordinarily be from one that shares the worldview of the boy's community. Often the *shadchen* will surprise the young man by suggesting a girl that the boy has known for years—but one that he had never thought of as a potential marriage partner.

Men and women are expected to be chaste prior to marriage, and premarital sexual activity is probably uncommon. Boys and girls do not date as they do in the larger society. After the *shadchen* suggests a partner, the parents meet and arrange a get-together between the couple. The boy arrives at the girl's home with his parents. The parents then leave the couple alone to talk about whatever they wish, usually for not more than an hour. Often a decision is made after the first date. If, after three such meetings, no decision has been made, there is usually no further interaction. All parties involved, boy, girl, and parents, must agree to the marriage. Should an agreement be reached, the parents may agree to support the couple while the young man continues his Talmudic training.

Following the marriage agreement, the young man goes to the *rebbe* with a petition and asks his blessing. Few such petitions are denied, and a marriage date is set, usually within a few months of the agreement. Couples are not allowed to meet during the betrothal period, and strict families will not even tolerate telephone conversations between the betrothed.

Hasidic weddings are festive occasions. The ceremony itself is performed under a *huppa* (marriage canopy). The bride in her white gown is led into the wedding hall, where she circles the groom seven times.

Bride and groom then sip from a silver goblet offered by the rabbi performing the ceremony. After reciting the wedding rite, the groom
smashes a wineglass on the floor. Following the ceremony, the couple
dine alone, consummating the marriage.

When they return to the wedding hall, two parties are in progress,
one for the men, one for the women; the sexes never mingle. Both
parties are lively. The men sing loudly, and dance vigorously into the
night. The bride is the star of her party, and all the women want a dance
with her. Near evening's end, the bride is brought into the men's portion
of the hall where she dances with close male relatives before dancing
with her husband. The dancers each hold to the end of a handkerchief; a
Hasidic man may touch no woman other than his wife.

Marriage denotes full participation into Hasidic community life. For
the first year, the couple are considered newlyweds, and the husband is
expected to spend all his time with his wife, except for hours spent at
work, in Torah study, or in prayer.

Divorce is possible but extremely uncommon in Hasidic communities.
The *mitzvahs* command that a wife bear her husband at least one son and
one daughter within the first ten years of marriage. Failure to produce
offspring is demeaning to a family, but divorce even on those grounds is
almost unheard of. Those who do divorce remarry quickly, and the few
single-person households that exist are usually those of the widowed
elderly.

Sexual Norms

Sexual norms are clearly spelled out in the *mitzvahs* and in rabbinical
interpretations of the *mitzvahs*. That the sexes may not touch is carried to
an extent that outsiders consider extreme. For example, if a woman
purchases an item at a market from a male clerk, she will lay her money
next to the purchase. The clerk then puts her change on the counter, and
their hands never touch. Hasidim feel uncomfortable sitting next to the
opposite sex on a bus or subway. Even public displays of affection between husband and wife—a hug or kiss—are very uncommon.

To keep from arousing men, Hasidic women wear dresses with high
collars, sleeves below the elbow, and skirt hems below the knees. A
woman may not sing in front of a man; the lips and mouth of a woman
are considered highly erotic. Men may sing in front of women, however;
women, the more spiritual sex, are not prone to erotic stimulation.
Women clip their hair at marriage and cover the stubble with a wig or
kerchief; natural hair is considered too erotic for the average man to bear.

Conduct during a woman's menstrual flow and for seven days after is
clearly spelled out in Jewish law. As previously noted, a man may touch

no woman other than his wife, and he may not even touch his wife during this period. Any object passed between the two must be set down first before it is picked up by the other. The couple must sleep in separate beds until the woman, her cycle completed, has cleansed herself in a *mikvah*.

If the community learns that a child has been conceived in a period after menstruation has begun and before the ritual ablutions have been performed, it is considered the equivalent of a bastard, and the offspring will not be permitted to marry an Orthodox Jew. There is little discussion of sex in the community, and many women find it embarrassing to be seen at a *mikvah*. Everyone knows she is there to make herself sexually acceptable.

Even the act of sexual intercourse is subject to religious proscriptions. A man must not look at a woman's sex organs, so intercourse is restricted to the night hours with the lights off. Men are encouraged to rise above animal instincts, and are urged to think of the Torah or the teachings of a religious wise man during the act. With all this in mind, he must remember not to lose his *yarmulke* (skullcap); by law his head must be covered at all times.

A Hasidic man is not permitted to use prophylactic devices for any reason. A woman may, with the permission of a rabbi, if she can provide evidence that childbearing would adversely affect her health. Rabbinical permission is not given unless serious cause is shown, and some rabbis will not acquiesce under any circumstances. A less effective alternative for women who wish to avoid pregnancy is to wait until after the peak time for conception has past before performing ablutions, in that way extending the period her husband may not touch her. Most women who wish to avoid pregnancies, however, seek out a sympathetic rabbi.

The Role of Women

Socialization does not turn out identical people like pennies cast from a die. Nevertheless, most Hasidic women (like Mormon women, Amish women, Gypsy women, and women in the Jehovah's Witnesses) accept roles that their counterparts in the larger society often define as second class. When asked about the religious proscriptions that seemingly relegate them to inferior roles, Hasidic women claim they are equal to men in the eyes of God, and the earthly roles of the sexes are part of his plan.

During their morning prayers, Hasidic men thank God that they were not born women, ostensibly because women are excused from performing many Torah duties. For example, women are not obligated to teach the Torah, pray daily outside the home, or read the morning prayer. It is argued that men, who are innately less spiritual than women and more exposed to contaminating other-worldly influences, need more time in prayer and Torah study.

In reality, Hasidic men are extremely protective of their position in relationship to the Torah. Recently, in Jerusalem, forty or so women attempted to pray at the wailing wall, considered the holiest site in Judaism. The women were attacked by a mob of angry Hasidic men. The following report appeared in the *New York Times:*

> [The] women infuriated the men by trying to hold morning prayers while reading from the Torah and wearing prayer shawls. Orthodox Jewish men insist that women are forbidden even to carry a Torah scroll, and only males have the right to don the shawls.
>
> Several women were knocked to the ground and one suffered a gash on her neck when an Hasidic man threw a heavy metal chair at the heads of the praying women. . . . The worshipping women were forced to flee before finishing their prayers when they were overcome by tear gas fired at the Orthodox men by police.
>
> "I keep coming back," said Susan Kahn, who runs a women's Torah school in Jerusalem. "I believe that women have the right to express themselves spiritually at the wall. Men, Hasidic men, do not own the wall."[8]

The dominant obligations of women are maintaining a *kosher* home and bearing children. There is no women's prayer thanking God that they were not born men. Physical separation and rules against touching are constant reminders that different worlds exist for Hasidic men and women.

Hasidim are segregated by sex at all public events, the men usually accorded the better facilities. Harris described a meeting she attended held at a Hasidic synagogue:

> There were about four thousand people crammed into the synagogue—a space that, estimating generously, ought to have comfortably sheltered two thousand. About a third of those present were women, but the area consigned to them seemed hardly large enough to contain half that number. To enter a women's gallery—two windowless, airless balconies blocked off from the men's section by a black Plexiglas panel—one simply allowed oneself to be swept forward by a tidal wave of female[s] . . . .[9]

One of the few occasions when women are permitted on the same floor and in the same section of the synagogue as men is the circumcision ceremony. Circumcision is viewed as a sign of God's covenant with Abraham, and all male children are circumcised on the eighth day after birth, by the *rebbe* in front of the congregation. The operation is begun by

---

[8]"Hasidim Attack Women at Prayers," *New York Times*, March 21, 1989.
[9]Harris, *Holy Days*, p. 122.

a *mohel* (professional circumciser) who prepares both baby and surgical instruments for the rite. After the *rebbe* performs the operation, the *mohel* binds the wound. A few days later, he checks the child to be certain there is no infection. Removed from a clinical setting, the rite of circumcision further underscores the importance of being male. Mothers, along with female relatives and friends, must stand behind the men during the ceremony.

Hasidim, like everyone else in the United States, are subject to the laws of the land. It is rare, however, to see a Hasid in an American court of law. Hasidim have their own rabbinical courts, composed of one or more rabbis, which handle internal community affairs.

Based on the Torah, women have property rights equal to men. They may enter into contracts just as men do, and litigate in cases for damages. Women's testimony is often disqualified in religious courts however; not much credence is given to their abilities to get the facts straight, and in criminal prosecutions, the testimony of a woman is not deemed sufficient grounds to obtain a conviction.

Employment

Most boys, long before the twelfth year of *yeshiva*, drop English studies to concentrate on religion. What Hasidic boy would want to arrive two hours later than his peers to a Torah study session carrying an American history text or calculator? It is surprising that even a few Hasidic boys graduate from high school. Fewer still go on to college even though, as residents of New York City, they are eligible to attend tuition-free universities. Hasidim do not object to college subjects such as business, mathematics, physics, or chemistry, but university accreditation also requires exposure to contaminating subjects such as sociology and psychology—subjects that often contradict the teachings of the community.

Yeshiva training, essentially, is relatively ineffective training for anything but work within the Hasidic community. And that is precisely where young Hasidim want to work. In his study of Hasidic males, Kamen found that nearly 75 percent of the boys indicated preferences for positions such as *yeshiva* teacher or working for the *rebbe*. Only a privileged few are offered such positions, and most must find work elsewhere.

Some become self-employed as wholesalers or retailers within the community, catering to needs peculiar to the Hasidim. These would include the preparation of *kosher* foods, tailoring, wig-making, and the manufacture of religious items. Other young men become self-employed in service professions such as plumbing and heating. It should be noted, however, that nothing in the *yeshiva* curriculum prepares a young Hasid for self-employment, and most young men who enter business professions do so because their fathers have established businesses.

The majority of Hasidim must find work outside of the community, and fields of opportunity are limited. Since Shabbes begins on Friday at dusk, Hasidim can only work half-days on Fridays during the winter months. Sunday is not part of the Shabbes, but the *goyim* usually close their businesses on Sundays. In addition, not only do Hasidim observe the major Jewish holidays, they require time off to observe a variety of minor holidays and celebrations. Piety, not occupation, is the "key status" of the Hasid. Because they work to live, not live to work, Hasidim have jobs, not careers.

Two major New York industries, the diamond industry and the garment industry, have accommodated the Hasidim and their schedules. The diamond exchange, in Manhattan, provides work for the Hasidim at every level, from importers to cutters to polishers to janitors. Yellow busses bearing the names of Hasidic congregations transport groups of workers to the city from their home communities. In the garment industry, Hasidim often work as pattern cutters and sewing-machine operators.

Before entering the world of work, a Hasid is expected to get permission from the *rebbe*. If the young man is entering a traditional field, the *rebbe*'s approval is perfunctory. Being a Hasid comes first, and the *rebbe*'s blessing is never given when a proposed job conflicts with Hasidic teachings, community life, or obstructs the observance of traditions.

Hasidic Problems

Welfare   Religious affiliation is not required on welfare applications, so it is impossible to know the exact number of Hasidim on welfare rolls. In the 1970s, as part of a documentary, CBS News featured a segment on the Hasidim entitled "The Poor Jews of New York." Because work cannot conflict with religious observances, Hasidic Jews often work part-time or at poor-paying jobs. This coupled with a high birthrate (Hasidim average 7.5 children per household)[10] entitles a great many families to welfare assistance. It is usually subsidy welfare as opposed to total welfare. Food stamps are commonly used in *kosher* shops; and hospitals and doctors serving the community expect that some share of the bill will be paid by the city, state, or federal government.

Like most groups with large numbers relying on assistance, Hasidim would rather earn their keep than be dependent on the government. Some of the self-help services instituted in Hasidic congregations in-

[10]Douglas Martin, "In Brooklyn, Hasidim Find Door of Hope," *New York Times,* March 8, 1989, p. A17, p. B1.

clude private community bus services, walk-in clinics, ambulance services, first-aid services, nursing services, summer camps for youth, employment agencies, and free loan services.

Many of the communities fund all or part of their educational system.
Nevertheless, a large proportion of the tax dollars paid the government
by the Hasidim are returned to them in some form of subsistence. It is
doubtful, given the structure of their educational system and time-
consuming religiosity, that this circumstance will change markedly in the
near future.

Mental Health   Pesach Tikvah (Door of Hope) in Brooklyn, is one of the
few mental health clinics that treat Hasidic patients. According to the
director, a rabbi, the rate of mental illness among Hasidim is likely lower
than in society in general. Because Hasidim connect mental illness to
sin, however, it is difficult for them to acknowledge or treat such problems when they arise. Psychotherapy is viewed, for the most part, as a
contaminating outside influence.

The rabbi director also disclosed that "parents can be seen walking
with [developmentally disabled] children late at night [to his clinic] to
avoid detection."[11] Hasidim fear that if mental illness or retardation is
diagnosed in one of their children, it will reflect negatively on all of their
children.

The rabbi feels that his clinic is playing a catch-up game. "We seem to
be re-inventing the wheel at a time when everybody else is in modern
automobiles."[12] He cited, as an example, a funeral oration he had recently performed for a young Hasid who had died of a drug overdose—
the first in Williamsburg. The rabbi dealt with the death openly and
honestly and asked those present at the funeral for compassion and
introspection. He received many anonymous phone calls. All said his
remarks were "very distasteful."

Anti-Hasidim   There is little question that anti-Hasidic sentiment exists
in some quarters of New York. Recently, for example, the management
of a Manhattan hotel near the diamond district was accused of racial
discrimination. A complaint lodged by the American Jewish Congress
contended that "the hotel . . . discriminated against Hasidim and other
Orthodox Jews because the way they dressed did not fit the hotel's
trendy image."[13]

A hotel employee alleged that Hasidim, who sometimes dropped by

---

[11]Ibid.
[12]Ibid.
[13]"Manhattan Hotel Called Biased against Hasidim." *New York Times,* March 9, 1989, p.
A16.

to visit and sip soft drinks, were told falsely that "public" accommodations were for guests only. Rooms at the hotel rent for about $190 a night, and a suite can cost more than $1,000. According to management, "the hotel was fashioned as a place for the sophisticated literary crowd to meet and mingle."[14]

Ironically, the hotel owner is Jewish.

Lubavitchers and Satmarers

Much of the variation within Hasidim is demonstrable in a brief survey of the Lubavitchers and Satmarers. In the many books and articles written about Hasidim—mostly produced by non-Hasidic Jews—the Lubavitchers, for the most part, seem to be accorded better treatment. Judaic scholar Arthur Cohen described the Satmarers as ". . . a paranoid extreme of Hasidic orthodoxy, rigorous in their sense of judgment and lacking in mercy."[15]

Photojournalist Philip Garvin wrote, "I learned quickly that there are significant differences among the groups. . . . [A] number of young Satmarer threatened me and tried to take away my cameras, and would have become more violent had I not retreated immediately. In the years of my work in Brooklyn, I never became fully accustomed to the aggressive nature of the Satmarer, and I photographed in Williamsburg only when I felt it was absolutely necessary."[16]

Criticism of Satmar Hasidism is directly related to the insular attitudes of the group. Life in the Satmar ghetto is much as it was in Hungary in the beginning of the century. No compromise is made with the Western world. The men wear their *peyes* so that they are clearly visible. Women crop their hair close to the scalp. The Satmar Rebbe admonishes his followers to keep every letter of the Torah, fearing that even the smallest divergence will lead successive generations to still further transgressions and, ultimately, to the demise of Hasidim.

Satmar children learn English at a later age than other Hasidim, and their orientation to the larger culture is much more limited. It is difficult for most Satmarers to communicate with those in the outside world, and, for most, employment opportunities are limited to factory work. The goal of the community is social isolation.

By contrast, at least in an external sense, the Lubavitcher congregation is the most Westernized of the Hasidic communities. The men wear their

[14]Ibid.

[15]Philip Garvin and Arthur A. Cohen, *A People Apart; Hasidism in America* (New York: Dutton, 1970), p. 30.

[16]Ibid., p. 9.

peyes shorter, sometimes tucked behind their ears or tied over their heads. There is much more color in their clothing, and no edict demands that they wear black only. Married women wear wigs, but do not crop their hair severely. Some families have a television—taboo by Satmar standards—allegedly to keep up with events in the outside world that might affect their community.

Lubavitcher children are expected to learn English, and secular studies are more acceptable in their classrooms. Most Lubavitchers can communicate with outsiders, and this gives them at least an appearance of friendliness.

A radical difference between Satmar and Lubavitch is their relationship to non-Hasidic Jewry. The Lubavitchers believe that all Jews are capable of achieving the Kingdom of Israel and actively proselytize. The Lubavitchers have outreach programs in American cities and on college campuses. Their worldwide program extends to Jewish settlements in such far-flung places as Australia, Italy, Turkey, and South Africa. Lubavitcher books are published in many languages, including Russian, Danish, and Arabic.

The planned proselytizing by the Lubavitchers has been effective, and this, coupled with a high birthrate, has dramatically increased their numbers. The Satmarers, on the other hand, do not proselytize and are content to grow through normal increase. Satmar is still the largest community. If Lubavitch continues to be successful in recruiting new members, however, it may surpass Satmar in numbers.

"Who Is a Jew" Issue   The Lubavitcher Rebbe's political activism is not confined to local political arenas. In Israel, before the November election in 1988, voting cards with a picture of the Brooklyn Rebbe were handed out, imploring voters to cast their ballots for Agudat Israel, a major religious party. On the back of the card, in Hebrew, it read:

> This is the time to vote for Row 3 for the unity of the nation. In merit of this it will be fulfilled in you and your family the blessings of the Rebbe and the Hasidic masters and the holy men of our generation, who bless those who vote for Row 3—with children, long life and abundant prosperity.[17]

At issue was "who is a Jew." Agudat Israel supports a legislative initiative that would force the Israeli parliament "to pass a law that would recognize only Orthodox conversions for those converts seeking to enter Israel as full citizens."[18] The majority of Conservative and Reform Jews in the United States are, of course, unalterably opposed to the

---

[17]Ari L. Goldman, "Israelis Vote, and Lubavitchers Rejoice: At Last, Many Hasidim Feel, the Law of Return Will be Changed." *New York Times*, Nov. 14, 1988, p. A5, p. A13.
[18]Ibid.

proposal. When interviewed, a spokesperson for the Lubavitcher Rebbe commented:

> Jews have been a people because of the Torah; it has kept us together as a people. . . . When you break away from the Torah and its command-ments, you fragment the people.
> Lubavitch has nothing against Conservative and Reform Jews. . . . The Rebbe loves all Jews, but we cannot stand by as their leaders alter the laws to the detriment of Jews everywhere. [Conservative and Reform rabbis] are causing other Jews to unwittingly assimilate. . . . Jews didn't go to the gas chambers or suffer the inquisitions so that their children could be assimilated.[19]

Four religious parties won 18 of the 120 seats in the Israeli election and these parliamentarians could tip the balance of power to either of the major parties, Labor or Likud. Reform and Conservative spokespeople in the United States have asked the majority parties in Israel not to give in to pressure from the religious parties. What will be the outcome? Only time can tell.

Zionism   Amish clergy are nominated by their congregations and chosen by lot to allow heavenly influence into the process. Although the clergy are respected in the communities, the Amish do not consider them anything but human. Occasionally, districts fall out of full fellow-ship over disagreements regarding traditional methods, such as which gadgets are allowable, modes of dress, and other church matters. In Lancaster County, Pennsylvania, bishops meet regularly, twice each year, to work out their differences.

Unlike the Amish, Hasidic congregations do consider their *rebbes* above ordinary humans, and when differences occur between *rebbes*, resolution is at best difficult. Each *rebbe* is believed by his followers to be closer to God than the *rebbes* of other congregations. Because a *rebbe* converses with God, he expresses God's will when he speaks. In the past, minor differences between congregations have been worked out, but one issue, Zionism, has caused a rift within Hasidim that appears far from resolution.

In 70 A.D., the Jewish commonwealth in Israel was destroyed by the Romans. Although some Jews remained in Palestine, most fled to other parts of the world and have lived in what Jews refer to as the Diaspora (any place other than Palestine). Ever since their exile, religious Jews have prayed for the restoration of King David's throne in Zion—that is, Jerusalem. Triumphant return to the holy land is expected to be led by a God-sent Messiah.

[19]Ibid.

Although attempts had been made prior to World War II to repopulate Jerusalem with Jews—notably, during the 1890s through the efforts of Baron Edmond de Rothschild—Zionism, without messianic leadership, was considered sacrilege by most Jews. It wasn't until after the war, with the perceived need for a homeland, that religious barriers against Zionism broke down.

The Satmar Hasidim remain steadfastly anti-Zionist. This unique position within Jewry, argued by the Satmar Rebbe, attributes both past and present problems in the Middle East to misguided Jews working in opposition to God's messianic plan. If the Zionists were to give up their fight for a homeland and wait for the Messiah, God would lift his wrath from the Jewish people.

The Satmar position has not been confined to debate, and, on occasions, violence between congregations has erupted. The Satmarers have picketed pro-Zionist rallies, and demonstrated outside the United Nations. Zionist rabbis from other congregations have been attacked and beaten. The depth of discord within Hasidim received national media attention a few years ago when the Belzer Rebbe, who now lives in Israel, returned to visit his followers in Brooklyn. It was rumored that the Rebbe's life had been threatened, and ultimately New York's mayor, Ed Koch, was asked to intercede.

While enmity exists between the Satmarers and all congregations that profess or condone Zionism, the Satmarers direct most of their anti-Zionist hostility toward the Lubavitchers, whose support for Israel has been highly visible. The Lubavitcher Rebbe denies an ideological argument with the Satmar Rebbe and agrees that only the Messiah can rule Israel, but the Lubavitcher Rebbe contends that Israel is occupied by Jews, and since Jews are the chosen people, Israel must be supported.

There are no arguments within congregations as to which *rebbe* is correct. The Satmarers and Lubavitchers are squarely behind their respective *rebbes*. Because *rebbes* are believed to have a mystical relationship with God, the character of a Hasidic community is in essence the character of its *rebbe*. On most issues, as with Zionism, the Lubavitch and Satmar represent polar positions within Hasidism. *Rebbes* of other congregations, more often than not, seek a comfortable, if tenuous, position on a scale somewhere between the larger, more powerful Lubavitch and Satmar.

The Future

According to sociologist W. I. Thomas, "if a situation is perceived as real, it is real in its consequences." Hasidim will remain a people apart as long as they continue to perceive themselves as God's chosen people living the Torah as only they are capable. What Hasid would give up the God-given right to enter heaven for contrived, earthly pleasures? Children are raised to conform to the norms and values of the community, and few are seduced by negative social influences—material pleasures, promiscuity, drug use, immorality, and corruption. These are problems of the *goyim,* an inferior people. As long as all that is *goyish* is suspect, Hasidim will erect barriers against integration into the larger community.

Despite the self-created isolation of the New York communities, Hasidim express concern about the contaminating influences of urban life. Their communities in Europe were, for the most part, rural communities, often much like self-sufficient manors with their own *kosher* slaughterhouses, shops, and artisans. Many of the New York congregations have expressed an interest in returning to a life-style as free from *goyish* influence as possible. Enclaves have been established, for example, in New Jersey, and in Westchester and Rockland Counties, New York, and one homegrown *tzaddik,* the Bostoner Rebbe, heads a community in Brookline, Massachusetts.

Impressive physical isolation has been achieved by the Skvira (anglicized to Squarer) Hasidim. In 1961, 132 acres of land, two miles north of Spring Valley in Rockland County, New York, was incorporated by the Squarers as the Village of New Square. The Village is fenced on all sides, and isolated in such a way that outside traffic is uncommon. New Square now has a full range of Hasidic businesses, and outsiders rarely enter the community except for business reasons. By law, property transactions within New Square cannot be made without permission of the community council, and permission to sell to a non-Squarer would never be granted. Some observers feel that the urge for separation may cause whole Hasidic communities to move as did the Squarers.

Of utmost importance to the Hasidim is a personal relationship with a *rebbe,* a holy man, who can solve their personal, business, and spiritual problems. As the congregations grow numerically, it is inevitable that distance will increase between man and holy man. Religio-bureaucratic structure is now limited, since only *rebbes* have special influence with God. And while such structures could expand, this is unlikely given Hasidic religious convictions.

It is more probable that new *rebbes* will emerge and move to different parts of the country, a diffusion not unlike the scattering of wise men that occurred after the death of Dov Baer in Europe. Hasidim are extremely loyal to their *rebbes* and such diffusion could not occur without the blessing of the established *rebbe.* It would not be surprising, however, to learn that a Detroit, Baltimore, or San Diego *rebbe* had joined the Bostoner Rebbe in the trek to the hinterlands.

SELECTED READINGS

Arden, Harvey. "The Pious Ones." *National Geographic*, 148, no. 2, August, 1975.

Bodek, Mendel, and Dresner, Samuel H. " 'Devekut'—The Essence of Hasidism," *Judaism: A Quarterly Journal*, 36 (Winter 1987).

Garvin, Philip, and Cohen, Arthur A. *A People Apart; Hasidism in America*. New York: Dutton, 1970.

Harris, Lis. *Holy Days: The World of a Hasidic Family*. New York: Summit Books, 1985.

Kamen, Robert Mark. *Growing Up Hasidic*. New York: AMS Press, 1985.

Kranzler, George C. *Williamsburg: A Jewish Community in Transition*. New York: Phillipp Feldheim, 1961.

Mahler, Raphael. "A Marxist View of Hasidism." In *Social Foundations of Judaism*, ed. by Calvin Goldscheider and Jacob Neusner. Englewood Cliffs, NJ: Prentice-Hall, 1990.

Mintz, Jerome R. *Legends of the Hasidim*. Chicago, IL: University of Chicago Press, 1968.

Newman, Louis I. *The Hasidic Anthology*. New York: Schocken Books, 1963.

Poll, Solomon. *The Hasidic Community of Williamsburg*. New York: Free Press, 1962.

Rabinowitsch, Wolf Zeev. *Lithuanian Hasidism*. New York: Schocken Books, 1971.

CHAPTER SIX

THE FATHER DIVINE MOVEMENT

The U-shaped banquet table is decked in spotless linen, shining silverware, and fresh flowers. Each place setting includes a goblet with a cone-shaped napkin, in the center of which stands a small, bristling American flag. Just above the head table is a neon sign, "Father Divine's Holy Communion Table," and underneath the sign there are three large American flags. On the left wall is a felt banner with "PEACE" embroidered in large, even letters. On the right wall is a printed sign with the unsurpassable message: "FATHER DIVINE IS GOD ALMIGHTY." All in all, it is a striking scene, and the 250 assembled guests—a mixture of blacks and whites—seem well aware of the fact.

The room itself vibrates with excitement and anticipation. Suddenly the tempo increases. There are several screams and shouts. From somewhere, a female voice rings out, "He's here! Father's here!" There is mass movement toward the doorway, where the curtains are parting. Then Father Divine—accompanied by Mother Divine on his right—breaks into the room with no uncertain step.

He is a short, squat African-American man with smooth skin. His head is shiny bald, and while at the moment his face is impassive, his eyes are quick and penetrating. He wears jewelry: a diamond ring, an expensive-looking wristwatch, a gold chain across his vest, and two emblematic lapel buttons. Yet the overall effect is not one of pomp or flash. Father Divine's suit is dark and well cut, his tie is a conservative stripe, and his shoes are black.

Perhaps the most striking aspect of the man is his height, or the lack of it. He seems to be no more than four feet ten inches. (Both in photographs and in real life, Father Divine is invariably seen as the shortest person in the group.) But despite his diminutive size, it is apparent—to those present, at least—that he is a commanding personality. Every step of his buoyant walk, every gesture, every nod of his head brings gasps of delight from the onlookers. Several of the women jump high into the air.

Although Father Divine appears to be of indeterminate middle age,

Mother Divine is clearly much younger. (She is his second wife, his first wife having died several years earlier.) A striking looking white woman, Mother Divine is immaculately dressed. Almost a head taller than her husband, she gazes at him from time to time with genuine adoration. In addition to being his wife, it is obvious that she is also one of his most devoted followers.

Together they make their way to the head table. Although the throng presses in closely, no one so much as touches Father. On his part, Father Divine seems to take the adulations for granted. Neither condescending nor overbearing, he acts with good-natured dignity and restraint. It is apparent that he is in command of the situation at all times.

The Communion Banquet

Father and Mother Divine are seated, and since Father's feet do not reach the floor, a cushioned stool is placed under them. His followers return to their tables, and the noise subsides. The communion banquet is about to begin.

And what a banquet it is! A dozen different vegetables, roast beef, fried chicken, baked ham, roast turkey and duck, meat loaf, steak, cold cuts, spareribs, liver and bacon, four different kinds of bread, mixed salad with a choice of dressing, celery and olives, coffee, tea, and milk, and a variety of desserts, including layer cake, pie, pudding, fresh fruit, and great mounds of ice cream.

A corps of waitresses—immaculately clad in white—stand by, ready to help with the food. Each dish is first placed in front of Father Divine, who blesses it by touching the dish or adding a serving fork or spoon. The dishes are then passed on to the guests. The waitresses enthusiastically pour coffee, refill empty plates, help circulate the dishes, and otherwise encourage the diners to enjoy what Father Divine calls "the abundance of the fullness." (As we shall see, food has always played an important part in the Father Divine movement.)

With so many courses, so much food, and so many people, the serving and eating process takes a good deal of time—two and a half hours, to be exact. There is never a dull moment however; in fact, there is so much happening that it is difficult to follow it all.

A thickset black woman suddenly jumps to her feet and thrusts both arms upward. "I was paralyzed!" she shouts in a throbbing voice. "No movement in the legs—none at all. And then I met you, Father, and you cured me. I am yours forever, Father, with true devotion!" She sits down and buries her head in her arms.

A middle-aged white woman stands up. "I had tuberculosis real bad. It was consumption. I coughed all day, and I coughed all night, and they told me I was a goner. Then you came into my life, Father, and made me well again overnight. I love you, Father, truly love you."

A thin black man with gray-white hair gets up slowly. "Before I was twenty, I was put in jail twice for stealing. Each time, I told the judge I didn't do it, but in my heart I knew I did. I was a bad boy, and I grew up to be a bad man. I set my neighbor's car on fire and never told nobody— till now. It was only when God came to me in the form of Father Divine that I was able to resolve myself. Thank you, Father."

Festivities   The Rosebuds, the young women's choir, break into song at this point. They range in age from about ten to thirty-five, and all are dressed in red jackets and navy blue skirts. On the left side of their jackets is a white V—for virtue.

> Just as a Rosebud with its fragrance so sweet,
> A perfect Rosebud, FATHER, we want to be,
> Devoting, directing, dedicating our whole lives
> All to YOU, all to YOU, all to YOU . . .

There are approximately forty Rosebuds in the choir, and they sing their hearts out on every song. Their spirit is indomitable, inexhaustible. Although they are accompanied by a pianist, they have no sheet music to read. All their songs—dozens of them—are memorized. The words are original, although some of the music are well-known melodies like "White Christmas" and "Anchors Aweigh."

During many of the songs the chorus is repeated, at which point the young women clap their hands and stamp their feet. When this happens, the audience joins in—and the chorus is likely to be repeated several more times. Unmistakably, the room is filled with happy singers. The only person not visibly affected is Father Divine himself, who acts as though the festivities were a routine part of his life. (Which indeed they are!)

Following the Rosebuds' songs, there are more confessions of sin and some additional tributes to Father Divine. One woman stands on a chair and shouts, "I love you, Father! Truly!" There is a chorus of agreement, after which individual testimonials are heard from all parts of the room.

"Blessed is the Lord!"

"I owe you everything, Father! Thank you, Father!"

"Bless his heavenly body!"

"Father Divine is *God Almighty!*"

At this point, the Lilybuds stand up and render a song. Dressed in attractive green jackets with white trim, the Lilybuds are an older version of the Rosebuds. There are perhaps fifty of them, and their ages seem to range from thirty-five up. Although they are not as vivacious as the Rosebuds, they do not lack enthusiasm. And their devotion to Father Divine is obviously unsurpassed. Their song has the ring of utmost sincerity.

> We want to be a real true Lilybud,
> Basking in our FATHER'S LOVE every day.
> We want to be a real true Lilybud,
> Obeying and doing what our precious FATHER says.

Now, for the first time, people are beginning to dance in the aisles. The dancing is unrehearsed, spontaneous, and individualistic. No two steps are alike, and no two people touch one another. Subdued at first, the movements and gesticulations accelerate as the evening wears on.

Following the Lilybuds' rendition, there is much shouting and applause, and then—as if led by an invisible cheerleader—the entire audience stands up and chants:

> Two, four, six, eight. Who do we appreciate?
> FATHER DIVINE! MOTHER DIVINE! Yea!

> One, two, three, four. Who are we for?
> Five, six, seven, eight. Who do we appreciate?
> FATHER DIVINE! MOTHER DIVINE! Yea!

Throughout the proceedings, Father Divine remains impassive. Much of his time has been spent in blessing the food plates and starting them on their way. Now he himself eats—slowly and sparingly. If he is impressed by the goings-on, he does not show it. He seems to look at no one in particular, and, with the exception of an occasional comment to Mother Divine, he is silent.

It is time now for a song from the Crusaders—the mens' group. Although they include men of all ages, the Crusaders are a much smaller group than the Rosebuds or the Lilybuds. In fact, a large majority of those present, both uniformed and nonuniformed, are female. There are about fifteen Crusaders, and they are dressed in powder blue coats, white shirts, and dark trousers. They sing lustily and—like their predecessors—with obvious devotion.

> I want to love YOU, FATHER,
> A little bit more each day,
> I want to love YOU, FATHER,
> In all I do and say.
> I want to love YOU, FATHER,
> For the wondrous works YOU do,
> For I know YOU'RE GOD ALMIGHTY,
> And I've given this heart to YOU!

At the end of the song, the audience erupts with an outburst of clapping and shouting. There are more testimonials, more dancing, and more of the women leap into the air. One oldster lies down across three chairs, sobbing uncontrollably. But all such behavior appears to be taken for granted by the group itself. There seems to be a tacit sequence of events, and if the activity is becoming more feverish, it is because the sequence dictates that the program is coming to a climax. And sure enough, there is a stirring at the head table. Father Divine is getting up to speak.

The Sermon   As Father Divine looks into the eyes of his followers, there are shouts of "God! God! God!"; "Peace, Father!"; "Thank you, dear one!"; "Hallelujah!"; "I love you, Father!"; "God Almighty!" Once he commences to speak, however, all noise stops. For the duration of his talk, the audience gives him their full attention.

As he speaks, twenty-five young female secretaries take up their notebooks and write down Father's words in shorthand. As a matter of fact, everything Father Divine says—sermons, discourses, speeches, interviews, extemporaneous remarks—is recorded by the ever-ready secretaries. Their shorthand is then transcribed and appears in *New Day*, the movement's biweekly newspaper, thus preserving Father Divine's words for posterity.

(The secretaries have always held a rather exalted position in the organization, since the nature of their work—when the movement was at its peak, at least—required them to stay close to Father Divine day in and day out. The secretaries include both black and white members, most of whom are ex-Rosebuds. Mother Divine had been both a Rosebud and a secretary.)

Father Divine speaks in a strong, resonant voice, with a distinctive tone quality. Though he starts slowly—almost methodically—his audience is spellbound from the very first word. The sermon itself is a combination of the practical and the profound, the esoteric and the absurd, yet his phrasing is such that it is often difficult to tell which is which.

> Though we have Blessings unlimited economically, and though we have physical comfort and convenience for ourselves and for millions of others, yet back of all of it is IT, which said, "Let there be light, and there was light."
>   Back of all of it was, as it is, the same, that while on the water, as so to speak, invisible, and spoke into visibility the earth upon which we are living, the beginning of the material and economic things of life![1]

Several times in the course of his sermon, Father Divine punctuates an affirmation with "Aren't you glad!" And each time the audience answers with a resounding "Yes, so glad!" or "So glad, Lord!"

---

[1]Full texts of sermons such as the above are reprinted periodically in the *New Day*, New Day Publishing Company, 1600 W. Oxford Street, Philadelphia, PA.

When the sermon is finished, there is a tumultuous burst of applause, and shouts of "So true, Father!" "Thank you, Father!" "Lord God Almighty!" People jump and whirl, and a number have tears in their eyes. Almost all are visibly moved. One woman clutches herself and screams, "I love you, sweetheart!" Another lies on the floor motionless, scarcely noticed by the others. An elderly man takes his cane and whacks it against the table as hard as he can, the vibrating silverware adding to the din.

In the midst of all the exuberance, the Rosebuds rise and sing one of their inimitable songs, and there is more stamping and clapping. Additional testimonials and confessions follow—and further expressions of adulation for Father. Then the Lilybuds rise and sing. Then the Crusaders. Genuine ecstasy. Genuine rapture. No doubt about it. Only Father Divine manages to take it all in stride. In a few minutes, he and Mother Divine—with their entourage of secretaries and others—will leave and, quite possibly, visit another of their "heavens," where a similar spectacle will unfold.

"God in a Body"   Although it may read like fiction, this description of a Father Divine communion banquet is based on fact. The foregoing scene is a composite picture of actual happenings. Father Divine died in 1965, and while the movement continues, the "enthusiasm" has been necessarily dampened. Nevertheless, while he was alive he was a phenomenally successful leader. It is quite possible that at the height of his career Father Divine was more ardently acclaimed and revered by his followers than any religious leader in United States history. To those who believed, he was more than just an exalted person. He was, quite simply, God.

Who was this man, this superman, this "God in a body"? When and where was he born? What was his youth like? When did he first aspire to be God? Whence cometh his financial support? How did his movement get to be worldwide in scope? Can it survive, now that "God" is no longer on earth?

Some of these questions are answerable; some—at the moment, at least—are not. From World War I to the present, the Father Divine story is traceable. It is far from complete, but the broad outlines are known. The period prior to World War I is the stickler. Here the picture is murky and tantalizing, and this is unfortunate. For if we knew the real origin and background of Father Divine the man, we would have a much better understanding of Father Divine in his role as God.

The George Baker Story

Relatively few books have been written about Father Divine, and these—as well as most of the articles—have tended to be of World War II vintage.[2] For the most part, furthermore, the output has tended to be journalistic in nature, and there are some gross differences in reporting. Fortunately, there has been some recent academic interest in the subject, and during the 1970s and 1980s several scholarly books and dissertations have appeared.[3]

In a historical sense, nevertheless, our knowledge of Father Divine's early period is admittedly spotty and stems largely from the aforementioned journalistic accounts. But according to these accounts, such as they are, it is said that there once was a man named George Baker . . .

His date of birth is reported as anywhere between 1860 and 1880, depending upon who is doing the reporting. Since no official birth certificate has ever been uncovered, the specific date is largely guesswork. His place of birth is said to be around Savannah, Georgia, although there is no proof of this, either. Some observers believe George Baker's parents were slaves, which might account for his obscure background. Others believe they were sharecroppers, of Baptist persuasion.

Between the time of his birth and the turn of the century, George Baker's whereabouts and activities remain unknown. There are isolated reports of his refusing to attend Jim Crow schools, of being jailed for riding in the "whites only" section of a trolley car, of being a Sunday school superintendent, and of spending six months on a chain gang. None of the accounts has been proved—or disproved. It is not until around 1900 that the various biographical accounts tend to converge.

By that year, George Baker had apparently settled in Baltimore, working as a gardener during the day and as an assistant preacher at night and on Sundays. He was neither more nor less successful than other ministers of the period who were forced to take outside jobs. Until fate intervened in the form of one Samuel Morris.

Although reports differ on how the two men met, the meeting itself had a profound and lasting influence on George Baker. Samuel Morris rejected the usual hellfire-and-damnation approach to salvation and in-

---

[2]See Robert Allerton Parker, *The Incredible Messiah* (Boston: Little, Brown, 1937); John Hoshor, *God in a Rolls Royce: The Rise of Father Divine* (1936; reprint ed., Freeport, NY: Books for Libraries Press, 1971); Sarah Harris, *Father Divine: Holy Husband* (1953; reprint ed., New York: Macmillan, 1971, with a preface, introduction, and afterword added). See also the series by St. Clair McKelway and A. J. Liebling, "Who Is This King of Glory?" *New Yorker,* June 13, 1936, pp. 21ff; June 20, pp. 22ff; and June 27, pp. 22ff. There have been hundreds of articles about Father Divine in publications such as *Time, Newsweek,* and the *New York Times.* The principal historical sources, however, seem to be those just cited.

[3]Stephen Zwick, *The Father Divine Peace Mission Movement* (Princeton University: Senior thesis, 1971); Roma Barnes, *"Blessings Flowing Free": The Father Divine Peace Mission Movement in Harlem, New York City, 1932–1941* (Ph. D. diss., University of York, England, 1979); Kenneth E. Burnham, *God Comes to America: Father Divine and the Peace Mission Movement* (Boston: Lambeth, 1979); and Robert Weisbrot, *Father Divine and the Struggle for Racial Equality* (Urbana, IL: University of Illinois Press, 1983).

stead taught that God dwells within every person. One report has it that Morris proclaimed himself to be God—and, upon being evicted from the church where he was preaching, was befriended by George Baker. Another report makes no mention of this episode but states simply that Baker was drawn to the religious philosophy of Samuel Morris, returning "again and again" to hear him preach.[4]

In any case, it may have been at this time that George Baker caught the idea of becoming God. Prior to his association with Morris, his sermons had given no inkling of heavenly aspirations, but by 1907 he seems to have become intertwined—apparently forever—with the Deity.

Although the details at this point are not clear, Samuel Morris and George Baker evidently worked out an arrangement whereby they shared the godship. Also, at this time, both men apparently changed their names (or were "reborn"). Samuel Morris was henceforth known as Father Jehovia, and George Baker became known as the Messenger. In 1908 they were joined by a third man, John Hickerson, a tall, African-American minister with an imposing voice. Not to be outdone by his companions, Reverend Hickerson also adopted a more spiritual name, St. John the Vine. Although Father Jehovia (Samuel Morris) seems to have been number one, the three men were somehow able to share their divinity, and for the next several years they were as flamboyant a preaching team as the area had ever seen.

The Messenger In 1912 the triumvirate broke up. Presumably they were no longer willing to share their divine authority, and in any case they went their separate ways. St. John the Vine Hickerson traveled to New York City, where he founded his own church. Father Jehovia passed from the picture and for all intents and purposes was never heard from again. The Messenger (George Baker) turned southward, gained some converts, and—if we can believe his biographers—ran into a pack of trouble.

At Valdosta, Georgia, in 1913, the Messenger was preaching the gospel in his own unique style. The townspeople were entranced and turned out in large numbers to hear the man who called himself God. While reports vary, there were some in the audience who were not impressed. Among the skeptics were a number of local pastors, who had the Messenger arrested and taken to court. The charge: any person who believes himself or herself to be God must be of unsound mind.

For reasons best known to themselves, the jury upheld the charge, and the Messenger was declared insane. Instead of committing him to a

---

[4]See works in footnote 2 for historical details—and variations—of the pre–World War I period under discussion.

mental institution, however, the court ordered him to leave the state of Georgia forthwith. He did so, and as far as we know he never returned.

In spite of the resistance and harassment he met in the South, however, the Messenger did succeed in gaining converts. They were few in number, to be sure—probably not more than a dozen—but they were dedicated believers, and they would form the nucleus of his forthcoming religious organization. One person is worthy of particular mention: a stout, African-American woman called Peninah, or Sister Penny. Before the group left the South, Sister Penny was reportedly the Messenger's chief angel.

The New York Maelstrom

In 1915, the Messenger and his disciples arrived in New York City, undaunted by their troubles and apparently none the worse for wear. After a brief stay in Manhattan, the little group settled in Brooklyn. Starting in a rooming house, they began to develop the format for what would one day be a worldwide religious organization.

As they struggled to survive in the big city, the Messenger himself was in touch with his old friend and fellow deity, St. John the Vine Hickerson. Hickerson's own church—the Church of the Living God—had been fairly successful. The Messenger attended Hickerson's services, checked his methods, asked questions, and otherwise borrowed from. St. John the Vine's repertoire.

Along with modest success, however, Hickerson was also having some difficulty. Like his mentor, Father Jehovia (Samuel Morris), St. John the Vine taught that God was not in heaven but within every person. This meant that although Hickerson could be God, there could be any number of auxiliary Gods—and this is exactly what was happening. Wearing "gold" and "silver" crowns and royal purple robes, these deities clogged the path to Hickerson's church. There were Father Obey, Joe World, Elijah of the Fiery Chariot, Saint Peter, Father Paul, Steamboat Bill, Father Joshua, and many others. Later on there would be cult leaders and other exotic personalities, like Barnaby Bill, Sufi Abdul Hamid, and Daddy Grace. New York was fast becoming a religious maelstrom.

Before long, St. John the Vine's church fell under the weight of its own gods. Although he did not pass into oblivion like Samuel Johnson, John Hickerson became a relatively obscure figure. Following World War I, he is heard from less and less.

The Messenger himself severed all connection with John Hickerson and never referred to him publicly again. The little group in Brooklyn, meanwhile, was holding its own—perhaps even growing a bit. A few of the original members had left, but new ones kept joining. The Messenger was a persuasive speaker, and his followers genuinely revered him. He ran a tight ship, however, and unlike St. John the Vine, permitted only one God—himself. He made all the rules and brooked no interference, and he followed that practice all his life.

As to its living arrangements, the group operated communally. The Messenger himself did no outside work—nor would he, ever again. Instead, he ran an employment service, supplying domestics and menial workers to those who were looking for honest, reliable help. Whether or not they got their jobs through his employment service, however, the Messenger's followers presumably turned their wages over to him. He then paid the rent, bought the food, and took care of the necessary bills.

Peninah was in charge of the actual household management—including shopping and food preparation—and from all accounts she was an indefatigable worker. In fact, some observers believe that the Messenger married her during this period, though others set the date much earlier. But whatever the date, the marriage was spiritual in nature. It may also have been legal—though no marriage license has been uncovered—but it was not sexual. Quite early in the movement, the Messenger declared that sex was unclean, a mark of depravity, and hence was forbidden. Neither he nor his followers have been known to violate the decree.

Name Changes

During the New York period, another interesting phenomenon occurred: the Messenger underwent further name changes. The reason is not entirely clear, but presumably he felt the need for a more appropriate title. In any case, just as George Baker evolved into the Messenger, so the Messenger evolved into Major Jealous Divine. (More than one biographer has suggested that the Messenger borrowed not only St. John the Vine's ministerial techniques but his surname as well!)

To complete the cognominal sequence, Major Jealous Devine was eventually shortened to M. J. Devine, and finally—over a period of years—*M. J. Devine* became *Father Divine.* These latter changes, though gradual, are a matter of record and are not really in dispute. The dispute arises over the earlier sequence: the transition from George Baker to the Messenger, and from the Messenger to Major Jealous Devine. Before continuing with the rest of the story, therefore, let us pause and examine a genuine mystery.

Man, Myth, or Both?

The George Baker-Messenger-Father Divine story told in the preceding pages is based largely on the handful of available biographies. It is most certainly *not* the account told by Father Divine's followers, or for that matter by Father Divine himself. Whenever he was asked when he was born, he might reply, "I wasn't born. I was combusted." He also answered queries about his birth with a scriptural "Before Abraham was, I am."

Not all of his replies were nebulous, however. On one occasion, a radio news commentator stated in no uncertain terms that Father Divine's real name was George Baker. An excerpt from Father Divine's reply (by letter) follows:

> MY name is MAJOR J. DIVINE, better known as FATHER DIVINE. . . . MY name has never at any time been George Baker, as stated by you and many others who have filled the press and the air with radio broadcasts with false, erroneous and perjured testimonies endorsed as though they were true.[5]

Predictably, Father Divine's followers totally reject the George Baker story; indeed, they go out of their way to "set the record straight." Mother Divine, for example, recently wrote to the Library of Congress, requesting that their records be corrected. Their reply was as follows: "The Library of Congress heading created in 1936 for Father Divine under the spurious name 'George Baker' has been corrected. Our heading now reads: 'Father Divine.' The change . . . is being reflected on all records going into our new catalog."[6]

Kenneth Burnham, an authority on the subject, makes the following point:

> All attempts to describe Father Divine's history have been rejected by his followers on the ground that his life can be understood only from his own words in the publications of the Movement. They believe that the only true statements about him have come from his own lips.[7]

But what does the best evidence really indicate?

The early biographers—who presumably researched their subject—all believed that Father Divine was indeed George Baker, and that his divinity had its inception around the turn of the century in Baltimore. Moreover, most of the biographies were written in the 1930s, when those close to the movement would have been expected to know something

---

[5]Mother Divine, *The Peace Mission Movement* (Philadelphia: Imperial Press, Inc., 1982), pp. 106–107.

[6]Ibid., p. 108.

[7]Burnham, *God Comes to America*, p. 6.

about Father Divine's early background. By implication, at least, the biographers actually talked to informants of this type.

On the other hand, there were only a handful of biographies, and—as was mentioned earlier—none was written by a trained social scientist. References, research sources, and general documentation are largely lacking. The methodology is not rigorous, and there are some time gaps in the narratives. It is hardly surprising that there are some sharp discrepancies among the various accounts. In brief, they are popular books—no more, no less.

Certain logical questions present themselves. Is there any extant documentation that would link Samuel Morris, George Baker, and John Hickerson in place (Baltimore) and time (early 1900s)? Are there no local or state records available to establish that George Baker was in fact convicted in a court of law? Are there no documents that shed light on his movements during the developmental (1908–1914) period?

The one key witness in this historical entanglement is St. John the Vine. It is he, principally, who identifies Father Divine as George Baker. Writing in the early 1950s, for example, Sarah Harris pointed out that St. John the Vine Hickerson was *the only person then alive who knew Father Divine before he became God.* According to Hickerson:

> Sure, he was just plain little George Baker in 1899. He lived in Baltimore. You know what he did? Gardening. Working around the white neighborhoods for fifty cents a day. He used to live for Sundays because he used to teach Sunday School and be an assistant preacher.[8]

But how much credence are we to put in this statement—knowing of Hickerson's bitterness? After all, St. John the Vine was a failure, and Father Divine a success, and since Hickerson blamed much of his own failure on Father Divine, the George Baker allegation should be weighed carefully. Hickerson's story may be true, but what is needed is some independent corroboration.

Why, for instance, was Samuel Morris never interviewed regarding the authenticity of the George Baker story? Morris had no ax to grind, and he was certainly in a position to know the facts of the case. Yet he apparently made no statement on the subject. Indeed, there is no indication that he was ever asked, though he did turn up as a caretaker in New Jersey during the 1930s.

But John Hickerson and Samuel Morris are long since dead—as are the earlier biographers. If further evidence is forthcoming, therefore, it will probably be from new sources. Here is a ready-made research project for someone!

---

[8]Harris, *Father Divine*, p. 6.

Frederick Edwards?   One fascinating episode remains in the attempt to identify Father Divine's secular origins. In 1936, one Elizabeth Maysfield claimed that Father Divine was her son, and that he had been christened Frederick Edwards some fifty years earlier in North Carolina. She added that she had seen him only once during the past fifteen years (in Richmond). At that time, she said to reporters, "He told me not to recognize him as son, and that he would not recognize me as mother any more."

The woman further claimed that Father Divine had never helped her financially, even though she had been in need of help for some time. She charged, finally, that Father Divine had deserted his wife and children in Baltimore in 1926.

Although parts of Maysfield's story did correspond with reports of Father Divine's Baltimore background, her credibility was weakened by the 1926 desertion charge. For, as we shall see, in 1926 Father Divine's whereabouts were well known—and they were nowhere near Baltimore.

Father Divine himself did not reply directly to any of the charges, though his personal secretary, John Lamb, "curtly denied all." And while the story made headlines initially, it soon faded from the news. The general feeling seemed to be that Elizabeth Maysfield was one of the many who were trying to capitalize on Father Divine's good fortune.

The entire episode might have been forgotten completely had it not been for a remarkable coincidence in 1960. In May of that year, Father Divine entered the Bryn Mawr (Pennsylvania) Hospital in the throes of a diabetic coma. While he lay semicomatose in his hospital room, he gave as his first name none other than Frederick![9]

(He was released a week later, lived for several more years, and nothing further ever came of the incident. It did, however, add yet another angle to an already multidimensional mystery.)

Sayville—the Turning Point

But let us pick up the chronological thread of our story. Starting in 1919, fortunately, the activities of Father Divine and his followers become increasingly clear—and more and more a matter of record. During that year, he and his little group, numbering not more than two dozen, moved from Brooklyn to Sayville, Long Island. The house they moved to—an attractive, twelve-room dwelling at 72 Macon Street—still stands. It is used by the followers as a kind of shrine, for it was here that the movement first gained national and international recognition.

Things started off peacefully enough. The deed to the house was in the

[9]The account of Frederick Edwards is taken largely from Weisbrot, *Father Divine*, pp. 9–10.

name of Major J. Devine and his wife, Peninah. And if the white community was less than enthusiastic at the prospect of blacks setting up in their
midst, no overt reaction was apparent. In fact, for several years Sayville
and its environs made good use of Father Divine's services. Operating an
employment office—as he did in Brooklyn—Father Divine was able to
supply reliable domestics for the many nearby estates.

From all accounts, Father Divine was a good neighbor. He kept 72
Macon Street spic and span. He worked in the garden. He was polite
and friendly, with a ready smile. His followers did not inundate the
neighborhood, as some had feared. The group did manage to grow in
number—but slowly. They were not loud or unruly. There was no drinking. And there were never any sex problems.

Things went on this way for ten happy years.

Father Divine appeared to be consolidating his position. He was, in
effect, learning how to combine the role of businessman with that of
deity. On both counts he was successful. As a businessman he had the
confidence and respect of the community—in spite of the general racial
situation. And in his role as deity he was superb.

African-Americans of the 1920s were likely to be disadvantaged individuals. Faced with both social and economic discrimination, they often
had a low level of aspiration and—more than occasionally—a feeling of
hopelessness. Father Divine succeeded in imbuing his followers with a
sense of hope and purpose.

He gave them economic security in the form of lodging, food, and
employment. He encouraged self-respect by insisting that they give their
employers an honest day's work for a day's pay. He forbade them to
accept tips. He gave them a sense of self-discipline by prohibiting smoking, drinking, swearing, and "immodest behavior." And—above all
else—he gave them spiritual security. For if he, Father Divine, was God
Almighty, then his followers were assured of everlasting life.

To be sure, his followers had to make certain sacrifices. They had to
renounce sex and marriage. They had to abide by Father Divine's rules
and regulations, for he did not tolerate backsliders. And again, they
presumably all turned their wages over to him. But these were small
sacrifices compared to the economic and spiritual benefits involved.

Slowly but surely the fame of M. J. Devine—better known as Father
Divine—spread. As the 1920s wore on, membership increased steadily.
On Sundays, busloads of visitors would arrive at 72 Macon Street to see
and hear God and partake of the mighty meals. Thirty to forty courses
every week, and all for free! No collection plate was ever passed, no
request for donations was ever made. When—invariably—the question
was asked, "But where does the money come from to pay for it all?" the
answer was always the same: "It comes from God."

In 1930, the Sunday bus excursions were joined by private automobiles. First dozens, then hundreds. To local residents, it seemed like an endless caravan. The banquets also grew in size and vigor. There were testimonials and increasing reports of miraculous cures. (Father was clearly omnipotent.) Then came the songs and the clapping. And the sermon. And the hallelujahs. And so on. To the good citizens of Sayville, at least, things seemed to be getting out of hand. It was time that something was done.

At first there was police harassment—tickets for traffic and parking violations in wholesale lots. When this tactic failed, the district attorney planted a female undercover agent at 72 Macon Street. Dressed as a poor African-American working woman, the agent tried to verify rumors of sexual relations between Father Divine and his female followers. When this also failed, she tried to seduce Father Divine, but—by her own account—he ignored her. The only thing she could report was that everyone treated her with sympathy and kindness.

Next there were town meetings, with groups of angry residents demanding Father Divine's ouster. A committee of leading citizens was selected to visit 72 Macon Street and make their demands known. Father Divine received the group and listened patiently while they explained their point of view. Then he explained his. He and his followers were good citizens. They had broken no laws. He himself had helped Sayville economically by providing an employment service and by buying large quantities of food and supplies from local merchants. Furthermore, Father Divine pointed out, the Constitution guaranteed freedom of religion. So he was not going to leave Sayville. On the contrary, he was quite likely to expand his activities.

Father was polite, speaking in an even tone. But something in his manner told the committee that further discussion was futile, and they left. A short time later—during one of the Sunday services—police broke into 72 Macon Street and arrested Father Divine and eighty of his followers for disturbing the peace. The Sunday in question was November 15, 1931, a date that quite possibly marks the real beginning of the Father Divine movement. While the arrest itself was peaceful enough, the entire episode was a shot heard round the African-American world.

Judge Lewis J. Smith Despite the flimsiness of the case, Father Divine was indicted by the grand jury and held (on $1,500 bail) for trial. The black press—and a sizable segment of the white press as well—took up the cry of racial discrimination, and the fight was on. News stories made the front pages, and publicity grew by leaps and bounds. Within a few weeks, Father Divine had become a cause célèbre. He himself, though not visibly perturbed, vowed to fight the case   and if necessary to "rot in jail" rather than succumb to the forces of intolerance and bigotry.

John C. Thomas, an African-American lawyer who had been assistant United States district attorney, offered his services to Father Divine, who accepted. The presiding judge in the case was Lewis J. Smith, who was white, and who—the record would show—was clearly antagonistic in his attitude toward the defendant. One of the judge's first acts was to cancel Father Divine's bail and remand him to prison for the duration of the trial. This action, based on a legal technicality, set the tone for the entire trial.

The actual proceedings were fairly clear-cut. The prosecution contended that Father Divine and his followers had annoyed the neighbors, disturbed the peace, obstructed traffic, and were a public nuisance. The defense naturally denied the allegations. Most of the witnesses were either neighbors (prosecution) or Father Divine's followers (defense). The only thing really noteworthy during the trial was the antagonism shown by Judge Smith toward several of the defense witnesses. It was easy to see where his sympathies lay.

Even in his charge to the jury, the judge showed partiality. He stated that Father Divine was a bad influence in the community, that his real name was not Father Divine but George Baker, that Mother Divine was not his legal wife, that he was not an ordained minister, and that he was able to induce others to turn their wages over to him.

After deliberating a short while, the jury—not unexpectedly—returned a verdict of guilty. They did, however, recommend leniency. Judge Smith adjourned the court for several days while he contemplated the sentence. The defendant, meanwhile, stayed in jail.

Public reaction was mixed. Some felt that Father Divine was in fact guilty as charged. Many fair-minded people, however, had come to the conclusion that he was innocent, a victim of unadulterated race prejudice.

Undaunted, Judge Smith reconvened the court and imposed the stiffest sentence the law allowed: one year in jail and a fine of five hundred dollars. Also undaunted, Father Divine went to jail, a quizzical expression on his face.

Three days later, Judge Lewis J. Smith was dead!

Only fifty years of age and apparently in good health, he reportedly had died of a heart attack.

When asked—in his cell—whether he had any comments regarding Judge Smith's demise, Father Divine replied, somewhat mournfully, "I hated to do it."

Afterwards, the appellate court overturned Father Divine's conviction, basing its decision on the "prejudicial comments" voiced by (the late) trial judge. The fines levied against Father Divine and his co-defendants were also rescinded.

Why They Joined

The death of Judge Smith had an overwhelming effect on large segments of the African-American community. Although most white newspapers carried the story in routine fashion, the black press used banner headlines. In some neighborhoods, African-Americans held parades and rallies. On June 26, 1932, for example—the day after Father Divine's release from prison—a "Monster Glory to Our Lord" rally was held at the Rockland Palace in Harlem. Lines started to form at five A.M., even though Father Divine wasn't scheduled to appear until noon. Over 7,000 persons jammed the auditorium, and thousands more were turned away.

Father Divine did not let his followers down. Shunning his usual figures of speech, he delivered one of the clearest talks of his career. Among other things, he said:

> You may not have seen my flesh for a few weeks, but I was with you just the same. I am just as operative in the mind as in the body. There were many who thought I had gone someplace, but I'm glad to say I did not go anywhere.
>
> I held the key to that jail all the time I was in it, and was with you every time you met. They can prosecute me or persecute me, or even send me to the electric chair, but they can never keep me from you or stop me from doing good![10]

When Father Divine finished his talk, the human explosion almost tore the roof off Rockland Palace. Eruptions of "Hallelujah!" "Sweet Savior!" "Father Divine is God Almighty!" rocked the auditorium. People jumped, screamed, shouted, shook, and whirled. Most were ecstatic, but some were overcome and wept. Harlem had never seen anything like it before.

After the waves of acclaim had passed, testimonials were heard. One woman had been cured of cancer through Father's intervention, another of arthritis. A cripple had been healed and had thrown away his crutches. On and on they went, a spontaneous cascade of miracles.

Then the tone of the audience changed, and people began to complain not of their physical afflictions, but of their social oppression. They were poor and hungry. They lived in squalor and could not get jobs. They had no hope. No future. They needed help, and they needed it now—from God! Little by little, louder and louder, the chant was taken up: "Need you, Father! Need you! Need you! Need you!"[11]

What were the sociological factors that accounted for this mass attraction? To answer the question in generalized terms is easy: the right

[10]Harris, *Father Divine*, pp. 42–44.
[11]Ibid.

person was in the right place at the right time—with the right people. A more specific answer would involve a number of points.

To begin with, the nation was in the grip of a wicked depression, and as low person on the economic totem pole, the African-American was the hardest hit. In many African-American neighborhoods the housing was dreadful: run-down buildings, congestion, rats and roaches, three and four families sharing one toilet, no hot water, inadequate heat in the winter. Year after year after year. Sickness, ill-health, inadequate medical facilities, poor sanitary conditions, a high death rate. Year after year. Unemployment, desertion, drug addiction, hopelessness. Year after year. The African-American—particularly the lower-class member—did indeed need someone. And in the absence of a more appropriate candidate, it looked as though that someone might be Father Divine.

Of particular relevance here is the food factor. Social security, unemployment compensation, Medicare and Medicaid, Aid to Families with Dependent Children (AFDC), United Fund, old-age assistance—such programs were still many years away. One of the first problems facing an unemployed person, therefore, was hunger. It is easy to see why Father Divine—whose daily services included huge quantities of free food—had such ready appeal. And whenever the question was asked, "But where does all the food come from—who pays for it?" the answer was the same. "It comes from God, and God don't need money."

The Racial Stereotype   The depression was not the only cause of African-Americans' economic difficulties. Prejudice and discrimination were so widespread that even when jobs were available, African-Americans were likely to be excluded. In the 1930s, even clerical and semiskilled occupations were generally closed to black applicants. One did not see black sales clerks in stores or black secretaries in offices. One did not see black bus drivers, or mechanics, or tradespeople.

In fact, in the 1930s, racial stereotyping was the order of the day. Originally defined as "pictures in the head," *stereotype* can best be described as a kind of conceptual shortcut, often of an erroneous nature. Thus, the belief by whites that blacks were lazy or inferior is a typical racial stereotype. And while sociologists are well aware that stereotyping still occurs, it is probably not so prevalent as it was a generation or two ago. In the 1930s, certainly, it was commonly believed by prejudicial whites that blacks were listless, unreliable, happy-go-lucky, and largely incapable of holding a job.

Because so much of Father Divine's program was aimed at the elimination of racial stereotyping and job discrimination, it is easy to see why he had such an impact on the African-American community. It is no accident that his appeal was greatest in those areas where congestion, unemployment, and discrimination were rampant: Brooklyn, Manhattan, Newark, Jersey City, Philadelphia.

Alienation   Things were so bad for African-Americans in the 1930s that a feeling of alienation often prevailed. As used by sociologists, *alienation* refers to a sense of futility and insignificance. Alienated persons feel that those in power have neglected them, and that there is nothing they can do about it. They believe that they have little or no control over their own destiny, and that—in effect—they have become dispensable.

More than any other leader of his time, it was Father Divine who fought against the spread of alienation, and he was a superb practitioner. He understood the masses. He could talk to them. He could engender feelings of self-respect, and he could play the role of God. Most important, he never lost sight of the two basics: food and jobs. These were the bedrock. As long as he was at the helm, Father Divine's followers would have ample food at little or no cost. And—through his employment service or within his own economic establishment—they would have jobs.

Overview   Food, jobs, and a joyous war against racism and alienation. No wonder large numbers of African-Americans flocked to Father Divine's banner. Add to these his personal magnetism, his heavenly claims and obvious knowledge of the Bible, his penetrating voice and allegorical speech, his presumed healing powers, his spontaneous and vibrant manner, his intense concentration on goodness and fairness—for his followers, the result spelled God.

The Economic Structure

Over the years, there has been a good deal of misunderstanding regarding Father Divine's economic operations. His followers tended to believe that since he was God, he could "materialize" all the money he wanted, a notion that Father took no steps to dispel. The Internal Revenue Service, which had some genuine doubts about his deification, wondered why he never paid any income tax. After all, they reasoned, a man who wore expensive suits and diamond rings, who rode in Cadillac limousines and ate lavishly—such a man must also have a lavish income. Father Divine denied the imputation, and in a series of showdowns between "church and state," the state lost.

During his long career, Father Divine never paid a penny in income taxes. His critics contended that, under the mantle of the Lord, he used his workers' salaries to line his own heaven with gold. His supporters countered with the argument that Father Divine had never asked anyone for money in his life, and that even in his own churches there was no such thing as a collection plate.

Actually, Father Divine's economic operations were not so complicated—or so secretive—as his critics claimed. While much of the day-to-day procedure never became public knowledge, enough is known to permit a reasonable description. The basic economic principle was remarkably simple: to feed and house ten people communally did not cost ten times as much as it would cost to feed and house a single individual, especially if the ten were willing to let the Lord handle the fiscal details. This was the principle Father Divine (as the Messenger) had followed in Brooklyn during the World War I period, and he adhered to it throughout his entire career.

The Hotel Business   Of all the economic enterprises under the aegis of Father Divine—and there were many—none was more successful than the hotel business, the structural network around which the movement revolved. For example, although the organization had a number of churches, or missions, many of the meetings and rallies were held in the hotels. Communion banquet services, like the one described earlier, were held in the hotels.

When it came to labor, problems were minimal. Instead of being staffed by employees demanding union wages, the hotels would employ Father Divine's followers, who would work for no wages whatsoever. Instead, they received room and board and the eternal care of a loving God, whom they were privileged to serve on a regular basis. And, of course, because they served outsiders, the hotels were profitable. This in turn enabled the movement to feed thousands of needy people virtually free of charge. One further point should be mentioned. Father Divine and his followers did not build their hotels; they bought them. Often in run-down condition, the buildings were refurbished— with the help of the faithful—and then opened for business. Father Divine had a remarkable eye for real estate values, and much of his success stemmed from his uncanny ability to ferret out bargains. Once he made his intentions known, it was not difficult to find the necessary backers. Large urban hotels such as the Divine Tracy (Philadelphia), the Divine Hotel Riviera (Newark), the Divine Fairmount (Jersey City), and the Divine Lorraine (Philadelphia) were all acquired in this manner, and all were operated successfully—in fact, all are still in operation today.

Father Divine was a strong believer in racial integration, and his hotels gave him the opportunity to practice what he preached. Blacks and whites not only worked together side by side but—as a matter of policy—were assigned to the same room. Father Divine said the hotels were his "demonstrators of democracy in action."

Employment Service   Father Divine first started his employment service during the New York period (1915–1919). He had an obvious knack for placing domestic workers, and throughout his career the employment service remained his most successful operation, with the possible exception of the hotels.

The reason for his success is that, as previously mentioned, Father Divine insisted on an honest day's work for a day's pay. Over the years, his workers' reputation—for honesty, reliability, and devoutness—grew. Indeed, as many housewives in the New York-New Jersey-Philadelphia area can attest, the demand for domestics was greater than the supply. Father Divine forbade his workers to accept tips or gifts. The following announcement has been printed and reprinted in *New Day* hundreds of times:

To Whom It May Concern

A true follower of Mine does not want or desire a gift, or present, or anything of that type for Christmas or any holiday, and considers it to be unevangelical, unconstitutional, and not according to scripture. . . . MY true followers, as long as they receive just compensation for their labor, will not accept tips, gifts, or presents. . . .

This leaves ME Well, Healthy, Joyful, Peaceful, Lively, Loving, Successful, Prosperous and Happy in Spirit, Body and Mind, and in every organ, muscle, sinew, joint, limb, vein, and bone, and even in every ATOM, fiber, and cell of MY BODILY FORM.

> Respectfully and Sincere, I AM
> REV. M. J. DIVINE
> (Better known as FATHER DIVINE)

The ending is one that Father Divine used in his written communiqués. The message in the body of the letter is self-explanatory and is another example of how he could be crystal clear—when he wanted to be.

It should also be mentioned that Father Divine's followers could work inside or outside the movement. If they worked inside—in a hotel, restaurant, or larger business establishment—they toiled in the service of the Lord, without wages. If they worked outside—as domestics, for example—what they did with their wages was up to them. Presumably, many of them did turn their wages over to the movement, but they were not forced to do so.

Social Organization and Nomenclature

All the groups discussed in the present volume are, in one way or another, outside the mainstream of American life. To help in their adaptation to the larger society, each of the groups has utilized certain techniques aimed at enhancing internal solidarity. The Father Divine movement has employed a combination of the sacred and the secular. Their churches, for instance, not only serve as places of worship but are designed to house and feed people.

Formerly known as "heavens," the churches and their branches are officially designated as "kingdoms, extensions, and connections," and many of the followers live in these buildings. Not all of the followers, to be sure: it is permissible to live at home. But the dedicated followers—sometimes called the "inner circle" or "holy family" of Father Divine—do live within the walls of the kingdoms. (It is from this group that the Rosebuds, Lilybuds, Crusaders, and secretaries have traditionally been drawn.)

Actually, the kingdoms, extensions, and connections are no more—and no less—than hotels, apartments, rooming houses, and other buildings used for all-purpose quarters by the faithful. Outsiders may also live in the kingdoms, but while they are on the premises they are subject to the same strict rules of living as the followers. When the movement was at its peak—which is the historical present we are now discussing—there were over 175 kingdoms, extensions, and connections.

Followers who live in one of the kingdoms are closely knit and—like the Oneida Community discussed in Chapter 2—would comprise a genuine primary group. Describing an assembly of followers who were waiting for the appearance of Father and Mother Divine, Burnham writes as follows:

> It was here that it was possible to experience the primary-group nature of the rank and file of the Movement. They have known each other from five to forty years. They have worked together, traveled together in the church cars, lived together in buildings they own jointly, and eaten together at Communion served by fellow believers, and in restaurants owned and staffed by "brothers" and "sisters."[12]

Dedicated followers are united in ways other than by living and working together. *They also believe together.* They are convinced that Father Divine is God and that all his statements are literally true. They believe in the Bible, but for spiritual guidance they frequently turn to the *New Day,* which carries the sermons of Father Divine over and over again. True followers help the movement in every way they can. They even change their names for Father.

Name Changes It is quite likely that the followers of Father Divine have the most picturesque names of any religious group in the world.

---

[12]Burnham, *God Comes to America,* pp. 81–82.

Although the press has sometimes derided their nomenclature, the names themselves—when one thinks about it—do capture both the essence of the movement and the benevolent nature of Father Divine. The following are some names picked at random from *New Day:*

Miss Great B. Love	Mr. Brilliant Victory
Miss Merriness Truth	Miss Magnetic Love
Mr. Enoch Mental	Miss Melchizedec Peace
Miss Glad Tidings	Mr. Joseph Pilgrim
Miss Sunshine Bright	Miss Meekness Branch
Mr. David Guilelessness	Miss Evangeline Faithful
Miss Happy Word	Miss True Sincerity

When she was asked about the reason for the various name changes, Mother Divine replied as follows:

> If you are familiar with the Scripture, you know where Nicodemus came to JESUS and JESUS told him that he must be born again if he was to enter the kingdom of Heaven. . . .
>
> So many people, in order to lose their identity, have prayed to God, and the Spirit has given them a New Name. And you also know that Paul, when he was converted, changed his name from Saul to Paul. . . .
>
> The followers are all striving to have a new nature, the nature of CHRIST, and lose their mortal or Adamic nature and characteristics.

While not all of Father Divine's supporters change their names, practically all of the inner circle, the true followers, do. And, of course, this name bond serves as another link in the chain of group cohesion.

No Sex—No Marriage—No Family

Sociologists use *cultural theme* to refer to broad, axiomatic principles that serve as guides to behavior. In the Father Divine movement, the theme "It is better to be celibate than to marry" pervades the entire organization. True followers do not believe in sex, marriage, or family. Married couples can join, but if they live in one of the kingdoms they must separate. (The usual procedure is for males to live on one floor, females on another.) If there are children, they must be reared separately.

With regard to family life, dedicated followers see themselves as children and Father and Mother Divine as parents, and they believe that this type of relationship is more gratifying—and more exalted—than normal family arrangements. Point seven of the Crusaders' "Declaration Concerning God" shows the intensity of their feelings:

> I believe that FATHER DIVINE is my Real FATHER, and that MOTHER DIVINE is my Real MOTHER, and that I never had another.

True followers also abstain from all sexual relationships. In fact, men and women have very little to do with one another. Before and after communion banquets, it is quite common to see the men talking among themselves and the women among themselves. There is no hostility or antagonism, merely a gentle avoidance.

The "International Modest Code," formulated by Father Divine, is the behavioral guide used by all dedicated followers. The code—in whole or in part—is prominently displayed in the various kingdoms, extensions, and connections. It is also reprinted in issue after issue of *New Day*, as follows:

International Modest Code
Established by Father Divine

NO SMOKING * NO DRINKING * NO OBSCENITY
NO VULGARITY * NO PROFANITY
NO UNDUE MIXING OF THE SEXES
NO RECEIVING OF GIFTS, PRESENTS
TIPS OR BRIBES

True followers adhere to the code, word for word, almost by second nature. But they seem to give special attention and credence to the section "no undue mixing of the sexes." Celibacy, virginity, purity, chastity, virtue—by whatever term, the followers seem almost to flaunt the idea of sexual abstinence.

The Rosebuds wear a white V (for virtue) on their jackets, and of their "Ten Commandments," number six reads, "We will endeavor to let our every deed and action express virginity." The Lilybuds' "Endeavor" says that they will "live pure, holy, virtuous, and clean." And the Crusaders pledge to "live a righteous, useful, consecrated Life which is devoted to holiness, purity, . . . self-denial."

One final word on the sexual theme. Several observers have contended that the followers are able to achieve a measure of sexual gratification through their intense physical/spiritual reactions. Harris, in describing the "vibrations" of Miss Holy Light, writes as follows:

Tears come to her eyes. . . . She screams, falls on the floor. . . . She rises and stands rigid. . . . Then she closes her eyes and dances away. She jerks her hips again, and her breasts. "Hallelujah!" she screams out. "I love you—love, love, love you!"

She stops moving and sits down with a happy look on her face. Her vibration has finished. It is apparent that, in her testimony to Father Divine, she has reached a sublime climax of fulfillment. This is apparent in the way she holds her fists clenched and her eyes tight shut as though she cannot bear to open them, and in the harsh breathing she could not stop if she wanted to.[13]

Other writers—including Dr. Burnham, who has observed the Divinites over a period of several decades—have never reported a physical reaction of the type mentioned above. On occasion, the communal banquets have been spirited affairs, certainly, and the love expressed for Father Divine is something to behold. But it stops far short of any physical-sexual manifestation. As far as can be determined, the followers do not consider sexual deprivation a major problem. They look upon it, rather, as a willing and loving sacrifice, made in accordance with the word of God.

The Rewards

It should not be thought that the followers of Father Divine lead a completely sacrificial life. Far from it. They must renounce normal marital and familial relationships and abjure the profit motive, but the rewards—from their point of view—are far greater than the sacrifices.

Dedicated followers will never get rich, obviously, but then they have no need for riches. Their expenses are near zero. They have no family to support, no parents to look after. They pay no rent, have no mortgage or other expenses connected with a house. Their recreational and travel costs are minimal. They have no food bill. What need have these followers for wealth? The movement will care for their material needs as long as they live. And they in turn will provide the movement with a lifetime of dedicated service.

In the intangible sphere, dedicated followers' rewards are even greater. They have the day-to-day satisfaction of serving and being close to their God. They have the comfort of living and working with like-minded people. They are spared the worries of family living. They have no financial woes. They have peace of mind and a sense of spiritual well-being that outsiders often envy.

This latter point is perhaps the most important, for no one can be around the group very long without being intrigued by their spiritual outlook. They give the impression of inner security because they *understand*. Their love of God—Father Divine—is so great that it has given them an understanding, both of themselves and of the outside world.

The Here and Now   Nowhere in Father Divine's teachings is any provision made for the hereafter, for the dedicated follower has everlasting

[13]Harris, *Father Divine*, p. 118.

life. Father Divine spoke literally, not symbolically, on this point. Over and over again, he promised his followers that if they adhered to his teachings faithfully, they would have perfect health and eternal life. On the basis of these pronouncements, followers refuse to buy insurance of any kind.

Good will toward all people, racial integration, righteous government, international modesty—all these things are *desired now,* in this world, not the next. It is on this premise that the plans, policies, and actions of the movement are based. And it is this "here and now" philosophy that gives true followers a sense of abiding satisfaction. They feel that if they can unashamedly express their love for Father, put his teachings into practice, and show that the system works, then human salvation will be at hand.

But is it really true that Father Divine's followers do not get sick or die? Of course not. Their morbidity and mortality rates seem to be the same as for the population at large. When followers do die, however, it is attributed to the fact that they somehow failed to live up to the principles set forth by Father. Had they abided by those principles, they would not have died.

Present-day followers are realistic on this point. They realize full well that their members die. The point they make, however, is that Father Divine's teachings represent a *goal,* and that while the goal is difficult, it is not impossible. Successful or not, the true follower is one who devotes his life to the attainment of that goal. Mother Divine writes as follows on the subject:

> In the Peace Mission Movement there are no funeral services. Followers of Father Divine believe in giving flowers to the living. . . .
>
> If a follower dies in the faith, the body is taken care of in a very simple, legal, unobtrusive way. Followers believe that the body returns to the dust from whence it came, and that the Spirit goes back to the GOD that gave it. HE will give it another body as it pleases HIM.
>
> A true follower who brings his body into complete subjection to the Law of the Spirit of Life that gave JESUS CHRIST the victory *will not die.* This goal of Perfection is something great to which to aspire, but nevertheless it is Jesus' command: "Be ye therefore perfect, even as your Father which is in heaven is perfect." (Matthew 5:48)[14]

Enemies and Defectors

Despite his phenomenal success as a religious leader, both Father Divine and the movement he founded have experienced considerable opposi-

[14]Mother Divine, *The Peace Mission Movement,* p. 51. Italics added.

tion. Segments of the African-American community have been scornful of the fact that one of their members had the audacity to play God. The popular press has often ridiculed the movement, while serious scholars— with some exceptions—have remained largely aloof.

In the early period, much of the opposition came from the outside clergy. There was, of course, St. John the Vine Hickerson, who contended that "God" was none other than little George Baker, from Baltimore. Daddy Grace was a more formidable opponent. Wearing colorful costumes and denouncing Father Divine as a false god, he set up "houses of prayer" along the East Coast and—at a dollar a head— performed special baptismal rites on thousands of enthusiasts. He was apparently more adept at baptism than he was at filing his income tax, however, and after running afoul of the Internal Revenue Service, he fled to Cuba.

The next opponent was Bishop Lawson. Unlike so many of the others, Lawson was not an exotic or a cult leader, but a legitimate—and fairly well known—African-American minister. He denounced Father Divine in the press and on the radio, calling him an unscrupulous faker. On and on he railed, week after week, month after month. But in the end, the result was the same. He was forgotten, and Father Divine's followers increased by the thousands.

And so it was with all Father Divine's competitors. Decade after decade they sallied forth, only to be whirled back like pursuers before the Pillar of Fire. In retrospect, none of Father Divine's outside antagonists gave him much cause for concern. His real grief came from those who were within the gates. Of all his flock, however, Verinda Brown probably caused Father more trouble than all his other "problem children" combined.

An Apostate   Verinda Brown had a respectable background. She had no vices, no jail record, no physical debilities. In fact, when she first met Father she was a happily married woman. She and her husband, Thomas, worked as domestics for a wealthy New York family. They made good money, and one would not have expected them to join the celibate world of Father Divine. But join they did.

Somehow—they could never explain why—they were drawn to Father, and after attending several communion banquets they were ready to accept him as God. To put aside temptations of lust, Thomas Brown relinquished his job and went to work in one of the kingdoms. Verinda Brown kept her outside job as domestic.

A short while later they adopted new names: Thomas Brown became Onward Universe, and Verinda became Rebecca Grace. To show their allegiance to the movement, they began to convert their insurance, their building-and-loan holdings, and their real estate to cash. Some of the cash they gave to Father Divine outright. With the rest they bought him gifts. At least, that is what they said they did.

Then Father Divine began to treat them coolly. Apparently, he was not convinced that they had kept lustful thoughts out of their minds. At first Verinda Brown felt hurt, then resentful, then bitter. After thinking things over, she decided to leave the movement, and a short while later her husband followed suit.

But Verinda Brown was not finished. She had, in effect, given Father Divine nearly $5,000—and she wanted it back. She hired a lawyer and took the case to court. Father denied the claim, and produced a host of followers who swore that he never took money in any way, shape, or form. The judge ruled in favor of Verinda Brown, and Father Divine was ordered to pay the full amount plus court costs. Father refused and promptly appealed the case but to no avail. The appeals court upheld the original verdict, and the decision stands to this day.

The decision stands legally, that is. Not morally. For Father Divine refused to pay. Not a dollar, not a dime, not a penny. Instead, he simply left New York, and in July 1942 moved his headquarters to Philadelphia, where it has been ever since. The only time he returned to New York was on Sundays, when, according to state law, process papers cannot be served.

Father Divine's refusal to obey the court order was strictly a matter of principle. Over and over, he proclaimed, "The charge was false. The decision was unjust. I would rather rot in jail before paying one cent." Even his lawyers were never able to get him to change his mind. It was their view that the $5,000 was little more than a nuisance claim, and that paying it was preferable to the onus of moving. But Father never budged from his position.

There is no doubt, however, that Father Divine was hurt by the court decision—in a number of ways. For one thing, adverse publicity always hurts, especially in the case of a religious movement. For another, the subsequent move to Philadelphia led to a noticeable decline in numbers,[15] and while there were other factors involved, the move itself was probably instrumental. Many of the key personnel moved with their leader to Philadelphia. A number of the kingdoms, extensions, and connections closed down, and today only a handful remain in New York. (It was for these very practical reasons that Father Divine's attorneys advised him to pay the claim.)

But there is another side to the story, for if Father Divine was hurt, was not New York hurt even more? After all, as Weisbrot points out, "The stress on independence, honesty, and self-discipline all contributed to a

[15]Weisbrot, *Father Divine*, p. 211.

dramatic lowering of the crime rate wherever new Peace Missions established themselves."[16] A number of judges and police officials attested to this fact.

In a similar vein, because of their honesty and reliability, true followers were in great demand as workers. Additionally, Father Divine was feeding tens of thousands of unemployed New Yorkers every year, virtually free of charge. And, of course, none of his followers were permitted to go on welfare or relief of any kind. In brief, he was saving New York taxpayers a good sum of money on a more or less regular basis. Ironically enough, therefore, it looks as though New York's loss was Philadelphia's gain!

Scope and Operation of the Movement

Most of his followers worshiped Father Divine, and it seems that the closer they were to him the greater was their reverence. Indeed, it is a tribute to his leadership that there were so few Verinda Browns. But how, specifically, did the organization operate? How did one go about joining? Was Father the sole executive and administrator, or did he have deputies and assistants? How large was the membership? In how many states and countries?

Some of the above questions are answerable, some are not. The most difficult ones are those pertaining to numbers, for membership lists were never kept, and neither Father nor Mother Divine has ever given any figures, even though they have been asked hundreds of times. The ban on published statistics extends to financial transactions, bank statements, tax returns, and other fiscal records.

The actual procedure for joining Father Divine's organization must have been extremely informal. Several years ago, when the movement was closer to its peak, a follower was asked how one went about joining. "Well," the man replied,

> you come to the meetings and services, and show them you're really interested. You keep meeting people and, like, you give them a chance to size you up. Then if you want, you can stay on and try it for a while. It all works out. The wrong kind don't last long.

Actually, there are two classes of members: the true or dedicated followers, who live and work within the movement, and the adherents, who live at home. The latter group has always had varying degrees of affiliation and loyalty, and it is this group that has made it difficult to estimate numbers.

---

[16]Ibid., p. 94.

It seems likely that the magnitude of the Father Divine movement has been exaggerated. True, in its heyday, substantial numbers were involved. Standing-room-only crowds were in evidence almost every place that Father spoke, and there was often danger that fire laws were being broken. The demands on his time were such that he could scarcely keep up with his schedule.

But there was another side to the vociferation. Many of the standing-room-only crowds included quasi-members, or simply spectators who were eager to see what "God" looked like. On many occasions, busloads of Father's followers accompanied him from place to place, adding to the impression that there were followers everywhere.

To the press, also, God and his angels were good copy, and reporters constantly played up the movement's circus-like atmosphere. When Father Divine bought an airplane, one would have thought—according to the headlines—that he was taking off for heaven. Many of the newspaper stories, furthermore, were clearly inaccurate. Press reports that the movement numbered 15 to 20 million members represented a figure that was higher than the total African-American population of the United States at that time.

Nevertheless, by World War II, there were traces of the movement in some twenty-five states, although many of the organizations were short-lived. Although Father Divine himself continually stressed the international flavor of the organization, membership abroad never amounted to much numerically. A limited number of countries were involved— Australia, British West Indies, Canada, Switzerland, England, Germany, and Panama. Today, most of the foreign branches appear to be either inactive or defunct. The hub of the movement was always New York, New Jersey, and Philadelphia.

The peak period for the Father Divine movement came in the 1930s and 1940s. It was during these years that membership reached a maximum, that the movement became national and international in scope, and that Father Divine became a renowned religious leader. The organization remained moderately strong during the 1950s and early 1960s, although the vigor was clearly waning. After 1965, however—the year of Father's death—the movement seemed to go downhill rather sharply. Today the organization survives, reduced in both numbers and energy.

How large was the membership during the peak period? No one can say for sure. The number never approached the 22 million repeatedly claimed by Father Divine or the "millions" regularly headlined in the press. If the hangers-on and the spectators are excluded, it is doubtful whether the figure even ran to the hundreds of thousands. Membership probably could be counted in the tens of thousands, but only at the height of the movement. Today the number of followers appears to be quite small, perhaps a few hundred dedicated believers, perhaps less.

There have always been more blacks than whites in the movement. During the peak period, the black-white ratio was about 90:10 or 80:20. Also, females have always outnumbered males, by perhaps three or four to one. And—predictably—the movement has had more appeal to the middle and older age groups than to the young.

Leadership Not too much can be said about the subject of leadership. Writing in the period when the movement was at its peak, Arthur H. Fauset contends that

> in the Father Divine Movement, Father Divine *is* the organization. There are no assistant leaders, nor directors, vice-presidents, vice-chairmen, or elders. Whatever directive is carried out is assumed to have been issued by Father Divine.[17]

The contention is largely true. It was Father Divine—and no one else—who formulated policy, gave talks, bought property, established businesses (although not in his own name), counseled the followers, dealt with the public, made the major decisions, and otherwise controlled the destiny of the movement. None of the other religious leaders discussed in the present volume had anything like the authority vested in Father Divine.

Structurally, the movement encompasses five mother churches, all rendering allegiance to Father Divine. Some of the churches have branches, although each church and each branch—in a legal sense—is independent. In fact, each of the five churches is incorporated, although the movement itself is not.[18] And since the church buildings are designed to house and feed people, there are day-to-day management problems, paperwork, service details, and so forth, responsibility for which resides in duly elected officers and trustees.

Nominally, each church holds yearly meetings, at which time the officers are elected. Actually, it was an open secret that Father Divine made the selections, with the congregation joyously approving them. (*New Day* invariably carried the proceedings, and the same officers tended to be reelected year after year.) When he was alive, Father could count on a group of faithful lieutenants who assisted in local operations. In the years since his death, these individuals have often continued their local functions.

The Rosebuds, Lilybuds, Crusaders, and secretaries have generally been drawn from the inner circle of the movement, and—in terms of helping Father and Mother Divine—they can be counted on to do what-

[17]Arthur H. Fauset, *Black Gods of the Metropolis* (Philadelphia: University of Pennsylvania Press, 1944), p. 56.
[18]See Mother Divine, *The Peace Mission Movement*, p. 26.

ever has to be done. The secretaries (whose numbers have dwindled from a high of around twenty-five to a mere handful today) have always had high status in the movement. Their duties include handling appointments, greeting visiting dignitaries, taking care of correspondence and other paperwork, and, of course, recording and transcribing the various talks given by Father (and now by Mother) Divine.

This, then, is the leadership structure of the movement. On the one hand, there is no doubt that Father Divine had some much needed help; after all, he was running an organization of thousands. On the other hand, when the movement was at its peak, there was scarcely a person in the organization who could make a significant move without prior approval from Father. This was the way he wanted it, and this was the way his followers wanted it.

The current leader of the movement is Mother Divine, who has proved to be a remarkable woman. Since she has always occupied a special place in the leadership structure, let us examine both her sociohistorical and her present role.

Mother Divine

In spite of tribulations involving Daddy Grace, Bishop Lawson, and Verinda Brown, the movement continued to grow and prosper all during the 1930s. Father Divine was emerging as a man to be reckoned with, and a variety of political figures—including the mayor of New York—courted his favor. But what of Sister Penny, Father's first wife? She was seen at his side less and less often. Finally, her appearances ceased altogether, and she was not heard from after 1940.

It was not until August 1946, however, that Father Divine broke the sad news to his followers. Peninah had died six years earlier. She had had a protracted illness, had grown old and weary in body, so—acceding to her wishes—Father Divine had permitted her to "pass." He had been reluctant to do so. He had also been reluctant to tell his followers the sad news and had waited until the right time to do so. But the right time had come, and on April 29 he had taken a new bride: Sweet Angel, one of his young, white secretaries. (As was previously noted, Father Divine's followers were not allowed to marry. Father felt he was the only one strong enough to marry and keep sexuality out of the bargain.)

As might be expected, the announcement of Father Divine's second marriage came as something of a shock, both to the public at large and to those within the movement. Most Americans in the 1940s were intolerant of interracial marriages. In sociological terminology, such marriages were against the *mores*, that is, those customs or beliefs about which the majority of people have strong emotional feelings.

In fact, at the time, interracial marriages were illegal in no fewer than thirty states. (It was not until 1967 that the Supreme Court declared such laws unconstitutional.) At any rate, the public was shocked and angered at Father Divine's action. Even for some of the followers, the announcement of Peninah's death plus the second marriage was too much. They simply left the movement.

After the first shock waves had passed, however, the new marriage proceeded to work out remarkably well. The public grew accustomed to seeing the couple together, true followers soon took Sweet Angel to their hearts, and Sweet Angel herself proved to be more of a help than even Father had foreseen.

So successful was the marriage that at the end of the first year a giant wedding anniversary banquet was held. From all accounts, it was something to behold. Indeed, it just may have been the most lavish ever given in the United States: 60 different kinds of meat, 54 vegetables, 20 relishes, 42 hors d'oeuvres, 21 different kinds of bread, 18 beverages, 23 salads, 38 different desserts. All told, there were some 350 different kinds of food served, with the marathon meal lasting a full seven hours. Since then, the wedding anniversary celebrations have become one of the movement's most important yearly events, with followers attending from across the nation.

For the record, Mother Divine was born Edna Rose Ritchings, in Vancouver, Canada. Her father was a well-established florist, who would have been able to send Edna Rose to college. But her interest lay more in religion, particularly in Father Divine's brand. She became acquainted with the movement in Canada, and when she was twenty-one she came to Father's headquarters in Philadelphia. A few weeks later, she was made one of the secretaries. At the time of her marriage, Sweet Angel had not yet reached her twenty-second birthday. She would eventually carry heavy responsibilities.

According to the pronouncement made by Father Divine, Mother Divine was the reincarnation of Sister Penny, his first wife—and this is the view of all true followers today. But reincarnated or not, Mother Divine, formerly Sweet Angel, formerly Edna Rose Ritchings, has worked out very well indeed. When Father Divine was alive and in good health, she was at his side during virtually all the communion banquets, meetings, and interviews. During his declining years—roughly 1961 to 1965—she and the secretaries took over more and more of the movement's managerial duties.

After Father's death, Mother Divine became head of the movement. She now presides at the communion banquets and other meetings, handles correspondence, grants interviews, visits the various branches, gives talks, and makes the major decisions necessary in day-to-day operations.

There is no doubt that the Peace Mission movement has been going downhill, a trend which at the moment appears irreversible. If it were not for the efforts of Mother Divine and a small group of followers who work closely with her, the entire organization might already have dissolved.

Father Divine: The Man and the God

What manner of man was this Father Divine? How was he able to convince tens of thousands of followers that he was God Almighty? Circumstantial phenomena such as alienation, racism, and the Judge Lewis Smith episode have already been mentioned. But what of Father Divine himself? What was there in the way of personal characteristics that would help explain his charisma? What was there about him?

Physical and Mental Traits Father Divine's height, paradoxically, might have worked to his advantage. Just as a tall person stands out in a crowd, so does a short one—at least, if he or she is the center of attention, which Father certainly was. Actually, Father Divine had many of the traits we associate with a tall person. He had a resounding—some would say strident—voice that could fill an assembly hall without benefit of microphone. His voice had an inimitable, attention-commanding quality, a quality that comes through even today when we listen to recordings of his talks made several decades ago.

In everything he said and did, Father Divine exuded enthusiasm, zeal, and self-confidence. His walk, his motions and gesticulations, his facial expressions, all attested to the fact that he was on earth to help humanity—and that all the forces of evil combined would not stop him.

His energy was prodigious. Sermons, talks, interviews, conferences, business meetings, consultations, trips to the various branches—day after day, year after year—all on four hours of sleep a night! As he himself might have put it, his energy was embedded "in every organ, muscle, sinew, joint, limb, vein, and bone, and even in every ATOM, fiber, and cell of [HIS] BODILY FORM."

His health, also, was little short of phenomenal. If he had any physical ailments, they did not manifest themselves while he was still active. As Mother Divine says, "He never complained." This is all the more remarkable considering his age. If—as those close to him contend—he married Peninah in 1882, he would have been over 100 years old when he died (1965). This in turn would mean that when he was actually guiding the movement (1930–1960), Father Divine was between 65 and 95 years old.

Some biographers feel he was closer to 85 when he died, although there is no proof of this. His death certificate lists him as being 101. But even if we accept the lower estimate, Father Divine was well up in years during the time he actively engineered the movement. In either case, the overall picture is close to incredible.

But, say his followers, Christ was also incredible. And that is the point. For if, when God periodically returns to earth, He does so in the form of an unlikely human figure, then Father Divine's physical characteristics were all positive attributes. This is the position of the true followers.

Father Divine was intelligent, witty, quick, and had a sharp memory. He abounded with original ideas. He had an excellent understanding of human nature and was a remarkably good businessman. He knew the Bible and could quote long passages verbatim. Despite the fact that he gave hundreds of sermons, talks, and addresses over the years, he never prepared for any of them. So far as is known, *they were all extemporaneous!*

The Father Divine Idiom   In the case of any orator, two essential ingredients are voice power and word power. And to anyone who ever heard him, there was no doubt that Father Divine had both. He had a mighty voice, which seemed even more compelling than it was because of the small body that housed it. And when it came to words and sentences, he was a veritable magician.

Unheard-of expressions rolled off Father Divine's tongue like counterfeit bills off a high-power press. Words like invisibilate, unfoldment, contagionized, convincement, transnipotent, physicalate, convictable, omnilucent, tangibilated—all these and countless others enlivened both his writing and his oratory. And when he was not tangibilating new expressions, he was, as Hoshor puts it, tossing out words that never before had been used in the same sentence.[19] For example, from one of his sermons:

> Someone tries to measure GOD with the measure of the mortal versionated concept of man, but THEY CAN'T DO A THING! "WHERE DID GOD START AND WHERE DID HE BEGIN? EVEN IF SO, WHY, YOU COULD GO BACK THERE AND THEN, AND FROM THENCE ON FROM THERE, AND THEN WHERE WOULD YOU FIND HIM STARTED AT? AREN'T YOU GLAD?"
>
> ("We're so glad, ALMIGHTY GOD!" came the eager response.)

It was not only in his public addresses that Father Divine employed his unfoldment. The following is taken from a personal interview:

> QUESTIONER: You did not say you were God, did you?
> FATHER: I don't need to say it. Did you not hear ME say "the personification of the Fundamental made real, and the universalization of the Personification of God"?
> QUESTIONER: I notice that YOUR followers claim that YOU are GOD.

---

[19]Hoshor, *God in a Rolls Royce,* p. 50.

FATHER: (*softly but firmly*) I do not deny it.
QUESTIONER: YOU do not deny it, but YOU do not actually claim it—is that right?
FATHER: I need not claim anything for MYSELF. I do what I AM and express it in the Actuated Words of Expression.
QUESTIONER: I see.

In spite of his omnilucence and verbal agility, Father Divine could be as clear as the blue sky when he wanted to be. On those occasions when he resorted to obfuscation—as in the foregoing interview—there was probably a reason for it.

Was Father Divine aware of his own grammatical looseness and his questionable agility with words? Indeed he was. He simply considerd himself immune from laws of syntax, as the following sermon-extract indicates.

They may hang me on a grammatical cross. Aren't you glad? And you may say within yourself again, "If he is all intelligent," while I am on the grammatical cross of your consideration, "why is it he does not take himself down off the grammatical cross? Why is it he splits so many verbs and makes so many grammatical errors?"

I do as I please mentally, spiritually, and physically, I am exempt. The law of diction cannot bind me. If the law of diction could bind me, I would be limited to the versions of men.

Personality and Character   It is difficult to characterize Father Divine because he was not a simple man. He refused to discuss his past. He did not keep statistical records pertaining to the movement. And his formal statements were frequently unclear, as can be seen from the above quotations. He also had both a conservative and a flamboyant side, and this duality resulted in different writers having different impressions of the man.

On the conservative side, Father was never known to smoke, drink, or gamble. He did not use profanity. He ate sparingly and evidently renounced all forms of sex quite early in life. Throughout his career he dressed moderately and never wore ceremonial garb of any kind. At a time when other cult leaders in Harlem arrayed themselves in garish costumes, Father Divine wore plain business suits. He worked hard, was intensely patriotic, and preached a more or less standard sermon: honesty, modesty, a day's work for a day's pay, peace on earth. . . .

But did he not also have a flamboyant style? After all, how many people have Cadillacs and Rolls Royces, an airplane, and twenty-five secretaries? How many people coin new words, write to heads of foreign governments, and date their letters A.D.F.D. (*anno Domini* Father Divine)? How many serve hundred-course meals to their guests? And how many claim to be omniscient, omnipotent, and omnilucent?

All things considered, it is probable that Father Divine's so-called flamboyance was not an inherent part of his personality. In both his personal habits and official pronouncements, he revealed himself to be a basically conservative individual. All the rest—the secretaries and the Cadillacs—were probably features that he felt added to the effectiveness of his role. And even in these instances—which were overblown in the daily press—there was often a logical reason involved.

The secretaries, for instance, were not simply stenographic frills. They actually served as the nucleus—a center of loyalty—around which the movement revolved, and as such they comprised a stratum of subleadership. To transport the secretaries and other members of his staff from one meeting to another, it was necessary to have several large cars, and Cadillacs served this purpose as well as adding a touch of elegance to the entire movement.

Father Divine did not throw money away on status symbols, however. His much-publicized airplane—which he scarcely used—was bought secondhand for $700. And his Rolls Royce, bought as a used car in 1933, cost only $150. The other things—the sumptuous communion banquets, the linguistic idiom, the omnilucence—were not so much acts of flamboyance as necessary components of the movement as he was shaping it.

In his economic and financial operations, Father Divine was clearly a person of rectitude. As Weisbrot points out, "He returned all outside contributions to the movement, usually with a note 'explaining' that God provided for his needs."[20] Also, despite the fact that he was in great demand as a public speaker, he refused offers as high as $10,000 "on the grounds that it was wrong to charge for spreading the word of God. And unlike many other cult leaders, he denounced attempts to sell buttons and other items with his endorsement, calling it racketeering."[21]

There were other indications that he was indeed a person of principle. At Sayville he went to jail rather than give in to racial prejudice. In the case of Verinda Brown, he left New York—and took his staff with him—rather than pay what he felt was an unjust claim. In fact, when one considers the size of his organization, the number of branches involved, and the rather complicated economic system he used, it is remarkable that so few charges were ever brought against Father Divine.

Unknown Factors   It must be admitted that many—perhaps most—of Father Divine's personality traits remain unknown to the world at large. Even today, his dedicated followers will talk at great length regarding his attributes as God—but not of his traits as a person. Next to nothing has been released with respect to his personal likes, his habits, his leisure, his temperament, his moods and idiosyncracies.

[20]Weisbrot, *Father Divine*, p. 92.
[21]Ibid.

Most of what we know stems from his overt actions, his published talks, and his sermons. In both talks and sermons, he spoke sometimes as God, sometimes as preacher. But he seldom conversed as an ordinary mortal, and hence his "human" side remains sketchy at best.

The Movement: Weaknesses and Strengths

Weaknesses   The basic weakness of the movement was that it developed as a one-person operation. Like the Oneida Community—but unlike the Jehovah's Witnesses and the Mormons—the movement made virtually no provision for succession. It was assumed that Father Divine would go on forever. Although present followers may deny it, his illness and death apparently decimated the movement. Father himself taught that true followers would not experience illness or death—and when he died, large-scale disaffection followed.

Granted, Father Divine's death would have created problems even if provisions for succession had been made. But the problems could have been solved. Other groups have faced and overcome similar obstacles. Oddly enough, however, the movement seems to be compounding the error in the case of Mother Divine: her death is not contemplated, and no successor has been designated. When the question of succession was raised with one of the followers, the answer was unmistakably clear: "But Mother Divine will always be with us, just as Father has always been with us. . . ."

The movement's position on celibacy is related to their belief in immortality; that is, if dedicated followers live forever, there is no need for procreation. Of course, the fact that they do die means that the movement has no effective means of growth.

Exactly why Father Divine invoked the celibacy rule is not clear. Some writers feel that since the movement was interracial and since—at that time—attitudes toward miscegenation were decidedly negative, Father solved the problem neatly by prohibiting both sex and marriage. This explanation seems a little far-fetched. If he thought he was in the right, Father Divine would never have been deterred by public opinion. A more likely explanation is simply that he desired his followers to live the life of Christ, a position that was—and is—expressive of the very heart of the movement.

Irrespective of the reason, celibacy must be listed as one of the weaknesses of the organization. All groups grow in one of two ways: by natural increase and/or by proselytizing. The Mormons have utilized both methods, and they have grown rapidly. The Amish have rejected all forms of birth control, and they have also shown rapid growth. The Shakers embraced celibacy and, in later years, made few attempts to proselytize—and they are now close to extinction. Is the same fate in store for the Father Divine movement?

Strengths   The movement has already made some positive contributions. During the depression, the various branches fed thousands of destitute people at little or no charge. The homeless were provided with a clean room at a dollar or two a week. Prostitutes, beggars, thieves—all were welcomed into the movement and given respectable jobs.

Once they joined, followers were taught the value of honesty and hard work, and the importance of building self-respect. They were forbidden to accept gifts or gratuities, and they were admonished to dress moderately, eschew vulgarity, and act kindly toward their fellow humans.

In the field of race relations, Father Divine was clearly a generation ahead of his time. The movement of the 1930s and 1940s was pressing for reforms that would not be enacted until the 1960s and 1970s: laws prohibiting segregation in schools and public places, laws establishing fair employment practices, removing "race or color" designation on personnel forms and official records, outlawing restrictive covenants in housing, and so on.

In the political field, also, Father Divine proved to be a seer, for many of the planks in his Righteous Government platform came into being in the decades following World War II: affirmative action programs, changes in welfare policy, changes in tariff schedules, expansion of civil service coverage, and the like.

It may be true that the various reforms would have come about with or without the assistance of Father Divine. But it is equally true that he spoke out in no uncertain terms when many others were silent. Without the impetus of the Father Divine movement, these reforms might have been slower in arriving.

There is one other feature of the movement that should be mentioned: the great emphasis on peace. Father Divine probably desired peace as fervently as any person who ever lived. Peace between nations. Peace between races. Peace between ethnic groups. Peace among people, and peace with oneself. This is what he stood for, and this is what he preached. He called his organization the Peace Mission movement, a name it is known by even today.

The Present Scene

The Peace Mission movement provided large numbers of blacks with an escape from the dismal reality of a white world. It gave them a sense of physical and spiritual well-being. And it tried to develop self-pride. On a societal level, the movement served as the tip of the spear, penetrating into the murky areas of civil rights and international peace. It also served as a reminder that Righteous Government principles could be adopted by persons other than politicians.

Yet today the Peace Mission movement is in trouble. Times change, and the 1930s are a far cry from the 1990s. The societal context has shifted, and a new set of societal problems has emerged. But the movement has not changed. Its goals, organization, and method of operation are much the same today as they were fifty years ago.

In the 1930s, the urban masses—both black and white—needed food, and Father gave it to them. During recent decades in the United States, fewer people suffered from starvation or lack of housing, and not many people sought the services of Father Divine's organization. Social service programs, however, suffered cutbacks during the 1980s, and it is possible that there will again be a need for Divinite programs.

Affirmative action programs also suffered setbacks in the 1980s, and there is evidence that racial discrimination is on the rise. Nevertheless, discriminatory levels today are not nearly as great as they were fifty years ago when blacks were excluded from hotels, restaurants, movies, and even organized sports. Although to some extent African-Americans today are still handicapped by their color, they have better opportunities for getting a college education and making their mark in the business and professional worlds.

Fifty years ago, African-Americans, particularly those in the lower classes, needed an inspirational leader who could stand up to the white world and show some results. And Father Divine filled that role. Today, leadership in the Peace Mission movement is white, and one suspects—given the temper of the times—that this fact may have a negative effect on black recruitment.

Sayville, Judge Lewis Smith, and the days of retribution are far behind. Father himself is no longer physically present to spark the membership and expand the organization. As a group, the followers are aging. Many have already died, and others have left the movement. The social climate that spawned the Peace Mission program has changed drastically. In brief, aside from self-perpetuation and the continuation of traditional rituals—such as publication of *New Day*, convocation of communion banquets, and the observance of holidays—there doesn't seem to be a great deal for the organization to do.

In some ways, the movement is still a going concern. Thanks to Father Divine's perspicacity, the organization is well endowed financially and owns a number of valuable properties. True followers can still put on a spirited performance at their get-togethers. They are absolutely devoted to Mother and Father Divine, and to the movement itself. Inexorably, however, celibacy continues to block the main arteries of growth. New converts are hard to come by, and—numerically—the membership is at an all-time low.

This, then, is the present status of the movement. It is rapidly reaching the point—if it has not already—where the entire membership will consist of a small, spiritually elite group. One follower compared the present state of the movement with an earlier quiescent period of Christianity, the implication being that sooner or later there would be an inextinguishable resurgence for the Divinites.

All of which may be true. To an objective observer, however, there is nothing on the secular or spiritual horizon to suggest a rejuvenation. But whether there is or not, Father Divine will remain one of the indelible figures in the history of twentieth-century religious thought. He was—with the possible exception of Brigham Young—the most remarkable of all the leaders discussed in this book. He was also a person of infinite goodness.

SELECTED READINGS

Barnes, Roma. *"Blessings Flowing Free": The Father Divine Peace Mission Movement in Harlem, New York City, 1932–1941.* Ph.D. diss., University of York, England, 1979.

Braden, Charles. *These Also Believe: A Study of Modern American Cults and Minority Religious Movements.* New York: Macmillan, 1949.

Buehrer, Edwin. "Harlem's God." *Christian Century,* 52 (December 11, 1935): 1590–93.

Burnham, Kenneth E. *God Comes to America: Father Divine and the Peace Mission Movement.* Boston: Lambeth, 1979.

Calverton, V. F. *Where Angels Dared to Tread.* New York: Bobbs-Merrill, 1941.

Cavan, Ruth. "Communes: Historical and Contemporary." *International Review of Modern Sociology,* 6 (Spring 1976): 1–11.

Crumb, C. B. "Father Divine's Use of Colloquial and Original English." *American Speech,* 15 (October 1940): 327–37.

Fauset, Arthur H. *Black Gods of the Metropolis.* Philadelphia: University of Pennsylvania Press, 1944.

Galanter, Marc. *CULTS: Faith, Healing, and Coercion.* New York: Oxford University Press, 1989.

Gordon, Suzanne. "Life after Heaven." *Philadelphia Inquirer Magazine* (December 11, 1989), 28ff.

Harkness, Gloria. "Father Divine's Righteous Government." *Christian Century,* 82 (October 13, 1965): 1259–61.

Harris, Sarah. *Father Divine: Holy Husband.* 1953. Reprint, New York: Macmillan, 1971.

Higginbotham, A. Leon. *In the Matter of Color.* New York: Oxford University Press, 1980.

Hoshor, John. *God in a Rolls Royce: The Rise of Father Divine.* 1936. Reprint, Freeport, NY: Books for Libraries Press, 1971.

Hostetler, John. *Communitarian Societies.* New York: Holt, Rinehart and Winston, 1974.

Howell, Clarence. "Father Divine: Another View." *Christian Century,* 53 (October 7, 1936): 1332–33.

Kelley, Hubert. "Heaven Incorporated." *American Magazine,* 221 (January 1936): 40ff.

Kephart, William M. *The Family, Society, and the Individual.* Boston: Houghton Mifflin, 1981. See chapter seven, "The Black Family," pp. 175–201, and chapter 20, "Communes," pp. 529–34.

McKay, Claude. "Father Divine's Rebel Angel." *American Mercury* 51 (Sept., 1940): 73–80.

McKelway, St. Clair, and Liebling, A. J. "Who Is This King of Glory?" *New Yorker,* June 13, 1936, pp. 21ff.; June 20, pp. 22ff.; June 27, pp. 22ff.

Moseley, J. R. *Manifest Victory.* New York: Harper & Row, 1941.

Mother Divine. *The Peace Mission Movement.* Philadelphia: Imperial Press, 1982.

New Day. Published biweekly by the New Day Publishing Company. 1600 W. Oxford Street, Philadelphia, PA.

Ottley, Roi. *New World A-Coming: Inside Black America.* Boston: Houghton Mifflin, 1943.

Parker, Robert Allerton. *The Incredible Messiah.* Boston: Little, Brown, 1937.

Shey, Thomas. "Why Communes Fail: A Comparative Analysis of the Viability of Danish and American Communes." *Journal of Marriage and the Family,* 39 (August 1977): 605–13.

Staples, Robert, ed. *The Black Family: Essays and Studies.* Belmont, CA: Wadsworth, 1978.

Stinnett, Nick, and Birdsong, C. W. *The Family and Alternative Life Styles.* Chicago: Nelson-Hall, 1978.

Washington, Joseph R. *Black Sects and Cults: The Power Axis in an Ethnic Ethic.* New York: Doubleday, 1973.

Weisbrot, Robert. *Father Divine and the Struggle for Racial Equality.* Urbana, IL: University of Illinois Press, 1983.

CHAPTER SEVEN

THE MORMONS

Of the nearly 1,200 different religions in the United States, none has had a more turbulent history than that of the Mormons. It would not be much exaggeration, in this respect, to say that the Mormons are in a class by themselves.[1] Born in controversy and vilified throughout most of the nineteenth century, they have nevertheless succeeded in establishing a socioreligious organization of unbelievable vitality.

The "Burned-Over" District

The groundwork and foundations of Mormonism were laid out in the 1820s in western New York State. The area came to be known as the "burned-over" district; that is, burned over by the fires of religious ardor. Never in our history has so much religious fervor been packed into one geographical area. Bibles, revelations, preachers, and prophets came (and went) with astonishing rapidity.

The Millerites proclaimed that the world was coming to an end. Ann Lee's Shakers renounced sex and marriage, and formed a nearby settlement. Jemima Wilkinson, ruling by revelation, built her colony of Jerusalem. John Humphrey Noyes started the Oneida Community. The Fox sisters, claiming to have communicated with the dead, founded the modern spiritualist movement. All of this occurred in western New York between, roughly, 1825 and 1850. Even the older denominations—Methodists, Baptists, Presbyterians—were torn by schism and dissent.

Into this religious maelstrom came Joseph Smith. Taken to Manchester, New York, as a teenager, young Joseph soon became disturbed by "this war of words and tumult of opinions." Which group was right? Which group was wrong? In genuine perplexity, according to his own account, he turned to the Bible and was struck by a passage in the Epistle of St. James: "If any of you lack wisdom, let him ask of God . . . and it shall be given him" (James 1:5).

---

[1]For a recent account of the Mormon experience, see John Heinerman and Anson Shupe, *The Mormon Corporate Empire* (Boston, MA: Beacon Press, 1985).

Accordingly, Joseph Smith "retired to the woods" to ask God the all-important question. It was here that he had his first religious experience, for he was visited by both God the Father and his son Jesus Christ. Among other things, he was told that he was to join none of the existing sects, for "they were all wrong." Smith was only fifteen years old at the time, and the visitation remained engraved on him forever.

Smith made no attempt to hide the fact of his heavenly visitation. With the natural exuberance of a teenager, he divulged what had happened, but his story fell on deaf ears. "I soon found," he said, "that my telling the story had excited a great deal of prejudice . . . and though I was an obscure boy of only fifteen, yet men of high standing would take notice sufficient to excite the public mind against me, and create a bitter persecution."[2]

Although he could not know it at the time, Joseph Smith's persecutions would continue as long as he lived. In fact, they would accelerate. But despite the rising tide of troubled waters, he never once recanted nor wavered in his spiritual beliefs. His alleged revelations and heavenly visitations continued right up to the day he died.

The Golden Plates   The next visitation came three years later (1823), when Smith was eighteen. This was the most noteworthy of all his religious experiences, since it involved the angel Moroni and the discovery of the golden plates. These plates, or tablets, form the very foundation of Mormonism, so let us read Joseph Smith's own account:

> After I had retired to my bed for the night, a personage appeared at my bedside, standing in the air, for his feet did not touch the floor. He had on a loose robe of most exquisite whiteness. . . .
>
> He called me by name, and said that he was a messenger from the presence of God, and that his name was Moroni; that God had work for me to do. . . .
>
> He said that there was a book deposited, written upon gold plates. He said that the fullness of the everlasting Gospel was contained in it. Also, that there were two stones in silver bows—and these stones, fastened to a breastplate, constituted what is called the Urim and Thummim, and that God had prepared them for the purpose of translating the book.[3]

After several more visits—in which Moroni repeated his instructions—Joseph Smith was ready to unearth the plates. On the west side of the highest hill in the county, he came across a large stone. "Having removed the earth, I obtained a lever which I fixed under the edge of the stone, and with a little exertion raised it up. I looked in, and there

---

[2]Joseph Smith, *Pearl of Great Price* (Salt Lake City: The Church of Jesus Christ of Latter-day Saints, 1974), p. 49.
[3]Ibid., pp. 50–51.

indeed did I behold the plates, and the Urim and Thummim, as stated by the messenger."[4]

Eventually, Joseph Smith removed the plates from the hill (now known as Cumorah) and took them home. Each of the plates measured eight inches square, and since there were a number of them—the stack was six inches thick—the total weight must have been considerable. Yet young Joseph Smith experienced no difficulty in transporting them, or at least made no mention of the fact. He did, however, have trouble keeping them out of evil hands. "For no sooner was it known that I had them, than the most strenuous exertions were used to get them from me. But by the wisdom of God, they remained safe in my hands, until I had accomplished what was required."[5]

Although the golden plates were written in an ancient tongue, Joseph Smith—aided by the Urim and Thummin—translated them with relative ease. When he had finished, the angel Moroni came and took back both the original set of plates and the Urim and Thummim. The translation, of course, remained on earth and became known as the Book of Mormon.

Considering the theme of the book and the circumstances surrounding the writing, it is little wonder that the Book of Mormon has become a source of contention. Indeed, it is one of the most controversial books ever written. Its author, or translator—only twenty-three years old at the time—remains one of the most perplexing figures in American social history.

Joseph Smith—Man of Controversy

Joseph Smith was born in 1805 at Sharon, Vermont, of old New England stock. Whether any of his early activities foreshadowed future events is a matter of opinion. His grandfather claimed to have had heavenly visions and actually had his experiences published in book form. Joseph himself was fond of using a "peep-stone," a kind of native quartz or crystal, to locate hidden treasure. And while the digging never unearthed anything of value, the boy did show evidence of lively imagination and—quite important—the ability to lead people older than himself. Use of the peep-stone, incidentally, was a rather common practice of the period.

In a strictly religious vein, Joseph Smith was not precocious. He seemed neither more—nor less—attracted to the Lord than other children his age. Nor was he bookish or intellectual in any known sense. He could read and write, but his education, like that of most of his peers,

[4]Ibid., p. 53.
[5]Ibid., p. 54.

was severely limited. He seems to have been a pleasant, likable young man, not significantly different from others of his age group—except, perhaps, for his preoccupation with treasure hunting.

Although the Smiths were never destitute, Joseph's father had some difficulty earning a living. When they moved to New York, their fortunes did not improve—and neither did young Joseph's luck with treasure hunting. How he would have fared in a competitive economy will never be known, for at an age when most young men were serving their apprenticeships, Joseph Smith was discovering and translating the golden plates. And at an age when most of his childhood acquaintances were starting up in business or agriculture, Joseph was founding a church.

The Book of Mormon   As transcribed by Joseph Smith, the Book of Mormon is a mammoth and fairly intricate work. The present edition runs to 531 double-column pages, divided into fifteen books—Nephi, Jacob, Enos, Jarom, Omni, and so forth. Each book is subdivided into chapter and verse, so that in style it is like the Bible; indeed, a number of Old and New Testament passages are quoted verbatim.

The Book of Mormon tells the story of a family who left Jerusalem around 600 B.C. Lehi, the father, was a Jewish prophet who had been notified by God that the city was doomed to destruction. Under Lehi's direction, the family, together with some friends and neighbors, built a small ship and sailed eastward. Their probable route was the Arabian Sea, the Indian Ocean, and the South Pacific, for eventually they reached the western coast of America.

The little group established itself in this New World of promise and soon began to expand and multiply. When Lehi died, the group split into two factions, one following Nephi, the youngest son, the other following Laman, the eldest. The Nephites and the Lamanites eventually became hostile to one another, and fighting ensued.

Although there were exceptions on both sides, it appears that the Nephites were a more vigorous people than the Lamanites. The Nephites were industrious, well versed in the arts, and prayed to God for guidance. The Lamanites were often in trouble and became slovenly and idolatrous. They incurred God's displeasure: as a result their skins became dark, and they were reduced to savagery. They were, according to the Book of Mormon, forebears of the native Americans.

In brief, the Nephites advanced and the Lamanites declined, and while both groups had an Israelite background, it was no great surprise when Jesus appeared among the Nephites. Indeed, he taught the same things he had taught in Palestine and set up his church in much the same way. As the Nephites grew and prospered over the years, however, they tended to fall away from Christ's teachings. Prophets such as Mormon—who had kept a chronicle of the Nephites—exhorted them to mend their ways, but to no avail. God eventually lost patience with the Nephites and permitted their hereditary enemies, the Lamanites, to prevail.

The final battles took place around the hill Cumorah in A.D. 400, and the Nephites were destroyed as a nation. The last remaining Nephite was Mormon's son, Moroni, who took his father's chronicle, wrote the concluding portion, and buried the entire record—in the form of gold plates—on Cumorah. This was the same Moroni who, as a resurrected personage, divulged the hiding place to Joseph Smith.

The idea of a spiritual bridge between the Old World and the New had a natural appeal for many Americans, especially since there was then much speculation about the origin of the native American. And while the account of the Nephites and the Lamanites represents but one small portion of the Book of Mormon, it does illustrate one of the central themes of the book: the cycle of good and evil. Humans follow the commandments of God; hence they thrive and prosper. But prosperity leads to pride, and pride leads to selfishness and a rejection of God's ways—hence humans fall. To rise again, they must repent and ask His forgiveness.

Over and over again, in a variety of different contexts and with a host of different peoples, the sequence is repeated: from goodness to prosperity, from prosperity to pride and selfishness, from pride and selfishness to downfall, from downfall to repentance. Repentance leads to goodness, and the cycle starts once more. There is litle equivocation or obscurity in the Book of Mormon. Good and evil are portrayed with crystalline clarity. And as more than one commentator has pointed out, it is this clarity that adds to the appeal of the book.

Doubters and Believers   As was mentioned earlier, the golden plates—and the story inscribed thereon—provoked an avalanche of controversy. Critics denounced them as fakes, and Joseph Smith was decried as a mere yarn spinner. If scholars had difficulty with hieroglyphics, how could an uneducated twenty-three-year-old possibly have translated them? The Book of Mormon, furthermore, contains a number of internal errors. The steel sword of Laban is reported as existing in 600 B.C. (1 Nephi 4:9), long before steel was invented. Cows and oxen are reported in the New World about the same time (1 Nephi 18:25), although the first cattle were actually brought from the Old World by Columbus on his second voyage.

Some critics also question the Hebraic origin of the native Americans, since archeological evidence indicates that the native Americans are a Mongoloid strain who reached the American continent via the Bering Strait. Leone contends that many Mormons seem to have no idea that there is an alternative explanation outside *The Book of Mormon* for the peopling and history of the New World before the arrival of Columbus—and that it was not all Nephites and Lamanites as stated in the First and Second Nephi. They are unaware of what the rest of the world has concluded.[6]

Other critics see the Book of Mormon as a not-too-subtle attempt to paraphrase the Bible. They call attention to similarities in name-style and wording. The phrase "And it came to pass," for example, appears no fewer than 2,000 times.

Defenders of Mormonism reject all the above arguments in no uncertain terms. They believe that since Joseph Smith was a true prophet of God, he had no need of formal education to translate the golden plates. The Urim and Thummim, as instruments of the Almighty, were all that was necessary.

As for the plates themselves, Mormon supporters point out that eleven witnesses testified—by sworn statement—that they had actually seen the plates. A number of these witnesses later withdrew from the Mormon church and renounced their ties completely, but *none ever repudiated their sworn testimony concerning the golden plates.* To this day, every copy of the Book of Mormon contains a facsimile of the sworn statements, together with the eleven signatures.

As far as archeological evidence is concerned, Mormon defenders claim that it is unclear, that the authorities themselves have differing interpretations, and that new discoveries are constantly being made. It is held that, when all the evidence is in, the account contained in the golden plates will be confirmed. The other criticisms—involving word meanings, grammar, and phraseology—are dismissed as inconsequential points that arise whenever a manuscript is processed for publication.

Most followers believe strongly that the Book of Mormon is an internally consistent document that has stood the test of time. They feel it is beautifully written, eternally instructive, and a true reflection of the word of God. They accept it—along with the Old and New Testaments—as Scripture. The net result, as Leone states, is that "Mormonism is not a part of traditional Christianity; it is a whole new version."[7]

Formation of the Church

On April 6, 1830, six young men gathered together not far from the hill Cumorah. In addition to Joseph Smith himself, there were his two

---

[6]Mark Leone, *Roots of Modern Mormonism* (Cambridge, MA: Harvard University Press, 1979), p. 203.
[7]Ibid., p. 171.

brothers, Hyrum and Samuel, as well as Oliver Cowdery, Peter Whitmer, and David Whitmer. All had seen the golden plates—they had so testified—and all had been profoundly moved by the inscribed message. Indeed, they were gathered for the purpose of founding a church based on that message. The laws of New York State required a minimum of six members for incorporation, and these were the six. When the meeting opened, Joseph Smith announced that he had received a revelation from God which said, "Behold there should be a record kept among you: and in it thou shalt be called a seer, a translator, a prophet, an apostle of Jesus Christ, an elder of the church through the will of God."

By this revelation, and by the unanimous consent of the original six members, Joseph Smith was acknowledged to be a prophet of God and the undisputed leader of the church. Even today, in routine conversation, Mormons refer to him as the Prophet. It should be mentioned, however, that the term "Mormon church" was never adopted, the original designation being simply the Church of Christ. (Outsiders referred to members as "Mormons" or "Mormonites.") A few years later (1838), the present name was made official: the Church of Jesus Christ of Latter-day Saints. ("Latter-day" refers to the Western Hemisphere period of scriptural history.) Members of the church do not mind being called Mormons. They use the name themselves. They are more likely, however, to use terms like "Saints," "Latter-day Saints," or "LDS."

The church grew rapidly—a thousand members in less than a year. It soon became apparent that, being American in both setting and theology, LDS had a natural attraction for many people. Then, too, in this early period the church was blessed with a number of extremely able, vigorous leaders. In addition to Joseph Smith, a genuinely charismatic leader, there were Oliver Cowdery, Sidney Rigdon, and Parley Pratt. There was also a man named Brigham Young.

Death of the Prophet   Mormon growth, however, was accompanied by prolonged and vicious persecution. In New York State, Joseph Smith was arrested several times for disturbing the peace. To escape harassment, the Prophet and his followers moved westward—to Ohio, Missouri, Ilinois—but in each state they encountered real trouble. Raids, attacks by mobs, pitched battles—the trail of persecution seemed endless. Joseph Smith himself was assaulted, beaten, and jailed on a number of occasions.

The end came on June 27, 1844, when a mob stormed the jail at Carthage, Illinois, where four Mormon leaders were being held. Willard Richards and John Taylor managed to escape with their lives, but Joseph Smith and his brother Hyrum were brutally shot to death.

The Aftermath—and Brigham Young

The death of the Mormon leader shocked both the citizens of Illinois and the nation at large. Even the demise of such well-known figures as Ann Lee and John Humphrey Noyes brought nothing like the publicity accorded Joseph Smith. To be sure, the Prophet was brutally murdered, while the others died of natural causes, but the reaction was based on more than that. It was as though the public sensed that—unlike the Shakers, the Oneidans, and scores of others—the Latter-day Saints presaged a major movement.

The skeptics thought otherwise. Many outsiders felt that the Mormons could never survive the death of their leader. And some insiders tried to weaken the movement by forming splinter groups. One faction followed Sidney Rigdon eastward. Another group went with James Strang to Wisconsin and Michigan. Still another followed William Bickerton to West Virginia and Pennsylvania. Not all of these offshoots failed—small groups of Strangites and Bickertonites still exist—but none had any appreciable effect on the health of LDS proper. The only apostate organization to achieve any size and importance was the Reorganized group, which will be discussed later.

In any event, the Church of Jesus Christ of Latter-day Saints not only survived but grew and prospered. The death of Joseph Smith did not result in a bankruptcy of leadership. On the contrary, LDS had any number of able and enthusiastic people. There was, of course, only one Brigham Young.

Born in 1801 at Whitingham, Vermont, Brigham Young reportedly came from the poorest family in town. Instead of going to school, he worked—with his hands. He became a skilled carpenter, painter, and glazier, and—on the side—learned to read and write. He evidenced no special religious leanings until he was twenty-two, when he became a Methodist. A few years later, after reading the Book of Mormon and becoming convinced of its authenticity, he converted to LDS.

In 1832 he met Joseph Smith, and the two had a long talk. From then on, Brigham Young was one of the Prophet's staunchest supporters— and one of Mormondom's most enthusiastic workers. As a carpenter, he helped build temples; as a planner, he laid out whole cities; as a missionary, he achieved a brilliant record in England. His rise within the church was rapid, and following Joseph Smith's death in 1844, he was the dominant figure in LDS for over thirty years. It is difficult to imagine what form Mormonism would have taken without his leadership.

"This Is the Right Place"

After a short—and uneasy—truce, persecution of the Mormons was resumed. The alleged murderers of Joseph Smith were tried but were acquitted, and from then on things went from bad to worse. Mobs attacked Mormon families. LDS buildings were set afire. Attacks and counterattacks accelerated. At one time, both sides were using artillery pieces. By the end of 1845, it had become obvious that the Latter-day Saints would have to leave Illinois.

The exodus began on the morning of February 4, 1846, and the going was rough. It took the Saints nearly five months to reach Council Bluffs, Iowa, four hundred miles away. But the Rocky Mountains were still five hundred miles distant—and beyond the mountains was another stretch of a thousand miles, most of it unsettled land.

In the spring of 1847, an advance group of some 150 Mormons, headed by Brigham Young and Heber Kimball, set out to blaze a new path. Their success was startling. Known as the Mormon Trail, the new route was eventually followed by both the Union Pacific Railroad and U.S. Highway 30.

The trailblazers pushed on across the Rockies, and on the morning of July 24, 1847, Brigham young caught his first sight of the Great Salt Lake Valley. He held up his hand and said, "It is far enough. This is the right place." His followers knew what he meant. Thenceforth, July 24 would be celebrated among the Mormons as Pioneer Day, their greatest holiday.

Miracle of the Gulls   One of the striking stories concerning early Mormon hardships is the so-called miracle of the gulls. The summer of 1849, thanks largely to innovative irrigation, was a good crop year. The vegetation was thick, and the leaves were lush. But just as the Saints were visualizing full storehouses for the winter, hordes of locusts swarmed over the plants and began to devour them. Horrified, the residents tried to beat the insects off with everything at their command. They also opened up the irrigation canals to try to drown the invaders. But for every 1,000 killed, 10,000 more appeared. Finally—after all human effort had failed—the Mormons knelt down beside their crops and prayed to God for help.

Suddenly, in the distance, a dark cloud appeared. It proved to be a large flock of gulls, and for a time the Mormons feared further crop destruction. But to their unbounded joy, the gulls began to devour the locusts, and soon the danger was over.

The story is a true one, and today there is a monument to the gulls in Salt Lake City. The gull is also the official state bird, and—understandably—is protected by Utah law.

Overseas Missions   It had always been Joseph Smith's feeling that Mormonism needed a strong overseas base, and as early as 1837 an LDS mission had been established in England. The actual flow of converts from Europe to America began shortly afterward, but not until Brigham

Young took office did Mormon immigration flourish. During the thirty years of his presidency (1847–1877), tens of thousands of converts arrived in America, nearly all of whom remained loyal to the church.

The chief source of LDS immigration was England and Scandinavia, although some converts were also received from Germany and Switzerland. Mormon attempts in other countries—Italy, Spain, China—failed. There is no doubt, though, that much of Utah today is of Anglo-Scandinavian stock. As Turner puts it, "A summer day's walk down any street in Salt Lake City's business district shows a constant parade of blonds with blue eyes and skins tanned golden brown under the sun of the high desert."[8]

Polygamy

Once the Salt Lake region was consolidated, the Mormons experienced steady and rapid growth. Like all organizations, they had problems and conflicts. But there was one issue that dwarfed all the others, one issue that almost brought the edifice down. The issue was polygamy, and it is ironic that the very practice that came close to being fatal is the one which, in the public mind, seems interminably linked with Mormonism.

(Strictly speaking, polygamy refers to plural spouses—husbands *or* wives—while polygyny includes only plural wives. However, writers of the period used the term polygamy when referring to the Mormons, and somehow the term has persisted. Accordingly, polygamy will be used throughout the present account.)

How did the Latter-day Saints come to adopt polygamy in the first place? A number of explanations have been offered, most of them false. It has been suggested that plural marriage was utilized in order to take care of excess Mormon females. Census figures indicate, however, that—as in most of the West—the Utah area had an excess of males, not females.

It has also been suggested that polygamy was simply a convenient method of satisfying the high male sex drive, yet prurient interests can hardly have been paramount. Before a man could take a second wife, he was required to get the permission not only of his bishop but of his first wife. Only by so doing could he be assured of a sanctioned LDS marriage.

Some observers feel that plural marriage was a not so subtle attempt by the church to increase the Mormon birthrate. But this contention is not true either. Polygamous wives, on the average, had fewer children than did monogamous wives.

The Latter-day Saints adopted polygamy for one reason and one reason only. They were convinced that the practice had been ordained by

[8]Wallace Turner, *The Mormon Establishment* (Boston: Houghton Mifflin, 1966), p. 69.

God—as revealed through the Prophet Joseph Smith. Virtually all modern scholars are in agreement on this point.

Beginnings   While the history of Mormon polygamy contains numerous gaps, the following information has been fairly well documented. Joseph Smith reported that he had received a revelation from God prescribing polygamy. The date of the revelation is unclear. It was recorded, however, on July 12, 1843, for on that date the Prophet carefully dictated the lengthy revelation, later known as the Principle, to his clerk, William Clayton.

It should be emphasized that in the early period, polygamy was never publicly admitted; indeed, the revelation itself was locked in Brigham Young's desk for many years. Gradually, however, as more and more of the church hierarchy took plural wives, the element of secrecy was lost. When Orson Pratt and Brigham Young made the public announcement in 1852—based on the Prophet's earlier revelation—the Principle had become a more or less open secret.

By this time, of course, the Mormons had "escaped" from the East and the Midwest. Well beyond the Rocky Mountains, they were—or thought they were—safely ensconced in their territorial domain. Church leaders did not expect that the Principle would go unchallenged. They anticipated some intervention by the United States government, but thought that—in the interest of religious freedom—the courts would be on the side of LDS. This was an incorrect assessment.

Nevertheless, for a period of almost fifty years the Latter-day Saints not only practiced polygamy but did so with a fair amount of success. It may well be that this exercise in marital pluralism was the most unusual large-scale experiment in American social history.

The Operation of Polygamy   At the time, there were many misconceptions about Mormon polygamy, and some of them still remain. According to the lurid accounts of the eastern newspapers, Mormon patriarchs were simply gobbling up unsuspecting girls in wholesale lots—for lewd and lascivious purposes. And while such charges were obvious nonsense, they did much to inflame public opinion.

The "typical Mormon patriarch" was quite content to have but one wife, for in any group which permits polygamy, most people still practice monogamy. This is because at the marrying ages, males and females are roughly equal in numbers. When there is an excess of one sex, it is usually slight, so that—generally speaking—every plural spouse means that someone else is deprived of matrimony altogether.

What percentage of Mormons actually practiced polygamy? An accurate answer remains elusive. The figure doubtless varied over the years, peaking around 1860. The overall figure—the proportion of Mormon men who ever practiced the Principle—is estimated at 3 percent by LDS. Critics of Mormonism have placed the figure as high as 20 to 30 percent. When most scholarly calculations are considered, perhaps a fair estimate would be in the neighborhood of 10 to 15 percent. Whatever the figure, one very important fact is often overlooked; namely, that it was the upper-level Mormon men—especially those at the top of the church hierarchy—who were most likely to take plural wives.

Of those LDS men who were involved in polygamy, a clear majority had but one additional wife, which fact also ran counter to public impression. The misconception regarding numbers arose in part because of the prejudice of certain anti-Mormon elements. But it was also true that there were some church leaders who did indeed have a plurality of spouses. Orson Pratt had ten wives; his brother Parley had twelve. John D. Lee had eighteen wives and sixty-five children. Heber Kimball had forty-five wives and sixty-eight children. Brigham Young had twenty-seven wives and fifty-six children. And there were many others. Joseph Smith himself apparently had numerous wives, although the exact number remains in doubt.

A common polygamous practice was for the man to marry sets of sisters, the feeling being that such a procedure would reduce connubial tension. Whatever the reason, Joseph Smith is reported to have married three sets of sisters. Heber Kimball married four sets. John D. Lee married three sisters and also their mother! And so it went.

What about the economic aspect of plural marriage? Was having plural wives (and plural children) an asset or a liability? In many cases, it was a liability. True, an extra wife and children for a Mormon farmer meant that he would have additional help for the farm. But a fair number of Latter-day Saints were not farmers, and even among those who were, there was a point of diminishing returns. A Mormon farmer with fifteen wives and forty-five children could hardly hope to keep them all productively engaged in farming. And with all those mouths to feed. . . .

Little wonder that so many Mormon polygamists were from the upper economic bracket. Poorer members could hardly afford the practice, a fact of life that was well understood by all concerned. Plural marriage held status advantages for Mormon women as well as for men. Foster puts it as follows:

> [A]t least until 1880, polygamous wives held higher status through association with the most influential men, and through the sense of serving as religious and social models for others. . . . In some cases, a first wife actively encouraged her reluctant husband to take a plural wife so that they could both reach the highest state of exaltation in the afterlife. . . .[9]

[9]Lawrence Foster, *Religion and Sexuality* (New York: Oxford University Press, 1981), pp. 211–12.

Celestial Marriage One of the revelatory doctrines promulgated by Joseph Smith and practiced by LDS is *celestial marriage*. According to this concept, there are two distinct types of marriage: one for time and the other for eternity. The former is regarded as a secular marriage that is broken at the death of either husband or wife. Celestial marriage, on the other hand, serves to "seal" a man and woman not only for time but for all eternity. Such marriages are always solemnized in a Mormon temple and include rites and rituals that are never divulged to non-Mormons. Other types of ceremonies—civil or religious—are held to be valid only until death. (Marriages with non-Mormons run counter to LDS policy and are not performed in the temples.)

The point is that celestial marriage dovetailed nicely with polygamy. For example, if a man who had been sealed for time and eternity died before his wife, the latter could—if she desired—marry another man for time only. Some of the women married to Joseph Smith for time and eternity, later (after the Prophet's death) married Brigham Young for time only, even though they bore him children

It was also possible to marry for eternity rather than time. A woman who had died without ever having married could be sealed for eternity to an LDS male—after her death. The fact that he might already have a legal wife would make no difference, since plural wives were perfectly acceptable.

It should be pointed out that celestial marriage is not a dated concept. It has always been—and still is—an integral part of LDS religion. One Mormon woman puts it as follows:

> The principle of celestial marriage was considered the capstone of the Mormon religion. Only by practicing it would the highest exaltation in the Celestial Kingdom of God be obtained. According to the founders of the Mormon church, the great purpose of this life is to prepare for the Celestial Kingdom. . . . The tremendous sacrifices of the Mormon people can be understood only if one keeps in mind this basic philosophy.[10]

Affectional Considerations Living arrangements varied among the polygamous families. In some instances, the wives lived with the husband under one roof. In the larger families, however, there were usually separate dwellings for the respective wives and their children. At any rate, a considerate husband was not supposed to show any favoritism. Hypothetically, at least, he was obligated to spend an equal amount of time with (and money on) each wife. In some cases, evidently, the husband would practice "rotation": he would spend one night with each of his spouses.

---

[10]Annie Turner Clark, *A Mormon Mother: An Autobiography* (Salt Lake City: University of Utah Press, 1969), pp. 1, 116. Quoted in Hill, *Joseph Smith*, p. 361.

Although polygamous arrangements may have been onerous for some plural wives, most of them seemed to have adjusted rather well. The wives of Brigham Young, for instance, were devoted to him and quite compatible with one another. Susa Young Gates, one of his daughters, writes:

> The wives of Brigham Young lived together without outer friction. They were ladies, and lived their lives as such. The children were never aware of any quarrels, and indeed they could not have been serious or the children would have been aware of them.
>
> None of Brigham Young's wives ever married again after his death, though some were comparatively young women. Mother's love of father . . . and of his memory after his death amounted almost to worship. That all the others felt as did my mother is proved by the way in which they cherished his memory and respected their widowhood.[11]

(There was one exception to the above claim. Ann Eliza, Brigham Young's twenty-seventh wife, was reported to be a hellion. She not only sued him for divorce on grounds of cruelty but toured the nation denouncing the entire system of plural marriage.)

The question is sometimes asked whether this sharing of love, as the Gentiles (non-Mormons) called it, did not have a sexually frustrating effect on the plural wives. In a strictly factual sense, there is very little information on a subject as sensitive as this. The fact that plural wives voiced no complaint along these lines suggests that the problem was not too significant.

It should be kept in mind that during the nineteenth century, American women, both Mormon and non-Mormon, were regarded as having a procreative function. Birth control was by no means accepted in society at large and is still frowned upon by the Mormon church. The point is that sexual intercourse was not considered by most females to be the pleasure-giving activity that it is today. On the contrary, it was more or less openly held to be a "wifely duty."

Other Problems   Sex was not the only problem associated with polygamy. Jealousies, economic disputes, child-rearing and in-law conflicts—these too were involved. In a monogamous pairing, for example, there are usually four in-laws, and the resultant problems are a well-known factor in marital discord. Where there were two, or six, or ten wives, the in-law problem must have indeed been formidable.

Conflicts over child rearing also occurred, especially when the wives and children all lived in one house. Children always knew who their real

[11]Susa Young Gates, *The Life Story of Brigham Young* (New York: Macmillan, 1930), pp. 340–41.

mother was, and they generally bowed to her authority. (The other wives were called aunts.) But with a half-dozen or so aunts in the house, such things as discipline, punishment, and lines of authority must have presented some real problems.

Instances of jealousy, also, were hardly unknown. It was only natural that there would be a certain amount of vying for the husband's attention—and for him to show total impartiality would have required superhuman effort. Conflict apparently occurred when a middle-aged husband took a young woman for his second (or fourth, or seventh) wife.

Culture Conflict   All things considered, it is remarkable that polygamous marriages worked as well as they did, for there is no doubt that some mighty problems existed. One of the best accounts of Mormon pluralism is by Kimball Young, a grandson of Brigham Young. Through personal interviews, as well as an examination of newspapers, journals, diaries, and autobiographies, Young estimated that about half the polygamous marriages were highly successful, a quarter were reasonably successful, and perhaps a quarter had "considerable or severe conflict."

Although there is no satisfactory way to compare these figures with those of monogamous marriages, it does appear that Mormon pluralism frequently presented a stern challenge to the good ship of matrimony.

> The real problem was that the difficulties could not be easily settled, because the culture did not provide any standardized ways for handling these conflicts. For the most part, these people genuinely tried to live according to the Principle. But when they applied the rules of the game borrowed from monogamy, such as not controlling feelings of jealousy, they got into real trouble.[12]

The End of Plural Marriage

Mormon polygamists had their share of domestic discord—perhaps a bit more than their share. Given time, however, the system of plural marriage probably could have been made to work. The problems were not insurmountable, and the Saints were a dedicated people. Unfortunately for all concerned, the real difficulties were external rather than internal, and as time went on the situation deteriorated. It soon became apparent that as far as the outside society was concerned, polygamy was creating a lesion of unhealable proportions.

As portrayed in the Gentile (non-Mormon) press, Mormonism was a

[12]Kimball Young, *Isn't One Wife Enough?* (New York: Henry Holt, 1954), p. 209.

false religion—with many evil connotations. But the target attacked most was polygamy. Over and over and over again, the perfidies and traumas of plural marriage were emblazoned in bold headlines. Some of the stories were factual, but—given the nature of American newspapers— many were the products of reportorial imagination. And as Carl Carmer points out:

> The published "feature stories" found eager readers among Gentile women. The latter wept over the first wife who, on being informed that her husband was bringing a second to the home, climbed through a window and up to the roof, where she sat under the gleaming pattern of western stars until the pitiless cold of a Utah winter stopped the beating of her heart.
>
> Another young spouse, when told that her husband had built a nearby house for a prospective second bride, snatched her rifle from its rack, and for a week or so sent bullets spaced at regular intervals into the honeymoon cottage. This action postponed the contemplated wedding indefinitely.[13]

Such stories clearly tended to inflame public opinion. And when that happens, political reaction is sure to follow. In 1862, President Lincoln signed a bill outlawing polygamy in the territories of the United States, and after the Civil War federal agents began "swarming over Utah." The difficulty was, however, that the agents could not always gain access to church marriage records. Also, Mormon polygamists became adept at scattering and hiding their wives, and—if necessary—themselves.

Brigham Young died in 1877 and was buried in a walnut casket he had designed himself. But even he had not escaped the long arm of the law, having been arrested and jailed on charges of polygamy. However, he was freed after an overnight confinement when he was able to convince the judge that in a *legal* sense, he had only one wife—the first.

After Brigham Young's death, things seemed to go downhill rapidly for the Saints. In 1882, a new federal law provided punishment for anyone found living in "lewd cohabitation," and Mormon leaders found themselves going to jail in droves. During a single year, 1887, some two hundred polygamists were imprisoned.

Still the fight went on, with many Saints building secret passageways, hidden rooms, and underground tunnels between houses. Carmer writes that when federal officers appeared, "the 'cohabs' suddenly disappeared into church steeples, haystacks, cornfields, old cellars, or disguised themselves in women's dresses and sunbonnets. The whole countryside was playing a wild game of hide-and-seek."[14] John Taylor, Brigham Young's successor and a devout polygamist, was in office for ten years but had to spend practically all of it in hiding.

---

[13]Carl Carmer, *The Farm Boy and the Angel* (Garden City, NY: Doubleday, 1970), pp. 174–75.
[14]Ibid., p. 181.

To many, it must have seemed as though the conflict between the "cohabs" and the "feds" was a standoff. On the one hand, no matter how many federal agents were sent in—and no matter how many polygamists were brought out—the Latter-day Saints continued to abide by the Principle. This was especially true of the leadership, practically all of whom remained steadfast in their beliefs. On the other hand, it had become clear that the government was prepared to take whatever steps were necessary to obliterate the remaining "relic of barbarism."

The year 1887 marked the beginning of the end of plural marriage, for in that year the Edmunds-Tucker Act was passed. This bill dissolved the church as a corporation and provided for the confiscation of church property. Cost to the Mormon church was over 1 million dollars, nearly half of it in cash. And the raids and imprisonments continued. In all, there were 573 convictions for polygamy.

By this time, many Mormons had wearied of the struggle. Then too, LDS leaders—who remained resolute to the end—wanted statehood for Utah, a goal they realized was unattainable so long as polygamy was being practiced.

During 1887, John Taylor died (while still in hiding), and he was succeeded in the church presidency by Wilford Woodruff. In 1890, the Supreme Court upheld the Edmunds-Tucker Act as constitutional, a decision that marked the end of the line for plural marriage. Shortly after the decision was handed down, Woodruff made the following official pronouncement, known in subsequent years as the Manifesto.

> Inasmuch as laws have been enacted by Congress forbidding plural marriages, which laws have been pronounced constitutional by the court of last resort, I hereby declare my intention to submit to those laws, and to use my influence with the members of the church over which I preside to have them do likewise. . . .
>
> And I now publicly declare that my advice to the Latter-day Saints is to refrain from contracting any marriage forbidden by the law of the land.[15]

There is one extremely interesting footnote to the long-running battle over polygamy. The various statutes outlawing polygamy were generally ineffective until 1890, the year the Supreme Court upheld the Edmunds-Tucker Act. Note that it was not the Edmunds-Tucker Act itself, which was aimed at destroying the Mormon church, but the supporting Supreme Court decision that spelled doom for polygamy.

What has been almost entirely overlooked, however, is the fact that *the Supreme Court ruling was based on a 5-4 decision!* If a single justice had changed his vote, the Edmunds-Tucker Act would have been voided!

---

[15]Joseph Smith, *Doctrine and Covenants*, (Salt Lake City: The Church of Jesus Christ of Latter-day Saints, 1974), last section.

And then what? Would polygamy—in one form or another—have continued? It is an intriguing question.

Although the Manifesto caused some internal resentment, both Mormons and non-Mormons were generally glad that the long battle was over. Woodruff's pronouncement was (and is) treated as a revelation. When asked about it, he replied simply, "I went before the Lord, and I wrote what the Lord told me to write." The pronouncement apparently ended the long conflict over plural marriage.

Or did it?

Epilogue   Woodruff's Manifesto put an end to the open practice of plural marriage, and United States President Benjamin Harrison granted a pardon to all the imprisoned polygamists. In 1896, Utah was admitted to the Union as the forty-fifth state. Nevertheless, for a decade or so following the Manifesto, a few Mormon leaders continued to take plural wives.

In 1902, Reed Smoot, an LDS official, was elected to the United States Senate. There was opposition to his being seated, however, and during lengthy hearings the facts concerning "secret" polygamy came to light. The Mormon church, while not condoning plural marriage, had taken no steps to remove those officials who were continuing the practice.

At the final Senate vote, Smoot was confirmed by a narrow margin, and political opposition to Mormon office seekers came to an end. In fact, over the years, any number of ranking government officials have been Mormons. After the highly publicized Smoot hearings, LDS adopted a policy of excommunicating any member known to practice polygamy, a policy that remains in effect today:

> With the zeal of converts, (LDS) became ultra monogamous. Utah . . . became by far the most active state in prosecuting polygamists. In the more relaxed sexual climate since the 1960s, however, a live-and-let-live attitude has developed. . . . In recent years, apart from occasional sackings of people in sensitive jobs, the state authorities in Utah have left polygamists in peace.[16]

Organization of LDS

The Mormons have one of the most complicated—and successful—clerical organizations in America. Every "worthy male" is expected to take his place in the hierarchical priesthood. There are now more than a million LDS priests, a figure that far surpasses the number of Roman Catholic priests in the entire world.

Although they are not professional in the sense of being seminarians

[16]"Polygamy under Siege," *The Economist* (January 30, 1988), p. 21.

or receiving pay for their work, it is the priesthood that provides the bones and sinew of present-day Mormonism. Within the priesthood there are two orders, or subdivisions: the Aaronic and Melchizedek. Both orders are subdivided into ranks, and these ranks, or gradations, form a kind of promotional ladder that the Mormon male ascends during his lifetime. Which rung he reaches depends largely on the effort he is willing to put forth in carrying out the Word.

A worthy male starts his priestly career at age twelve, when he is admitted to the Aaronic order with the rank of deacon. This is the lowest rank in the priesthood, usually attained a few years after baptism. Chief duties of the deacon include helping at church meetings, collecting fast offerings, and otherwise assisting the higher ranks.

After three years or so as deacon—if all goes well—the boy is promoted to the rank of teacher. This is a kind of apprenticeship, for while teachers do occasionally preach, their primary role is helping their superiors. When he reaches eighteen or thereabouts, the boy advances to the highest rank in the Aaronic order, that of priest. The duties of the priest include preaching, teaching, baptizing, and administering the sacraments.

Assuming he has performed his duties in the Aaronic order satisfactorily, the boy is ready for the higher order, the Melchizedek, which also has three ranks—elder, seventy, and high priest. Elders are generally ordained in their early twenties and are invested with authority to take charge of meetings, to bestow certain blessings, and to officiate during rites when the high priest is unable to be present.

Seventies are essentially elders who have been chosen to be traveling missionaries, usually for a term of two years. Top rung in the ascending hierarchy is the rank of high priest. Once he has reached this level, there is no higher priestly rank a Latter-day Saint can aspire to. There are, however, any number of administrative and executive positions available—if he has the necessary qualifications. LDS is a huge operation, and its management requires immense effort.

Wards and Stakes   The Church of Jesus Christ of Latter-day Saints has two forms of administration, horizontal and vertical. Horizontal, in this context, refers to the various ward and stake organizations, while vertical refers to the overall administrative hierarchy of the church.

The basic horizontal or geographical unit of LDS is the ward, roughly corresponding to the Protestant congregation or the Catholic parish. Since Mormondom is growing, the number of wards is constantly increasing, the present figure reaching into the tens of thousands.

Although each ward contains both priesthood orders—with all the ranks thereof—the ward itself is administered by the bishop. It is he who baptizes and confirms, counsels members, receives contributions, conducts funerals, and so forth. He often gives a prodigious amount of his time, but neither he nor his assistants receive any pay for their work. All Mormons, incidentally, including those at the head of the church, must belong to some ward.

A stake—corresponding to the Catholic diocese—is made up of from five to ten wards. At the head is the stake president, who is assisted by two counselors. The president nominates the various ward bishops, holds conferences, and is generally responsible for the management of the wards under his jurisdiction. Although his is also an unpaid job, the stake president—like the ward bishop—spends an enormous amount of time on church-related activities.

The General Authorities   The vertical, or hierarchical, structure of LDS is more complicated than the horizontal. At the top of the Mormon establishment is the first president, also known as "prophet, seer, and revelator"—Joseph Smith's original title. The first president holds office for life. Since his mantle of authority is believed to be inherited from the Prophet himself, and as his title "revelator" signifies, the first president is the only member of the church empowered to voice revelations. This power is seldom used, however. The system is theocratic, and authority comes from the top. Indeed, some observers believe that the first president holds more power than any other church leader except the pope.

In addition to two presidential assistants, there is also an executive council of twelve apostles, another council of seven members who oversee missionary activities, and a three-member bishopric that looks after the church's business activities. These twenty-five people are often referred to as the general authorities, for together they hold practically all the top LDS offices. Stake and ward officials are under the control of the general authorities.

Participatory Involvement   To outsiders, at least, the participatory involvement of Mormons is staggering. There are ward activities and stake activities and temple ceremonies. There are constant family visitations by teachers and bishops. Streams of missionaries flow to faraway places, and the conversion rate is high. There are annual and semiannual conferences and visits by the apostles. There are sealings for time and eternity. New religious tracts and publications are constantly being issued. There are weekly social events and Mormon holiday celebrations. There are recreational and musical activities and sporting events. There are a host of subsidiary organizations: women's relief society, young men's and young women's mutual improvement associations, scout troops, the Sunday school union, the genealogical society, the church welfare plan, the Tabernacle Choir, and so on. LDS even has a department of education which, among other things, administers a series of institutes and seminaries. The church also maintains Brigham Young University, founded in 1875.

From the outside, LDS gives the appearance of being a beehive of activity—which in fact it is. (It is no accident that a figure of the beehive, prominently displayed on so many LDS buildings, was chosen to be the state symbol for Mormon Utah.) Both literally and figuratively, Mormons are always on the move. In fact, the Latter-day Saints themselves good-naturedly define a Mormon as "one who is on his way to a meeting, at a meeting, or returning from a meeting."

In addition to the meetings, there are always new jobs to do, new conversions to make, new challenges to meet. And while the personnel requirements are enormous—it takes hundreds of thousands of dedicated workers to staff the various organizations—the church has never had any recruitment difficulties.

This is not to say that all Latter-day Saints are dedicated. Some young men are considered unworthy and are not accepted into the priesthood. Some adults of both sexes are only moderately active, and others (called Jack Mormons) are inactive. But somewhere between one-half and two-thirds of LDS members not only are active, they are hyperactive. This participatory involvement—this hyperactivity—is one of the distinguishing marks of Mormonism.

Vitality of the Family

Another feature of Mormon social organization is the strong emphasis placed on family relations. Whether the family member is young, middle-aged, or old—or even deceased—he or she is assured a meaningful place in the kin system. Conversely, Latter-day Saints are against those things that they feel are harmful to family life. Premarital and extramarital sex are frowned upon, along with abortion, masturbation, indecent language, immodest behavior, birth control, and divorce. While the church mounts no special campaign against these practices, most Mormons seem to have little difficulty abiding by the rules.

There are lapses, to be sure. Some young Mormons do engage in premarital sex, though the incidence is much lower than for non-Mormons. Some LDS marrieds do practice birth control, and in fact the Mormon birthrate has fallen somewhat. However, it is still twice as high as for society at large. As the Campbells point out, "Mormons take the Biblical injunction to multiply and replenish the earth very literally and seriously."[17] Predictably, Latter-day Saints have comparatively few divorces, and the Utah abortion rate is the lowest of any state.

[17]Bruce Campbell and Eugene Campbell, "The Mormon Family," in *Ethnic Families in America*, eds. Charles Mindel, Robert Habenstein, and Roosevelt Wright, Jr. (New York: Elsevier, 1988), p. 483.

The familistic orientation of LDS is revealed in a variety of other ways. Whereas most Americans are accustomed to pursuing individualized interests, hobbies, and activities, Mormons tend to participate as families. Their social life is largely a function of church and family. Ward dances, parties, outings, and sporting events are all attended by families and are designed to encourage the intermingling of different age groups.

Another example: Monday evening is designated as home evening. On this occasion, all members of the household stay home and devote themselves to family recreation, such as singing, games, instrumental music, and dramatics.

The Kin Family Network   In view of the stress on family, it is understandable why kinship plays such an important role throughout Mormondom. Brothers and sisters, aunts and uncles, nieces and nehews, grandparents, cousins, in-laws—all maintain an active and enthusiastic kin relationship. During reunions of the kin family network—one of the Saints' favorite summer pastimes—it is not uncommon to see several hundred people in attendance! Special consideration is often shown to direct descendants of pioneer Mormon families, particularly those whose forebears had direct contact with Joseph Smith or Brigham Young.

It should not be thought that their emphasis on family and kinship serves to fragment the Mormon community. On the contrary, every effort is made to extend and apply familistic feelings to the community at large. One has but to attend any of the ward activities to see the closeness and camaraderie involved. The entire social fabric of Mormonism is designed so that "no one feels left out." And in their routine dealings with one another, this same type of we-feeling is evident. Mullen writes:

> Mormons almost always refer to each other as brother or sister. It is Brother Petersen this, or Sister Evans that. A group is composed of brethren, and this word is also applied frequently to the leadership. . . .
>
> To Mormons, there is the feeling that we really are the children of God. . . . Some have one gift and some another; some may be stronger or wiser than others; but each has a duty to help the other.[18]

Search for the Dead   Before leaving the subject of family, one final observation is in order; the Latter-day Saints' predilection for extending their range of kinship to those long dead. The problem is basically simple. Mormons believe that they themselves are following God's word, as revealed to the Prophet Joseph Smith. But what about those who died without ever hearing the Prophet's revelations?

The answer is also simple. Ancestors who died before the religion was

[18]Robert Mullen, *The Latter-day Saints: The Mormons Yesterday and Today* (Garden City, NY: Doubleday, 1966), pp. 27–28.

founded in 1830 may be baptized or sealed by proxy. That is, the living person stands in for the deceased during a baptismal or sealing ceremony. The ceremony itself takes place in a Mormon temple, and the deceased is accorded full rites.

Difficulty arises from the fact that, as one goes back in time, (1) the number of ancestors becomes enormous, and (2) they become exceedingly difficult to track down. LDS does not do things halfway, however, with the result that the search for ancestry has become one of the major functions of the church.

The Mormon Genealogical Society, an administrative arm of LDS, is located in downtown Salt Lake City. An additional seventeen branches are maintained in other parts of the United States and abroad. The amount of genealogical research undertaken at the various branches is staggering. Vital statistics, census materials, church records, poll books, official documents of all kinds—such things are constantly being microfilmed for use by Mormon (and non-Mormon) researchers.

Some of the figures are hard to grasp. Close to a thousand people a day come to the Mormon Genealogical Society to use the hundreds of microfilm reading machines available. (There is no charge for using either the records or the machines.) The number of temple ceremonies for the dead has now passed the 50 million mark. The number of names on file exceeds 10 billion. For some states—and nations—*all the pertinent records have been microfilmed!*

To protect the records from fire or explosion, the negative films are stored in a safe place. Here is Mullen's description of it.

> In Little Cottonwood Canyon, 12 miles into the (Wasatch) mountains from downtown Salt Lake City, there is a solid face of granite from which was taken much of the stone used in the Temple. A narrow mountain road leads to a leveled-off place where one confronts six large concrete portals resembling entrances to a railroad tunnel. If you walk into the main portal and proceed about 150 feet, by which time you are under 800 feet of solid granite, you come across a tunnel, or room, some 402 feet long and 50 feet wide. This is lined in corrugated steel. Between the rough-hewn granite and the exterior of these ten-gauge steel linings has been pumped waterproof concrete. This vast room is the central office for the genealogy records.
>
> You see three huge barnlike vault doors. One weighs 15 tons and could withstand almost any known blast. Each door leads to a 350-foot room, extending even farther into the granite mountain. Beyond these rooms is still another. . . .
>
> The vaults have their own self-contained power plant, their own emergency supplies, fresh air filters, and other equipment to endure even a severe atomic attack, which one can only suppose was at the back of the minds of the designers and builders. . . .[19]

[19]Ibid., pp. 193–94.

In recent years, medical researchers have taken an interest in Mormon family histories. According to Ray White, co-chairperson of genetics at the University of Utah: "The million or so Mormons here—some of whom have thousands of members of their extended families living nearby—are mostly descendants of about 20,000 pioneers."[20] In Utah, scientists have been able to identify dozens of kin-groups with extensive bloodlines.

Geneticists have determined, by comparing Mormon genealogical records with cancer treatment records, that clustering exists in colon, prostate, lung, cervix, and stomach cancers. At this time, a responsible and trackable gene has not been identified. If the gene can be flagged, those with hereditary predispositions to these illnesses could be periodically tested, affording them the opportunity of early treatment.

Distinctive Mormon Customs

"To us, the greatest day of all time is today." These words, spoken by a former Mormon leader, exemplify LDS philosophy. Few other groups are as present-oriented as the Latter-day Saints. It is not that they disregard or play down the significance of the hereafter. Their emphasis on genealogy, ancestral baptism, and sealing for time and eternity shows the importance they attach to the next world. But the way they prepare for the next world is to keep religiously active in the present one.

> Mormonism de-emphasizes contemplation, and fosters an activist pragmatism. Children growing up in an orthodox Mormon home will be urged to apply themselves to their studies, to cultivate recreational interests such as music, art, and hobbies, and to apply the rule of moderation to all facets of life.
>
> Regular church attendance is expected, but *speculation about theological problems or the religious answer to modern movements such as existentialism or Freudianism is discounted.* Nothing could be further from the spirit of Mormonism than the Trappist monk—celibate, contemplative, withdrawn from the world.[21]

Group Identification   Mormons place great stress on cultural and recreational activities, but in both instances the emphasis is on group rather than individual participation. Team sports, organized recreation, dancing and ballet, orchestral music, choir work, theater—all such activities

[20]Michael Waldholz, "The Mormons' Genetic Legacy," *Saturday Evening Post* (November 1988), p. 52.
[21]William Whalen, *The Latter-day Saints in the Modern-Day World.* (New York: John Day, 1964), p. 213. Italics added.

are felt to have a religious base in the sense that *they enhance group identification.* May writes convincingly on this point:

> In contemporary Mormon society there is discernibly greater emphasis on the performing arts than on the visual arts. There is widespread emphasis on group singing, the well-known Mormon Tabernacle Choir being a great source of local pride. Musical ensembles, especially bands, have been widespread among the Mormons since the mid-19th century.
>
> Plays and theatrical productions have also been a favorite cultural activity of the Mormons. . . . Today Salt Lake City supports six professional theater companies, an impressive number for a metropolitan area of 500,000.
>
> Dancing has also been popular since the 19th century, both as a social activity and as a form of creative expression. The city's five dance companies have made Utah a center for dance in the West. Ballet West and the Utah Repertory Dance Theater have a national reputation for excellence.
>
> More individual forms of creative expression have not received the widespread support given to performing arts.[22]

Devout Mormons never forget that they are Mormons. The fact that they are helping to carry out God's word reinforces group identification. Even their *individual* involvements—baptism, tithing, prayer, genealogical research, and certain temple investitures—serve as reinforcement factors.

One of the more interesting of the latter is the issuance of special undergarments. These derive from one of the temple ceremonies called the endowments. When they receive their endowments, Mormons are issued a special set of underwear, which they are supposed to wear at all times. Originally the temple garments, as they were called, gave the appearance of a union suit. They were made of knit material and covered the body from ankle to neck. Although they are still worn by devout Mormons of both sexes, the undergarments themselves have been shortened in length and modified in appearance. They still contain the embroidered symbols that remind the wearers of their temple obligations.

(A few of the older church members follow the rules literally: they keep at least a part of the fabric touching them at all times. Even when taking a bath, they keep a small portion of the sleeve in contact with the body until fresh undergarments are ready to be worn.)

Word of Wisdom   It is a common observation that Mormons do not drink or smoke, a proscription that derives from one of Joseph Smith's revelations:

---

[22]Dean L. May, "Mormons," in *Harvard Encyclopedia of American Ethnic Groups,* ed. Stephan Thernstrom (Cambridge, MA: Harvard University Press, 1980), pp. 723–24.

That inasmuch as any man drinketh wine or strong drink among you, behold it is not good. . . .

And again, strong drinks are not for the belly, but for the washing of your bodies.

And again, tobacco is not for the body, neither for the belly, and is not good for man, but is an herb for bruises and all sick cattle. . . .

And again, hot drinks are not for the body or belly.[23]

The revelation is known throughout Mormondom as the Word of Wisdom. Included in the prohibition are tobacco in any form, alcoholic beverages of any kind (including wine and beer), tea, and coffee. LDS has even substituted water for wine in the Sunday communion service.

Although they themselves abstain, Mormons have no objection to drinking or smoking on the part of visitors or outsiders. At the same time, however, "the Word of Wisdom makes Mormons uncomfortable at cocktail parties, coffee breaks, and other such gatherings that serve the rest of American society as important occasions for social interaction."[24]

In any case, the Latter-day Saints are convinced they are right, and point to the fact that LDS prohibited smoking long before the surgeon general of the United States and the Royal College of Surgeons affirmed that tobacco was a cancer-causing agent. Mormons are permitted to drink hot chocolate, lemonade, fruit juice, and a variety of other nonalcoholic beverages.

But does the membership really abstain, abiding by the Word of Wisdom? The answer is yes, *all worthy* Mormons do abstain. Indeed, abstinence is one of the traits most clearly separating the true believer from the Jack Mormon. The Word of Wisdom is looked upon as a commandment. Those who disobey are not considered to be worthy Mormons and are denied admission to the temple—which means that they cannot participate in ceremonies involving sealing, baptism of the dead, endowments, and the like.

Tithing   In addition to their adherence to the Word of Wisdom, Latter-day Saints have two other customs that should be mentioned. One is tithing; the other is missionary work. Taking them in order, *tithing* comes from *tithe*, meaning "one-tenth." And in simplest terms, this is exactly what LDS expects: 10 percent of one's income "for the support of the Lord's work." Authority for the tithe comes from another revelation of Joseph Smith, this one in 1838.

Those who have been tithed shall pay one-tenth of all their interest annually; and this shall be a standing law unto them forever . . . and all those

---

[23]Smith, *Doctrine and Covenants,* 89:5.
[24]May, "Mormons," p. 730.

who gather unto the land of Zion . . . shall observe this law, or they shall not be found worthy to abide among you.[25]

It should be noted that the 10-percent figure is not based on the income that remains after normal living expenses have been deducted; it is a flat 10 percent "off the top." Tithes are collected by the ward bishops and forwarded directly to the general authorities in Salt Lake City, a procedure that also stems from one of the Prophet's revelations.

The membership does not ask—and the general authorities do not disclose—exactly how much money is collected or what happens to it. It appears, however, that the two major expenditures are for missionary work and education, including the support of Brigham Young University.

It is true that all Mormons are not full-tithers. Occasionally, members are permitted to give less than 10 percent and still remain in good standing. Others—the inactive group—may give little or nothing. The typical Mormon, however, not only gives his or her 10 percent but is quite happy to do so. By being worthy members, Mormons maintain their place in the Mormon community, are assured of full temple privileges for themselves and their families, and have the inner security that comes from carrying out the word of the Lord as revealed to the Prophet Joseph Smith.

Missionary Activity   As Turner aptly points out, "It is foolish to pick any *one* aspect of this remarkable religion and assert that 'this is its strength.' Yet the temptation is strong . . . to select the missionary program."[26]

Like so many aspects of their religion, the Mormon missionary program is considerably different from that of other groups. It is larger, more vigorous, more youthful, more systematic—and more successful. Latter-day Saints consider it an honor to be missionaries, and many young Mormons look forward to the time when they will be selected. The selection is made by the ward bishop, who forwards a detailed application to the missionary committee in Salt Lake City. The applicant must be young (nineteen or twenty), of good character, and worthy in the eyes of the church. Also he or she (or his or her family) must be able to afford the cost, for the expenses incurred during the fieldwork are not borne by LDS.

Either sex may apply, although males outnumber females by a wide margin. If an applicant is accepted by the committee, he or she receives a "call," a letter with a territorial assignment. This may be in any one of the fifty states or abroad, but in either case the young missionary is expected to stay for the stipulated period of time, usually

[25]Smith, *Doctrine and Covenants*, section 119.
[26]Turner, *Mormon Establishment*, p. 89.

one-and-a-half or two years. Before departing for his or her post, the missionary spends a week or so in Salt Lake City attending a brief training course.

Those who have been approached by Mormon missionaries may have wondered how these young people manage to learn so much about Mormonism in so short a time. But the fact is that they have been trained in Mormonism all their lives. The short intellectual period in Salt Lake City is merely to explain the operational details.

Once they have reached their assigned areas, the young emissaries work hard. It is not at all uncommon for them to put in eight to ten hours a day, seven days a week. They operate in pairs, living together and visiting the homes of potential converts together. They have strict rules of conduct, and are not permitted to date during the missionary assignment.

When they discuss Mormonism with potential converts, the missionaries are sincere but not insistent. They patiently and systematically explain their point of view in accordance with a routine mapped out by LDS authorities. They leave pamphlets and other literature, and often make return visits to the same home. The work is occasionally tiring and—like all door-to-door efforts—more than occasionally discouraging. Nevertheless, most missionaries are happy in their assignments. There are close to 30,000 of them in the field at any one time, and when their tour is over, memories of their experience will undoubtedly remain with them for the rest of their lives.

In recent years, LDS began using self-supporting senior citizens as missionaries. Today, there are more than 1,250 couples in the field. They do not go door-to-door, spreading the word, as do their younger counterparts. Often they work as tour guides at LDS historical sites, as genealogical researchers, in campus ministries, or in foreign missions. Many are retired married couples. Singles who volunteer are assigned same-sex partners, and sent into the field.*

Effort and hard work aside, is the missionary effort successful? Indeed it is. First, the conversion rate is fantastically high. The number of yearly converts is reported to be in the neighborhood of 80,000. This is what accounts for much of the phenomenal growth of LDS. Second, Mormon missionary efforts have been so successful that in many parts of the world permanent missions have been established. In fact, in Hawaii, Canada, Brazil, England, South Korea, Switzerland, New Zealand, the Philippines, Guatemala, Peru, East and West Germany, South Africa, Sweden—and many other countries—Mormon temples have been erected or are under construction.

*1989 interview with Marge Land, Oklahoma City Public Information Officer, LDS.

Some Mormon Problems

All large organizations have their problems, and LDS is no exception. In fact, in a historical sense, the Mormons have probably had more than their share. That they have managed to solve most of them is due to good management plus—always—the conviction that God is with them. Of the problem-areas that remain, five seem to merit particular attention.

The Intellectuals   In view of the origin and nature of Mormonism, the church has a special problem with the intellectual element. That is to say, intellectuals are by definition challengers. They challenge accepted beliefs and try to apply a so-called rationality to various issues. Through their critical insights, they are able to provide concepts—new ways of looking at things—not obtainable from other sources.

The Mormon church, on the other hand, is based on revelation. It is active rather than contemplative; it maintains a set of long-cherished beliefs; and, of course, it holds to the view that the Book of Mormon, and the Bible (correctly translated) are literally true. As a result, disagreements between LDS and the intellectual members of the church crop up every now and then.

Some Mormon leaders acknowledge the problem. Others do not. When interviewed, one church official responded, "Oh I suppose you could call it a problem, but it doesn't amount to too much. I don't think the 'intellectuals,' as you call them, would feel comfortable in any church. Personally, I think we have more important things to worry about."

The Women's Movement   LDS does not prohibit their female members from joining the labor force, and Mormon women are to be found in all walks of life, including the professions. At the same time, there is no doubt—in terms of priorities—that the church leaders feel that "woman's place is in the home." May notes: "The leaders see the women's liberation movement generally and the Equal Rights Amendment (ERA) in particular as causes that divert women from their primary role."[27]

For the first time in the state's history the Utah fertility rate is declining. Although the birthrate has dropped—from 3.2 to 2.5 births per woman—it is still considerably higher than the national average of 1.8. Women are postponing the birth of their first child. The average woman in Utah now bears her first child when she is 23.3, up from 22.2 at the close of the last decade. When women delay childbearing, they have fewer children.

[27]May, "Mormons," p. 729.

Demographers attribute the decline in fertility to economic necessity—women having to work to make ends meet. The trend, however, has not gone unnoticed by the Mormon church. In a recent address, church president Ezra Taft Benson told young families:

> With all my heart, I counsel you not to postpone having your children. Do not curtail the number of children for personal or selfish reasons. Material possessions, social convenience and so-called professional advantage are nothing compared to righteous posterity.[28]

Although they have their own organization within the church, women are not permitted to ascend the LDS hierarchy. All Mormon leaders, from ward bishop to church president, are—and always have been—male. Some Mormon women have resented their exclusion and have complained bitterly. A few have even been excommunicated for "preaching false doctrine, and undermining church leadership because of their public statements."

On the other hand, most Mormon women not only support the church's position but sincerely believe in the more traditional sex roles. Based on their survey research, which compared attitudes of Mormons and non-Mormons, the Hartmans report as follows:

> Attitudes toward appropriate roles for women and role conflict are strongly affected by religious affiliation. LDS members are more traditional in attitude than non-LDS members.
>
> LDS emphasis on the importance of the family and women's roles at home is not accompanied by an ideology that women cannot perform in the economy or are inferior in any sense. On the contrary, women's roles and contributions in the family and home are highly valued because of the importance of the family in their religion.[29]

This, then, is the problem: although the large majority of Mormon women seem to be quite satisfied with the role accorded them by the church, some are clearly dissatisfied. There is no denying that the women's movement has had some impact on Mormon women. It would be an exaggeration, however, to say that the impact was critical.

What the answer is, only time will tell. But it should be pointed out that African-Americans formerly had a somewhat similar problem; that is, while they were welcomed into church membership, they were not eligible for the ranks of the priesthood. It took a revelation—reported by church president Spencer W. Kimball on June 9, 1978—to change the rules. Whether a similar change might someday occur regarding the role of women is problematical.

---

[28]*New York Times*, December 29, 1988. p.A7; p.A14.
[29]Moshe Hartman and Harriet Hartman, "Sex-Role Attitudes of Mormons vs. Non-Mormons in Utah," *Journal of Marriage and the Family* (November 1983), p. 901.

All that can be said is that since Joseph Smith's death, revelations have been announced by the church in only three instances: once by Brigham Young when he was guided to Utah; once by Wilford Woodruff when he was commanded to put an end to plural marriage; and once by Spencer W. Kimball, whose revelation indicated that "all worthy male members of the church may be ordained to the priesthood without regard for race or color."

The Salamander Incident   In the early 1980s, Mark Hofmann, a former Mormon missionary, gained attention when he claimed discovery of papers written by early Mormon leaders. Hofmann's first discoveries confirmed church history, including accounts of how the angel Moroni had led Joseph Smith to write the Book of Mormon. After gaining a reputation as an expert in church documents, Hofmann began delivering letters to church leaders, purportedly written by early Mormons, which *undermined* official church history.

The most damaging of these letters was said to have been written by Martin Harris, Smith's first convert outside the Prophet's family. The letter alleged that Smith, while practicing folk magic, had been led to the "golden plates" by a "white salamander," rather than an angel. The letter, later shown to be a forgery, had been authenticated by FBI document experts as legitimate. Church officials bought the letter and other potentially embarrassing documents from Hofmann and stored them in a vault, in order to hide them—at least, so critics claimed—from LDS members and historians.

The documents were not exposed as forgeries until 1985, when Steven Christensen and Kathleen Webb Sheets were killed, on the same day, in separate pipe bombings. Utah prosecutors alleged that Hofmann killed Christensen, his associate, because Christensen was threatening to expose Hofmann as a forger. Sheets, along with her husband, Gary, were also document traders. Prosecutors alleged that Kathleen Sheets was killed to divert attention away from Hofmann.

On the day after the double murder, Hofmann was seriously injured when a pipe bomb exploded in his car. Prosecutors alleged that Hofmann had planned a third murder that day, and the bomb went off by accident. Hofmann, who sold more than $2,000,000 in forged documents to LDS and private collectors, pled guilty to two counts of second-degree murder. He is now serving a life sentence in the Utah state penitentiary.

The Apostates   Over the years, LDS has had its share of trouble with apostates—those who have left the fold. During the nineteenth century, much of the anti-Mormon propaganda could be traced to disgruntled Mormons. Some of the apostates were simply individuals who became dissatisfied with certain policies of the church. Much more serious, however, were those who, finding themselves unable to accept church doctrine, defected as a group in order to pursue their own set of religious beliefs.

A number of such withdrawals occurred after polygamy was officially proclaimed in 1852. The most significant was that of the Josephites, who rejected not only the doctrine of plural marriage but also the leadership of Brigham Young. The Josephites held that church leadership should have followed a hereditary line, and that the rightful heir, following Joseph Smith's death, was his son Joseph Smith III.

Organized in 1852, the Josephites grew steadily if not spectacularly, and at the end of the decade proclaimed themselves the Reorganized Church of Jesus Christ of Latter Day Saints, with Joseph Smith III as head. Today the Reorganites are a large, active organization, with some quarter-million members.

The relationship between LDS and the Reorganites is amicable enough. Indeed, the two groups have much in common, including their founder, Joseph Smith. Like LDS, the Reorganite hierarchy includes a president, twelve apostles, and a quorum of the seventy. The Reorganized church likewise relies on the nonsalaried services of elders and priests for the handling of their local congregations. Most important, perhaps, both LDS and the Reorganites accept the Book of Mormon as divinely inspired. The original manuscript, dictated by Joseph Smith from the controversial golden plates and written in longhand by Oliver Cowdery, is owned by the Reorganized church and kept in a temperature-and-humidity-controlled bank vault in Kansas City.

On the other hand, there is little likelihood that LDS and the Reorganites will bury their differences and unite. The division is too pronounced. In addition to the leadership factor mentioned above, the Reorganites do not maintain a volunteer missionary system. Also, they have no secret temple rites of any kind, no endowments, no special undergarments, no sealings, and no celestial marriage. The temples—and the meetings—are open to the public.

Although the Reorganites do tithe, their 10 percent is not "off the top" but is figured after normal living expenses have been deducted. The difference between the two kinds of tithes is substantial and goes a long way toward explaining why LDS has grown so much faster than the Reorganized church.

The Reorganites were not the only apostates who seceded as a group. There were the Cutlerites, the Strangites, the Rigdonites, the Bickertonites, and the Hedrickites. Except for the Reorganites, however, none of these groups ever grew to any size. And none of them—including the Reorganites—ever caused the Mormon church any real problem or embarrassment. But there was one group that did.

The Fundamentalists   Just as the official adoption of polygamy created a number of schisms within the Mormon church, the Manifesto announcing an *end* to plural marriage had the same effect. Small groups of Mormons—or more accurately, ex-Mormons—have continued to practice plural marriage, even though it is against both the law and the tenets of LDS. These fundamentalists, as they are called, have had the unfortunate effect of prolonging the association between Mormonism and polygamy. Hence it is little wonder that they are denounced by LDS.

After the Manifesto was proclaimed, some of the fundamentalists migrated to Mexico, but others stayed in the United States—mainly in the Arizona-Utah-California area—where they have continued their polygamous practices down to the present. Exactly how many fundamentalists there are is not known, since their operations are generally underground. Melissa Merrill, herself a plural wife, places the figure at between 20,000 and 30,000. She goes on to make the interesting contention that "there are probably more living plural marriage in the periphery of the church now than had ever lived it while it was an official practice."[30]

A number of observers—including, perhaps, most LDS members—look upon the fundamentalists as deviants, and of lower socioeconomic status. Fundamentalists themselves say that they come from all walks of life. They also claim to be devout rather than deviant. In point of fact, they seem to be both.

Fundamentalists contend that just before he died in 1887, First President John Taylor called together five of his followers and told them that the practice of polygamy must, at all cost, be retained. His message had great impact on the five men for two reasons: (1) in defense of the Principle, he himself had spent the last years of his life in hiding, and (2) since he was president of the church at the time, the five men felt that his counsel was based on revelation.

Whatever the rationale, there is no denying that the spark of polygamy is still very much alive—despite the fact that the pluralists have long since been cut off from the Mormon church. The fundamentalists may have some sort of clandestine organization, although not too much is known about it. From time to time they publish and distribute literature, and every so often the popular press runs an exposé of their plural marriages. But responsible information is hard to come by.

The reason for our dearth of knowledge is twofold. In the first place, despite their agreement on the Principle, the fundamentalists are not united or organized into one cohesive organization. They are spread over several states and Mexico, and their geographical area encompasses thousands of square miles. A number of different sects, or cults, are involved, most of them quite small. Indeed, many of those who adhere

[30]Melissa Merrill, *Polygamist's Wife* (Salt Lake City: Olympus, 1975), p. 116.

to the Principle do so as individuals; that is, they have no connection with *any* group or organization.

The second reason for the lack of information is that polygamy is illegal, and those involved never know when the authorities will crack down. To circumvent possible court action, most polygamists take but one *legal* wife. Subsequent marriages—and some polygamists are reported to have as many as eleven wives—are performed by some sort of religious officiant, and do not involve a marriage license.[31] Utah, in turn, has made cohabitation a felony—provable merely by the presence of children. (In retaliation, fundamentalists have reportedly planted spies in both LDS and the police departments to warn of impending raids.)

Actually, authorities have been increasingly reluctant to take legal action against the polygamists. For one thing, cohabitation is far from uncommon in society at large, with the public apparently taking a rather tolerant position. For another, there is the welfare problem. If a polygamist is prosecuted and sent to prison, his wives and children can—and do—go on welfare. And local governments may not have budgetary provisions necessary to handle such cases.

In any event, legal action against polygamists has become more and more infrequent. The last man to be convicted of polygamy left Utah State Prison in 1969, having served a year and a half of a five-year sentence.

Nevertheless, whether or not anyone bothers them, the fundamentalists will continue to be an embarrassment to LDS. The last thing the Mormons want is to continue to be associated with plural marriage. But as long as fundamentalism exists, that association seems inevitable.

Mormonism Today

Irrespective of what criteria are employed—total membership, rate of growth, wealth, devoutness, education, vigor—the Church of Jesus Christ of Latter-day Saints has an extraordinary record. There is no evidence, furthermore, that its various activities are diminishing, either in scope or tempo. On the contrary. . . .

Business and Financial Interests   To say that the Mormon church is wealthy would be a clear understatement. There are no figures available, but a number of observers—including the *New York Times*—believe that on a per capita basis, LDS is the richest church in the world. It is known, for example, that the church carries hundreds of millionaires on its rolls.

---

[31]Ibid., p. 107.

An Associated Press report indicated that the Mormon church, with its corporate control, "has revenues of more than three million dollars a day."[32]

Tithing has already been discussed. But in addition to the "off-the-top" 10 percent, each Mormon is expected to contribute *another* 2 percent toward the upkeep of the local ward. Total tithing, therefore, is far greater than the contributions in most other churches and has enabled LDS to invest in a number of profitable businesses.

The Mormon church owns some of the choicest hotels and motels in the West. It owns department stores, insurance companies, radio and television stations, and a newspaper. It has vast real estate holdings, both in the United States and abroad. It owns skyscrapers in such diverse places as Salt Lake City and New York City.

LDS also has a major interest in the United States beet sugar industry. It owns 700,000 acres of Florida ranchland, which means that the church is probably the largest landowner in the state. Additionally, LDS has 100,000 acres of ranchland in Canada and a large sugar plantation in Hawaii. It owns dozens of mills, factories, and stores—and hundreds of farms. The church also has large holdings in a number of well-known corporations. And the list of assets could be extended.

The Mormon church has been powerfully successful. This is a safe statement despite the fact that no yearly financial statements are released. The economic prosperity of LDS stems from a generous and enthusiastic tithing system, plus sound business practices. The money generated is used for the maintenance and continued expansion of the church.

Welfare   All Mormons are not rich, naturally. Most of them belong to the broad middle class. And, of course, there are some at the lower end of the economic ladder. LDS, however, takes care of its own needy, and the latter seldom have to depend on public relief. The system employed is most effective, for it permits those in need to be helped without drawing on general church revenue.

The program has two main features. First, each stake has one particular welfare project. Some stakes have farms, others have orchards, others have canneries or factories, others raise cattle, and so on. All project-labor is performed without charge by LDS members. Each stake has a quota, and the interchange of commodities takes place on the basis of administrative conferences.

Turner, who studied the distribution system, shows how extensive the program is:

---

[32]Cited in Marilyn Warenski, *Patriarchs and Politics* (New York: McGraw-Hill, 1978), p. 82.

Peanut butter comes from Houston; tuna from San Diego; macaroni from Utah; raisins from Fresno; prunes from Santa Rosa, California; soup from Utah; gelatine from Kansas City; toothpaste and shaving cream from Chicago; orange juice from Los Angeles; grapefruit juice from Phoenix and Mesa; sugar from Idaho.[33]

The second half of the welfare program involves "fast money" contributed by LDS members. On the first Sunday of the month, each Mormon family skips two meals. The estimated price of the meals is then given as a welfare contribution, most of the money being used for items not obtainable from the exchange program, such as clothing, razor blades, light bulbs, and so forth. Although the fast money collected from each family may not seem like much—perhaps fifteen to twenty dollars a month—the LDS welfare program takes in millions of dollars every year by this method.

All the welfare items, both produced and purchased, are stocked in the various bishops' storehouses scattered throughout Mormondom. The storehouses—some 150 of them—resemble fair-sized supermarkets, except that no money changes hands. The needy simply present a written order from the ward bishop, whereupon the necessary supplies are dispensed. (If money is needed, there is a special bishop's fund available.)

Some contend that no Mormon ever goes on public relief, and while this may be true in some wards, it is probably not true in all. Also, in spite of the obvious success of its welfare program, it is doubtful whether LDS could handle the need that would arise, say, in the event of a major depression. But then, neither could most other groups. All in all, the Mormon welfare program is one of their more successful undertakings.

Education For some reason, the general public seems unaware that LDS places great stress on education. But the fact is that the Mormons founded both the University of Utah—the oldest university west of the Mississippi—and Brigham Young University.

Whalen makes the following eye-opening statement:

Traditionally dedicated to education, the Mormon church boasts that it furnishes a higher percentage of entries in *Who's Who in America* than any other denomination. (The Unitarians may dispute this claim.) The church has produced an army of chemists, agronomists, sociologists, recreation specialists, and educational administrators.

Utah leads the nation in literacy, and in the percentage of its college-age young people actually enrolled in a college or university. LDS itself sponsors the largest church-related university in the country: Brigham Young University, in Provo, Utah.[34]

[33]Turner, *Mormon Establishment*, p. 98.
[34]Whalen, *Latter-day Saints*, p. 17.

One of the two major educational efforts of the Latter-day Saints is their system of seminaries and institutes. The seminaries are programs held as supplements to high school, while the institutes are socio-religious centers for Mormon college students. There are well over 2,000 institutes and seminaries in the United States and abroad, and at any one time some 100,000 Mormon youth attend them. These programs are used "to bridge the critical period of life when young Mormons must make the transition from the blind faith of their childhood to the reasoned acceptance of the faith the church hopes they will achieve."[35]

The second major thrust of the Mormon educational program is in higher education itself. Utah leads the country both in the percentage of college enrollees and in the percentage of college graduates. Latter-day Saints are justifiably proud of this accomplishment, and of the fact that they have supplied the presidents for many colleges and universities outside Utah. (The number of eminent people who have been Mormons—corporation heads, scientists, engineers, governors, senators, presidential cabinet members—is too great to attempt even a partial listing.)

Brigham Young University (BYU), of course, is the capstone of the Mormon educational effort. The buildings and campus are magnificent, and—in terms of physical plant—would probably rank at or near the top of U.S. colleges and universities.

In the last thirty-five years, enrollment has gone from roughly 5,000 to well over 25,000, making it, as mentioned earlier, the largest church-related university in the nation. The fact that it is church-related, however, does not signify any curtailment in extracurricular activities. In fact, 1984–1985 was a banner school year for BYU. The football team was ranked number one in the country; and Sharlene Wells, a twenty-year-old Brigham Young student, was crowned Miss America at the Atlantic City pageant.

It should also be mentioned that tuition at BYU is low—just a little more than $1,700 a year. (For non-LDS, the tuition is nearly $2,600.) And although the university receives no federal aid of any kind, building and other expenses present little problem. As elsewhere in Mormondom, tithing supplies fuel for the educational machinery.

BYU is primarily an undergraduate institute, although it does offer the doctorate in a number of fields. The large majority of the student body are Mormons, and they come from all fifty states as well as dozens of foreign countries.

Why the stress on education? The impetus can be traced to a revelation of Joseph Smith in 1833: "The Glory of God is intelligence, or, in other words, light and truth." This motto, encircling the figure of a beehive, can be seen on university literature and letterheads.

[35]Turner, *Mormon Establishment*, p. 123.

While BYU is a major university in every sense of the word, it is still a *Mormon educational institution.* The campus is organized into wards and stakes, as is Mormondom at large. Also, student attire and behavior are conservative, in keeping with the tenets of the church. The men, for example, are not permitted to wear beards, while for women "the no-bra look is unacceptable." The following blurb appeared in a recent BYU Introductory Brochure:

> BYU students agree to be honest in all behavior, respect the rights of others; sustain the law; avoid drug use; abstain from alcoholic beverages, tobacco, tea, coffee; live the law of chastity; and observe high standards of taste and decency.
>
> Students are asked to dress and be groomed in a manner that is modest, neat, clean and becoming the dignity of a representative of BYU and the Church of Jesus Christ of Latter-day Saints.

The Outlook

During World War I, LDS membership stood at approximately half a million. At the outbreak of World War II, the number had risen to around a million. Today, total membership exceeds 6 million! Clearly church membership is not only growing, it is accelerating.

A dozen or so years ago, there were—worldwide—fifteen Mormon temples (for rituals such as the endowments, baptisms, and sealings). Today there are more than fifty such temples built or under construction!* There are now wards and stakes in all fifty states. LDS membership is also increasing sharply in a number of foreign countries.

There is nothing secret about this phenomenal rate of increase. The Mormon church grows because it wants to grow. The Latter-day Saints have not only a high birthrate, but a low death rate. On the average, they live several years longer than other Americans. (This they attribute to their prohibitions against alcohol, caffeine, and tobacco.)

As mentioned earlier, the Mormons have a high conversion rate. This, coupled with their high birthrate and low death rate, has led to astounding growth. For example, "the church gained 247,000 members in 1987, bringing the total to 6,440,000 members."[36] The number of new missionaries added the same year was 2,947, bringing that figure to a record 34,750.

The same avenues of growth are open to other groups but are seldom used in conjunction with one another. The Old Order Amish and the

---

[36]"Mormons Grow," *Christian Century* (May 5, 1988), p. 448.
*1989 interview with Marge Land, Oklahoma City Public Information Officer, LDS.

Hasidim, for instance, have exceptionally high birthrates, but their conversion figures are near zero. True, not all LDS membership is active, but the ratio of active to inactive is probably higher than in most other denominations.

The Latter-day Saints have had more than their share of problems. They have been criticized for not assimilating, for not caring enough about the larger community. They have been troubled by apostates and plagued by polygamy. They have been rebuked because of their position on women. And they have been condemned by other denominations for stealing their members.

In the early days, of course, persecution was rampant. Time after time, in state after state, entire Mormon settlements were forced to flee. LDS leaders were jailed, and substantial amounts of church property were confiscated. Despite the many problems, however, both old and new, the long-term vitality of the movement has remained unimpaired. If anything, the tempo has increased. The fact is that Mormonism is more than a religion or a set of theological beliefs. For most of its members, it is a whole way of life.

SELECTED READINGS

Albrecht, Stan, Bahr, Howard, and Chadwick, Bruce. "Changing Family and Sex Roles: An Assessment of Age Differences." *Journal of Marriage and the Family,* 41 (February 1979): 41–50.

Alexander, Thomas, and Embry, Jessie, eds. *After 150 Years.* Midvale, Utah: Charles Redd Center for Western Studies, 1983.

Arrington, Leonard. *Brigham Young: American Moses.* New York: Knopf, 1985.

Baer, Hans. "Sex Roles in a Mormon Schismatic Group: The Levites of Utah." In *Sex Roles in Contemporary American Communes,* ed. by John Wagner, pp. 111–54. Bloomington: Indiana University Press, 1982.

Barlow, Brent. "Notes on Mormon Interfaith Marriages." *Family Coordinator,* 26 (April 1977): 143–50.

Campbell, Bruce, and Campbell, Eugene. "The Mormon Family." In *Ethnic Families in America,* ed. by Charles Mindel, Robert Habenstein, and Roosevelt Wright, Jr., pp. 456–94. New York: Elsevier, 1988.

Carmer, Carl. *The Farm Boy and the Angel.* Garden City, NY: Doubleday, 1970.

Clark, Annie Turner. *A Mormon Mother: An Autobiography.* Salt Lake City: University of Utah Press, 1969.

Foster, Lawrence. *Religion and Sexuality.* New York: Oxford University Press, 1981.

Gates, Susa Young. *The Life Story of Brigham Young.* New York: Macmillan, 1930.

Hartman, Moshe, and Hartman, Harriet. "Sex-Role Attitudes of Mormons vs.

Non-Mormons in Utah." *Journal of Marriage and the Family*, 45 (November 1983): 897–902.

Heinerman, John, and Shupe, Anson. *The Mormon Corporate Empire*. Boston, MA: Beacon Press, 1985.

Ivins, Stanley. "Notes on Mormon Polygamy." *Western Humanities Review*, 10 (Summer 1956): 229–39.

Leone, Mark. *Roots of Modern Mormonism*. Cambridge, MA: Harvard University Press, 1979.

May, Dean L. "Mormons." In *Harvard Encyclopedia of American Ethnic Groups*, ed. by Stephan Thernstrom, pp. 720–31. Cambridge, MA: Harvard University Press, 1980.

Merrill, Melissa. *Polygamist's Wife*. Salt Lake City: Olympus, 1975.

Mullen, Robert. *The Latter-day Saints: The Mormons Yesterday and Today*. Garden City, NY: Doubleday, 1966.

Porter, Blaine. *Selected Readings in the Latter-day Saint Family*. Dubuque, IA: Wm. C. Brown, 1963.

Stegner, Wallace. *The Gathering of Zion*. New York: McGraw-Hill, 1964.

Thornton, Arland. "Religion and Fertility: The Case of Mormonism." *Journal of Marriage and the Family*, 41 (February 1979): 131–42.

Turner, Wallace. *The Mormon Establishment*. Boston: Houghton Mifflin, 1966.

West, Ray B., Jr. *Kingdom of the Saints*. New York: Viking, 1957.

Whalen, William. *The Latter-day Saints in the Modern-Day World*. New York: John Day, 1964.

Whipple, Maurine. *This Is the Place: Utah*. New York: Knopf, 1945.

Wilkinson, M., and Tanner, W. "The Influence of Family Size, Interaction, and Religiosity on Family Affection in a Mormon Sample." *Journal of Marriage and the Family*, 42 (May 1980): 297–304.

Young, Kimball. *Isn't One Wife Enough?* New York: Henry Holt, 1954.

CHAPTER EIGHT

THE JEHOVAH'S WITNESSES

Most Americans in the 1990s separate their religious and secular lives, and there is relatively little condemnation of competing religious ideologies. But there are certain religious groups that are often thought of as being beyond the pale.

One such group is the Society of Jehovah's Witnesses. Americans exhibit a range of attitudes toward the Witnesses from indifference to derision to occasional hostility. Yet the group continues to grow and prosper, not only through natural increase, but also through proselytizing.

Why have they been so successful? To answer this question, it is necessary to know the group's history, understand their belief system, and examine the "supports of faith" that bind them together.

Charles Russell

Charles Russell, founder of the Jehovah's Witnesses, was born in 1852 in Allegheny, Pennsylvania, now a part of Pittsburgh. Both his parents, Joseph L. and Eliza Russell, were of Scottish-Irish descent. The Russells were religious people, members of the Presbyterian church. Eliza Russell died when Charles was nine, so it is difficult to know how much religious influence she had on her precocious child. As to child and father, it is probable, at least in a religious sense, that the son had greater influence on the father than the father on the son.

An exact date does not appear in Witness literature, but some time during his adolescence, young Charles left the Presbyterian church and joined a Congregational church, ostensibly because its attitudes were more liberal.

Joseph Russell, a haberdasher, owned a chain of five shops. After only a few years of formal education, Charles joined his father in business. By day, Charles sold shirts; at night, he studied the Bible. He was most interested in the prophetical books, particularly Daniel. By the time he was fourteen, he was on the streets with colored chalk writing Scriptures on the sidewalk. Nevertheless, at age seventeen, Russell encountered a spiritual crisis. He found himself no longer able to accept the concepts of eternal punishment and predestination. Surely, he believed, a good and just God would offer a plan of salvation for all of humankind. And certainly a loving God would not eternally damn even the worst of his children. For a period of time he rejected religion.

During Russell's youth, there was an industrial depression. Foreseeing a revolution on the horizon, he declared that "the old order of things must pass away, and the new must supersede it. . . . The change will be violently opposed by those advantaged by the present order."[1] Russell wrote: "Revolution world-wide would be the outcome, resulting in the final destruction of the old order and the introduction and establishment of the new."[2] His words share the tone of the *Communist Manifesto*, but there is no evidence that he ever read Marx.

During his religious renunciation, which lasted about a year, Russell stated, "I'm just going to forget the whole thing and give all my attention to business. If I make some money, I can use that to help suffering humanity, even though I cannot help do them any good spiritually."[3] By the time he was thirty, he had accumulated $300,000, a fortune in the 1880s. There is no indication that any of this money was used to aid humanity in a secular sense. Russell soon showed, however, that he was quite willing to use his fortune when it came to the expansion of his religious beliefs.

The Millerites   Russell's return to faith came as a result of his contact with the Second Adventists, or Millerites, a group founded by William Miller in 1829. Millerite membership was, for the most part, confined to the middle Atlantic states, and most followers were economically disadvantaged. Miller preached that the Second Coming of Christ would occur in the 1840s. The failure of this prophecy, of course, was already evident by the time Russell encountered the group. Russell believed the Millerites were "called of God," but had miscalculated the date for the Messiah's return. The Millerites were the only religious group Charles Russell did not denounce during his lifetime.

After Miller's death, his followers recalculated and decided Christ's Second Coming would occur in 1873 or 1874. In 1870, Russell organized a Bible study group in Pittsburgh. He and his group—there were only six members—determined that the Second Coming would occur later, and that Christ's return would be invisible. To set the record straight, Russell published, at his own expense, 50,000 copies of a booklet entitled *The Object and Manner of the Lord's Return*. An early

---

[1]Barbara Grizzuti Harrison, *Visions of Glory* (New York: Simon & Schuster, 1978), p. 43.
[2]Ibid., p. 43.
[3]*Yearbook of Jehovah's Witnesses*, (New York: Watchtower Bible and Tract Society of New York).

convert was his father, Joseph, who lent Charles both emotional and financial support.

Russell's following began to grow, and in 1879 he began publication of a periodical called *Zion's Watch Tower and Herald of Christ's Presence*. The new magazine had an impact. By 1880, there were some thirty congregations established in seven states. Also, in 1881, the Zion's Watchtower Tract Society was organized as an unincorporated body in Pittsburgh.* Stipulated in the organization's charter was the intent to "disseminate Bible truths in various languages by means of publication of tracts, pamphlets, papers, and other religious documents. . . ." Society pamphlets sold for five cents, books for twenty-five cents. Potential converts with no money were given the literature free. This practice has not changed.

By 1909, the organization had grown so large that it was decided to move its headquarters to Brooklyn, New York. The original building on the site was the manse of the noted abolitionist Henry Ward Beecher.

Personal Characteristics   Charles Russell was a small, thin man with an ascetic demeanor. A spellbinding speaker, he possessed charm and appeared to enjoy meeting people. He welcomed the press and photographers, and a large pictorial account exists of his ministry. He studied the Bible, and quoted Scripture readily in support of his beliefs. In his later years, his long white beard gave him the appearance of a sage patriarch. He was, indeed, a genuinely charismatic leader.

Russell was a workaholic. It is estimated that in the forty years of his ministry, he travelled a million miles, delivered 30,000 sermons, and wrote more than 150,000 pages of biblical exposition. While doing this, he managed a worldwide evangelistic ministry that employed more than seven hundred speakers.

Hints of Scandal   The Witnesses had to overcome several scandals during their formative years, but none was as far-reaching and caused as much disruption as Russell's marital difficulties. In 1879, Charles Russell married Maria Ackley. No children were born to the union. In the early years of the marriage, Maria Russell worked side by side with her ambitious husband, answering correspondence and addressing women's groups in his stead. But by 1909, the marriage had deteriorated to such a point that she sued for divorce, alleging, among other complaints, that Pastor Russell, as he had become known, had sexual relations with

---

*The Jehovah's Witnesses are now officially incorporated as: Watchtower (sic) Bible and Tract Society of New York, Watch Tower (sic) Bible and Tract Society of Pennsylvania, International Bible Students Association, Brooklyn. Most of the organization's work is conducted by the New York corporation. In 1931, at a convention held in Columbus, Ohio, the membership voted that they should, henceforth, be known as Jehovah's Witnesses.

female members of the congregation. Russell always denied these charges, but the divorce was granted.

During his ministry, two serious scandals, apart from his marital difficulties, received much press attention and caused some loss of Society membership. In his Brooklyn congregation, Russell sold bushels of a western wheat that was alleged to have marvelous properties. The wheat sold for sixty dollars a bushel. Grandiose claims for the magic grain brought vigorous press attacks, particularly from the *Brooklyn Eagle,* a popular local newspaper of the period. Pressure from the press finally forced the preacher out of the wheat business. Russell sued the *Eagle* for $100,000, but lost.

A similar episode involved Russell's endorsement and sale of a cancer cure, a compound of chloride of zinc, which may have sped some of his followers to an early reward. Not only was the caustic paste ineffective as a cure, it was damaging to those who used it. Although the cancer paste and wheat did not have marvelous properties, there is no reason to suggest that Russell himself did not believe in the products. It is often said that no one is easier to sell than a salesperson; Russell, a superb salesperson, may have been sold on the usefulness of these products— he even offered to return the purchase price of the merchandise to anyone who was dissatisfied.

Russell was often sued and was quick to use the courts in retaliation. He had unshakable faith in the invincibility of his own rightness. Because he was quick to attack Christians of every denomination, it is not surprising that those he denounced were often eager to attack him. His belief that only he understood the Bible made him an anathema to most religionists of his time. On October 31, 1916, the stormy life of Charles Russell came to an end. While on a nationwide lecture tour, he died in a Pullman car near Pampa, Texas.

Charles Russell, the moving, dynamic organizer of the Jehovah's Witnesses, is now but a footnote in the history of the organization. When a knowledgeable elder was asked how it all began, he answered, "It began in Pennsylvania when a group of Bible students wanted to learn the 'real truth.' They studied the Bible just as we are studying." Then, as though it were an afterthought, he added, "One of them, Charles Russell, was probably a little more prominent than the others."

Witnesses and the Federal Government

Judge Joseph Rutherford was elected president of the Jehovah's Witnesses shortly after Russell's death. Within a few months of Rutherford's election, his convictions were tested. At the beginning of World War I, there was much pro-war sentiment in the United States. The

Witnesses do not believe in war for any reason; also they do not believe in silence when secular beliefs conflict with Witness worldview.

In 1917, Rutherford and seven other Witness leaders were indicted for violation of the Espionage Act. The federal indictment charged the group with conspiracy to cause insubordination in the armed forces; a second charge accused the Witnesses of obstructing military enlistment. The Witnesses argued that they owed allegiance to no person, flag, or nation; they owed allegiance only to Jehovah. They were "of another world."

Rutherford and his followers were convicted, and all but one was sentenced to serve twenty years in the federal penitentiary at Leavenworth, Kansas; the seventh man received a ten-year sentence. The Witnesses began serving their sentences in June 1918. A petition for a new trial was filed, and in March 1919, all of the jailed Witnesses were released on bail. By then the war was over, and the government chose not to retry the case. Many people considered the jailing of the Witnesses a travesty of justice, and Society membership grew rapidly in the decade that followed.

Rutherford, like Russell, was a prolific writer. The Witnesses, however, deemphasize individuality and stress the importance of the "group." Since the death of Rutherford in 1942, none of their publications bears an author's signature. When knowledgeable Witnesses are asked about authorship, the usual response is that the article in question was probably written by a committee of Bible scholars.

Following Rutherford's death, Nathan Knorr was elected third president of the Society. He, too, had to stand up for Witness pacifist beliefs in the face of a draft. During the First World War, Witness leaders had been jailed; the government took a different tack during the Second World War. Instead of jailing a few leaders, more than 4,000 of the rank and file were arrested and jailed for failure to comply with draft laws. The Witness argument continued to be that they were "of another world."

Harassment of Witnesses on other issues was evident as well. During the war, Witness children were targeted in public-school systems. Harrison, an ex-Witness, describes in her book, *Visions of Glory*, a grade school experience:

> Having to remain seated . . . during flag salute at school assembly was an act of defiance from which I inwardly recoiled. . . . Not saluting the flag, being the only child in my school who did not contribute to the Red Cross, . . . and not bringing in tinfoil balls for the War Drive did not endear me to my classmates. I wanted to please everybody—my teachers, my spiritual overseers, my mother; and, of course, I could not.[4]

[4]Harrison, *Visions of Glory*.

Many Witness children were expelled from public schools for failing to conform to the system's expectations, and the Witnesses brought court suits in response to the expulsions. A 1940 Supreme Court decision, *Minersville v. Gobitas*, held that children who did not salute the flag were subject to expulsion. In 1943, the issue was returned to the Supreme Court in *West Virginia v. Barnette*. The Court ruled that the previous case had been "wrongly decided," and it was a Fourteenth Amendment violation to force children to salute the flag.

Following Knorr's death in 1977, Frederick Franz was elected president of the Society. There has been little conflict between the Witnesses and the outside world during his tenure in office. Witness convictions remain the same on issues of the draft and saluting the flag. There has not been a draft, however, since Franz assumed the presidency of the Society, and there has been no attempt by anyone to bring the flag-saluting issue back into the courts.

Franz is nearing his one-hundredth birthday. He is still to some extent active in the day-to-day affairs of the Society. The Witnesses believe that all major decisions should be the consequence of a committee process, and, since all the members of the governing committee are considered competent Bible scholars, it matters little if one committee member—even the president—requires a reduced workload.

Organization

During the early years, the Society's work was carried on by a board of directors. Anyone who donated ten dollars to the Society was eligible to cast one vote at board elections. Contributors could cast one additional vote for each ten-dollar increment contributed above a minimum donation. During his lifetime, Russell was the Society's unquestioned leader, and voting for the presidency was perfunctory.

In 1944, the Society's charter was amended to remove monetary contributions as a means of access to the governing body. Today, there is a governing body made up of eighteen men that meets weekly in Brooklyn to make both secular and religious decisions. In 1976, to assist the governing body, the following standing committees were formed: Service Committee, Writing Committee, Publishing Committee, Teaching Committee, and Chairman's Committee, term of appointment to any committee not to exceed one year.

At the next echelon are district and circuit overseers. Charged with the responsibility of visiting each congregation twice each year, these men (there are no women overseers) often accompany local Witnesses on home visits, ostensibly to help them with proselytizing techniques.

When leadership positions open, all baptized male Witnesses over age twenty are eligible for consideration.

At the head of each local congregation is a presiding overseer chosen from among the elders. It is a rotating position, the appointment not to exceed one year. The transience of the position fortifies the authority of the New York Society, emphasizing that no one man at the local level is indispensable.

Headquarters   The Witness headquarters complex in Brooklyn is called Bethel (House of God). Residents at Bethel, including married couples, live two to a room. Baths and toilets are shared. Most of the needs of the Bethelites are met within the confines of the complex, which includes its own barber shop, tailor shop, laundry, and bakery. Food and housekeeping services are provided. The rooms are pleasant and the food is good. Staff members, including the president of the Society, receive a monthly stipend of ninety dollars for personal needs. A few Witness detractors make much of the fact that headquarters personnel travel first class when on tour. It would seem, though, that Witness leaders move about in no greater style than leaders of other religious organizations.

The Society also owns and operates a number of farms, including a 1,698-acre farm near Walkill, New York, which provides most of the food required by the more than 3,500 headquarters workers. Witness farmworkers produce a large vegetable crop, maintain a herd of beef cattle, raise broiler chickens and laying hens, and milk a dairy herd. They also process what they produce. Eight hundred workers are required to operate the farm, processing facilities, and the two large printeries located on the farm.

Printeries   The printing operation at Walkill produces the magazines *Watchtower* and *Awake!* The farmworkers and printing-plant workers are classified as minister-volunteers and live a dormitory life-style similar to the Bethelites. They, too, receive a ninety-dollar per month stipend.

It is difficult to know just how much printed material is produced by the Jehovah's Witnesses. A recent edition of *Awake!* noted an average printing of 11,250,000 copies. A recent edition of *Watchtower* reported an average printing of 13,030,000 copies. Each magazine is produced semimonthly. The printeries at Walkill, which produce the magazines, are not nearly as large as the Bethel printeries, which produce books and pamphlets, where six of the ten multistory buildings are devoted to production of the written word. Sterling described what he saw:

> The sheer magnitude of the printing and publishing operation of the Watchtower Bible and Tract Society is most impressive. There is no loitering around the water coolers here. There are no clusters of workers wast-

ing Jehovah's time standing around the entrance doorways during work breaks—if indeed there are such events. Everyone is busy at his job producing warnings of the nearness of the last days. There is a distinct "work for the night is coming" flavor and aura to this publishing hive. . . .

They are not printing in modest numbers, as most of the 36,000 books that are printed annually by the American publishing industry are. . . . There is no way of knowing how their output compares with other publishing companies and printing houses, but the Witnesses appear to be ahead of who is in second place.[5]

Today, *Watchtower* and *Awake!* magazines sell for twenty-five cents, a standard Bible for four dollars, and a deluxe version for seven dollars. And no book is overpriced, based on materials and labor costs in today's marketplace. A fair portion of Society literature is given away. Individual ministers, in carrying out the work of the Society, prepay the printing costs of tracts, books, and magazines needed in their daily work, and many ministers who feel they have come in touch with someone open to their views will leave literature with a potential convert and not ask for payment.

Finances

Each year, the Society places a notice in an issue of the *Watchtower* soliciting contributions. In order to facilitate planning, the notice asks contributors to specify how much the Society can expect to receive and when contributions will be made. Collections are not taken at the Kingdom Halls, and the elders do not solicit money from the pulpit.* Every Hall has a contribution box, but contributions from this source seem to be few and far between. Most donations come from self-imposed tithes.

Classified as a charitable religious organization, the Society is not required to make public its financial statements. Many denominations, similarly exempt, choose to make public disclosures of income and assets; that the Witnesses do not may be linked to past problems with tax collectors. The most notable of these occurred in 1971, when the state of New York enacted a law permitting taxation of property not exclusively used for religious purposes. The Society paid $2,000,000, under protest, to the city of New York. On July 11, 1974, tax exemption was restored to the Society by the New York State Court of Appeals. The court's written decision stipulated that the Society was organized exclusively for religious purposes within the meaning of the statute.

---

[5]Chandler Sterling, *The Witnesses: One God One Victory,* (Chicago: Regency, 1975), p. 120.
*Kingdom Halls are places for education and worship. Witnesses do not use the term "church." A body of believers is termed a "congregation."

Charity   Members of other faiths, legislators, and the public in general do not understand the Witness position on charity. There are no charitable entities within Witness organizational structure: no hospitals, no clinics, no food programs. The Society believes that the last days are so near that all available funds must be spent on the "promulgation of the truth" (spreading Jehovah's word).

The edict to be charitable permeates Society literature. Charity is up to the individual, however; it is not viewed as an organizational responsibility. Aid usually involves services such as baby-sitting, marketing for the elderly, transportation, and reading scriptures to the infirm. It is difficult to know the private transactions of the Witness "in-group," but it is probable that they help each other financially as well.

Building Construction   Erecting new buildings is not a problem for most Witness congregations, which are willing to expend their own time and energy. For example, a Minnesota congregation has a new Kingdom Hall, built almost entirely by the members, many of whom are skilled laborers. Nothing was spent for outside help. When they had difficulty planning and installing the electrical system, a call for assistance was sent to nearby congregations, and the problem was resolved quickly. When the building was dedicated, members of the congregations who lent assistance were honored. Great pride was felt in the accomplishment. An investment of time and labor is apparently more rewarding than a monetary contribution.

Financing construction of Kingdom Halls is a relatively simple matter. Congregations need only finance the cost of building materials; there are no labor costs. The elimination of labor costs creates built-in equity for the lender. For example, a Kingdom Hall valued at $100,000, minus the cost of labor, may necessitate only a $50,000 loan. There is almost no risk for the lender. The parent Society maintains a list of bankers and institutional investors eager to invest in Kingdom Halls.

Witness congregations save money in many ways. For example, they do not hire janitors. In most congregations, janitorial and maintenance duties are assigned to Bible study groups on a rotating basis. Most Witnesses are skilled or semiskilled laborers, so maintenance is never a problem for them, and thus, the Kingdom Halls are well cared for.

The organization pays as it goes; it does not accrue unnecessary debt. And Russell's statement in a 1914 *Watchtower* appears to be as true today as it was then:

> We have no church organization in the ordinary sense of the word, no bondage of any kind, no obligation to pay, either to the parent society or anybody else, either ten percent or any other sum. . . . No solicitations for money in any way are authorized by the society. . . . Every amount there-

fore, that has come into our hands, and been used, has been a voluntary donation from a willing heart. . . . It is true of the Lord's people in general . . . that among them are not many rich, not many learned, not many noble, but chiefly the poor of this world. . . .[6]

What Witnesses Believe

In the Beginning   Before earth there was heaven and in heaven was God (Jehovah) and he was alone. His first creation was a son, the Archangel Michael. Michael "was used by Jehovah in creating all other things."[7] Michael's first creations were other spirit sons for God, angels numbering in the millions. Among these sons was Lucifer, who would later be called Satan, which means "Resister."

After creating the earth, Jehovah said to Michael, "let us make man in our image."[8] Their purpose was to create a perfect paradise (Eden), for a perfect man (Adam) and woman (Eve). Adam and Eve, in turn, were expected to bear perfect children, who would live according to Jehovah's laws and glorify him.

The Fall   It was Jehovah's intent that humans should live in perfect harmony with their environment and never die. Lucifer was put in charge of Eden. Jealous of Jehovah, he wanted followers who would adore him. To accomplish this, he had to alienate Adam and Eve from God. While Jehovah rested at the beginning of the seventh day (Genesis 2:2), Lucifer found the fatal flaw in Adam and Eve.*

Jehovah had given Adam a single prohibition: Do not eat the fruit of the tree of knowledge of good and evil, or you will die. Satan, using a snake as a medium, convinced Eve to eat the fruit. She then seduced Adam, and he, too, ate the fruit. Jehovah's punishment was death to Adam and Eve, and death for all of their kind to follow.

Witnesses do not attribute the Fall to the sex act. Interestingly, original sin is tied to intellectual freedom. Eve's act led to freedom of choice, which didn't exist before the forbidden fruit was eaten. Before the Fall, Adam simply obeyed Jehovah's laws, as he had been commanded:

> The woman was the first human sinner. Her temptation by God's adversary . . . was not through an open appeal to immorality of a sensual na-

[6]Watchtower Bible and Tract Society of New York, 1914.

[7]*Insight on the Scriptures*, vol. 1 (New York: Watchtower Bible and Tract Society of New York, 1988), p. 527.

[8]Ibid., p. 527.

*All biblical references are from *New World Translation of the Holy Scriptures* (New York: Watchtower Bible and Tract Society of New York, 1961; 1971 revision).

ture. Rather, it paraded as an appeal to the desire for supposed intellectual elevation and freedom. . . . He [the snake] asserted that eating the fruit from the proscribed tree would result, not in death, but in enlightenment and godlike ability to determine for oneself whether a thing was good or bad. . . .[9]

The Ransom   Jehovah loved Adam despite his failure, and chose to release Adam's children from the death penalty. Viewed by the Society as the head of a theocratic legal system, even Jehovah must act according to law. Humankind could be released from the certainty of death, but only through a legal ransom. Witnesses define "ransom" as an exact corresponding price. Adam was a perfect man, therefore a perfect man had to be sacrificed to redeem humankind.

Witnesses reject the concept of a Holy Trinity—the idea that Father, Son, and Holy Spirit are one. Jesus is believed to be God's first son, the Archangel Michael. Because Adam was human, Michael was sent to earth in human form. As Jesus, he was capable of sin, but in order to pay Adam's "ransom," he had to live a sinless life. After the Resurrection, he was restored to a spiritual being.

Prophecy Failure   The most important date in Witness chronology is 1914. Witnesses believe that on October 4 or 5 of that year, Christ fought the devil in heaven, won the battle, then hurled Satan and his demons to earth. Russell and early Witnesses thought that Christ would establish his earthly kingdom in that same year. When Christ did not make a visible appearance, the date for his advent was recalculated to 1918. Despite the recalculation and Russell's charisma, there was some decrease in Society membership in the years that followed.

Judge Rutherford, Russell's successor, studied the Scriptures and concluded that the Society had erred. It was decided that Christ had established his "invisible heavenly kingdom" in 1914 but that he would not establish his "earthly kingdom" until after a "generation had passed." A generation was defined as the life span of all those living in 1914 who were old enough to understand the horrors of that year. The Society cites the beginning of World War I, along with other disasters that occurred in that year, as proof that an angered Satan, cast out of heaven, was displaying his wrath.

Contemporary Witnesses believe that an infant would not have understood the horrors of 1914 but, perhaps, a precocious child of three or four could have. If there is to be a second prophecy failure, it cannot occur until the Witnesses are convinced that all those who understood the events of 1914 have died. The following excerpt from *Awake!* reminds

[9]*Insight on the Scriptures*, vol. 2 (New York: Watchtower Bible and Tract Society of New York, 1988), p. 963.

Witnesses that only a few of this generation are still living:

1914 Assassin Dies

One member of the revolutionaries who assassinated Archduke Francis Ferdinand of Austria in 1914 now remains living after another member, Cvetko Popovic, recently died at the age of 85. The assassination at Sarajevo, Yugoslavia, triggered World War I. The survivor, historian Vasa Cubrilovis, is 83 years old. This is further evidence that the "generation" of persons that saw those events continues, though nearing its end.[10]

Eschatology Christian eschatology is concerned with the Second Coming of Christ, the resurrection of the dead, the last judgment, and the nature of human existence upon the completion of history.

Russell's final dispensation, "The World to Come," begins with the "Miliennial Age." Christ, and those already in heaven, are waiting to begin the battle of Armageddon—the final, decisive battle between good and evil. Satan will be defeated in the battle and cast into an abyss for a thousand years, a millennium.*

Witnesses do not believe in a fiery hell. Most of the billions of people who died before the battle of Armageddon have been turned to dust from which they will be resurrected. The few who will not return are those that in life were "willfully wicked." Witnesses define the "willfully wicked" as those who knew the will of Jehovah but defied him. There appears to be no consensus among Witness rank and file as to who had been "willfully wicked," but the number is deemed small. Adam and Eve, Judas, and Nimrod are certain to remain in dust.

Paradise By the end of the millennium, humankind will have reached a perfected state; vice, disease, corruption, and death will disappear from the earth. But at the end of the millennium, Satan will be freed from his bondage. He will gather demons around him, and together they will try to persuade humankind to follow them. Witnesses believe that few will. After experiencing paradise, how could humankind want to lead an immoral and degrading life? Satan's small army will be defeated, and a second judgment day will follow.

Jehovah's first judgment, after Adam's failure, was against all of humankind. The final judgment, following the destruction of Satan, will be of individuals. All those deemed unworthy will be condemned to eternal dust. Even this untoward group will not have to suffer the agonies of a tormenting hell.

After the millennium, Christ will return a perfected earth to Jehovah.

---

[10]"Watching the World," *Awake!* (October 8, 1980), p. 29.

*Witnesses believe, based on their interpretation of Scripture, that only 144,000 will know the heavenly kingdom. All others returned from the dust will live in an earthly paradise ruled by Jehovah.

Jehovah will become an active king in his theocratic system. Survivors of the final judgment will live in harmony with their creator in paradise for eternity. There is little speculation as to what life will be like in "the Ages to Come." Most Witnesses simply believe that it is beyond the power of mortals to comprehend all the goodness Jehovah has in store for them.

Social Characteristics

Voting Behavior   Most Jehovah's Witnesses do not vote. Those who do ordinarily confine their ballots to local issues such as zoning, taxes, and school board elections. At a group meeting in Minnesota, an elder was asked if he didn't think it was in the interest of the Society for members to vote for national candidates who might best represent Witnesses' moral convictions. His response was that it didn't make much difference who was elected, nothing would change. Satan's evil plan would be followed until Jehovah establishes his kingdom on earth. The wife of the congregation's presiding elder ended the conversation when she asked the interviewer, "If you were a citizen of France, would you expect to vote in Great Britain's elections?" The interviewer said he would not. "Well," she continued, "we are citizens of Jehovah's Kingdom. Not only should we not want to vote, we really don't have the right to vote."[11]

Sexual Attitudes   Witnesses do not consider sex to have been the downfall of Adam and Eve. But this has not led to "liberated" sexual attitudes. On an NBC *Today Show,* a Methodist minister explained the explicit sexual films he had recently produced. His purpose was to help people understand the normality of the sex drive. The films could not be shown on television; apparently little was left to the imagination. Part of his project dealt with oral sex, one segment depicted homosexual love, and still another segment dealt with sex between the elderly. That same afternoon, by contrast, one of the "brothers" at a district convention of Jehovah's Witnesses spoke sharply on the evils of masturbation.

Masturbation is considered self-love, and most Witness children are told early and often about the Scriptures that forbid the practice of self-adoration. Witness children are warned that masturbation can inhibit a happy marriage, noting that it is a man's responsibility to ensure that his wife derives pleasure from the sex act. If a habit of premarital masturbation develops, one thinks only of oneself, and it becomes difficult to satisfy a partner.

---

[11]William Zellner, *Of Another World: The Jehovah's Witnesses* (Ph.D. diss., South Dakota State University; Brookings, SD: Brookings 1981), p. 60–61 (All subsequent references to the "Minnesota Study" were extracted from this thesis.)

Witnesses take the unique position that masturbation can lead to homosexuality. One of the Witness books, *Your Youth*, states:

> Masturbation can lead into homosexuality. In such instances the person, not satisfied with his lonely sexual activity, seeks a partner for mutual sex play.
>
> This happens much more frequently than you may realize. Contrary to what many persons think, homosexuals are not born that way, but their homosexual behavior is learned. And often a person gets started when very young by playing with another's sexual parts, and then engaging in homosexual acts. . . .[12]

Homosexual behavior is considered an unnatural abomination and is grounds for disfellowship. Homosexuals are counseled before action is taken against them.

The Witness term for excommunication is "disfellowship." During Zellner's two-year study of Minnesota congregations it was found that two young women were disfellowshipped from one of the congregations, each deemed guilty of fornication; both were living unwed with a male friend. On several occasions, "brothers" visited and counseled the errant "sisters." Members of the congregation all felt the sisters were censured fairly, but all hoped the women would repent: Society doors are opened to repentant sinners.

Note, the brothers counseled the women. Sisters are considered the weaker vessel; their position in the Society is one of support. In the Minnesota study, a rather stable, seemingly strong young woman was asked if she resented the secondary role assigned women by the Society, if she didn't think it was unjust that she couldn't counsel, in an official way, those who faltered, or that she couldn't hold a leadership position in the church. "Oh, no!" she replied, and looked at the interviewer with a somewhat puzzled expression. "Women are not emotionally strong enough to handle those kinds of things."[13]

Witnesses recognize Jehovah's biblical commandment to be fruitful and multiply. Members are, however, permitted to practice birth control. Witnesses are opposed to abortion, so birth control must not include the use of intrauterine devices (IUDs), on the grounds that these devices act to abort the egg after fertilization has occurred. Such methods as the pill, a diaphragm, or prophylactics may be used at the discretion of the individual. There are no available statistics on average Witness family size. Most members are blue-collar workers, however, a group with a higher birthrate than middle-class families.

---

[12] *Your Youth: Getting the Best out of It* (New York: Watchtower Bible and Tract Society of New York, 1976).

[13] Zellner, *Of Another World*, p. 62.

The Society suggests that young Witnesses consider singleness—celibate singleness—as a viable alternative to marriage. Missionaries are particularly encouraged to give extra thought before marrying. The Society warns that marriage could limit their ability to carry out their duties properly. The Society further makes the point that, with Armageddon so near, there is no need to hurry parenting; it might be better to wait and bring children into a perfected world.

Marriage and Family   Idyllically, the Witness marriage is the kind of marriage that was supposed to have existed in the United States before the sexual revolution of the 1960s. The husband is responsible for meeting the family's economic needs, while the wife is responsible for the care and maintenance of the home. A good wife defers to her husband on all matters of importance. Many Witness texts, however, such as *Happiness, How to Find it*, suggest that the husband—to promote marital happiness—give in to the wife on unimportant matters.

In practice, the familistic orientation of the Witnesses is very similar to that of the Mormons. Families are encouraged to do things together or with other Witness families. Congregational functions are to be attended by all members of the family, and families are encouraged to work together, play together, and worship together. There are no separatist bodies within the Society—no men's groups or women's groups.

The Society does, however, recognize that some married couples are so mismatched that it is impossible for them to live together. Charles and Marie Russell were such a mismatch. In such cases, separation is condoned, but divorce is permissible only on the Scriptural ground of adultery.

The Society recommends that women whose husbands live outside the Kingdom defer to their spouse on all matters except those which contradict Jehovah's teachings. It is thought that if a wife continues to exhibit a "sweet nature," the husband may eventually mature.

Integrated Community   The Witnesses evidently do not practice racial discrimination, and Society literature clearly denounces the practice. On several occasions during the Minnesota study, an observer attended meetings (they are never called services) in a racially mixed urban neighborhood. The congregation reflected the makeup of the larger community. Intermarriage is quite common, and it is not unusual to see a white grandparent making a fuss over a black grandchild. In observing the interactions within this congregation, it was evident that racial harmony is the norm. Male African-American Witnesses are eligible for, and do attain, leadership roles in the organization's hierarchy.

Medicine   Jehovah's Witnesses do not accept blood transfusions, regardless of medically defined need, but this does not mean they categorically reject the medical profession. The Society does not object to the use of medicinal drugs, inoculations, internal medicines, or necessary surgery, provided blood transfusion can be avoided. The ban against the use of blood is based on Leviticus 17:10: "God told Noah that every living creature should be meat unto him; but that he must not eat blood, because the life is in the blood." Witnesses cite the currrent AIDS epidemic as proving this long-held belief to be correct.

Witnesses do not believe in faith healers. Such individuals are considered absolute frauds. The Society acknowledges that a select few, prior to Christ, had the ability to heal, as did Christ and the apostles, but the gift was lost with the death of the last apostle.

Education   At one district convention, a Witness speaker encouraged young people of ability to attend trade schools and stay away from colleges, insisting that college instruction contradicts Jehovah's teachings. Society literature directs the Witness father to train his sons to use their hands. When he repairs his car, his son should be allowed to help. Daughters should be trained by their mothers and taught to sew, cook, and maintain a clean house. At one Bible study, a well-attired young man had the floor. "No, you won't find much of man's education in this room," he said. "You won't find no bachelor's degrees, no master's degrees. This is not what we seek. Our education is of God's word."[14]

Holidays   The "Memorial Supper," the observance of the death of Christ, is the only Witness holiday. It is not a festive occasion, but a very solemn meal of unleavened bread and wine. There is no thought of the bread and wine as symbolic of the body and blood of Christ. Only those who are convinced that they are part of the "remnant" (those still living who will ultimately rule in heaven with Christ) actually partake of the meal; all others simply pass the bread and cup. When members are asked how they know they are part of the "remnant," the response is always, "You just feel it." Only two persons in a Kingdom Hall in Minnesota, where an observer regularly attended meetings, felt justified in eating the meal.

The Witnesses find reasons for not celebrating other holidays. The Easter rabbit is a pagan symbol of fertility; New Year's celebrations are debaucheries; Halloween is associated with Catholicism's celebration of the dead; secular holidays, such as Labor Day, Independence Day, and Columbus Day, glorify humans. In *Reasoning from the Scriptures*, the Society debunks Christmas and birthday celebrations in a single paragraph:

[14]Ibid., p. 66.

Suppose a crowd comes to a gentleman's home saying they are there to celebrate his birthday. He does not favor the celebration of birthdays. He does not like to see people overeat or get drunk or engage in loose conduct. But some of them do all those things, and they bring presents for everyone there except him! On top of that they pick the birthday of one of the man's enemies as the date for the celebration. How would the man feel? This is exactly what is being done by Christmas celebrations.[15]

Media Relations   In the decades following Russell's leadership, press coverage of Witness events had not been encouraged. Witness positions were simply Witness positions, and the Society exhibited no concern for public image. Recently, at one Minnesota district convention, there was a pressroom set up and staffed by elders, who could quote Scripture in support of any Witness viewpoint. The existence of the press center may have been significant, evidencing a sensitivity to the "other world," a sensitivity that has not existed in the past.

When one of the elders was asked by an observer why a press center had been established, he said that the Society had taken positions against draft registration and the Equal Rights Amendment, and they wanted the public to understand that their views were based on Scripture.

There were many chairs in the large pressroom; half were occupied by elders, half were empty. There were press releases, books, and pamphlets. The only thing missing was the press.

Gaining Converts and Maintaining the Faith

Why people join and maintain membership in a group that is often deprecated is an interesting question. The answer has remained somewhat elusive. Witnesses themselves are often less than cooperative. The few studies we do have contain little more than demographic data. The important issues, such as how members of the Society come to agree on rules, definitions, and values, are not addressed.

In the Minnesota study, Zellner went beyond collecting demographic data, and chose, instead, to observe Witnesses as they function in the day-to-day world. He attended meetings and participated in a home Bible study. Questions were asked in a conversational way and recorded later. Often, the questions did not have to be asked. Witness converts, like most other religious converts, have a penchant for comparing their former unfulfilling life-styles to their new, much improved life-situation.

---

[15]*Reasoning from the Scriptures* (New York: Watchtower Bible and Tract Society of New York, 1985), p. 179.

The questionnaire that follows contains typical answers. The respondent was a forty-nine-year-old white female identified by the pseudonym Kate Williams.

Q. What is your marital status?
A. Widow.
Q. Do you have any children?
A. Eight.
Q. Are they members of the group?
A. Three participate fully. Five are, at this time, living outside of Jehovah's Kingdom. It is difficult to raise children in Satan's world. They are sent to school and taught by teachers who know nothing about Jehovah, or have rejected him. Then when they get a job, they are surrounded by more people who either don't know or won't accept Jehovah's word. It is my sincerest hope that all my children will eventually enter Jehovah's Kingdom.
Q. What kind of work do you do?
A. Material sorter.
Q. How long have you been a member of the Jehovah's Witnesses?
A. Twenty-six years.
Q. How did you first encounter the group?
A. They came to the door when we were living in California. I wasn't at home the first time they came, but I remember my husband was very excited about their visit. We studied over the literature for many hours.
Q. Were the Jehovah's Witnesses any different in California than they are here [Minnesota]?
A. Jehovah's people are Jehovah's people wherever you meet them.
Q. Were you at a time in your life when you were experiencing some sort of unusual strain?
A. We had not been living in California very long, and we were having some difficulty getting adjusted to that way of life. We felt we were surrounded by godless people.
Q. Do you feel that a pattern for life is important?
A. Everyone should have direction in life. My husband and I both felt that need.
Q. Did your becoming a Jehovah's Witness fulfill that need?
A. Most definitely.
Q. Did you believe in the existence of God before encountering the Jehovah's Witnesses or would you have considered yourself an agnostic or atheist?
A. My husband and I both believed in God. We went to a Lutheran church before moving to California.
Q. Before attending formal group [Witness] meetings, did you form a close tie with one or more of the Witnesses?
A. We liked the people who came to our house, and we began attending meetings right away. We went to the Kingdom Hall and met people who wanted to live according to God's will. It was very different from what we had previously experienced in California.

Q. Did your becoming a Witness cause a strain between you and other family members?

A. All of my family was alienated; so was my husband's.

Q. Did your joining the group strain relationships between you and your friends?

A. We had no friends to speak of in California. But when we got back to Minnesota, I lost a friend who was like a mother to me. I still feel bad about that.

Q. Has being a Witness caused you any problems in your work situation?

A. No. Most of the people I work with are very nice. I do feel sorry for them, though. They search and search and what they are looking for is right under their noses. Jehovah has laid out his plan for us all.

Q. How many hours a week do you spend in organizational activity?

A. Twenty-two to twenty-three hours a week. [This included attending meetings and proselytizing.]

Q. How long was it before you moved from verbal agreement with the group to commitment, attending regular meetings, and so on?

A. We began right away.

Q. Do you seek to gain new members for the group? How?

A. Of course. We are obligated to spread the word. When I feel that I can talk to someone at work, or someone in the neighborhood, I talk to them about Jehovah. Also, I go door-to-door like all Witnesses who are able.

Q. Do you subscribe totally to the belief system of the Jehovah's Witnesses or do you have some doubts or disagreements?

A. I believe totally.

Q. Do you consider membership in the group the most important aspect of your life?

A. Yes, I do. I have brought at least ten people into the "new system." If my life wasn't fully committed, I couldn't have done that. [Kate Williams is an extremely pleasant woman and her claim of conversions is probably accurate. Most Witnesses are not nearly so successful at bringing new members into the group despite their dedicated activity.]

There are more than 4 million Witnesses worldwide, and their further growth is more or less guaranteed by the process of natural increase. Witnesses, however, are not content with only that kind of growth. Because they believe that the end is near, the Society has defined its mission as bringing as many as possible into the "new system" before Armageddon.

On three occasions, Zellner spent half a day proselytizing with a Jehovah's Witness. He was not convinced that the Witness liked the idea of his tagging along. Since Zellner had not completed his home Bible study, the elder felt Zellner's training was inadequate to the task. It was only after Zellner assured the elder that he would be friendly, but leave the Bible talk to him, that the elder reluctantly allowed him to go along.

Two of the trips were to working-class neighborhoods, the other to a middle- to upper-middle-class area. Very few doors were opened to the pair, and what little success they did have was in the working-class neighborhoods. The Witness making the calls was employed by a janitorial service. When he got his foot in a door, he not only talked about the Bible, but about his family and job as well. He had much in common with most of the working-class people to whom he spoke—shared backgrounds, experiences, and problems.

Not surprisingly, a proselytizing butcher does not attract a college student, rather he or she tends to attract a carpenter or plumber. A working-class housewife is more likely to develop rapport with a widow working in a school lunchroom than she is with a banker. As a group, Jehovah's Witnesses have similar social-class backgrounds, one of the consequences of the proselytizing process.*

Bonding   Forming an "affecive bond" (an emotional relationship) with one or more members of the group is the keystone to conversion for most Witnesses. Kate Williams's response to the survey question "Before attending formal group meetings, did you form a close tie with one or more of the Witnesses? was typical. Thirteen of the eighteen Witnesses interviewed had their first encounter with the Society when Witnesses called on them at their homes. All of the Witnesses interviewed reported having formed an affective bond with one or more Witnesses before becoming active in the group.

Bonding is more important than dogma. The differences between Witness dogma and conventional Christian dogma are not emphasized in the proselytizing process. What is emphasized are the similarities. Zellner made the following observations concerning his home Bible study program:†

> It was several months before my instructor revealed that Christ was not God incarnate, long after an affective social bond, under ordinary circumstances, would have been formed. It would have been very difficult to break a strong interactive bond based on that one bit of information. The dogma comes in bits and pieces.
>
> I was never lied to, but when I did not initiate the "hard" questions associated with doctrinal differences between the Witnesses and normative Protestant denominations, the differences were not revealed until my instructor thought I was ready for the "truth."[16]

---

[16]Zellner, *Of Another World*, pp. 101–2.

*There are notable exceptions. Rock star Michael Jackson is a Jehovah's Witness, as is Mickey Spillane, creator of fictional detective Mike Hammer.

†Zellner was working as a Pinkerton security guard during the course of his "participant observation" of the Jehovah's Witnesses. He did not reveal to the Witnesses that he was a sociologist.

There are no half-hearted Witnesses. The price for not buying wholeheartedly into the belief system, after a reasonable length of time, is possible loss of interaction and the cutting of affective bonds. The potential convert must accept Society teachings or risk losing interaction in the form of primary-group relationships.

Meaningful bonds are apparently formed very quickly. Kate Williams responded to the survey question "How long was it before you moved from verbal agreement with the group to commitment, attending regular meetings, and so on?" that she and her husband began attending meetings right away. This was not an unusual response. Of the eighteen Witnesses interviewed, most became active in a period varying from a few weeks to a few months; only one held out as long as six months.

Need for Certitude   It appears that a "need for certitude" is a necessary but not sufficient condition for conversion to the Jehovah's Witnesses. All eighteen converts felt that their lives lacked direction before encountering the group; all felt that a pattern for life was important; and all felt that their conversion satisfied this need. The Witness belief system is conformity-demanding.

Prescriptions for action cover every situation. Converts are told exactly what is required of them in family situations, job situations, and how to act in the presence of nonbelievers. The Society provides a way to cope with the suffering and inequities of Satan's world. The plan meets the human need for certitude, provides light beyond death, and becomes the convert's *raison d'etre*.

Primary-Group Relationships   It may be logically assumed that some people are more receptive to religious proselytizing at certain times during their lives. Five of the eighteen converts interviewed had just moved to a new community where they had no family and few or no friends. Four had weak or nonexistent family ties even before they encountered Jehovah's Witnesses. Family ties, in most cases, suffer further strains after conversion. The Society offers those who feel a need for primary-group relationships access to such relationships with like-minded people.

Shared Values before Conversion   The convert must accept new religious dogma, but most share similar social values before conversion. Society literature merely confirms and refines what most converts already believed about the world.

It appears, also, that most converts share many of the Society's social values before encountering the group. For example, the Society generally rejects voting; only two of the Witnesses interviewed voted before joining the group. Most were fundamentalists, and believed the Bible should be taken literally. All believed that the male should be dominant in the family unit. The Society emphasizes that people should work with their hands and strongly denounces higher education; all the converts worked with their hands before joining the group. The Society provides support for those who, for whatever reason, are not well educated in the traditional sense. Joining the Society adds group affirmation and justification for a life-style already chosen.

The Religious Perspective

Sociologists recognize three major "problem-solving" perspectives: religious, psychological, and political. Most people employ all three in their efforts to resolve life's problems. There are those, however, who tend to rely on only one perspective. Members of a radical political party emphasize a political problem-solving ideology, while people who buy self-help books from supermarket shelves tend to utilize the psychological perspective. Devoutly religious people almost exclusively answer life's questions with religious explanations. All eighteen Witnesses interviewed believed strongly in God, and had a religious problem-solving perspective before joining the movement.

House Calls   Conversionist religious groups do not convert atheists or agnostics. Any door-to-door vacuum cleaner salesperson can relate to this argument. Rarely does a salesperson knock on a door to have it opened by someone who shouts, "Hey! That's just what I was looking for!" Salespeople must knock on many doors; when they find one open, they must sell first themselves and then the sweeper. For the vacuum cleaner salesperson to have a chance, the potential customer must have a rug. For the Witness proselytizer, the customer's rug must be a religious problem-solving perspective.

Jehovah's Witnesses are believers; there is no doubt about that. Zellner discusses the rejection Witnesses encounter when seeking converts door-to-door:

> I will never forget the few field trips I made with a Witness proselytizer. Next to no-one-at-home, I considered polite indifference a good call. After the Witness introduced himself, the occupant usually said, "I'm a Presbyterian, Catholic, Jew, or whatever." What the prospect meant was "I'm not open to a new religious outlook," and doors closed to us very quickly.[17]

Proselytizing and perceived persecution are important "supports of faith." The Witnesses uniformly perceive the rejection they encounter in their missionary work as persecution; this common feeling creates inter-

[17]Ibid., p. 106.

nal cohesion and a strong "we" feeling. They are convinced that the world is on the brink of the millennium, the time when Satan's strength is on the increase. They talk endlessly about those they meet who are in poor spiritual condition, and the many good people deceived by Satan.

Past Relationships   Most Jehovah's Witnesses more or less sever relations with the outside world; meaningful relationships occur only within the microcosm. In response to the survey question "Did your becoming a Witness cause a strain between you and other family members?," only two of the eighteen converts reported any degree of normality in family relationships, and both felt there was room for improvement. Many had tried to convert relatives but had given up. All hoped their relatives would someday understand "the truth."

In response to the question "Did your joining the group strain relationships between you and your friends?," all eighteen Witnesses reported changing friends after joining the Society; a few reported having few or no friends before membership. The new friends were, of course, Jehovah's Witnesses.

Alienation   Eleven converts reported that they had, at one time or another, been chided at their workplace because of their beliefs. Through interaction, Witnesses share common definitions of situations, and all felt sorry for their tormentors. As part of the blue-collar class, Witnesses work with people who often exhibit little tolerance for nonnormative viewpoints. For the convert, religion is a matter to be taken seriously and never joked about. There is no question that Witnesses are alienated in most situations outside of the microcosm, yet it is alienation with hope. Not hope that they will someday fit in, but a hope that someday the rest of the world will join them.

Group Membership   As previously noted, the Society effectively promotes primary-group relationships. When the Sunday meetings are over, Witnesses do not leave their religion at the Kingdom Hall. They consider themselves "of another world," and spend as much time as possible in their self-created microcosm. In many ways, they are social isolates: most are alienated from their families, and most have few friends outside the group. What they do have is each other, and they interact much in the fashion of an extended family.

The Meetings

In general, Witnesses consider group membership the most important aspect of their lives. Most spend as much time as possible in organizational activity. Following is a schedule of formal meetings held at one of the Kingdom Halls. The structure of these meetings is not left to local congregations; a printed format outlining what is to be done during the entire year is sent from the Society in New York, and local congregations must not deviate from the plan. Only meeting hours may vary from one congregation to the next.

Witnesses have five formal meetings each week, and each represents an important support of faith. All Witnesses are expected to attend as many meetings as possible. Sickness and secular employment are acceptable excuses for missing, but if too many meetings are missed, a flagging Witness can expect a visit from a group of brothers.

The first hour each Sunday is labeled a "Bible Educational Talk." The talks range from denouncing "the evils of the United Nations" to "how to communicate within one's family." The speaker, an elder, always relates his topic to Scripture. In urban areas, the speaker is sometimes a

---

Know Your Bible

It can be an
Open Book to you.

Free Bible courses each week

Sunday

BIBLE EDUCATIONAL TALK   9:00 A.M.
   A different vital topic on current needs each week
WATCHTOWER STUDY   10:00 A.M.
   A question-and-answer meeting on selected Bible subjects

Tuesday

CONGREGATION BIBLE STUDY   7:30 P.M.
   A systematic discussion of religion's role in your life

Thursday

THEOCRATIC SCHOOL   7:30 P.M.
   A speaking course featuring the teachings of the Bible
SERVICE MEETING   8:30 P.M.
   Talks, demonstrations on practical use of Bible knowledge

All Interested Persons Welcome
Free   No Collection   Free

---

visiting elder from another congregation in the city; rural congregations as well will occasionally exchange speakers.

The second hour of the Sunday meeting is spent reading the current issue of the *Watchtower*. After a reader has read a paragraph from the text, the congregation is asked to respond to a question printed at the bottom of the page. The questions are numbered and correspond to the numbered paragraph in the *Watchtower* containing the answer. Many hands are raised. Ushers, usually teenage and always males, carry microphones on metal poles, and when the reader calls on one of the congregation to respond, an usher extends his pole down the aisle so the responder can read back the paragraph that has just been read. When a question appears easy enough, the reader will occasionally call on one of the children in the congregation to answer. If the child responds correctly, everyone beams approvingly.

This process of question and response is an important "support of faith," and often takes the form of friendly competition. Many Witnesses preread the questions and then underline what they think is the appropriate response. No abstract thinking is required. The following is from the *Watchtower*:

> 6   Do the scriptures speak of Peter as living in the "last days" of something away back there? Yes! Those particular "last days" began with the baptism of Jesus by John the Baptiser. . . . (Acts 10:37, 38).

Question at the bottom of the page:

> 6   When did the "last days" in which Peter was living begin?[18]

Pioneers and Publishers   To be a Jehovah's Witness is to surrender one's self to the group. Proselytizing—Witnessing for Jehovah—is expected, and almost every Witness is involved in the activity. Proselytizers are divided into four categories: special pioneers, pioneers, auxiliary pioneers, and publishers.

Special pioneers obligate themselves to a minimum of 150 hours each month in active fieldwork. Those in this category receive ninety dollars per month from the Society, the same as Bethel workers. This, of course, does not begin to cover their expenses. Special pioneers are often retired, or are the wives of working men who can economically support the activity. There were four such persons in the Minnesota congregation where Zellner regularly attended meetings.

There were four pioneers in the congregation, obligated to a minimum of ninty hours per month in the field. There were also four auxiliary pioneers working sixty hours per month. During the winter, there had

---

[18]"In the Last Days" Since When? *Watchtower* (October 1, 1980), p. 20.

been eighteen in the latter category. When the presiding elder of the congregation was asked about the drop in numbers, he winked and said "the numbers will improve again when cold weather sets in. Many Witnesses have lawns and gardens to take care of."[19] Witnesses who dropped from the rank of auxiliary pioneer for the summer, of course, did not stop proselytizing altogether; they became publishers.

There were 120 publishers in the Minnesota congregation, each obligated to 10 to 15 hours per month in the field. Almost every member of every congregation is in this category. Most male Witnesses work at low-income blue-collar jobs, and many have working wives. It is difficult for these people to attend all the Witness functions and also make field calls, but they do remarkably well.

Jehovah's Witnesses do not maintain formal membership rolls at either the national or local level; however, at any given time, they have more than just a vague idea as to their numbers. Each congregation maintains a territorial map, and a record is kept for each fieldworker. Because almost every Witness is an active proselytizer, a membership count is relatively simple. The Minneapolis congregation had 131 active fieldworkers. There were about 20 members who did fieldwork irregularly, mostly aged Witnesses, and 4 in Bible study. By simply adding categories, it can be deduced that there were about 150 adult Witnesses in the congregation.

Argots

Argots are a special language peculiar to a group. The Witness microcosm has a special language, uniquely its own, which adds to the desired feeling of separation of "we" from "they." Only a few examples need be cited to illustrate the depth and richness of this language.

Witnesses always refer to God as Jehovah, in the belief that he would prefer his people call him by his name. They note that Jehovah—not God—appears 6,961 times in the original Hebrew Scriptures.

"Sheep and goats" are commonly used argots. A sheep is a person receptive to a Witness proselytizer, a goat is not. Biblical justification for this usage rests in Matthew 24:32: "And all the nations will be gathered about Him, and He will separate the sheep from the goats."

"In the truth" is another common argot. This means an understanding of Jehovah's plan, and a willingness to live by it. A Baptist or Pentecostal might ask "Are you saved?" A Witness would ask, "Are you in the truth?"

The 144,000 who will serve in heaven with Christ are referred to as the

[19]Zellner, *Of Another World*, pp. 103–4.

"mystery class" or the "little flock." Christ told his disciples that this group would "know" the "mysteries" of the Kingdom of Heaven. More commonly, the 144,000 are called the "little flock," derived from Luke 12:32, in which Christ said, "Have no fear, little flock, because your Father has approved of giving you the kingdom."

Jehovah's Witnesses believe that they will survive Armageddon, should they be alive when the battle takes place. They refer to this survivor-class as "Jonadabs" or "other sheep." It is thought that this group, along with Witnesses returned from the dust, will be the leaders and teachers in the "new system." The "new system" is defined as Jehovah's kingdom on earth under theocratic law.

Interestingly, Witnesses never use B.C. (before Christ) or A.D. (anno Domini) as calendar designations. Their preference is for B.C.E. (before common era) and C.E. (common era). B.C.E. and C.E. are equivalent to B.C. and A.D., repectively; thus, 1991 C.E. is the same as A.D. 1991. All Witness publications use these designations.

Armageddon

Adult Witnesses are convinced that their religion is the only true religion, and salvation is possible only through Jehovah's plan as revealed by the Society. All other religions are false religions, and the Witnesses do not want their children associated with nonbelievers. But they have no choice. The Society does not maintain schools of its own, and Witness parents are required by law to send their children to secular schools. At a tender age, their young are forced out of the microcosm and into Satan's world.

Nevertheless, the Witnesses do everything possible to isolate their children from the contaminating effects of a public education. Their children are not allowed to salute the flag, vote in school elections, run for class office, sing the national anthem or school songs. They are not allowed to celebrate holidays, participate in extracurricular activities, date, attend school dances, or join school clubs. The Society has published a thirty-two-page booklet, *School and Jehovah's Witnesses*, setting out what their children can and cannot do in school. Witness children are instructed to give the publication to their teachers.

Despite efforts to isolate their offspring from mainsteam activities, children do not always share the religious zeal of their parents. But while the Society does lose some of its children, membership loss appears to be small. The Witness "socialization" process is effective, and although some do stray, it is usually only for a short period of time. Children raised in a close-knit social group often come to find life outside the group intolerable.

Kate Williams responded to the survey question "Are they [your children] members of the group?" that she was concerned for her children; she may well have been overly concerned. Although five of her eight children were living outside of the Kingdom, this does not mean that they had joined other religious organizations. To be fully part of the "new system" means that meetings must be attended regularly and field commitments met. Young people sometimes find it difficult to meet these obligations. The best guess is that Kate Williams's children will return to full-time Witness activity.

The Society is an established sect. Witnesses are "of another world," and it appears that they will remain so. The believers are uncompromising; they refuse to acknowledge the legitimacy of any other religious organization, and believe the direction that they have taken is the only path to salvation. The Society continues to grow, because the members work long and hard, with Matthew 24:14 always in mind: "And this good news of the kingdom will be preached in all the inhabited earth for a witness to all the nations; and then the end will come."

SELECTED READINGS

Aid to Bible Understanding. New York: Watchtower Bible and Tract Society of New York, 1969, 1971.

Beckford, James A. *Trumpet of Prophecy.* New York: Wiley, 1975.

Blackwell, Victor V. *O'er the Ramparts They Watched.* New York: A Hearthstone Book, 1976.

Gaylin, Willard. *In the Service of Their Country: War Resisters in Prison.* New York: Viking, 1970.

Harrison, Barbara Grizzuti. *Visions of Glory.* New York: Simon & Schuster, 1978.

Hoekema, Anthony A. *Jehovah's Witnesses.* Grand Rapids, Mich.: Eerdmans, 1974.

Insight on the Scriptures. Vol. 1. Watchtower Bible and Tract Society of New York, 1988.

Insight on the Scriptures. Vol. 2. Watchtower Bible and Tract Society of New York, 1988.

Manwaring, David R. *Render unto Caesar: The Flag Salute Controversy.* Chicago: University of Chicago Press, 1962.

Penton, M. James. *Apocalypse Delayed: The Story of Jehovah's Witnesses.* Toronto and Buffalo: University of Toronto Press, 1985.

Pike, Edgar Royston. *Jehovah's Witness: Who They Are, What They Teach, What They Do.* New York: Philosophical Press, 1954.

Reasoning from the Scriptures. Watchtower Bible and Tract Society of New York, 1985.

Rogerson, Alan. *Millions Now Living Will Never Die: A Study of Jehovah's Witnesses.* London: Constable & Co. Ltd., 1969.

Sterling, Chandler. *The Witnesses: One God One Victory.* Chicago: Regency, 1975.

Stevens, Leonard A. *Salute! The Case of the Bible vs. The Flag.* New York: Coward McCann and Geoghegan, Inc., 1973.

Stroup, Herbert Hewitt. *The Jehovah's Witnesses.* New York: Columbia University Press, 1945.

White, Timothy. *A People for His Name: A History of Jehovah's Witnesses and an Evaluation.* New York: Vantage Press, 1968.

Yearbook of Jehovah's Witnesses. New York: Watchtower Bible and Tract Society of New York.

Your Youth: Getting the Best out of It. Watchtower Bible and Tract Society of New York, 1976.

INDEX